GLOBALISATION, FDI, REGIONAL INTEGRATION AND SUSTAINABLE DEVELOPMENT

To the late Constant Munialo

Globalisation, FDI, Regional Integration and Sustainable Development

Theory, evidence and policy

ANTHONY BENDE-NABENDE
Postdoctoral Research Fellow
The Business School, The University of Birmingham, UK

Ashgate

Aldershot • Burlington USA • Singapore • Sydney

Published by
Ashgate Publishing Limited
Gower House
Croft Road
Aldershot
Hants GU11 3HR
England

Ashgate Publishing Company
131 Main Street
Burlington, VT 05401-5600 USA

Ashgate website: http://www.ashgate.com

British Library Cataloguing in Publication Data
Bende-Nabende, Anthony
   Globalisation, FDI, regional integration and sustainable
   development
   1.Globalisation 2.Investments, Foreign 3.International
   economic integration 4.Sustainable development
   I.Title
   338.9

Library of Congress Control Number: 2001096520

ISBN 0 7546 1937 0 ✓

Printed and bound in Great Britain by Antony Rowe Ltd.,
Chippenham, Wiltshire

Contents

List of Figures

List of Tables

Preface

The era of globalisation is opening many opportunities for millions of people around the world through increased trade, new technologies, foreign investments, expanding media and internet connections, and fuelling economic growth and human advances. There is more wealth and technology, and more commitment to a global community than ever before. All this offers enormous potential to continue the unprecedented progress of the twentieth century and eradicate poverty in the twenty-first century. Global markets, global technology, global ideas and global solidarity can enrich the lives of people everywhere, greatly expanding their choices.

Yet, it is also evident that these agents of advancement are also the same instruments for potential environmental derailment, increased North-South equity divide, growing human insecurity and consequently potential stimulants of unsustainable development, particularly, in the developing countries. Moreover, whereas it is being widely recognised that globalisation can engender both positive and negative effects on the growth process, the focus on positive effects has often overshadowed that on negative effects. This has been particularly true in the case of foreign direct investment.

The globalisation process has been triggered, encouraged or closely followed by transnational corporations and their associated foreign direct investment activities. The role of foreign direct investment in this process has become increasingly important. The dramatic growth of foreign direct investment in the 1990s and over time since the 1970 has brought about a greater degree of integration of the world economy than could have been achieved by trade alone. While foreign direct investment represents investment in production facilities, its significance for developing countries is much greater. Not only can foreign direct investment add to investible resources and capital formation, but, perhaps more important, it is also a means of transferring production technology, skills, innovative capacity, and organisational and managerial practices between locations, as well as of accessing international marketing networks. Surrounded by instability in equity markets and in international lending, foreign direct investment is also the most stable source of outside capital. Embodied in plant, equipment, or workforce, it may expand or contract in response to underling economic conditions, but not flee with that rapidity of stock market investors or commercial bank lenders. A vital part of the new context is the need to improve competitiveness, defined as the ability to sustain income growth in an open setting. In a liberalising and globalising world, growth can be sustained only if countries can foster new, higher value-added activities, to produce goods and services, which hold their own in open markets. Foreign direct investment and international production by transnational corporations can play an important role in complementing the efforts of national firms in this respect.

In March 1999, I launched a book entitled *'FDI, Regionalism, Government Policy and Endogenous Growth'*, whose contents included an assessment of whether the aforementioned potential foreign direct investment benefits had, in fact, been accrued by a selection of countries from Southeast Asia. Therefore, two of its nine chapters contained an empirical investigation based on econometric techniques. I have now considered it necessary to retreat from the Southeast Asian focus and present a more generalised text, which relates to a larger cross-section of countries and consequently should appeal to wider audience. In addition, I have found it essential to present the text in a more reader-friendly format, especially to that audience with limited knowledge about the technical econometric modelling. Most importantly, however, the discussion is now undertaken in the globalisation framework. More generally, the text now presents a balanced coverage of the theoretical, empirical and policy issues linking globalisation with FDI, regional economic integration, and economic growth and sustainable development. To begin with, it comprehensively explores the theoretical and empirical literature inter-linking the aforementioned factors from the anti-globalisation activists' viewpoint, and from the pro-globalisation proponents' perspective. It then prescribes policies that individual countries should pursue, based on the recognition that globalisation generates both positive and negative effects. That is, policies required to maximise the economic benefits globalisation may generate, and those that should be pursued to eliminate or at least minimise the negative development-oriented effects globalisation may engender and, hence, to propel sustainable development. Concomitant with its contents, the title of the text now changes to *'Globalisation, FDI, Regional Integration and Sustainable Development: Theory, Evidence and Policy.'* To achieve this, the following changes have been made:

• Three chapters have been eliminated from the 1999 edition. These are

Chapter 2 (Background of the Association of Southeast Asia (ASEAN) Economies), and the two econometric modelling-oriented empirical chapters (Chapters 6 and 7).

- Instead, two entirely new descriptive chapters have been introduced. One (Chapter 3) describes the trends of foreign direct investment in the recent past, and the other (Chapter 4) presents the views of anti-globalisation activists.
- Where applicable, the material that was in the eliminated chapters has been summarised in the literature and/or reference made to the 1999 volume.
- Needless to say, the literature for the chapters that are retained has been updated, and in some instances completely new material has been added. For example, a new component, i.e. the link between foreign direct investment and environmental protection and social responsibility has been added to Chapter 6. In addition, the growth theory is discussed in more detail. Most important, however, the literature is linked to globalisation.
- Additional features that might prove useful to the reader have also been introduced. These include an appendix comprising a brief background to the development of, membership of, and objectives for the formation of the respective regional economic blocs; and an author and subject index.

This book falls into either 'second reading' or 'research monograph' product category. In the academic arena, therefore, it should appeal to 2/3 level undergraduate students, graduate students and tutors from the disciplines of international economics, environmental studies, international relations, and growth and development studies. Outside the academics, it should appeal to policy makers particularly those associated with the investment boards and environmental bodies of the respective countries. Practitioners in international organisations (WTO, UN, World Bank) who are involved with trade, investment and development issues should find the book worthwhile and relevant. The business community, including local as well as international firms, will find this book invaluable in explaining the challenges of globalisation. The book should in principle appeal to both the anti-globalisation and the pro-globalisation schools of thought.

Of course, the book has benefited from direct and/or indirect contributions of different people. Needless to say, first mention goes to all those who were instrumental in the success of the first volume. First and foremost, I would like to thank my parents for their belief in education and, therefore, the academic foundation that they offered me. I must give considerable thanks to the administrative staff at the University of Birmingham Business School, who for many reasons of support, both direct and indirect made my study fruitful. Above all, special thanks go to Jim R. Slater and Prof. Jim L. Ford. These two were invaluable, particularly through their comments and guidance on the academic technicalities involved. I thank them for tirelessly offering the assistance that I required and for their patience while doing so. The original manuscript of the first volume was presented as a thesis for an award of a Ph.D at the University of Birmingham. I thank the University of Birmingham Business School and particularly the two officials, Collin Rickwood and Jim R. Slater, who were directly involved in making it financially possible for me to pursue this research. My further appreciation goes to Jim R. Slater for continuously making arrangements to ensure my financial 'survival'. Special thanks also go to all those, especially my brother Paul, who collectively or individually kept me at peace by taking care of some of my other responsibilities 'while I was away'.

Obviously, I must not forget my wife Gwen who not only had to endure my sporadic tempers but had to cope with a lot of typing as well during the first volume, and who gave me ample space and time, enabling me to complete the second volume. Needless to say, the arrival of 'Akakazi RTT' not only brought more happiness to the family, but also brought new inspiration and indeed justified the need for embarking on the second volume.

Last but not least, I thank the 'Lord' for the stamina and good health.

Abbreviations

ACM	Arab Common Market
ACS	Association of Caribbean States
AFTA	ASEAN Free Trade Area
AMEU	Afro-Malagasy Economic Union
ANCOM	Andean Common Market
APEC	Asia-Pacific Economic Co-operation
APTA	ASEAN Preferential Trade Area
ASEAN	Association of Southeast Asian Nations
ASEAN-4	Indonesia, Malaysia, Philippines and Thailand
ASEAN-5	Indonesia, Malaysia, Philippines, Singapore and Thailand
CACM	Central American Common Market
CAFTA	Canada-America Free Trade Area
CAP	Common Agricultural Policy
CARACOM	Caribbean Community and Common Market
CARICOM	Caribbean Community
CARIFTA	Caribbean Free Trade Area
CBD	Convention on Biological Diversity
CEAO	Communaute Economique de l'Afrique de l'Ouest
CEEAC	Communaute Economique des Etats de l'Afrique Central or Economic Community for Central African States
CEECs	Central and Eastern European countries
CEFTA	European Free Trade Agreement
CEMAC	Comunauté Economique et Monetaire d'Afrique Centrale
CEPGL	Communaute Economique des Pays des Grands Lacs or Economic Community of the Great Lakes Countries
CEPT	Common Effective Preferential Tariff
CIS	Commonwealth of Independent States
CMEA	Council for Mutual Economic Assistance
COMECON	Council for Mutual Economic Assistance
COMESA	Common Market for Eastern and Southern Africa

CSD	Commission on Sustainable Development
EAC	East African Community
EACM	East African Common Market
EACU	East African Customs Union
EC	European Community
ECCM	East Caribbean Common Market
ECOWAS	Economic Community of West African States
ECSC	European Coal and Steel Community
ECU	European Currency Unit
EEA	European Economic Area
EEC	European Economic Community
EFTA	European Free Trade Association
EMU	European Monetary System
EU	European Union
EUECA	Economic Union of Equatorial and Central Africa
EURATOM	European Atomic Energy Community
FAO	Food and Agricultural Organisation
FDI	Foreign Direct Investment
FTA	Free Trade Area/Agreement
FWAF	French West African Federation
GATT	General Agreement of Tariffs and Trade
GCC	Gulf Co-operation Council
GEF	Global Environment Facility
IPRs	Intellectual Property Rights
ISO	International Standards Organisation
LAFTA	Latin American Free Trade Area
LAIA	Latin American Integration Association
M&As	Mergers and Acquisitions
MERCOSUR	Southern Cone Common Market
MNCs	Multinational Corporations
MRU	Mano River Union
MTI	Multilateral Trade and Investment
MTS	Multilateral Trading System
NAFTA	North American Free Trade Area
NIEs	Newly Industrialising Economies
ODA	Official Development Assistance
OEEC	Organisation for European Economic Co-operation
OPEC	Organisation of Petroleum Exporting Countries
PTA	Preferential Trade Area

R&D	Research and Development
RDC	Regional Co-operation for Development
SACU	Southern African Customs Union
SADC	South African Development Community
SMEs	Small and Medium Sized Enterprises
SNA	System of National Accounts
TBT	Technical Barriers to Trade
TNCs	Transnational Corporations
TRIPs	Trade-Related Aspects of Intellectual Property Rights
UDEAC	Union Douaniere et Economique de l'Afrique Centrale or Customs and Economic Union of Central Africa
UEMOA	Union Economique et Monaitaire Ouest-Africaine
UN	United Nations
UNCSD	United Nations Commission on Sustainable Development
UNCTAD	United Nations Conference on Trade and Development
UNCTC	United Nations Centre for Transnational Corporations
UNDP	United Nations Development Programme
UNEP	United Nations Environment Programme
UNESCO	United Nations Educational, Scientific and Cultural Organisation
UNTCMD	United Nations Transnational Corporations and Management Division
UPE	Universal Primary Education
WAEC	West African Economic Community
WEO	World Environment Organisation
WHO	World Health Organisation
WWF	World Wide Fund for Nature

1 Introduction

Overview

The ongoing globalisation process characterised by 'shrinking space, shrinking time and disappearing borders', has swung open the door to more opportunities. These have resulted from breakthroughs in communications technologies and biotechnology, and led to integration of global markets, global technology, global ideas and global solidarity. Yet, rather than shrink the ideological borders as well, globalisation has instead indeed succeeded in widening them. The reason for this partly stems from the aforementioned opportunities, which are perceived by the pro-globalisation school of thought as dominantly positive to the welfare of mankind, but considered as a total negation to the well-being of nature by the anti-globalisation school of thought. Hence, the emergence of 'the globalisation debate'.

A traditional pro-globalisation economist defines economic growth as a process of change through time, which involves an interrelationship between economic, political and social factors. It can be envisaged as an almost uninterrupted increase year after year, in a country's per capita income. Thus, economic growth remains an urgent global need. Unsurprisingly, the development priorities of developing countries include income growth, rising investments and exports, creating more and better employment opportunities, and benefiting from technical progress. No wonder, developing countries are placed under considerable pressure to upgrade their resources and capabilities if they are to achieve these objectives. Consequently, factors that have the potential of acting as 'engines' of economic growth and hence, factors that may explain transition from an undeveloped economy to a developed economy have to be identified. Several factors have been hypothesised and empirically tested under several economic growth theories. These theories have evolved over time, beginning with the classical theory followed by the neo-classical theory and then the new or endogenous growth theory. However, the traditional factors that propel sustained economic growth have not changed over time. Instead, it is the global context for economic growth that has changed enormously over the past three decades. This change has affected not only the role of the engines of economic growth, but also the influence of government policies on the engines of economic growth. The traditional factors include the generation and efficient allocation of the basic factors of production, capital and labour. In addition, they include the application of technology and the creation of skills and institutions traditionally otherwise referred to as technical progress. Technical progress can be achieved through several channels. For instance, it may be stimulated by investment that augments and improves the productivity of national physical resources. Alternatively, it can be driven by innovations, which not only improve the productivity of existing activities, but also create competitive advantages in new activities. Additionally, it can be promoted by development of labour skills, or investment in human skills. The most recent focus of accounting for economic growth embraces factors such as human resources development, which include the role of quality improvements in the labour-force of an economy, improvements that come about from better health, more education and greater access to training. It also comprises technological change, international trade, and government policy. These factors not only determine how well each economy uses its factor endowments, but also affect how flexibly and dynamically each country adjusts to changes in economic conditions. Therefore, concomitant with this ideology, the pro-globalisation school of thought believes that globalisation is opening many opportunities for millions of people around the world through increased trade, new technologies, foreign investments, expanding media and internet connections, and fuelling economic growth and human advances. But, this is one side of the coin.

Anti-globalisation activists criticise the aforementioned ideas presented by the pro-globalisation economists for focusing on economic issues alone. For instance, when international economic comparisons are being made, there is often a temptation to measure development by economic growth alone. This provides a picture only of changes in quantitative indicators of the economic wealth of a nation, gross domestic product (GDP) and gross national product (GNP). Even if changes in these aggregates might provide a good index of the development of economic activities in a country, they say nothing about the composition and distribution of income between different groups in society. Nor does economic growth tell us anything about the human wealth of a country (i.e., the quality of food, health services, the school and university system, and safety). Moreover, traditional economic indicators are as uninformative about the state of the environment as they are about cultural and social aspects. Strong growth in national income may mask unbridled consumption of natural resources and intolerable human exploitation (child labour, for example). A good growth rate, then, can conceal situations where natural resources risk being exhausted in the short- or medium-term and where under-investment in 'human capital' threatens economic activity. From the anti-globalisation activists' viewpoint then, globalisation is more than the flow of money and commodities. It is the growing integration of not just the economy but culture, technology and governance and, hence interdependence of the world's people. Therefore, the dominant concern in the globalisation debate should not be just about economic flows. Rather, it should be about preserving biodiversity, addressing the ethics of patents on life, ensuring access to health care and respecting other cultures' forms of ownership. It should also go further to address the growing technological gap between the knowledge-driven global economy and the rest trapped in its shadows. They also argue that those agents of globalisation are also the same instruments for potential environmental degradation, increased North-South equity divide and human insecurity. Therefore, they are potential stimulants of unsustainable development, especially, in the developing countries. Specifically, globalisation leads to more violation of human rights, more disparity within and between nations, more marginalisation of people and countries, more instability of societies, more vulnerability of people, more environmental destruction, and more poverty and deprivation. Hence, it should address issues pertaining to ethics, equity, inclusion, human security, sustainability and development. In other words, economic issues should be amalgamated with ecological, and social-political issues so that the debate goes beyond examining just economic growth, to exploring issues in terms of sustainable development for all. To achieve this, the benefits of economic growth should be shared equitably, so that the increasing interdependence arising from globalisation should work for all people, and not just for profits. Additionally, the environment should be treated as a scarce resource so that some of the benefits derived from economic growth are utilised in its preservation. Thus, while economic growth combined with environmental protection leads to sustainability, economic growth coupled with less poverty deprivation results into development. This is why anti-globalisation activists are more concerned with *sustainable development*, which is an outcome of a combination of economical, ecological and social-political factors.

The number, range, co-ordination and activism among civil society groups on issues relating to globalisation has been expanding in the recent past. Although some groups organise around very specific products (e.g. tobacco and nuclear energy), most activism focuses on a relatively small set of major issue themes. These are then exemplified and addressed in terms of specific products, companies or events. Some of the most vigilant groups are Greenpeace, which is primarily concerned with environmental issues; Amnesty International and Human Rights Watch whose prime interests relate to human rights; and individual country Labour Unions, which focus on workers' rights.

It is worthwhile noting that the globalisation process has been triggered, encouraged or closely followed by transnational corporations (TNCs) or multinational corporations (MNCs) and their associated foreign direct investment (FDI) activities. Yet, FDI is a comparatively new phenomenon *vis-à-vis* international trade in the social, political and economic international relations. For instance, it was third placed among capital flows during the 1960s, 1970s and early-1980s, when aid and then commercial bank loans were larger. However, the significance of the role it plays in the global integration has been growing in the recent past. For instance, the dramatic growth of FDI in the 1990s and over time since the 1970s has brought about a greater degree of integration of the world economy than could have been achieved by trade alone. Specifically, FDI has been growing at a faster rate than exports since the mid-1980s. Unsurprisingly then, FDI is at the forefront of the ongoing globalisation process.

Prior to the 1970s, FDI and, hence, TNCs or MNCs (hereafter referred to as TNCs) were seen by developing economies as part of a problem to development, to be solved by minimising the role of TNCs. They were perceived by developing country politicians and development economist as an unnecessary evil that; made huge profits, imported obsolete technology, introduced unfavourable balance of payments, was a neo-colonial vehicle, milked the developing economies through transfer pricing, and introduced a dependencia syndrome which eroded their self-reliance. Unsurprisingly, this image is still held by anti-globalisation activists (albeit from a globalisation perspective), particularly, the extreme environmental activists, extreme development economists, and academics belonging to the extreme social-political discipline. They argue that FDI is the principal agent for the aforementioned negative globalisation tendencies. Nonetheless, some moderate anti-globalisation activists are increasingly recognising that globalisation can generate some good economic effects.

Advocates of pro-globalisation on the other hand note that the past three decades have witnessed unprecedented and sustained high rates of economic growth most notably in the Asian newly industrialising economies (NIEs), with substantial involvement of FDI. They therefore, argue that an awareness of the link between FDI and economic growth has been established. Moreover, many of the growth promoting factors identified by the endogenous growth theory have been hypothesised to form the foundation of the key positive spillover effects of FDI. For instance, FDI is said to stimulate economic growth through the creation of dynamic comparative advantages that lead to new technology transfers, capital formation, human resources development, expanded international trade, clean technologies and modern environmental management systems. Therefore, a vital part of the new context is the need to improve competitiveness, defined as the ability to sustain income growth in an open setting. In a liberalising and globalising world, growth can be sustained only if countries can foster new, higher value-added activities, to produce goods and services, which can sustain their market shares in an open world economy. FDI and international production by TNCs can play an important role in complementing the efforts of national firms in this respect. For this reason, national governments have recognised that TNCs can provide a package of external resources that can contribute to economic development. Therefore, it is not surprising that developing countries have changed attitude and are now considering FDI as part of the solution to their economic development. Subsequently, they have shifted from controlling and containing FDI to encouraging it. The growing importance and recognition of FDI is exemplified by the shift towards greater openness of national developing economies to FDI.

Nonetheless, concomitant with some of the anti-globalisation activists' views, the pro-globalisation school of thought (or at least some of its members) has recognised that FDI, the principal agent of globalisation, can indeed impact negatively on the development process of a country. This is partly because the objectives of TNCs may differ from those of host governments. For instance, whereas governments seek to spur national development, TNCs seek to enhance their own competitiveness moreover, in the international context. Thus, their strategies are not devoted to the development of the host country. Subsequently, their needs and strategies may differ from the needs and objectives of the host country. For this reason, not all FDI is always and automatically in the best interests of the host country. In fact, FDI can have adverse effects on the host country's development. Consequently, although there may be considerable overlaps, there are also significant differences. Thus, FDI offers a mixture of positive and negative effects. Unfortunately, even with this recognition, the solution offered is merely rhetorical. For instance, it is often concluded that 'it is then the task of the host country to disentangle these effects, and take measures that maximise the positives but minimise the negatives'. Yet, when it comes to practical policies on the ground, the emphasis put on the maximisation of the positive effects still far outweighs that, if any, put on the minimisation of the negative effects.

Another issue under contentious debate, and which has direct implications for free trade *vis-à-vis* trade discrimination is regional economic integration. Anti-globalisation activists argue that one of the channels through which sustainable development can be achieved is by pursuing free trade. Yet, numerous economic blocs continue to be formed all over the world. Those who support trade protection (not necessarily pro-globalisation advocates) on the other hand argue that a majority of developing countries have pre-union protection, suggesting that free trade is not viewed as desirable. Whereas welfare benefits generated from the static effects of regionalism are ambiguous, those derived from the dynamic effects, particularly, economies of scale and specialisation are well documented. The past decades have, therefore, seen a surge in regional trade arrangements involving developed countries partly formed for these reasons. This has increased developing countries' interest in similar arrangements based on the expectations of benefits such as economies of scale that may result from market size, market growth and tariff-discrimination, which act as additional incentives to lure FDI into the region thus accelerating industrialisation and economic growth.

But anti-globalisation activists argue that international specialisation, for example, that results from the comparative advantage model tends to alter the volume and geographical distribution of production activities in accordance with the resources available in each country (capital, labour, and natural wealth). In the case of primary resources (agriculture and mining products) it can consequently lead to the intensification of operating methods or to greater exploitation of untapped resources, not without effects on the quality of the environment. In addition, specialisation can sometimes lead to rich ecosystems or food crops being replaced by export crops. Moreover, it is developing countries that, impelled to specialise as part of structural adjustment policies, suffer the most severe social and environmental consequences.

For these reasons, globalisation, FDI and regional economic integration provide some important implications for all countries in general, and the developing countries in particular, especially those whose current image is unfortunately but rightly associated with civil unrest, war, poverty, diseases and mounting social problems.

Definitions

Globalisation

Globalisation refers to a world in which societies, cultures, politics and economies have, in some sense, come closer together. It can be defined as a set of economic, social, technological, political and cultural structures and processes arising from the changing character of the production, consumption and trade of goods and assets that comprise the base of the international political economy. It is an intensification of worldwide social relations, which link distant localities in such a way that local happenings are influenced by events occurring many miles away and vice versa. For instance, a miner's job in Country A may depend on events in Country B or C as much as on local management or national government decisions.

Globalisation is a result of a larger building process of a world market. There is an increasing structural differentiation of the goods and assets that have spread across traditional political borders and economic sectors, and consequently greatly influenced social-political and economic changes. These changes are transnational and multinational dynamics, which have a major impact on outcomes in determining 'issue-areas' (i.e., environment, trade and world regulation), and may induce global and local actors to be more autonomous from a traditionally exclusive State decision-making. But globalisation is more than the flow of money and commodities. It is the growing integration of not just the economy but culture, technology and governance and, therefore interdependence of the world's people.

Thus, globalisation is a complex process that affects not only the production and trading of goods and services but also culture and decision-making processes in all areas, including that of the environment. The most visible part of the iceberg, the globalisation of the economy, is closely linked to the globalisation of problems connected with development and the environment (Gueneau et al, 1998). This is characterised by:

- The integration of national economies into world markets.
- The transition from a 'high-volume' into a 'high-value' economy or rather from 'labour-intensive' to 'capital-intensive' production.
- The end of bi-polarity and traditional prize-fight between capitalism and socialism.
- Configuration of new trade blocs (Gueneau et al, 1998).

Yet it is arguable that globalisation is not a completely new phenomena. Rather, globalisation during the end of the twentieth century experienced distinctive features and was accelerated by specific agents. The resultant effect is that, many of the products bought in the high street have journeyed half way around the world, and people everywhere are becoming affected by events in far corners of the world. For example, the collapse of the Thai baht not only instigated a financial crisis in Southeast Asia, but also induced decline in global demand, which in turn led to slow-downs in social investment in Latin America and a sudden rise in the cost of imported medicines in Africa. In particular, the following features make this era much different:

- Shrinking space, shrinking time and disappearing borders as a result of greater connectivity.
- Blurring of traditional distinctions between greater international connectivity.
- Widening distribution of FDI, trade and opportunities for development across world regions and nations.
- Converging world economy, in which all places and people can, and generally do, find export market niches. For instance, foreign exchange and capital markets are linked globally, operating 24 hours a day, with dealings at a distance in real time. Trillions of dollars are now exchanged in the world's currency markets each day, and nearly a fifth of the goods and services produced each year are traded.
- Spreading media and cultural influences.
- Growing integration of people through immigration and communication, which are linking people's lives more deeply, more intensely, and more immediately than ever before. Each one of us is increasingly connected to people we will never meet, and from places we will never visit. This has been facilitated by new developments in form of internet links, cellular phones, and media networks which have eased communication.
- Emergence of new actors including the World Trade Organisation (WTO) with authority over national governments, the TNCs with more economic power than many States, the global networks of non-

governmental organisations (NGOs) and other groups that transcend national boundaries.
* New rules taking the form of multilateral agreements on trade, services and intellectual property, backed by strong enforcement mechanisms and more binding for national governments, reducing the scope for national policy (Gueneau et al, 1998).

Nevertheless, globalisation is neither uniform nor homogenous. In particular, there is a marked difference between the degree of globalisation as reflected in trade, FDI and international finance. Its boundaries are unclear and its constituent elements and multidimensional character have yet to be adequately explored. Some social scientists have considered globalisation as a second step to *complex interdependence*, which accepts that the notion of transnational interpenetration is not homogenous either. Others contend that globalisation modifies deeply the structural framework of rational choice in world relations, since the role of the key actor (i.e., the State), which commonly defined both the international and the domestic relations is subject to a critical structural transformation (Gueneau et al, 1998).

Foreign Direct Investment

FDI constitutes a resource flow, which is particularly useful for the economic development of developing countries, especially for their industrial development. It provides a unique combination of long-term finance, technology, training, know-how, managerial expertise and marketing experience. FDI comprises:
* Outlays for the establishment of a new enterprise or for the expansion of an existing enterprise whose operation is controlled by the foreign investor.
* Financial outlays for the acquisition of an existing enterprise (or part of it) either through direct purchase or through purchases of equity, with a controlling interest by the foreign investor. The notion of control is not defined, but control is assumed when the foreign investor owns at least between 10 and 51 per cent of the enterprise's value according to different definitions used by different governments.
* Intra-corporate long-term loans (OECD, 1978).

In a nutshell, FDI occurs when an investor based in one country (the home country) acquires an asset in another country (the host country) with the intent to manage the asset. In most instances, both the investor and the asset are business firms. In such cases, the investor is typically referred to as the 'parent firm', and the asset as the 'affiliate' or 'subsidiary'. This management dimension, which involves the transfer of control and direct involvement in the transfer of resources is what distinguishes FDI from portfolio investment in foreign stocks, bonds and other financial instruments. FDI is not only an exchange of the ownership of domestic investment sites from domestic residents to foreign residents, but also a corporate governance mechanism in which the foreign investor exercises management and control over the host country firm. In so doing, the foreign direct investors gain inside information about the productivity of the firm under their control, an obvious advantage over the uninformed domestic savers. Taking advantage of their superior information, the foreign direct investors will tend to retain the high productivity firms under their ownership and control and sell the low productivity firms to these uninformed savers. This adverse selection problem, which plagues the domestic stock market, leads to over-investment by the foreign direct investors even up to a point that, although first best capital inflows through FDI are not warranted, they nevertheless take place. FDI can be understood as capital invested for the purpose of acquiring a lasting interest in an enterprise and of exerting a degree of influence on that enterprise's operations. In sum then, FDI differs from portfolio investment in that it involves active control of part or the whole of the asset in question, while portfolio investors are passive investors, motivated only by the rate of return on the asset.

Economic Integration

Many international economists have come up with different definitions of integration. According to Balassa (1961), integration has been said to progress through the freeing of barriers to trade (trade integration), the liberalisation of factor movements (factor integration), the harmonisation of national economic policies (policy integration), and the complete unification of these policies (total integration) (Balassa, 1976). Kitamura (1966), however, criticises these definitions on the grounds that they conform to the principles of classical economic doctrines but do not apply to the present day market economies, which are characterised by a considerable degree of state intervention, and apply even less to developing and to socialist economies.

Pinder (1968) proposed to define economic integration as both the removal of discrimination as between the economic agents of the member countries, and the formation and application of co-ordinated and common policies on a sufficient scale to ensure that major economic and welfare objectives are fulfilled. His definition was criticised by Vajda (1971) for its excessive generality. Vajda introduced the distinction between 'market integration' and 'production and development integration'. The former is defined as 'the guarantee of unhindered sale of each other's products within the framework of the social system of participating countries'. The latter is on the other hand said to involve 'raising to an international level and programming the production of those branches of industry, which cannot be developed to an optimum size within national boundaries.'

International economic integration can, therefore, be taken to denote a state of affairs or a process involving attempts to combine separate national economies into larger economic regions. It can take on any of the following forms:

*   *Sectoral Integration*, which entails the removal of barriers to trade in the output of a single industrial sector as, for example, in the European Coal and Steel Community (ECSC).
*   *Preferential Trade/Tariff Areas,* which involve bilateral Tariff Agreements on selected groups of merchandise. The Association of Southeast Asian Nations (ASEAN) Preferential Trade Area (APTA) is an example.
*   *Free Trade Areas,* where member countries abolish all trade impediments among themselves but retain their freedom with regard to the determination of their policies *vis-à-vis* the outside world (non-participants). The North American Free Trade Area (NAFTA) forms a good example.
*   *Customs Unions,* which are very much like free trade areas except that member countries are obliged to conduct common external relations. For instance, they must adopt common external tariffs on imports from the outside world. The European Economic Community (EEC) was, in this sense, a customs union although much more was involved.
*   *Common Markets*, which are customs unions that also, allow for the free factor mobility across national member boundaries. For instance, capital, labour and enterprise should move without hindrance between the participating nations. The East African Common Market (EACM) is an example.
*   *Single Markets*, which are common markets that also allow for uniform product standards. The EEC was in a way a single market.

- *Monetary Unions*, which are single markets with fixed exchange rates and common monetary policy. The European Monetary Union (EMU) represented this.
- *Complete Economic Unions*, which are common markets that call for complete unification of monetary and fiscal policies. For instance, there is a central authority, which controls these aspects so that existing nations become regions of the union. The European Union (EU) has achieved this status.
- *Complete Political Unions,* where the participants become literally one nation. That is, the central authority not only controls monetary and fiscal policies but also has a central parliament with the sovereignty of a nation's government (El-Agraa, 1981). The United States of America in a way represents this.

Table 1.1 Effects of different types of integration

	Market			Economic		Political
Effect on integration	CU	CM	SM	MU	EU	PU
No trade restrictions and common external tariffs	*	*	*	*	*	*
Free movement of capital and labour	n.a.	*	*	*	*	*
Uniform product standards	n.a.	n.a.	*	*	*	*
Fixed exchange rates and common monetary policy	n.a.	n.a.	n.a.	*	*	*
Common economic policy	n.a.	n.a.	n.a.	n.a.	*	*
Common general policy	n.a.	n.a.	n.a.	n.a.	n.a.	*

Notes: CU - Customs union, CM - Common market, SM - Single market, MU - Monetary union, EU - Economic union, PU - Political union and n.a. - not applicable.

The effects of the more advanced types of integration are summarised in Table 1.1. Most of the discussion, which follows, concerns the geographical (regional) economic co-operation (integration). This form of co-operation is hereafter referred to as *regional economic integration* or for simplicity *regionalism*.

Sustainable Development

Sustainable development is a complex process that encompasses not only the ability of a population to achieve long-term growth in wealth, but also its modes of thought and social organisation. It therefore combines a quantitative aspect, a qualitative aspect and, unquestionably, an intangible aspect as well. In short, if growth and development are linked, the development process encompasses more than can be measured by growth alone. The concept of sustainable development demands multi-disciplinarity, an accommodation between hitherto distinct scientific logic, and harmonisation of the disciplines of ecology and economics. The three aspects of sustainable development, i.e. ecological, economic, and social political aspects express its interdisciplinary nature well.

The ecological aspect of sustainable development extends the issue of the industrial scale, which postulates the human needs that the economic system is required to satisfy. It proposes that nature places limits on industrialisation, and these need to be identified and respected. The aim is to manage and optimise the use of natural capital instead of running it down.

The economic aspect of sustainable development relates to the current and future effects of the economy on the environment. It raises the question of the choice, financing and improvement of industrial techniques in terms of natural resource utilisation. Sustainable development reconciles these two aspects by taking into consideration not just the conservation of nature but the entire relationship between nature and human actions. Based on the synergy between man and the environment, sustainable development favours the technologies, knowledge and values that make for longevity. It argues for an economic development process that takes long-term account of the basic ecological balances which support human, natural and plant life.

The social and political aspect of sustainable development is meant to turn development into an instrument of social cohesion and a process of political choice. This choice, first and foremost, must be for equity, both between generations and between States. In their concern for equity, current generations will preserve the development options of future generations and of different States, in both North and South. It is through this double imperative of equity that the environment and the economy must be reconciled.

Purpose and Plan of the Book

Considering the ongoing globalisation debate, it is somewhat surprising that no text has presented a comprehensive and balanced coverage of the core theoretical, empirical and policy issues representing the views of anti-globalisation activists on the one hand, and those of the pro-globalisation school of thought on the other hand. In particular, there is no text that extensively explores the globalisation debate by linking it to both FDI and regional economic integration. Instead, these three factors have often been examined either independently, or with specific emphasis on one of them.

While the issues relating to globalisation have received substantial coverage in the recent past, there has been a tendency for the authors to show a biased inclination to one school of thought. Consequently, the authors either present their 'skewed' views outright, or develop hypotheses based on them, which they then go ahead and either support or discredit. In fact, most of the globalisation debate has been dominated by presentations by anti-globalisation advocates. In particular, it has been overwhelmed by the environmentalists who have concentrated on environmental issues, and some development economists and social-political activists who have focused on the trade-linked North-South equity-divide.

Likewise, despite its current importance in the international economic, social and political environment, only a few texts offer a comprehensive coverage of the core theoretical, empirical and policy issues that link FDI to economic growth, let alone discuss them in the globalisation framework. Most of the available textbook material relating to FDI essentially focuses on the strategic responses of TNCs and, therefore, on their responses to the determinants of FDI. Those books that offer the literature, which links FDI to economic growth are often, either conference based and/or focus on specific regions and/or groups of countries. Additional published literature, which predominates the coverage of this subject is available in article form, mostly found in Academic Journals. Unfortunately, the depth of coverage of such publications is for obvious reasons often curtailed by the allocated 'premium' space. So far, only the United Nations (UN) has been able to cover this topic comprehensively. In 1975, the UN sought to further the understanding of the nature of TNCs and their contribution to development. The UN Centre on Transnational Corporations (UNCTC) undertook this programme between 1975 and 1992. However, it was transferred to the UN Transnational Corporations and Management Division (UNTCMD) between 1992 and 1993, and to the UN Conference on Trade and Development (UNCTAD) in 1993. The downside of the UN publications is that their annual releases are often published under specific themes. Therefore, one requires having access to almost the totality of these publications in order to get a comprehensive insight on the subject. Most importantly however, these texts do not offer literature on FDI in the context of the globalisation debate.

In contrast, the conceptual literature on regional economic integration, including its link to FDI has been extensively covered in many textbooks. But, the empirical component of the literature linking regional economic integration with FDI is often available as chapters in conference based editions and as articles in Academic Journals. Therefore, it is similarly exposed to the aforementioned shortcomings. However, the literature (both theoretical and empirical), linking regional economic integration to FDI and, hence the globalisation debate is rather scanty. In fact, what is abundant (and by its nature short-lived) in this respect are media reports linked to protests undertaken when for instance, meetings are organised to discuss regional trade agreements.

This text attempts to overcome these problems by acting as a 'one stop centre' for a balanced coverage of the theoretical, empirical and policy issues linking globalisation with FDI, regional economic integration, and economic growth and sustainable development. To begin with, it comprehensively explores the theoretical and empirical literature inter-linking the aforementioned factors from the anti-globalisation activists' viewpoint, and from the pro-globalisation proponents' perspective. It then prescribes policies that individual countries should pursue, based on the recognition that globalisation generates both positive and negative effects. That is, policies required to maximise the economic benefits globalisation may generate, and those that should be pursued to eliminate or at least minimise the negative development-oriented effects globalisation may engender and, hence, to propel sustainable development.

The book is, therefore, divided into eight chapters. The basic concepts relating to the theories of international integration and international production are encapsulated in Chapter 2. The first section presents a brief background to trade theories, and illustrates how they can be linked to the theories of international integration and international production. The second section highlights the conceptual aspects of the theory of international integration, but puts more emphasis on the dynamic effects and less emphasis on the static effects. For instance, regionalism leads to an increase in market size that promotes large-scale production and, therefore, economies of scale of production, making low unit-costs of production possible. Firms are then able to reap these economies of scale within the large single market. Furthermore, regionalism may provide a market large enough to support a sufficient number of optimally sized plants without resulting in the danger of monopolistic exploitation and hence X-inefficiency. This can then encourage competition and, therefore, innovation. The third section introduces the theory of international production, which suggests that the propensity for a firm to engage in foreign production depends on the combination of ownership-specific advantages, internalisation opportunities and locational advantages in the target market. Each of these determinants of FDI relates to an advantage of direct investment over alternative modes of serving the firms' customers abroad.

Since TNCs and their associated FDI activities are key ingredients of the ongoing globalisation process, Chapter 3 is devoted to the analysis of the recent trends of FDI. It briefly highlights the global and regional FDI trends during the past three or so decades when its economic influence became an issue of interest in the social, economic and political environment. It also identifies reasons responsible for the respective FDI booms and bursts, and provides explanations for the FDI inflow/outflow disparity between the developed and the developing countries. There is evidence to suggest that FDI has been one of the defining features of the world economy over the past two decades. It has grown at an unprecedented pace for more than a decade, with only a slight interruption during the recession of the early-1990s.

Chapter 4 presents the arguments put forward by the anti-globalisation activists from the environmental, North-South equity-divide and human insecurity points of view. Here, it is argued that instead of the acclaimed 'shrinking space, shrinking time and disappearing borders' effects of globalisation, there is in effect 'an incentive squeeze on the environment, a fiscal squeeze on public goods, and a time squeeze on care activities'. Thus, from the environmental perspective, globalisation leads to more environmental destruction. However, from the North-South equity-divide point of view, it causes more disparity within and between nations, and more marginalisation of people and countries. But, from the human insecurity viewpoint, globalisation engenders more violation of human rights, more instability of societies, more vulnerability of people, and more poverty and deprivation. For instance, trade liberalisation has led to increased production of goods and services that generate environmental damage. In addition, while the developed economies integrate more and more rapidly, the least developed countries are becoming increasingly marginalised. Furthermore, people are confronting new threats to human security, and sudden and hurtful disruptions in the pattern of daily life, dis-empowerment of the local communities, financial and economic insecurity, food security and food safety, job and income insecurity, health insecurity, cultural insecurity and criminal insecurity.

Chapter 5 presents the views of the pro-globalisation activists, but focuses on only the key agent of globalisation, TNCs and hence FDI. It is divided into two sections. The first section explores the classical, neo-classical and the new or endogenous growth literature, which suggests that economic growth may be stimulated by investment that augments and improves the productivity of national physical resources. That is, that it can be driven by innovation and technological change, development of labour skills or investment in human resources, and international trade. It establishes that many of these growth-promoting factors also form the essential characteristic spillover features of FDI. For instance, that the dynamic effects of FDI can also lead to new technology transfer, new capital formation, human resources development, and expanded international trade through its positive spillover effects. This then leads to a hypothesis that FDI also stimulates economic growth. The second section shifts focus, and examines the literature on the impact of FDI on human resources development, technology transfer, international trade, capital formation, environmental protection and social responsibility and, hence, economic growth in developing countries. Empirical evidence suggests that even if its impact is currently small, FDI is playing an increasingly important role in the economic growth process of developing countries. However, this mostly comes about as a spillover rather than a direct effect.

The review presented in Chapter 6 attempts to establish a theoretical and empirical link between the two theories. These include the possible investment responses of FDI to regionalism, the circumstances that lead to the respective responses, and the economic effects that may be derived by a regional bloc member host country when FDI is linked to regionalism. The first section explores the theoretical aspects of the link, while the second section examines the empirical evidence. The theory suggests that regionalism prompts three major integration effects namely, tariff-discrimination, market size and market growth which, in their individual and collective capacities have implications for the theory of international production. Needless to say, the most powerful argument for regionalism among developing countries is that the important benefits, which developing countries seek through integration arise from the exploitation of economies of scale. The removal of tariff barriers in a regional economic bloc (both internal and external) creates the confidence that these barriers will not be re-erected in the future. This increased certainty of access to a larger market stimulates both international trade and FDI, eventually inducing the economic growth of the economic bloc. From the pro-globalisation activists' viewpoint then, the FDI-related benefits generated from regionalism are bound to outweigh those that would originate from free trade.

Policy considerations on how to maximise the benefits and minimise the potential hazards of the globalisation process are presented in Chapter 7. The chapter first highlights the current problems being experienced by developing countries. It then suggests areas in which, and how developing country governments can maximise the positive dynamic effects that the key element of globalisation, FDI offers in order to enhance their economic growth rates. These include the liberalisation of their investment and trade regimes, the minimisation of both their internal and external conflicts, the eradication of the corruption culture, the reduction of defence budgets, and the consolidation of focus on factors that enhance economic, social and political stability. In addition, developing countries require to develop their resource bases to levels capable of exploiting the dynamic comparative advantages FDI offers. This may involve deepening the value-added content of production activity and building the capacity to sustain such a shift across a range of tradable activities in response to changing world demand and technologies. Additionally, benefits can be accrued from regionalism, which is based more on economic rather than political motives.

The second section concentrates on policies that can be pursued in order to eliminate, or at least minimise the negative effects globalisation may cause. It calls for an approach which gives developing countries a larger role and greater benefits; and which maintains the balance between economic growth and the ecosystem, so that natural resources can support growth over the long-term. It emphasises the need to revive economic growth, particularly in developing countries, as well as on the qualitative aspects of growth, particularly, the improvement of human insecurity. It also gives a special tribute to the vigilante groups which have not only come a long way, but have also played and continue playing an instrumental role in raising issues that were otherwise being ignored or overlooked by governments, international institutions and TNCs. While they should continue playing their vigilantism, however, the way forward now in the globalising world should not be to try to prevent change, but to look for reform that will improve life in the country and provide support for those who are losing out. Anti-globalisation activists' involvement should now shift away from confrontation to dialogue. It is time to change from being anti-establishment to being proactive.

Concluding remarks are encapsulated in Chapter 8. In sum, globalisation has come to stay. Most important, however, globalisation has an instrumental role to play in the development process of all countries. Therefore, the challenge of globalisation in the new century is not to stop the expansion of global markets. What is required are local, national, regional and global policy instruments that can maximise its potential benefits, and yet minimise its potential hazards. Therefore, on the one hand, besides improving the investment environment, developing country governments need to promote domestic capabilities, develop integrated strategies, build educational bases, strengthen technological institutions, encourage firms into export markets to test and advance their competitiveness, and pursue regionalism based on economic rather than political motives. This framework if properly planned and appropriately implemented, will enhance and sustain their economic growth rates. On the other hand, for globalisation to work, the aforementioned economic benefits should be distributed equitably while preserving the environment so that sustainable development for all is achieved.

2 Introduction to the Theories of International Integration and International Production

Introduction

This chapter introduces the basic concepts of the theories of international integration and international production. The theories of international integration combine elements of freer trade with elements of greater protection. They promote freedom of trade between the participating countries while providing more protection for producers inside the integration area against outside competition. In other words, they relate to discriminatory trade liberalisation, whereby two or more countries lower trade barriers against one another relative to the rest of the world. The theory of international production on the other hand suggests that the propensity for a firm to engage in foreign production depends on a combination of ownership-specific advantages, internalisation opportunities and locational advantages in the target market. Each of these determinants of FDI relates to an advantage of direct investment over alternative modes of serving the firm's customers abroad.

The chapter is divided into three sections. The first section presents a brief overview of the development of international trade theories, from which the theories of international integration and international production evolved. The second section summarises the concepts relating to the theories of international integration. The theories of international production are outlined in the third section.

International Trade Theories

Trade theories are theories that are developed in an attempt to explain trade motives, underlying trade patterns and benefits that are derived from trade between nations. A basic understanding of these factors enables individuals, individual firms and governments to determine better how to act for their own benefit within the trading system. Trade theories have evolved over time, beginning with the emergence of strong nation-states and the organisation of systematic exchanges of goods between these nations. The theories are associated with discrete time periods. The earliest of these periods was that of mercantilism followed by classical theory, neo-classical theory and modern trade theories.

Mercantilism

Mercantilism, which was popular in Western Europe in the late seventeenth and early eighteenth century, was based on the assumption that nations should be responsible for the transfer of goods between nations in order to increase the wealth of each individual nation. Individuals were at that time deemed untrustworthy. However, wealth meant the accumulation of precious metals, especially gold. Thus, it was the responsibility of governments to induce a favourable balance of trade by facilitating and supporting all exports while limiting imports. This was achieved through government intervention, which included export monopoly, subsidisation of domestic exporting industries and imposition of duties or quotas on imports (for purposes of limiting imports). No wonder then that Western Europe countries embarked on a strategy of colonising countries, which were to eventually provide sources of raw materials or precious metals. Trade opportunities with the colonies were thus exploited, with the colonies supplying the raw materials at very unrealistically low prices. Moreover, they were often required to buy processed and/or manufactured goods from their 'colonial masters' at extraordinary high prices.

However, mercantilism had its shortcomings. For instance, it falsely asserted that gold or precious metals have intrinsic value, when actually they cannot be used for either production or consumption. Thus, nations subscribing to the mercantilism notion exchanged the products of their manufacturing or agricultural capacity for this non-productive wealth. In addition, it capitalised on the role of volumes of exports and imports and failed to recognise the value of production efficiency particularly through specialisation. Moreover, it equated the amassing of wealth with acquisition of power.

The first deficiency was corrected by neo-mercantilism, which considered the overall favourableness or unfavourableness of the balance of trade in all commodities. This involved attaching a certain value to each traded commodity. Thus, the ideal situation was for a nation to have a positive balance of trade in all goods traded so that the value of total exports exceeded that of total imports. Following this, the term 'balance of trade' has to date become popular in the political and economic circles of all nations. The second shortcoming, was addressed in subsequent theories, including the classical theory of trade.

Classical Theory

Absolute advantage   The classical theory of trade, which rests on the doctrine of comparative advantage superseded the theory of mercantilism at the beginning of the nineteenth century. It coincided with three economic and political revolutions namely, the Industrial Revolution, the American Revolution and the French Revolution. The classical theory of trade was put forward by Adam Smith (1776) in his classic work, *The Wealth of Nations*. It was based on the economic theory of free trade and enterprise that was evolving at the time. Adam Smith rejected the idea that gold was synonymous with wealth by arguing that nations generate more benefits when they acquired through trade those goods that they could not produce efficiently and produced only those goods that they could produce with maximum efficiency. In a way then, Adam Smith advocated that costs of production should dictate what should be produced by each nation. This absolute advantage concept meant that a nation would only produce those goods that made the best use of its available natural (land, environmental conditions and climatic conditions) and acquired (skilled labour force, capital resources, and technological, management and marketing advances) resources.

This concept is best illustrated using an example (adopted from Khambata and Ajami, 1992). Take two trading nations, Country A and Country B, which both have the capacity to produce olives and martini glasses. Assume that Country A is endowed with resources suitable for the production of olives, while Country B is endowed with resources suitable for the production of martini glasses. Furthermore, assume that 500 crates of olives are equivalent to 100 crates of martini glasses in value terms. In Country A, 500 crates of green olives require 100 units of resources to produce, from cultivation and harvesting to processing and packaging. However, because of lack of manufacturing facilities and machinery in that country, each glass unit must be hand-blown. Therefore, 100 crates of martini glasses (an equivalent value to 500 crates of olives) take 500 resource units to produce. This contrasts with the situation in Country B, where the production of 100 crates of martini glasses can be easily mechanised and uses only 300 resource units. But, because of Country B's climate, olives can only be grown in greenhouses under man-made environmental conditions, a very expensive process requiring 600 units to produce 500 crates. Comparison of these figures leads to a clear conclusion as to how trade should be conducted. Olives should be grown in Country A and traded for glasses produced in Country B's glass factories, because the number of resource units required for each country to produce olives and glasses are as follows:

Country	Olives (500 crates)	Martini Glasses (100 crates)
Country A	*100 units*	*500 units*
Country B	*600 units*	*300 units*

Country A utilises a total of 600 resource units, while country B utilises a total of 900 resource units for the production of both items. If Country B concentrates on the production of martini glasses, its 900 total resource units are capable of producing 300 crates of martini glasses. In value terms, it earns an extra equivalent of 100 crates of martini glasses. Similarly, if Country A concentrates on the production of olives, its 600 total units are capable of producing 3000 crates of olives. In value terms, it earns an extra equivalent of 2000 crates of olives. In other words, production costs are minimised for both products at 100 resource units per 500 crates, and 300 resource units per 100 crates of martini glasses for a total of 400 resource units. In wealth terms, Country A doubles its wealth while Country B increases its wealth by 50 per cent.

In a nutshell therefore, each country should produce the good that it can manufacture at minimum cost. However, classical theory's absolute advantage of trade presented a major problem. For instance, what happens if a country produces both or several goods or commodities at costs lower than the potential trading partner country? Do both nations have the impetus to trade?

Comparative advantage The conclusion that a country should produce all the goods that it could manufacture at minimum cost was exposed to some criticism. This meant that if a country produced one or more goods at a lower cost than the potential partner country, then there was no impetus to trade.

David Ricardo's (1948) proposals under the paradigm of comparative advantage addressed this problem. This concept considers a nation's relative production efficiencies as they apply to international trade. In his view, the exporting country should look at the relative efficiencies of production for both commodities and make only those goods it can produce most efficiently.

Consider for example, in the previous illustration that Country A developed an efficient manufacturing capacity so that martini glasses could be produced by machine rather than being hand-blown. In addition, assume that because of its relatively newer productive capacity and capital plants (relative to Country B), Country A can produce 100 crates of martini glasses using only 200 resource units as opposed to the 300 resource units required by Country B. Thus, Country A's comparative costs would fall below those of Country B for both products and its comparative advantage *vis-à-vis* those products would be higher. The resource units required to produce olives and glasses would now be:

Country	Olives (500 crates)	Martini Glasses (100 crates)
Country A	*100 units*	*200 units*
Country B	*600 units*	*300 units*

Logically, Country A should produce both olives and martini glasses. In this event, Country B's capital and labour should be directed to Country A for purposes of attaining maximum production efficiencies. However, once more, there is a problem resulting from the relative immobility of capital and labour.

This led to the concept of *specialisation*. That is, since neither capital nor labour are entirely mobile, each country should specialise. In this case then, Country A should produce olives at 100 resource units per 500 crates while Country B should produce martini glasses at 300 resource units per 100 crates. Country A is still better off at maximising its efficiencies in olive production. By doing so, it produces twice as many goods for export with the same amount of resources than if it allocated production to glassmaking, even at the new, more efficient production level.

While Country B's production costs for glasses are still higher than those of Country A at 300 units, the resources of Country B are better allocated to this production than to expensive olive-growing. In this way, Country B minimises its inefficiencies and Country A maximises its efficiencies. Thus, the point is not that a country should produce all the goods it can more cheaply, but only those it can make cheapest. Such trading leads to maximum resource efficiency.

Deficiencies   Classical theories were only partial explanation for the exchange of goods and services between nations and had several limitations. For instance, they assumed the existence of perfect knowledge regarding international markets and opportunities. In addition, they assumed full mobility of labour and production factors throughout each country. Furthermore, they assumed full labour employment within each country. Moreover, they neglected motives such as traditional employment and production history, self-sufficiency, and political objectives and assumed that each country had as its objective full production efficiency. In fact, their simplistic assumption of a two-country, two-commodity trade is unrealistic. In reality, a country engages into trade activities with several countries over a wide range of commodities and goods. Thus, the trading situation is an ongoing dynamic process in which there is an inter-play of several forces and products. Classical theories consider only those costs associated with labour. They disregard the costs associated with the other factors of production such as transportation costs, cost of land, and cost of capital.

Factor Endowment Theory

The failings of the classical theories were addressed by subsequent trade theories, which attempted to address all factors of production. One such theory is the Eli Heckscher and Bertil Ohlin (Heckscher-Ohlin) theory of factor endowment, which addressed the question of the basis of cost differentials in the production of trading nations. They proposed that each country should allocate its production according to the relative proportions of all its production factor endowments, land, labour and capital on a basic level and, on a more complex level, such factors as management and technological skills, specialised production facilities and established distribution networks.

Therefore, the range of products made or grown for export would depend on the relative ability of different factors in each country. For example, agricultural production would be emphasised in countries endowed with land, and accompanying favourable environmental and climatic conditions. Conversely, in small-land-mass countries with high populations, export products would centre on labour-intensive articles.

Similarly, capital-rich countries might centre their export base on capital-intensive production.

In this way, countries would be expected to produce goods that require large amounts of factors they hold in relative abundance. Because of the availability and low costs of these factors, each country should also be able to sell its products on foreign markets at less than international prices.

Although the theory holds in general, it does not explain export production that arises from taste differences rather than factor differentials. In addition, like the classical theory, it does not account for transportation and transaction costs in its computation. Nor does it account for differences among nations in the availability of technology and economies of scale. In particular, it disregards the availability of new technology and how it can be diffused. For instance, if the same technology is given to two different countries, there is no guarantee that the efficiency of its diffusion and, therefore, its use will be equitable. In addition, the model did not incorporate the dissimilarity of labour (i.e. highly-skilled, skilled, semi-skilled and unskilled) and capital. Furthermore, world trade patterns may not reflect the expected trade system because of government interventions through tariff and quotas imposition.

Observations

In general, all the aforementioned theories assume that nations trade, when in reality trade between nations is initiated and conducted by individuals and individual firms within those nations. In addition, they assume perfect competition and perfect information among trading partners. Similarly, they do not explain the comprehensive dynamic flow of trade in goods, services and financial flows. Moreover, they are limited in looking at either the transfer of goods or FDI. Furthermore, they do not recognise the importance of technology, and expertise in the areas of marketing and management, which are associated with FDI. Because of these deficiencies, some scholars have investigated reasons why firms enter into trade or FDI. These issues now lead to the core objective of this book. That is, factors associated with FDI, trade discrimination and therefore, globalisation. These are addressed in the subsequent sections and chapters that follow. Consideration is first made on the theoretical aspects of the theories of international integration and international production.

Theories of International Integration

Static Effects

The theories of international integration are primarily based upon the concepts of the theory of customs unions. The economic theory of customs unions is of great practical relevance since it has an obvious immediate bearing on the formation of regional blocs such as the EU, NAFTA, APTA, CACM, and EACM. It combines elements of freer trade with elements of greater protection by providing freedom of trade between the participating countries, while providing more protection for producers inside the customs union area against outside competition. The most important characteristic of a customs union is the complete removal of tariffs between member countries. This constitutes a move toward free trade, at least within the regional bloc. In addition, a customs union is also characterised by the imposition of a common external tariff on imports from the rest of the world, and the higher its level the more adverse is its impact on outsiders. Whether a customs union is economically beneficial to its member countries depends, amongst other things, upon the two concepts of trade-creation and trade-diversion.

Trade-creation and trade-diversion   The breakthrough in the theory of customs unions was made by Viner (1950) in his classic book, *The Customs Union Issue*, in which he argued that a customs union has the effect of enlarging the volume of international trade on the one hand, and of diverting trade from old to new channels on the other. He used a partial equilibrium analysis to examine the effects on a single product. His presentation of the theory of customs unions put emphasis on the static effects on resource allocation in terms of trade-creation and trade-diversion. That portion of the trade between the member countries, which is wholly new trade, he called *trade-creation*, and that portion of trade between the member countries, which is a substitute for trade with third countries, he called *trade-diversion*.

These concepts are best explained by use of an example (adopted from Panagariya, 1998). For illustration purposes, assume that two countries, Country A and Country B are starting from a non-discriminatory tariff to form a free trade area. For simplicity, focus on the market of coloured television sets (TVs). Assume that TVs are homogenous goods and that Country B is a net importer of them. At $200 per TV, Country C is the cheapest supplier of the product in the world. Country A supplies the product at $220. Unit costs and, hence, the selling prices of Country C and Country A are constant.

Assume that Country B initially imposes a 50 per cent tariff on all imported TVs. This makes the tariff-inclusive price of TVs from Country C $300, and those from Country A $330. If decisions are based purely upon the cost factor, all TVs will come from Country C, and the price of TVs in Country B settles at $300. At this price, assume that Country B's residents buy a total of 150,000 TVs. Of these, 100,000 are supplied by Country B's sellers, who produce TVs at increasing marginal costs. The remaining 50,000 TVs come from Country C and Country B collects $5,000,000 in import duties.

Now suppose that Country B forms a free trade area with Country A. The two countries drop the tariffs on each other but retain them on outside countries including Country C. Because there is no longer any tariffs on TVs from Country A, these latter can be sold in Country B at $220, while Country C's TVs are priced at $300. All the imported TVs now come from Country A, and the price of TVs in Country B declines to $220. From the efficiency point of view, assuming for now fixed total demand of 150,000 TVs in Country B, two effects can be identified.

First, the original 50,000 TVs which came from low cost supplier, Country C, now come from the higher-cost partner, Country A. In Vinerian terms, this is trade-diversion and is associated with a loss for Country B. Thus, trade-diversion is a union-induced shift in the source of imports from lower cost external sources to higher cost partner sources. This involves: (*i*) an increase in the cost of the goods previously imported from abroad, owing to the shift from foreign to partner sources; and (*ii*) a loss of consumers' surplus resulting from the substitution of higher cost partner goods for lower cost foreign goods of a different description but suitable for satisfying the same needs. The loss is manifest in the disappearance of tariff revenue, which is recaptured only partially by consumers in the form of a lower price of TVs. The remainder of the tariff revenue goes to pay for less efficiently produced TVs of the partner country (Country A).

Second, because TVs are produced under increasing marginal costs in Country B, the output there declines with the decline in prices. TVs produced at a marginal cost higher than $220 in Country B are replaced by cheaper imports. This is trade-creation. Thus, trade-creation is a union-induced shift from the consumption of higher cost domestic products in favour of lower cost products from the partner country. This involves: (*i*) the reduction or elimination of the domestic production of goods that are identical with those produced abroad, the goods instead being imported from the partner country; and, (*ii*) increased consumption of partner country substitutes for domestic goods that formerly satisfied the need at a high cost. Trade-creation entails economic gains of two sorts. In (*i*) a saving in the real cost of goods previously produced domestically is attained (*production effect*), while the consumers' surplus arising from the substitution of lower for higher cost means of satisfying wants (*consumption effect*) is experienced in (*ii*). This trade-creation increases efficiency by replacing higher-cost Country B's production by lower-cost imports from Country A.

Trade-diversion reduces efficiency while trade-creation improves it. Therefore, the net effect of a free trade area is ambiguous in general. Basically, therefore, a customs union has an end effect of shifting the sources of supply for member countries either from lower to higher-costs or from higher to lower costs, depending on the circumstances. It will only be viable if all the members benefit from it either by appropriate distribution or compensatory transfers among member countries.

Ceteris paribus, the higher the initial tariff, the lower the difference between the prices of the two suppliers of imports; and the larger the economic size of the union, the more likely the free trade area will improve efficiency. A higher initial tariff means that potential gains from de-protecting the domestic industry even on a discriminatory basis are large, or, equivalently, the trade-creation effect is likely to dominate. A small difference between the prices of partner and outside source means that the terms-of-trade deterioration from switching to the partner is small, or, equivalently, the trade diversion effect is small. Finally, the larger the union, the more likely that the lowest-cost source of supply would be within the union. For instance, in this example, if Country C was also included in the union, there would be no trade-diversion in the TV market, and welfare would rise unambiguously.

It might be instructive to summarise this analysis graphically. In figure 2.1, DD' and SS', respectively represent Country B's demand for and supply of TVs of a given quality. The vertical axis shows the price of a TV in US dollars, and the horizontal axis shows the quantity of TVs in thousands. Under the non-discriminatory tariff of 50 per cent, the price in Country B is $300 and quantities consumed, produced and imported are 150,000, 100,000 and 50,000 respectively. All imports come from Country C at a border price of $200. Import duties sum to areas 1 plus 2.

A free trade area between Country B and Country A lowers the price in Country B to $220 per TV, and all imports now come from Country A. Of the original 150,000 TVs bought earlier, 40,000 are now produced domestically, and 110,000 are imported from Country A. The 60,000 additional imported units replace higher-cost domestic units. This is trade-creation and yields a gain of area 3 for Country B. The other 50,000 units replace cheaper Country C's units. This is trade-diversion and leads to a loss of area 1 for Country B. Note that all of tariff revenue represented by areas 1 and 2 disappears. But area 1 is recaptured by consumers via a lower price of TVs.

There is one more source of efficiency effect which, in the spirit of Viner, has not been identified so far. The reduction in price from $300 to $220 per TV expands the consumption of TVs and brings the marginal benefit from consumption closer to the marginal cost of it. This generates a further welfare gain represented by area 4. The net effect of the free trade area is positive or negative as the sum of areas 3 and 4 is larger or smaller than area 1.

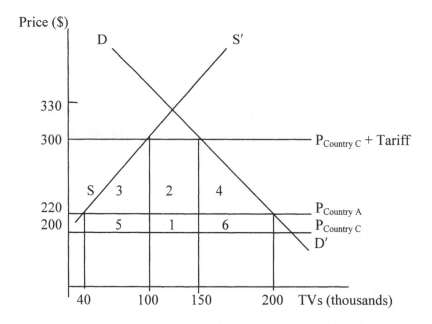

Figure 2.1   Trade-creation and trade-diversion effects
Note: Not drawn to scale.

Nonetheless, the dynamic effects relate more to the theory of international production than the static effects. As briefly highlighted below, these are mostly examined in relation to scale economies, specialisation, economic growth and terms of trade.

Dynamic Effects

Customs unions and scale economies Customs unions lead to an increase in market size that promotes large scale production and, therefore, economies of scale of production, making low unit-costs of production possible (originally, production in the home country would be limited by the size of the market). The enlargement of the market can be economically advantageous if the scale economies in production reduce the production costs to a lower level than production costs of non-members since this may induce higher demand.

Customs unions and specialisation If the member countries possess different comparative advantages, this opens up for specialisation between the different industries. The greater the relative differences in production costs are for the different industries, the greater the inter-industry specialisation will become among the member countries. The more uniform the production is with regard to product variants within a single industry, the less the companies in the different countries exploit the advantages of specialisation. The customs union allows the firms to exploit these advantages through specialisation, which leads to intra-industry trade.

Customs unions and economic growth Economies of scale will be facilitated if increased resource mobility can be stimulated, since the expanding industries could then draw those resources of which they are intensive users from a larger economic area. Giant firms are able to reap static and dynamic economies of scale within the large single market. These economies enable firms to meet greater market demand by moving down their long-run average cost curves. A customs union may provide a market large enough to support a sufficient number of optimally sized plants without resulting in the danger of monopolistic exploitation and hence X-inefficiency, which is often a problem of national segmented markets. Increased competition, which can stimulate a high level of efficiency, is another mechanism of dynamic gain provided by a customs union. Competition forces producers to improve their products and production processes through product and process innovation; and reduction of prices forcing the inefficient producers out of business. A large and expanding market is thus conducive to a greater level of both indigenous investment and FDI - *a key factor in raising the rate of economic growth* (see Chapter 5).

Customs unions and the terms-of-trade Economic benefits may be derived from a tariff levy and member countries can effectively exploit it under a customs union. It will, however, be beneficial to member countries but injure the rest of the world. A tariff not only diverts consumption from imported to domestically produced commodities (domestic in the entire customs union area), but also creates a change in favour of the tariff-levying country, the rate at which its exports exchange for imports which survive the tariff. This leads to an improvement in the national terms-of-trade and, therefore, an increase in the national total benefit from trade. The greater the economic area of the tariff-levying unit, the greater is likely to be *ceteris paribus* the terms-of-trade of a customs union area with the outside world resulting from its tariff. Unfortunately, customs union area terms-of-trade are not only influenced by its own tariffs but by tariffs levied by the outside world on its export products as well. Other things being equal, the terms-of-trade with the rest of the world will be less favourable, the higher the tariffs on its export products. The level of foreign tariffs can, however, be bargained, the bargaining being more effective the larger the customs union (bargaining unit).

High level integration schemes The dynamic concepts of the theory of customs unions can be extended to other integration schemes such as common markets. A common market involves not only the integration of product markets through the trade liberalisation that results from a customs union, but also the integration of factor markets through the elimination of obstacles to the free movement of factors within the integrated area. The main reason behind striving to establish a common market is the hope that the freedom of capital and labour to move from activities of a low marginal product to those with a higher one will lead to a more efficient allocation. The theory of common markets is, therefore, concerned with the additional gains that can be derived by adding the freedom of movement of factors to a customs union. A common market may speed up innovation and enforce changes in industrial structure. In addition, it may sharpen competition and thus lead to economies of scale, cost reduction, product improvement and better export potential.

A common market can also influence the process of international production. The larger market will offer prospects to specialist producers who would not have been viable in smaller nationally segmented markets. Should a common market present a sufficient diversity in production environments, then it will offer better opportunities for the location of firms in the course of the expansion and saturation stages of the product life cycle. A common market may also make it possible to find locations to accommodate within its territory and production of articles at the final stage of their life cycle, and thus postpone the movement or relocation of these activities to third countries.

Theories of International Production

Product Life Cycle

Vernon (1966) was among the first to explain the reasons for international production through the Product Life Cycle theory of investment. This theory, which focused on consumer durables was primarily based on the US experience. It suggests that FDI is a natural stage in the life cycle of a new product from its inception to its maturity and eventual decline. Thus, international firms expand into foreign markets on an incremental basis, giving management time to analyse and understand the foreign economic, political and social environments.

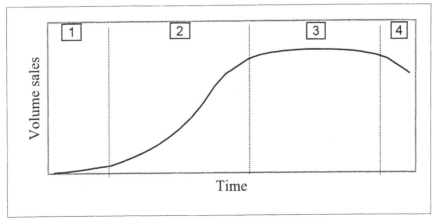

Figure 2.2   **The product life cycle stages**

Since this theory is best explained using a diagram, Figure 2.2 is employed to illustrate its four basic stages. Stage 1 marks the introduction of the new product. The socio-economic development, economies of scale, and oligopolistic competition that are found in most advanced industrial countries lead firms in these countries to undertake intensive research and development (R&D) efforts so that new technologically advanced or differentiable products are discovered. These new products are first introduced in the home market, and close co-ordination of production and sales undertaken while the products are improved. Cost consideration is not important here, since most of the costs are by nature fixed-costs. Furthermore, if customers like the new product, they are often willing to pay a premium price for it. Thus in US' case, the size of the market was big enough to generate benefits from scale economies, its per capita income was high, and its technological base was strong. Consequently, these factors served to stimulate the innovation and launching of new products in the home market. Besides, the fact that the product was close to the customers meant that it was possible to undertake research into customer needs and introduce them into the product. Stage 1 ends when the product has been introduced, and when increases in its demand indicate that it has been accepted.

Stage 2 relates to the period when the product is exported. At the beginning of this stage, the firm restricts itself to exporting until it has got a good understanding of the foreign environment. For the case of the US, the firms started exporting to the other developed countries. The product starts commanding a strong brand loyalty and its sales begin surging. However, because of its success, numerous aggressive companies start emulating it at this stage. Towards the end of Stage 2, industry competition stiffens after the market also accepts rival firms' imitations. Cost considerations then start coming into play. There is now a cost incentive to produce the product outside the home country. This may for instance, take the form of wanting to avoid export taxes and other tariffs imposed by the recipient country. Besides, a delay to undertake production in the target market may result into first-mover competitors undertaking early production and hence monopolising the market share.

The product eventually reaches maturity in Stage 3. In addition, competition from nearly similar products narrows profit margins and threatens margins in both export and home markets. Therefore, its production process is standardised. At this stage foreign manufacturing locations are sought, where market imperfections in the cost of factors of production create a chance for lower unit production costs. Consequently, production may be relocated to developing countries where skilled labour is abundant and cheap. Thus foreign investment is essentially a defensive investment designed to preserve profit margins in both export and home markets.

The inevitable occurs in Stage 4 when the sales start declining. There is now reason to further reduce costs by replacing labour-intensive production processes with automated ones. In that event then, there is strong reason for the production to go back to the home country where the technology for automation is abundant.

This theory is, however, no longer wholly appropriate since it is evident that TNCs introduce products simultaneously in several markets of the world. Moreover, they do so not just in a standardised but in a differentiated form as well. For instance, Japanese firms have simultaneously initiated innovative investments both at home and abroad.

Follow the Leader

Knickerbocker (1973) developed a follow-the-leader theory of defensive FDI. He noted that in oligopolistic industries when one competitor undertakes FDI, other competitors follow very quickly with defensive FDI into that market. He hypothesised that followers were motivated by a desire to deny any competitive advantage, such as the benefits of economies of scale, to the leaders. Defensive investments are even more apparent in the raw-material-producing industries. Control over sources of raw materials, and conversely denial of these sources to competitors, causes a number of pre-emptive, defensive-type investments, similar to those of market-seeking oligopolists. He suggested that investment can take on one of the following; investment to supply the local market, resource based investment and export platform investment.

Investment to supply the local market is undertaken when the firms investing have some competitive or ownership advantage over the local or other foreign firms. Should the firms choose to supply the market from a local production base rather than by exports, then it may be because locational advantages favour the host country rather than the home country.

Resource based investment is usually to supply the home firm or country and other countries with resources. The TNCs use their ownership advantages over domestic competitors derived from superior technology required for exploration, extraction and processing together with the large capital needs required. Raw material seekers extract raw materials wherever they can be found, either for export or for further processing and sale in the host country. Resource seeking FDI is usually undertaken to ensure availability, and reduce uncertainty and risk in the provision of raw materials. Firms in oil, mining, plantations, and forest industries fall into this category. Less advanced developing countries especially those based in Africa, still have natural resources that have not yet been tapped and this could be the one major source of hope of attracting foreign investment.

Export platform investment is mostly associated with production in countries where one or more of the factors of production are under-priced relative to their productivity. Labour-intensive production of electronic components in Southeast Asia is an example of this motivation. Of late, a distinction is being made between two types of production efficiency: production of complete goods and/or services, and sourcing components and assembling components. Production of complete goods and/or services will require TNCs to concentrate their production of labour or resource-intensive (natural) goods in labour and resource rich countries; and capital or technology-intensive goods in countries that are rich in capital and technology by taking advantage of specialisation and division of labour. The second kind deals with investment in labour-intensive parts of production process for sale in world markets, the capital or technology intensive part of the production being produced in capital or technology rich countries and the labour-intensive process being undertaken in the labour rich less developed countries. Sourcing components requires some form of skilled manpower and fairly sophisticated machinery and equipment, whereas assembling components requires minimum skill and machinery. The latter may become a target area for less advanced developing countries.

Eclectic Theory

The most recent view which in a way embraces the concepts of the earlier explanations is that which suggests that the propensity for a firm to engage in foreign production depends on the combination of ownership-specific advantages, internalisation opportunities and locational advantages in the target market. These reasons, which explain why FDI takes place at all have been given by Dunning (1981) under the eclectic theory of FDI. Each of these determinants of FDI relates to an advantage of direct investment over alternative modes of serving the firm's customers abroad.

The ownership advantage is necessary to outweigh the disadvantage of being foreign. That is, to overcome the better understanding of local conditions by indigenous firms. It arises from the possession of relatively large amounts of the three broad types of firm-specific assets, production technology, managerial resources and marketing techniques. The possession of relatively large amounts of these knowledge-based assets leads to two important theoretical expectations. First, it is likely to lead to more efficient production and marketing. Second, it gives such firms an international competitive advantage since the investing firms often have a strong ownership advantage over local firms.

The host country must also possess some locational advantage to attract investment, which will serve the market of the host country, or use it as an export base. This component of the eclectic framework, therefore, seeks to determine reasons why the use of a firm's ownership advantage should be implemented through production in foreign countries. This may take the form of factors such as a large or a potential domestic market, a low-cost effective export production base with abundant low-cost high quality labour, low transportation costs, generous investment incentives, lax pollution controls, political stability, and sound macro-economic policies. Locational advantages are highly dependent on the stage of development, the development path and the industrialisation strategy of the potential host country.

Finally, once ownership and locational advantages indicate that production in a particular country is desirable, there must be an internalisation advantage that induces the firm to choose between direct investment over the arms-length arrangements such as production licensing or franchising. This includes the desire to minimise the risk and/or costs of fluctuating exchange rates; to cushion the adverse effects of government legislation or policy; to be able to take advantage of differential interest rates and 'leads' and 'lags' in intra-group payments; and to adjust the distribution of its short-term assets between different currency areas.

It means, therefore, that a firm can only capture a foreign market through FDI if it has the capacity to exploit simultaneously all the three advantages. If for instance, it possesses only the ownership advantage without internalisation and locational advantages, then it will pursue other strategies such as licensing agreements or exporting as a means of entering the foreign market.

The eclectic model can, therefore, be perceived as a general theory of international production in as far as it provides an analytical framework for explaining all forms of such production. It explains that firms start production in home countries but shift abroad when their technology becomes more accessible to local competitors and the costs of production of the more mature and standardised product are more favourable abroad. It also helps to explain how regional economic integration changes locational advantages and the distribution of ownership advantages between firms of different origins.

Conclusion

There are a number of theories, which seek to explain international trade. These theories are descriptive in nature and mainly focus on trade patterns, and can be categorised as either traditional theory on recent theory.

Traditional theory is based on a number of assumptions. For instance, it assumes a situation of perfect competition in markets for finished goods and factor markets. In addition, it assumes no externalities. Therefore, de facto prices always reflect the social-economic costs of production, as well as the social-economic utility of consumption.

Recent theories assume that products are differentiated, and no longer assume constant returns to scale. There may be economies of scale and benefits in connection with product specialisation at the firm level. Nonetheless, there may be also external economies.

Traditional theory gives an exact account of the trade pattern. In the neo-classical factor proportion theory, the countries' factor endowments explain trade patterns. According to Ricardo's theory, differences in production conditions determine the pattern of trade.

The recent theories, which take account of differentiated products, as well as economies of scale and enterprise specialisation, succeed in explaining the substantial trade volume, but not the trade pattern.

The descriptive theories explain trade by using comparative static analysis, in which autarky is compared with free trade. These theories may also be used normatively by comparing welfare in autarky with welfare under free trade. Such static analysis leads to the conclusion that free trade is better than autarky. According to factor proportion theory, this can be explained by the utilisation of the relative differences in a country's factor endowments. According to Ricardo's theory, this is due to the utilisation of differences in production technology.

In recent theories, the benefit of free trade is related to economies of scale and enterprise specialisation being utilised to a greater extent under free trade because the market is larger. Free trade means that the competitive situation is different than in autarky. Increased competition gives advantages in the form of lower prices. Moreover, free trade opens up for a wider range of goods making it easier for individual consumers to choose between preferred types of products.

The dynamic concepts of scale economies, specialisation and terms of trade have enabled the understanding of the theories of international integration and international production. For instance, they provide reasons that support economic integration. In addition, they explain why firms may replace international trade with direct investment in a given country.

3 Global and Regional FDI Trends

Introduction

The globalisation process has been triggered, encouraged or closely followed by TNCs. This is partly why the significance of the role FDI plays in the global integration has been growing in the recent past. For instance, its dramatic growth in the 1990s and over time since the 1970s has brought about a greater degree of integration of the world economy than could have been achieved by trade alone. More firms in more industries from more countries are expanding abroad through direct investment than ever before, and virtually all economies now compete to attract TNCs. This trend has been driven by the complex interaction of technological change, evolving corporate strategies towards a more global focus and policy reform in individual countries. Therefore, it is essential to understand its recent trends.

This chapter briefly highlights the global and regional FDI trends during the past three or so decades when its economic influence became an issue of interest in the social, economic and political environment. It also identifies reasons responsible for the respective FDI booms and bursts, and provides explanations for the FDI inflow/outflow disparity between the developed and the developing countries. However, with the exception of a few outstanding countries and/or sub-regions, it is beyond the scope of this book to examine the detailed trends at the country or sub-regional level. These details are available in for instance the UNCTAD publications.

Global Trends

As Figure 3.1 illustrates, prior to 1973, FDI flows were relatively insignificant (see also Tables 3.1 and 3.2). FDI activity started to intensify in 1973 particularly in the developed countries. This intensity was partly in

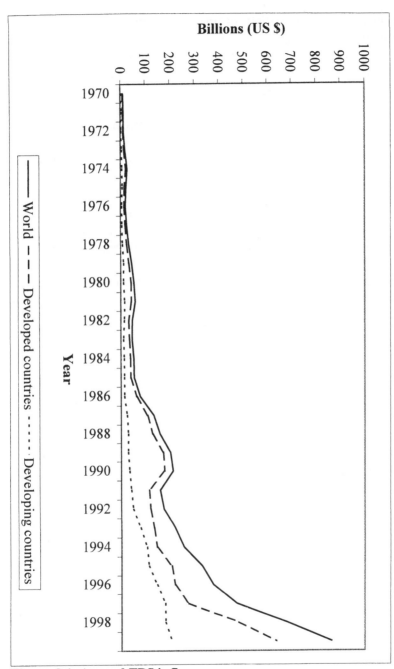

Figure 3.1 Annual FDI inflows
Source :   UNCTAD (varous years).

response to the formation of the European Community (EC) whose membership increased to 9 in 1973. Thus, FDI was defensive in nature, aimed at accessing the market and, hence jumping the anticipated tariffs concomitant with the formation of the community. These issues are discussed in more detail in Chapter 6 and in the Appendix.

However, the 1973-74 oil crisis caused a global economic recession, which in turn induced an FDI recession between 1975-76. Firms were forced to shift their investments to developed (mostly home) countries at that time in order to use their limited funds to support their affiliates during the recession.

Recovery was attained in 1977 eventually resulting into a boom, which lasted until 1981. Although substantial FDI was directed to the major oil producing countries because of the booming oil industry, the gap between flows to developed countries and developing countries started to increase. Not surprisingly, countries including the Netherlands, United Kingdom (UK) and the US, which are home to major petroleum TNCs led outflows.

The second oil crisis experienced in 1979-80 induced another global economic recession similarly resulting into an FDI recession in 1982 for the developed countries, and in 1983 for the developing countries. By 1984 recovery had been attained leading to an FDI boom that lasted until 1990. Specifically, the turning point came after 1985 following the Plaza Accord, which resolved to have an orderly appreciation of the major non-dollar currencies. This made the production of labour-intensive products more costly in the developed countries. Consequently, developed countries (particularly Japan) were forced to shift from their traditional approach of serving foreign markets explicitly through exports towards a greater reliance on FDI. In addition, there were some other factors. For instance, the expansion of the EC to 12 members triggered fears of stronger protectionism. This not only stimulated more FDI into the EC but, forced Japanese TNCs to also create their own 'fortress' in Asia. Therefore, production particularly by Japanese firms was relocated to the neighbouring labour-intensive countries endowed with semi-skilled or skilled labour. Furthermore, FDI was also facilitated by economic growth of developing countries, and by the development and adoption of information technologies by firms, which simplified the co-ordination with affiliates, management of affiliates and conduction of international transactions. Likewise, it was facilitated by surplus funds, which resulted from developed countries' economic booms, and by the locational advantages offered by some developing countries. These included

Table 3.1   FDI inflows by major region/country, 1989-99 (billion US $)

Region/Country	Year										
	1989	1990	1991	1992	1993	1994	1995	1996	1997	1998	1999
World	200.6	211.4	158.9	173.8	219.4	256	331.8	377.5	473.1	680.1	865.5
D'ed Countries	171.7	176.4	114.8	119.7	133.9	145.1	205.7	219.8	275.2	480.6	636.4
European Union	84.2	104.4	78.8	83.8	76.8	76.9	114.4	108.6	128.6	248.7	305.1
North America	72.8	55.8	25.5	23.4	48.3	53.3	68.0	94.1	117.2	208.0	300.6
United States	67.7	47.9	22.8	18.9	43.5	45.1	58.8	84.5	105.5	186.3	275.5
Other	10.4	10.1	10.5	12.5	6.9	8.7	18.7	10.8	19.0	12.7	20.7
Japan	1.1	1.8	1.7	2.8	0.1	0.9	0.04	0.2	3.2	3.2	12.7
D'ing Countries	28.6	34.7	41.7	49.6	78.8	104.9	111.9	145.0	178.8	179.5	207.6
C and E Europe	0.3	0.3	2.4	4.4	6.8	5.9	14.3	12.7	19.0	19.9	21.4
Africa	4.8	2.2	2.8	3.2	3.5	5.6	4.7	5.5	6.9	7.5	8.9
North Africa	1.6	1.1	0.9	1.6	1.5	2.3	1.2	1.2	2.4	2.3	3.0
Other Africa	3.2	1.1	1.9	1.6	2.0	3.3	3.5	4.3	4.5	5.2	5.9
L. A and C	7.5	9.0	15.4	16.2	20.0	30.1	32.8	45.9	69.2	73.8	90.5
South America	4.4	4.5	6.8	7.4	8.0	15.2	18.9	31.6	47.6	51.3	72.1
Other	3.1	4.5	8.6	8.8	12.0	14.9	13.9	14.3	21.5	22.4	18.4
Asia	16.0	23.1	23.1	29.6	54.8	68.6	73.3	92.4	101.6	96.5	105.6
West Asia	0.5	3.2	1.9	1.8	3.7	1.8	0.01	2.4	4.9	6.2	6.7
Central Asia	n.a	n.a	n.a	0.1	1.3	0.9	1.7	2.1	3.1	3.1	2.8
S and E Asia	15.5	19.9	21.?	27.7	49.8	65.9	71.7	87.9	93.5	87.2	96.1
China	3.4	3.5	4.4	11.2	27.5	33.8	35.8	40.2	44.2	43.8	40.4
The Pacific	0.2	0.3	0.3	0.4	0.2	0.2	0.6	0.2	0.1	0.2	0.2

Source: UNCTAD (various years).
Notes: D'ed: developed, D'ing: developing, C: Central, E: East, L. A and C: Latin America and caribbean, and n.a: no data.

Table 3.2   FDI outflows by major region/country, 1991–99 (billion US $)

Region/Country	Year								
	1991	1992	1993	1994	1995	1996	1997	1998	1999
World	198.1	201.5	247.4	282.9	357.5	390.8	471.9	648.1	799.9
Developed Countries	189.8	179.7	207.4	240.5	306.8	331.9	404.2	651.9	731.8
European Union	106.4	110.5	98.8	120.7	159.0	182.3	223.7	425.5	509.8
Germany	23.7	19.7	17.2	18.9	39.1	50.8	40.7	91.2	50.6
United Kingdom	16.3	19.0	26.8	32.2	43.6	34.0	61.6	119.0	199.3
North America	39.1	42.6	80.5	82.5	103.5	97.5	122.0	177.3	168.7
United States	33.5	39.0	74.8	73.3	92.1	84.4	99.5	146.1	150.9
Other	36.0	20.4	18.5	24.3	29.2	30.1	35.7	29.8	29.8
Japan	31.6	17.4	13.8	18.1	22.5	23.4	26.1	24.2	22.7
Developing Countries	8.3	21.7	39.8	42.1	50.3	57.8	64.3	33.0	65.6
Central and Eastern Europe	0.04	0.1	0.3	0.3	0.5	1.1	3.4	2.2	2.5
Africa	0.96	0.4	0.7	0.5	0.2	-0.04	1.6	0.6	0.9
North Africa	0.1	0.04	0.02	0.1	0.2	0.1	0.4	0.4	0.4
Other Africa	0.8	0.4	0.6	0.4	-.02	-0.1	1.2	0.3	0.6
Latin America and Caribbean	0.5	2.6	7.6	6.1	7.3	5.8	15.1	9.4	27.3
South America	1.3	0.7	2.9	3.1	3.8	4.1	8.6	8.4	8.3
Other	-1.8	1.9	4.7	3.0	3.5	1.7	6.4	0.9	19.0
Asia	7.8	18.7	31.5	35.5	42.7	51.9	47.4	22.8	37.2
West Asia	-0.3	1.3	0.8	-1.2	-0.9	2.4	-0.4	-4.3	1.2
South, East and Southeast Asia	8.2	17.4	30.7	36.7	43.4	49.5	47.7	27.0	35.7
Hong Kong	2.8	8.3	17.7	21.4	25.0	26.5	24.4	16.9	19.9

Source: UNCTAD (various years).

liberalisation of their FDI regimes, the availability of relatively cheap skilled labour and improved infrastructural facilities. Moreover, since the late 1980s, firms from the dynamic developing countries such as the Asian NIEs had developed strategic assets that enabled them also to invest abroad particularly in countries at comparatively lower levels of economic development.

Nonetheless, the share of FDI to the oil rich Western Asia countries as a percentage of flows to developing countries continued to decline during the second half of the 1980s, indicating that factors other than natural resources were acting as strong pull factors of FDI. In general China and the US dominated on inflows, and the UK and US on outflows. However, since the mid-1980s, the gap between FDI flows to developed countries and developing countries has widened. This is mainly attributed to three factors. First, the continued economic difficulties and political instabilities faced by many developing countries, making them less attractive to TNCs. Second, the increased importance of technologically-intensive investments favouring locations in developed countries. Third, fears of a rise in protectionist forces in the EU and US (NAFTA). Moreover, while the flows of FDI to developing countries continued to increase, this was restricted to only a few countries mostly situated in East and South Asia, and oil exporting countries.

An FDI recession was experienced in 1991 following the 1990 economic recession triggered by: the Japanese stock market collapse; slow down in economic activity in the US, which entered a recession in the mid-year; and rising private sector debt burdens and emerging structural weaknesses within the financial systems in a number of countries. However, this FDI recession was explicitly in the developed countries. Recovery in the developed countries was attained in 1992 leading to a boom that still existed at the time of writing (2001). It was in part driven by the formation of NAFTA in 1992 and the EU in 1993. However, the growth rate of FDI was faster in developing countries than developed countries in the early- 1990s. A new FDI record was set in 1997-99 when TNCs responded to economic growth and continued liberalisation, enabling them to expand their operations abroad through mergers and acquisitions (M&As). Many developed countries with large outflows also had large inflows. On the other hand, in response to the uncertainty caused by the 1997/98 financial crisis, the Asian countries' performance was exceptionally poor. Unsurprisingly then, the FDI growth rate for the developed countries surpassed that for the developing countries.

The expansion of FDI in the 1990s was driven by several inter-related factors: rapid technological change; trade and investment liberalisation at a national, regional and global level; privatisation; deregulation; demonopolisation and the switch in emphasis by firms from product to geographical diversification, involving a more balanced global distribution of production and sales for each company. A large number of stock market listings have also facilitated the sale of domestic companies to foreign investors. These factors interact at various levels as policy reform and technological change bring greater competition at a global level, which in turn drives firms to expand abroad and to invest in newer technologies. Governments in turn respond by trying to increase their attractiveness to foreign direct investors through further reform and liberalisation.

A central theme, which emerges from country studies is that the effectiveness of a given policy is not constant over time. Some host countries were able in the past to attract inward investment by offering a large and protected market. Market saturation and the lack of dynamism in the local economy as a result of protection eventually places a limit on the future growth of inflows as TNCs gravitate towards more dynamic markets. The same decline in effectiveness can be seen in terms of policies designed to maximise the potential benefits from inward investment. Many host countries made use of performance requirements in the past, such as exporting requirements or technology transfer agreements. As foreign affiliates of TNCs become more oriented towards global or regional markets and, hence, less dependent on the domestic market and as the number of countries eager to attract FDI grows, the tolerance of foreign investors for barriers and restrictions on their operations is likely to be much less than in the past. In this sense, the cost of investment restrictions has risen. Many of the remaining barriers to inward investment were erected at a time when foreign firms were investing in economies distorted by trade barriers, a lack of effective competition in product markets, under-developed financial markets and by many other policies associated with import-substitution. In this environment, host countries sometimes justified restrictions on inward investment on the basis of the theory of second-best, which argues that liberalisation in one area in the presence of distortions elsewhere may make the economy worse off. In the more competitive environment in many host countries today as a result of roughly a decade of economic reforms, many restrictions are at best ineffective and at worst counter-productive. The policy environment matters not just for its effect on FDI inflows but also because of the way it influences the potential benefits from those inflows. In the import-substituting environment found in many host countries in the past, the gains from FDI tended to be disappointing, particularly in the area of technology-transfer. After a decade of economic reforms, host countries are better placed to realise the full benefits from inward investment than they were in the past. These benefits could be further enhanced as the process of liberalisation continues (Ribeiro, 2000).

During the pre-industrial period (which has varied between countries and between regions), FDI was concentrated in raw material and resource-based extraction and processing, and to a limited extent manufacturing. It was characterised by oligopolistic activities almost exclusively by firms from developed countries. These firms had strong strategic assets that enabled them to invest abroad. For the case of developing countries, FDI was initially directed mostly to countries endowed with natural resources. The developing countries had neither the technology nor the skills necessary for the extraction and/or processing of raw materials, and for the development of the manufacturing sector. The foreign firms took advantage of this shortfall and provided both the technology and skills, enabling raw materials to be extracted for export or for further processing and sale at both home and abroad (Bende-Nabende, 2000). With increasing industrialisation and changes in consumer demand, FDI gradually shifted into the manufacturing sector until it started dominating the inflow shares. Further changes in consumer lifestyles, the technological revolution, and global deregulation has now promoted the services sector as the most favourable recipient of FDI particularly in the more developed countries. Thus in general, the dominance of FDI in the primary sector is currently characteristic of the very poor least developed countries or countries whose economies heavily rely on mineral and other natural resources. Although the services sector is showing signs of catching-up, FDI flows into most developing countries still dominate the manufacturing sector. For the developed countries and the NIEs, however, the services sector currently commands the largest share. UNCTAD (1999) reports that on a sectoral level, FDI stock declined by a half of the share in the primary sector between 1988 and 1997, globally as well as in developed and developing countries. The services sector experienced a corresponding increase, again in both developed and developing countries. Nonetheless, the share of the manufacturing sector remained stable, representing the single most important sector in developing countries.

The mode of investment has also changed with time. For instance, in contrast to the 1950s and 1960s when green-field investment was the most popular mode of market entry, cross-border mergers, strategic alliances and acquisitions have been used increasingly as a major means of entering foreign markets since the mid-1980s. Although it is now also picking up especially in the more dynamic developing countries, this is particularly the case in the developed countries. The reasons for the enhanced role of M&A are in part specifically commercial (e.g., over-capacity and low demand in certain industries), in part strategic (e.g., sharing high investment costs in information technology and high research and development expenditures) and in part related to the policy environment (e.g., the widespread adoption of deregulation and liberalisation measures). Cross-border mergers often occur when two companies of almost equal sizes come together under common ownership. This strategy is good if there is a potential synergy. Strategic alliances on the other hand take place when two companies come together in most cases for purposes of accessing each other's strategic assets, particularly new technology. Acquisitions are undertaken when bigger companies take over smaller ones, and act as one of the quickest ways of entering a new market. The sharp growth in the number and scale of cross-border M&As basically reflects the rising need to respond to international competition due to the globalisation of corporate activities, as well as the increased acceptance of M&As as a means of responding to this situation. At the same time, systems have continued to change in favour of M&As. These include the shift toward accounting standards that enable corporations to be compared on an international basis. While general trends such as privatisation and deregulation have created opportunities for M&As in a broad range of fields, conditions unique to each industry, especially the service industries in which M&As are heavily concentrated, have paved the way for more deals.

Developed Country Trends

The developed countries are the most important focal point for activities of TNCs for obvious reasons. For instance, their heavy investment in R&D makes them primary sources of innovation. Moreover, they have large markets and therefore large consumer demand. In addition, their investment environment is friendlier. Within the developed countries, FDI revolves within the Triad (i.e. the EU, Japan and the US). In addition, the regional divisions of labour have led to regional configurations often referred to as clusters. These were more pronounced during the mid- to late-1980s and the early-1990s. For instance, the Latin American countries and some Caribbean countries were clustered around the US. The East and Central European countries were clustered around the EU, while the Asian countries were clustered around Japan. Furthermore, the less advanced developing countries in Asia were in turn clustered around the Asian NIEs. Similarly, most of the inter-regional investment from Latin America went to the Caribbean Islands. These clusters are influenced by the geographic proximity of the developing country to the Triad member. Nonetheless, the African countries and some of the Caribbean countries were clustered around the EU mainly because of political and historical reasons. Since the late-1990s, however, there is an indication that the clusterisation is becoming less concentrated in some regions. For instance, the dominance of the US FDI share in Latin America is being challenged by heavy investment by European countries. This should indeed be attributed to the ongoing globalisation process.

UNCTAD (1992) reports that during the 1980s, approximately 81 per cent of FDI outflows originated within the Triad, while 71 per cent inflows went to the Triad. The factors responsible for this are the emergence of Japan as a significant investor after 1985, and the regionalisation of the European and North American markets. By 1998, the share of outflows had increased to about 92 per cent, while inflows had increased to 72 per cent (UNCTAD, 1999). In addition, they were responsible for over 90 per cent of all outflows and inflows to the developed countries in 1998. FDI between the US and EU jumped sharply, more than doubling from $109.6 billion in 1997 to $224.5 billion in 1998 and accounting for 34.6 per cent of global FDI. The EU's investment in the US has exceeded the US's investment in the EU since 1996. This is attributed to the large number and scale of M&As in the US by EU firms, which was particularly pronounced in 1998, when EU investment in the US exceeded US investment in the EU by a factor of 2.4.

Within the developed countries, the major single investor is the US which, in 1997, controlled 25.6 per cent of the world's FDI stock, compared to 45.1 per cent for the EU (15), and 8.0 per cent for Japan. More recent figures indicate that in 1998 the US was the world's biggest investor for the eighth year running, its investment having increased 20.8 per cent on the previous year's record of $110 billion to $132.8 billion. The other major investors were the UK (up 68.1 per cent to $106.7 billion), Germany (up 112.8 per cent to $87.7 billion), France (up 15.0 per cent to $40.8 billion), and the Netherlands (up 37.6 per cent to $39.8 billion). However, the US' monopoly was broken in 1999 when the UK with $199 billion became the largest outward investor. TNCs based in the EU invested $510 billion abroad, or nearly two thirds of global outflows (UNCTAD, 2000).

With respect to the inflows, the US registered strong growth of 77.0 per cent on the previous year to $193.4 billion, making it the largest recipient of FDI in 1998. It was followed by the UK (up 82.4 per cent to $67.5 billion), China (down 1.1 per cent to $43.8 billion), the Netherlands (up 163.1 per cent to $33.3 billion), and Brazil (up 62.4 per cent to $31.9 billion). Thus, as in the previous year, with the exception of China and Brazil, the top five recipients and sources of FDI were industrialised countries. In 1999, large M&As in the US and the continued strength of its economy made it the largest recipient of FDI ($276 billion, nearly one third of the world total) for the seventh consecutive year.

Developing Country Regional Trends

Asia

FDI has been a central part of capital inflows for many Asian countries during the recent years. For instance, since the general global liberalisation of the FDI regimes following the effects of the 1985 Plaza Accord, the percentage share of Asian FDI inflows grew steadily (except in 1989 and 1995) from 9.2 per cent in 1989 to almost one quarter in 1996.

There is a significant disparity in the regional distribution of FDI. Western Asia, which comprises mostly the oil rich 'Middle-east' countries, increased its share both world-wide and regionally, peaking during 1991-93. However, the share has slumped since 1994, perhaps indicating that oil-producing countries are no longer comparatively important FDI hosts. Consequently, the beneficiary sub-regions have been South and East Asia, which have attracted over 90 per cent of the annual FDI destined for Asia.

Even within this region, only about 10 countries dominate the FDI inflow share. For instance, the figures indicate that between 1986 and 1996, China, Hong Kong, Indonesia, Japan, Korea, Malaysia, the Philippines, Singapore, Taiwan and Thailand contributed close to 90 per cent of FDI share in 5 years, and over 90 per cent in the remaining 6 years.

However, the distribution of individual country shares varies considerably. In general, between 1986 and 1991, Singapore dominated the

Asian FDI inflows share averaging about 20 per cent, closely followed by China and then Hong Kong. Indonesia, Malaysia and Thailand then followed in the second group. In the last group were Japan, the Philippines and the two NIEs, Korea and Taiwan. However, the distribution changed drastically in 1992 when China's FDI inflows almost trebled from $4.4 billion in the previous year to $11.2 billion. UNCTAD (1997) attributed this mainly to the rush by investors to establish and implement FDI projects before the enactment of policies that would abolish some of the preferential treatment for foreign investors (i.e. on 1 April 1996, with an extension of six months for certain types of projects). Thereafter, its share not only remained significant world-wide and regionally but also grew annually to over 10 per cent world share and an amazing over 50 per cent Asian share. Singapore remained in a strong second position, followed by Malaysia and then Indonesia, which forced Hong Kong into fifth position. These were then followed by Thailand and the Philippines, and thereafter by Korea and Taiwan. Japan's FDI inflows have remained minimal apart from an increase in its share during the investment boom of 1990-92.

Nonetheless, the most recent trends indicate that investors and companies looking for growth in Asia are adopting a simple 'Go North' credo. These recent trends indicate that investors are getting more interested in the Northeast. The shift has forced Western companies to redraw their economic maps of the region, making China, Korea and Japan the new epicentres of opportunity (Frank, 2001). Between 1970 and 1991 the Northeast attracted FDI worth only $55.4 billion compared to the Southeast's $74.1 billion. However, between 1992 and 1996 the Northeast received investment to the tune of $175.7 billion, almost double the Southeast's $96.5 billion. The disparity increased further between 1997 and 1999 when FDI flows to the Northeast amounted to $213.1 billion, three and a half times the Southeast's $61.5 billion. If the preliminary estimates for year 2000 are to be believed, then the Northeast received record investment, and widened the investment disparity between the two sub-regions. For instance, China received $19.9 billion (the actual reported figure is $199 billion, but this might be a typing error) during the first seven months, Japan $6.8 billion during the first 6 months, Korea $6.3 billion during the first nine months, Hong Kong $33.2 billion during the first nine months and Taiwan $4.9 billion for the entire period. In contrast, with the exception of the Philippines and Cambodia, flows to the Southeast declined, including divestments in Indonesia (during the first three months). Frank (2001) reports that more than 80 per cent of the year 2000's mergers and acquisition (M&As) in Asia were in the Northeast, more than a third in Japan. In addition recent investments announced by the US and European companies in Asia largely target the Northeast. For example:

'...Motorola Inc. plans a $1.9 billion chip-making plant in China...General Motors Corp., which makes Buicks at a $1.65 billion plant in Shanghai, is making additional investments to launch two new cars this year...Newbridge Capital acquired a controlling stake in Korea First Bank...GE Capital, the US investment fund Lone Star Capital and American financier Wilbur Ross have recently taken control of Japanese finance companies and banks...Goldman Sachs & Co.'s Capital Partners Fund, has channelled its investments into Korea and Japan...' (Frank, 2001).

These recent trends can be traced to specific structural changes of the competitive advantages of the respective regions and countries, namely: market characteristics, investment environment (liberalisation, investment risk and uncertainty), labour costs, and technology.

While market size has implications for scale economies, market growth can proxy future market potential (see Chapter 6). For much of the 1970s, 1980s and early-1990s, the economies of both Northeast and Southeast Asia grew by 6 to 10 per cent a year (with the notable exception of Japan, the Philippines and former Indochina). Thus, disregarding the actual sizes of the individual countries, both the Northeast and the ASEAN-5 (Indonesia, Malaysian, Philippines, Singapore and Thailand) were more or less on the same level playing field *vis-à-vis* future market-potential, at least until the early-1990s. This trend, however, changed after the 1997/98 financial crisis. Although most of the countries recorded negative growth rates in 1998, the Southeast tended to be hit much more. For instance, whereas in the Northeast, China and Taiwan showed only minor signs of slowdown in growth, in the Southeast only Myanmar showed no signs of slowdown in growth. Furthermore, by the end of 2000, the growth rates of the ASEAN-4 (Indonesia, Malaysian, Philippines and Thailand) were still lagging behind the Northeast (excluding Japan), which had shown signs of almost full recovery.

The GDP levels for the Northeast Asian countries are far larger than those of the Southeast Asian economies. Even with its modest population of about 7 million, Hong Kong's annual levels of GDP exceed those of the Southeast Asian countries except Thailand and Indonesia. Even for these two, their GDP levels fell below that of Hong Kong after the 1997/98 financial crisis. However, Indonesia caught-up again in 2000. When the

1998 shares of aggregate GDP based on the purchasing power parity (PPP) value of a country are used to proxy market size, only those for Indonesia and Thailand are comparable with the NIEs of the Northeast. In fact, the PPP estimates indicate that the combined size of the Northeast (22.3) is almost five times as big as that for the Southeast (4.85).

Thus, combining the indicators of future market potential with those of current market size gives the Northeast a competitive edge over the Southeast. That is, the wealthy consumer base in Japan, Korea and Taiwan and the giant population in China (one fifth of the entire world) far outweigh any current benefits of the Southeast. Consequently, investors are betting on Asia's future and channelling more of their money to the large economies of the Northeast. For instance, China's fast-growing cellphone business is responsible for Motorola Inc.'s planned $1.9 billion chip-making plant. This fact is summarised in Mr. Broadfoot's (Managing Director of the Hong Kong-based Political and Economic Risk Consultancy) comment:

> '...For companies, it's not necessarily about the odds, but about how much you could win if things work out...The upside in the North is huge. But in the South, it's harder to see as much of an upside anymore...' (Frank, 2001).

Only a decade ago, Southeast Asia was leading the region in low-cost labour. However, having benefited from the flying-geese model of development, the ASEAN-4 lagged behind the NIEs in upgrading their created assets. Consequently, they have found themselves locked between two strong competitors. At the upper end are the NIEs with a comparatively superior infrastructure (including human skills), while at the lower end are several countries including China, former Indochina, and South Asian countries whose relative wage rates are more competitive. For example, a factory worker in the Chinese City of Shenzhen commands about half the wage of one in Bangkok (Thailand), while the salary for a middle-manager in Cebu (Philippines) is 47 per cent more than a middle manager in Shanghai (Frank, 2001). Consequently, when it comes to low wage costs in Asia, there is now a better alternative than the ASEAN-4.

Asia's model of development, i.e. the flying-geese (discussed below), requires at least two relatively developed countries, one to act as the 'lead goose' and the other to act as the 'support goose'. The lead goose, in the course of its own development process, constantly develops new industries and passes on to the next-tier countries those in which it has lost competitive advantage. Specifically, this flying-geese model is workable if the countries are at different levels of development; have the ability to restructure; posses sufficient demand and markets; have market verification of restructured industries through internationally competitive exports; posses enabling framework for the transmission of TNC assets; and have a favourable investment climate (UNCTAD, 1997). The Northeast satisfies all these conditions. For example, Japan plays the 'lead goose' role, while Korea and Taiwan play the role of 'support geese'. Therefore, with China's abundant cheap labour, this model of development can be sustained within the Northeast. In contrast, the Southeast cannot possibly survive under this model of development without support from the Northeast. For instance, Singapore, the most developed in the Southeast is incapable of playing the role of the 'lead goose'. Similarly, Malaysia and Thailand are incapable of playing the role of 'support geese'. Because of the slow ability to restructure, there is a similarity of comparative advantages among most of the Southeast Asian countries. This is pushing the Southeast Asian countries into a more competitive situation with each other for a shrinking pool of investment, lured by almost similar locational advantages.

During the mid-1980s, while the countries of the Southeast fast-tracked their liberalisation process, those of the Northeast remained comparatively less liberalised (except Hong Kong). This led to an upsurge in FDI flows to the Southeast. The attitude has now reversed. While the Northeast is opening to the world economy, the Southeast, which vigorously opened up since the mid-1980s is now switching back to regulation. Malaysia and Indonesia have for instance imposed capital controls, Thailand has largely halted its privatisation plans, and the Philippines' giant budget deficit has disqualified it from vital International Monetary Fund funds. For illustrative purposes, take Malaysia's case for instance: Following the crisis, Malaysia pegged the ringgit to the US dollar, and imposed exchange and capital controls. The controls prohibited offshore trading of the ringgit and restricted the repatriation of portfolio investment. In response, rating agencies downgraded Malaysia's credit ratings and removed it from major benchmark international investment indices. Consequently, Malaysia's risk premium in international markets increased markedly. Furthermore, the ringgit peg and control measures reduced activity in the offshore foreign exchange market, dampened trading activities in futures and options, and discouraged hedging activities. In addition, foreign investors now face higher administrative costs associated with additional verification and approval procedures. Subsequently, they perceive investment policy regimes as unpredictable and, hence, risky. This uncertainty has the potential of increasing Malaysia's risk ratings and eventually curtailing investment.

As if the failure to deregulate is not bad enough, politics in the Southeast is growing more volatile. For instance, in the Philippines, the president (Joseph Estrada) was ousted following angry protests, not to mention the increasing kidnaps undertaken by guerrillas. In addition, riots and ethnic cleansing are not uncommon in Indonesia, Thailand held controversial elections, and there is bitterness over the alleged suppression of the opposition party in Malaysia. After several years of relative political stability in the Southeast, could a political instability bubble be building-up?

In contrast, the Northeast is lowering barriers to foreign investment. For instance, South Korea has sold off major banks and eliminated foreign-ownership ceilings in almost all of its industries. This is exemplified by Newbridge Capital, which after being rebuffed in an attempt to buy a bank in Thailand, decided to acquire a controlling stake in Korea First Bank. Similarly, Taiwan has also torn down most of its foreign-ownership limits, and is allowing take-overs of its banks. Likewise, Japan, once among the world's most protected economies, is opening its financial and auto industries, its telecommunications and even its power-generation sectors (Frank, 2001). In addition, China's move to join the World Trade Organisation (WTO) is taken to denoted trade liberalisation. Moreover, the Northeast's political stability situation although by Western standards not perfect, is in fact improving. For instance, South Korea and North Korea have taken steps to make peace!

Thus, while the Northeast economies have been proactively embarking on reforms, stubborn opposition from those with vested interests has obstructed the much-needed economic restructuring and financial reforms in the Southeast.

TNCs are increasingly seeking world-class infrastructure, skilled and productive labour, innovatory capacities and an agglomeration of efficient suppliers, competitors, support institutions and services. With the exception of Singapore, the Southeast has failed to develop resource bases fast enough to facilitate their progressive shifts up the levels of technological complexity, and, hence, to participate in the state-of-art production activities. Frank (2001) reports that more than 20 per cent of the population of South Korea, Taiwan and Hong Kong was wired to the Internet in 1999 compared with about 1 per cent for the Philippines and 1.6 per cent in Thailand. In addition, Taiwan, Korea and Japan dominate computer and electronics production, as well as cellphone technology. Moreover, in terms of transnational cost theory, the advanced facilities help the investors to reduce information and other cost improving efficiency. Thus, with the exception of Singapore (in the Southeast), the potential for technical proficiency and innovation is in the Northeast. This is exemplified on the following statement:

> '...'When you look for technology investments, you have to go to the North. With the exception of Singapore, that's where the bulk of the technical proficiency and innovation is going to be.' Says Peter Rose, spokesman for Goldman Sachs in Asia' (Frank, 2001).

No wonder then that Goldman Sachs & Co.'s Capital Partners Fund, after buying a minority stake in a Thailand hotel in 1998, has channelled all of its investments into high-tech companies, principally in the Northeast. The company has spent most of its distressed-asset fund in Korea and Japan, and little in Thailand.

Amidst the 1997/98 financial crisis, there was some optimism regarding future investment in the region, particularly, in the Southeast. The expectation was that the financial crisis would provide an opportunity for some firms to enter the market or expand their existing operations. For instance, the domestic currency devaluation would reduce the cost of fixed assets. In addition, given the heavy indebtedness of the indigenous firms, many local companies would be available for purchase at very favourable prices. Foreign firms would require fewer financial resources in home currencies for the purchase of these properties. Furthermore, the large debts and rising interest rates could force some local firms to restructure and provide TNCs opportunity to undertake direct investment through M&As, boosting parent firms' equity shares in their affiliates at a cheaper price than might have been possible in normal times. In addition, disregarding the possible effects of inflation, currency devaluation would lower costs of production and make export-oriented FDI more profitable and hence attractive. However, there is no evidence to suggest that these advantages have been exploited in the Southeast. In effect only Thailand and the Philippines experienced an investment surge in 1998, but this was followed by a decline in 1999. Instead, the investment has been directed to the Northeast.

The US and the European colonial countries dominated FDI activities in Southeast Asia in the earlier decades. However, Japan emerged as a major investor in the 1970s, and the Asian NIEs started playing a significant role in the post-1987 years. The Asian NIEs and the economies of the ASEAN have benefited significantly from these shifts. For instance, in the past decade, the Asian NIEs have been the main recipients of the upsurge of Japanese outward FDI to non-OECD countries. In turn, the ASEAN-4 (Indonesia, Malaysia, the Philippines and Thailand) countries are the main destinations of the upsurge in outward FDI by Asian NIEs. This is concomitant with the *flying-geese* and *billiard-ball* models of development. The flying-geese model entails the relocation of production and FDI from countries at a higher level of economic development to those at lower levels, resulting in more efficient use of production factors, growth, and higher levels of industrialisation for both groups. Recipient countries utilise their surplus labour and accumulated capital, technology and management skills, advancing their industrialisation; while investing countries redirect excessive labour from sunset to sunrise industries thereby moving to an even higher level of industrialisation. Whereas the flying-geese type of economic development occurs at a macro level, the billiard-ball style shifts take place at the micro level. In this case, the transfer of technology and international division of labour between the developed and the developing countries arises from a shift in production of one product after another, to developing countries as the industry in the developed countries struggles to establish a new relationship based on international division of labour by developing new technologies and introducing new products. Even if Japanese, American and European annual investment shares in the ASEAN-4 are diminishing at the expense of the Asian NIEs, their invested stocks and investments in absolute terms still remain significant.

During the pre-industrial period, FDI in East and South Asia was concentrated in raw material and resource-based manufacturing. The exception to this was FDI in Singapore, which was directed largely to manufacturing and to commerce, finance and transport since it lacked natural resources and an agricultural base. This was followed by a spell of tariff-jumping FDI brought about by the import-substitution development strategy restrictions in the 1960s and 1970s. The recession of 1984-85 and its associated negative effects (i.e., declining external demand, large government budgets, balance of payments deficits, falling domestic savings, and increasing unemployment) acted as a big-push factor for the ASEAN-4 to revoke import-substitution and replace it with development strategies based on export oriented manufacturing policies. It is worthwhile noting that although vigorous action was undertaken in the mid-1980s, these policies had been gradually introduced in the 1970s. On the other hand, the Asian NIEs revoked the import-substitution development strategy much earlier. For instance, for Singapore, the withdrawal from the Federation, withdrawal of the British military forces and hence the anticipated effects on the economy, small market size, and lack of an agricultural sector were the causes of its turning point in the mid-1960s. Korea's policies changed between 1958 and 1963 from an inner-oriented economy toward an encouragement of export-orientation. Similarly, Taiwan began export orientation with reforms that started in the early-1950s. Hong Kong on the other hand represents a quintessential case of laissez faire. The British authorities did not undertake interventionist economic policies, but rather permitted free participation in the economy. However, it took a bit longer before the less advanced Asian countries also changed their development strategies.

This new outlook encouraged investment geared towards export production particularly export-platform investment and then sourcing and assembly which are associated with the host countries' individual sources of comparative advantage especially their relatively lower costs of production, particularly lower real wage rates (see Chapter 6). Consequently, relative to the primary and tertiary sectors, the manufacturing sector attracted most of the export-oriented FDI inflows. Needless to say, the sectoral distribution of FDI follows the ladders of economic development. For instance, the services sector dominates investment in Japan and the Asian NIEs, while the manufacturing sector dominates in most of the remaining countries. The exception to this is Thailand where the services sector dominates. This is attributed to the fictitiously high values attached to the housing and property industry.

In the process, many companies originating from particularly the Asian NIEs have evolved into internationally competitive companies with strategic assets capable of competing in foreign markets. Unsurprising then, more than 50 per cent of the FDI into the relatively newly liberalised countries such as Cambodia, Lao People's Democratic Republic, Myanmar and Vietnam currently comes from other developing Asian countries.

Africa

FDI flows into Africa were rather static prior to 1980, except in 1974 and 1979 when heavy investments were made in oil producing countries during and following the oil crises (UNCTAD, 1999, Figure 5.1). However, the trend started changing since the early-1980s with FDI peaking in 1989 following the liberalisation of FDI policies and then slumping in 1990 before recovering. Thereafter, there was on average a steady increase in the aggregate level of FDI flows. Among the reasons attributed to this increase is the degree of profitability of investments undertaken in Africa. For instance, UNCTAD (1999) reports that: (*i*) In the case of the US FDI, the rate of return in Africa was above 10 per cent between 1983-97 except in 1986; (*ii*) since 1990, the rate of return in Africa has averaged 29 per cent and since 1991 has been higher than any other region, including developed countries as a group, in many years by a factor of two or more; and (*iii*) in 1995, Japanese affiliates in Africa were more profitable (after taxes) than in the early-1990s, and were even more profitable than Japanese affiliates in any other region except for Latin America and the Caribbean and West Asia.

However, an assessment of the trends from a comparative perspective reveals that Africa's FDI position has been far below the average of developing countries since the mid-1980s when the realignment of the major currencies induced global liberalisation of FDI policies followed by an FDI boom. In fact, Figure 3.2 demonstrates that Africa's share of FDI to developing countries has indeed been declining, while that for Latin America and the Caribbean has been increasing and that for Asia although decreasing still remains dominant. UNCTAD (1999) observes that while inflows into developing countries as a group almost quadrupled, from less than $20 billion in 1981-85 to an average $75 billion in 1991-95, inflows into Africa only two folded during that period. Consequently, Africa's share in total inflows to developing countries dropped significantly.

Obviously, since all countries cannot have a similar performance, aggregate FDI flows conceal country-specific information. For example, although the share is gradually declining, owing to their oil reserves, Nigeria and Egypt have accounted for a substantial share of FDI flows to Africa ranging from 67 per cent in 1983-87, 54 per cent in 1988-92 to 38 per cent in 1993-97 (UNCTAD, 1999). Furthermore, in growth terms, UNCTAD (1999) reports that more recently a group of African countries including Botswana, Equatorial Guinea, Ghana, Mozambique, Namibia, Tunisia and Uganda have attracted rapidly increasing FDI. However, certain countries including Swaziland received FDI divestments, while FDI in some other countries (i.e., Mozambique and United Republic of Tanzania) had declined in the recent past but has now been reversed. Bennell (1994) reported that British Corporate investment fell drastically since mid-1994 following the TNCs' divestments in English speaking Africa.

Traditionally, most of the FDI in Africa originated from a few countries of Western Europe and the US (mostly 'colonial masters'). This later extended to OECD countries and in particular, the Triad. Nonetheless, since the mid-1980s, Africa started to attract significant FDI from non-Triad countries including the developing countries of Southeast Asia. Thus, if it were not for these other non-traditional sources, the position of Africa's share of FDI would in fact be worse.

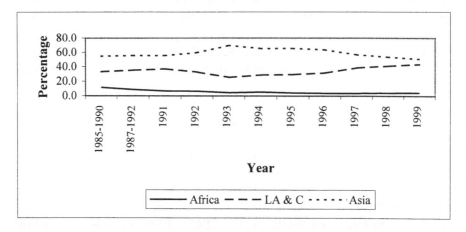

Figure 3.2 Percentage share of FDI flows to developing countries
Note: LA & C - Latin America and the Caribbean.
Sources: Data from various issues of UNCTAD's World Investment Reports.

FDI in Africa is no longer concentrated in the primary sector so much that services and manufacturing sectors are becoming key sectors even in oil-exporting countries. For example, the primary sector accounted for 30 per cent FDI stock in Nigeria in 1992, while manufacturing accounted for almost 50 per cent and services close to 20 per cent. Almost half of the FDI inflows to Egypt (48 per cent) went into services in 1995, with a further 47 per cent going into manufacturing and a mere 4 per cent into the primary sector (UNCTAD, 1999). Although the primary sector still dominates the FDI stock in Africa, the services and manufacturing sectors have surpassed it *vis-à-vis* the annual flows between 1988 and 1999. UNCTAD (1999) reports that in 1996, FDI from the US was almost as important in the manufacturing sector (mostly in food and kindred products, primary and fabricated materials, and other manufactures) as the traditionally most important sector, petroleum.

In sum, in the recent past, FDI to Africa has been very profitable, it has increased in absolute level terms, its sources have been diversified and it is no longer focused in only the primary sector. Despite this however, the region's FDI position is in fact deteriorating *vis-à-vis* other regions, probably suggesting a very serious problem with its locational environment. For instance, many African countries are not even listed for consideration by TNCs. In effect, they frequently do not make it to the short list when it comes to locational decisions for FDI. Consequently, the level of FDI flows to Africa has increased only modestly in recent years rendering the FDI position of the region comparatively poor. UNCTAD (1999) attributed the poor FDI performance in Africa to the negative image the region holds among many foreign investors. For instance, the continent tends to be associated with political turmoil, economic instability, diseases and natural disasters.

Latin American and the Caribbean

Typical of developing countries at the time, about three or so decades ago the Latin American and the Caribbean countries had negative attitudes towards FDI. These attitudes began to change in the early-1980s. Over the past years, the region's countries have undertaken a number of changes regarding the treatment of their FDI. These include significant improvement of their investment regimes through FDI liberalisation, bilateral investment treaties, and implementation of regional and sub-regional arrangements to deal with FDI. A large portion of the more recent investments relates to M&As partly made through the privatisation programmes.

In 1980, Latin America attracted 70 per cent of all FDI flows to developing countries. Then, as the crisis-ridden 1980's continued, Latin America lagged and Asia assumed a more dominant role. By 1994, the situation was almost entirely reversed, with Asia attracting over 60 per cent of the FDI flows to developing countries. Recent FDI statistics suggest that the pendulum may have begun to swing back towards Latin America again. By 1996, the region accounted for over 30 per cent of all the FDI received by developing countries. This share increased to over 40 per cent in 1997-1999 (see Figure 3.2). However, this is concentrated in only a few countries. For instance, of this, 38 per cent went to Brazil; Mexico and Argentina shared 25 per cent; while Bermuda, Chile, Colombia, Peru and Venezuela shared 24 per cent. In 1999, 80 per cent of FDI in Latin America went to Brazil, Mexico and Argentina. According to UNCTAD (2000), Latin America and the Caribbean attracted an estimated $90 billion of FDI in 1999, compared to $73.8 billion the previous year. Once more, only Brazil, Argentina, Mexico and Chile accounted for the largest share.

The manufacturing and services sectors overtook the primary sector's dominant share of FDI in the 1970s and 1980s. Needless to say, the precise pattern varies from country to country. For instance, in Mexico, much FDI went to the automobile industry, Chile consolidated in natural resources, Argentina and Venezuela in services and Brazil in manufacturing. By 1990, the trend indicated a greater share of FDI in the service sector and diminishing shares in the primary and manufacturing sectors. In fact by 1990, the primary sector's share for a number of countries was at an insignificant low of less than 5 per cent. The only exception to this trend was Argentina where the share of the services sector had been maintained over the period and Bolivia, Columbia and Venezuela where the share declined. UNCTAD (1992) reported that despite the general decline in the significance of the primary sector for most countries of the region, it still accounted for between 25 and 35 per cent of FDI stock in Ecuador and Peru. In addition, there were at least 5 countries where the sector was becoming more important (Argentina, Bolivia, Chile, Columbia and Venezuela) or had maintained its share (Costa Rica). Thus, the primary sector-related FDI liberalisation has influenced the dominance of the primary sector in countries endowed with abundant natural resources.

The US traditionally dominated the FDI in the region. By 1991 it was responsible for about one third of the FDI stock in the manufacturing sector, and over one half in the services sector. In 1997, accumulated US investment in Latin America was $97.5 billion (excluding the tax havens). Of these, $35.7 billion had been invested in Brazil, $25.4 billion in Mexico, $9.7 billion in Argentina, and $5.2 billion in Venezuela. However, European investment particularly in the manufacturing sector grew significantly during the 1990s. For instance in 1995-96, 82 per cent of FDI from the UK, 81 per cent from the Netherlands, 72 per cent from Italy and 67 per cent from Germany went into the manufacturing sector. In addition, the privatisation process enabled the services sector to attract investment from Spain and France. In fact, Europe's shares increased steadily and equalled the US share in 1997. No wonder, Latin America and the Caribbean region is currently the main non-OECD investment destination for some European countries including Germany, the Netherlands and the UK. A particular noteworthy feature has been large investments by Spanish TNCs.

There has also been a certain increase in Latin American intra-regional investment. Inter-regional FDI is significant since all countries except Mexico direct substantial FDI to other regional countries. In fact, inter-regional investment accounts for over 90 per cent of the region's investment by developing countries (UNCTAD, 1999). For instance, most of the inter-regional investment from Latin America goes to the Caribbean Islands.

The new all-time record set for FDI in Latin America in 1999 would appear to suggest that the region has managed to overcome most of the negative circumstances affecting investment flows to developing countries. It has been aided in this effort by the simultaneous appearance of new and interesting alternatives for foreign investors, most of which involve the acquisition of existing assets.

Transition Economies of Central and Eastern Europe, and Central Asia

In the immediate post-World War II period, the Central and Eastern Europe (CEE) and the Central Asia countries remained relatively isolated from the rest of the world and concentrated their attention on developing a 'socialist world market'. Unsurprisingly then, FDI is a very recent phenomenon in these economies, which opened up to capital inflows only in the late-1980s and the early-1990s. For example, significant inflows started only between 1992 and 1994 in Armenia, Azerbaijan, Georgia, Kazakhstan, Krygyztan, Russia, Tajikistan, Turkmenistan, Ukraine and Uzbekistan. Nonetheless, absolute values of FDI inflows have been growing during the last decade. For instance, Azerbaijan and to a lesser extent Turkmenistan have considerably improved their FDI positions. However, compared with its contribution to world GDP or world imports, the region's share in total world FDI stock is still relatively low. For example, FDI stocks in the Commonwealth of Independent States (CIS) during the period of 1990-1998 reached $23,694 millions, which represents 1.9 per cent of the total developing countries' share and 42 per cent of the total FDI stock in the CEE and the former Soviet Union economies.

Concomitant with other developing country regions, only a few countries dominate the FDI inflow shares. For example, between 1989 and 1998 Azerbaijan, Kazakhstan and Turkmenistan attracted the largest amounts of FDI in the CIS in terms of cumulative per capita inflows. Likewise, only Azerbaijan and Kazakhstan have managed to attract FDI above average level (in cumulative per capita terms) of the CEE and Baltic countries. In similar notion, Azerbaijan, Kazakhstan, Russia and Ukraine accounted for 87 per cent of the cumulative FDI stock in the CIS for the period 1989-98.

The sectoral distribution of FDI in the CIS countries in a way reflects the privatisation process and/or the nature of the respective countries' resource endowments. Manufacturing companies are usually the first targets of privatisation. Unsurprisingly, this sector's share has specifically been dominant during the early stages of FDI activities. For instance, it accounts for 40-60 per cent of the FDI stock in the CEE countries. Export-oriented green-field investments attracted by the cheap labour-force and, by generous incentives have in some cases been undertaken in the automobile and electronic industries. However, because of its strategic importance to the respective governments, the privatisation of the services sector is usually undertaken more cautiously than that of the primary and manufacturing sectors. Nonetheless, with the privatisation of telecommunications and electricity industries particularly in the more advanced transition countries such as the Czech Republic, Estonia, Hungary, and Poland, the significance of investment in the services sector is increasing.

In contrast to the global and the CEE trends, the primary sector has been more successful in the CIS region. This is most evident in Azerbaijan, Georgia, Kazakhstan, Kyrgyzstan, Tajikistan and Turkmenistan. This may be attributed to the fact that all of these countries, except for Georgia, are located in the Central Asia region endowed with natural minerals including oil, gas, and gold. Exceptions to this trend are Belarus, Ukraine and Uzbekistan where most FDI has gone into the manufacturing sector. In Belarus, FDI is mostly directed into food processing, machine building, textiles and wood processing. Nevertheless, FDI also goes into trade, transport and communication industries. Moldova has on the other hand attracted more investment in its agricultural industry, while FDI in the Russian Federation and Armenia has mostly gone into the services sector. While, management, financial and consulting services and retail trade account for most of the flows into Russia's services sector, flows into Armenia are mostly directed into telecommunication, although additional investment is undertaken in beverages, banking, mining (mainly gold), tobacco and pharmaceuticals industries.

According to UNCTAD (1999), FDI stock in the CEE countries is dominated by the direct investors from the EU, who accounted for almost two-thirds of the total FDI inflows in 1998. In this respect, the proximity of the CEE countries to the EU and the possible accession of some CEE countries into the EU partly explain this trend in the region. The region is catching up with the rest of the world. For instance, its FDI growth rate of 28.5 per cent between 1993-97 exceeded that of the developing countries (23 per cent) and the developed countries (19 per cent).

Conclusion

FDI has been one of the defining features of the world economy over the past two decades. It has grown at an unprecedented pace for more than a decade, with only a slight interruption during the recession of the early-1990s. More firms in more industries from more countries are expanding abroad through direct investment than ever before, and virtually all economies now compete to attract TNCs. This trend has been driven by the complex interaction of technological change, evolving corporate strategies towards a more global focus and major policy reform in individual countries. The past decade has witnessed an unparalleled opening and modernisation of economies in all regions, encompassing deregulation, demonopolisation, privatisation and private participation in the provision of infrastructure, and the reduction and simplification of tariffs. An integral part of this process has been the liberalisation of foreign investment regimes. Indeed, the wish to attract FDI has been one of the driving forces behind the whole reform process. Although the pace and scale of reform has varied depending on the particular circumstances in each country, the direction of change has not. The recent record levels of investment flows also owe much to several large cross-border M&As. The integration of the global economy through TNCs will nevertheless continue through the activities of smaller investors and their myraid transactions, whose importance is often underestimated. However, the current (2001) potential economic stagnation (or even recession) in the two leading world economic powers, the US and Japan, may have serious negative implications for FDI in the near future. As for Africa, there is indeed urgent need for it to integrate in the global economy, including integration into the regional or global production networks of TNCs and hence the international division of labour. The policies for achieving this are contained in Chapter 7.

4 The Globalisation Debate: anti-globalisation views

Introduction

All the recent summits dealing with the international economy have been besieged by many thousands of 'anti-globalisation' protesters. These advocates of anti-globalisation can be categorised into two, although not mutually exclusive groups. While one group objects to what the current pattern of world trade is doing to the world's poor by increasing the North-South equity disparity, the other group is more focused on the environmental consequences of globalisation with or without implications on the world's poor. Within both groups, there are extremists who totally denounce globalisation on the basis of its negative impact on the well-being of human kind and/or the environment. On the other hand are the moderates who acknowledge that globalisation has some good aspects, which should be shared equitably while measures are taken to protect the environment. Nonetheless, both broad groups are driven by the same ideology of *sustainable development*.

Unsurprisingly, the number, range, co-ordination and activism among civil society groups on issues relating to globalisation has been expanding in the recent past. NGOs in particular, have of recent played the dominant role. For example, through the NGOs' vigilantism, national governments have come to realise the need to protect the environment, and not to treat environmental damage as part of a price paid for development as was the case traditionally. Consequently, other stakeholders have joined arms in addressing environmental issues. These include, consumer groups, local communities, shareholders of companies and even employees of companies. National governments have responded by increasing stringency in environmental regulation. Although some groups organise around very specific products (e.g. tobacco and nuclear energy), most activism focuses on a relatively small set of major issue themes. These are then exemplified and addressed in terms of specific products, companies or events. Some of the most vigilant groups are Greenpeace and Friends of the Earth, who are primarily concerned with environmental issues; Amnesty International and Human Rights Watch whose prime interests relate to human rights; and individual country Labour Unions, which focus on workers' rights.

Characterised by 'shrinking space, shrinking time and disappearing borders', globalisation has swung open the door to opportunities. Breakthroughs in communications technologies and biotechnology, if directed for the needs of people, can bring advances for all of humankind. Therefore, global markets, global technology, global ideas and global solidarity can enrich the lives of people everywhere. For instance, on the one hand, freer global trade in manufactured products and services has been a great boon to those formerly poor countries that had the infrastructure, the educational levels, and the political stability to take advantage of it. For example, over the past two decades China, India, and a number of other Asian and Latin American countries have generated high export-driven growth rates, averaging over twice the rate in the old industrialised world. Of course, gross inequalities of income characterise all of these countries, but because of economic globalisation, they might, in the broadest sense, be 'catching-up'. Unfortunately, as their consumption soars, they weigh more heavily on the environment. Consequently, they are potentially a major source of future 'greenhouse gas' emissions. In addition, since the TNCs have moved much of their production there, and also need them as markets, there is relatively little political pressure at home to restrict trade with them. It is for these reasons that the moderate anti-globalisation activists are increasingly recognising that issues pertaining to environmental protection, North-South equity divide, human insecurity and economic growth should be pursued simultaneously, and that both the public and private sectors should get increasingly involved.

On the other hand, the really poor countries on the planet produce very little for export, except food and textiles. Moreover, much as they can produce these far more cheaply than anybody else, little FDI flows to these sectors, particularly in agriculture partly implying that they have no lobbies in the rich countries to open up markets for them. To make matters worse, the Western markets put some barriers on their products. For example, the highly subsidised and protected Western agriculture sector, above all, locks them out of global trade and into perpetual poverty. In fact, this instance suggests that the poorest countries of the world are damned not by globalisation, but by the lack of it. Therefore, the challenge is to ensure that the benefits are shared equitably and that this increasing interdependence works for people, and not just for profits. Additionally, the environment should be treated as a scarce factor input and, consequently, measures should be taken to preserve it.

But, the arguments by anti-globalisation activists go beyond just trade and the environment to cover all international social, political and economic factors that effectively relate to sustainable growth for all. For example, they also argue that markets go too far and squeeze the non-market activities so vital for human development. For instance, fiscal squeezes are constraining the provision of social services, a time squeeze is reducing the supply and quality of caring labour, and an incentive squeeze is harming the environment. Thus, globalisation may mean that the fish on our plate has travelled half way round the world to reach our table. But, it can also mean that the people in the region where it was fished find stocks so depleted that there's not enough left for their own families. Therefore, the long-term sustainability of the resource is threatened. Globalisation can bring consumers in richer countries more choice than ever. Yet, if their own subsidised surpluses are then 'dumped' on poorer countries, hundreds of local businesses in those countries will simply go burst. Worse still, globalisation is also effectively increasing human insecurity as the spread of global crime, disease and financial volatility outpaces actions to tackle them.

While a debate is meant to comprise two sides, the proposing and opposing schools of thought, this chapter focuses on the views put forward by anti-globalisation activists. The other school of thought is represented in Chapter 5, which concentrates on how one of the major components of global integration, FDI, can contribute to the economic growth process, particularly of developing countries. In addition, more evidence inter-linking FDI and regionalism and, therefore, economic growth is presented in Chapter 6. Rather than attempting to elaborate a grand theory of anti-globalisation or globalisation for that matter, the chapter takes a more concrete approach of examining globalisation as it is differentially viewed by the anti-globalisation activists. Specifically, this chapter highlights the three factors that although not mutually exclusive, form the nucleus of the globalisation debate. That is, globalisation and the environment, globalisation and the North-South equity divide, and globalisation and human insecurity. Some of the text in this chapter has been adopted from Gueneau et al (1998) 'Globalisation and Sustainable Development: 12 fact sheets'; and from Barker et al's (1999) 'Alternatives to Economic Globalisation: A Preliminary Report'.

Globalisation and the Environment

Impact on the Environment

Overview The environment comprises the four gifts of nature: land, water, air and the living organisms. The first three factors are basic necessities for the survival of all living things, be it animals or plants. Unsurprisingly then, environmental protection has of recent become a factor of interest to all nations, both developed and developing. No wonder, since the 1992 Earth Summit in Rio de Janeiro, heads of states nowadays gather together on an annual basis to discuss environmental issues.

The environmental issue forms one of the cornerstones in the globalisation debate. According to Gueneau et al (1998), environmental goods are referred to as public goods when they belong to everyone, and when there is no competition between users to consume them. Air is a good example of this. Consumption by one user is not in any way detrimental to consumption by other users, and no one can appropriate the good. On the other hand, because they have free access, many environmental goods are known as common goods. In practice, their free access subjects them to fierce competition, which can eventually lead to their exhaustion. For example, an individual who collects wood in a forest belonging to the community imposes costs on other users of the forest in the form of less wood and increase in travel time to reach a wooded area. Moreover, it is impossible to exclude this individual (who would have to be identified in the first instance) in many circumstances. People exploiting the forest have no market incentive to preserve it. This is in part because other individuals could nullify their own efforts as a result of over-exploitation. From the viewpoint of many environmentalists, trade liberalisation has led to increased production of goods and services that generate environmental damage and, therefore, to a tragedy of common goods. Arguably, the cost of this damage could be considerably greater than the expected commercial benefits. Nonetheless, even if the increase in income resulting from trade liberalisation outweighs the rise in environmental costs, there is no guarantee that this income will be effectively apportioned and allocated for environmental protection purposes. This is exemplified by historical evidence, which shows that during periods of prosperity, the gains from growth have not always been distributed equitably.

Environmental protection still remains a challenging issue most particularly in developing countries. For instance, policy makers in developing countries may be desperate to achieve projected economic growth rates and securing FDI, and in the process accept to undertake environmentally risky activities. In addition, investors may pursue a deliberate strategy of shifting the location of their pollution-intensive production in response to lax environmental standards. Likewise, the imported technology may be vintage and therefore, environmental-unfriendly. Alternatively, developing countries may simply lack the resources and technical expertise to inspect, monitor and enforce appropriate environmental legislation.

The facts and predictions Barker et al (1999) have enumerated the following facts and predictions. While it is still debatable, carbon dioxide is taken as the prime culprit of the greenhouse effect, followed by methane. The burning of fossil fuels (i.e., coal, oil and natural gas) and deforestation are the two main sources of atmospheric carbon dioxide emissions of human origin. The extension of aquatic rice growing in Asia and the increase in the number of ruminants reared on all continents are on the other hand held mainly responsible for methane emissions. However, emissions of other greenhouse gases are more difficult to estimate.

The earth's atmosphere acts as a filter that lets through some of the sun's rays and retains enough heat to keep the temperature on earth at a level propitious to life. However, certain gases (i.e., carbon dioxide, methane and nitrous oxide), found in very small quantities in the lower atmosphere are able to absorb some of the sun's rays reflected from earth. This causes what is now renown as the greenhouse effect. Scientific estimates suggest that without the greenhouse effect, the average temperature on the earth's surface would be -18°C instead of its current average of 15°C. The concentration of carbon dioxide and chlorofluoro carbons in the atmosphere has been rising since the beginning of the industrial era. Concomitantly, greenhouse gases not previously found in the atmosphere, such as the synthetic chlorofluoro carbons have made their appearance. At the same time, scientists have discovered that the temperature of the earth has been rising rapidly over the course of the twentieth century. Generally speaking, it is now estimated that if the present rate of greenhouse gas emission is maintained, the temperature will rise by between 2 and 4°C between now and 2100. At this rate, the speed of warming could be so great that ecosystems and human societies will be unable to adapt to these new conditions.

The aforementioned climatic changes are expected to lead to alterations in the composition and geographical distribution of all ecosystems. Environmental scientists predict that climate zones will shift towards the poles and higher regions too quickly for the vegetation and fauna associated with them to be able to adapt. In the process, biological and plant diversity will diminish. In addition, although agricultural production can be maintained at its present level, there is a danger that the food situation of certain regions will worsen.

The responsibility for the rising greenhouse effect has traditionally overwhelmingly belonged to the rich countries. Today, however, it is in developing countries that the increase is most rapid, with the share of these countries in carbon dioxide emissions being expected to rise from 25 per cent in 1990 to 37 per cent in 2020. The worrying news is that under the influence of demographic and economic growth, world energy demand will necessarily continue to increase, at least over the first half of the twenty-first century. This should be the case even if the most efficient energy production and consumption techniques go into widespread use.

In the past, the tendency for aridity to become more acute has been confirmed in several regions, in particular the Sahel and Central Asia. But, existing evidence demonstrates that extreme climatic phenomena, such as droughts and cyclones, seem to have become more intense and to have shifted towards the temperate zones. No wonder then that, the question of what impact the accumulation of greenhouse gases is having and, over and above that, how much responsibility certain human activities have for recent climate changes is of major concern to the scientific community.

Precipitation should increase on average, but with very uneven distribution in space and time. At present, the 19 countries that suffer from water shortages, are concentrated in the Middle East and North Africa. This number could double by 2025. In Southeast Asia, increased precipitation could exacerbate the sometimes devastating effects of the monsoon. In addition, problems of drinking water access could worsen. The World Health Organisation (WHO) expects a resurgence of certain serious diseases such as yellow fever and cholera. Moreover, a rise of between 3 and 5°C would lead to malaria spreading over an additional 4 to 17 million square kilometres, threatening almost three quarters of the world's population, compared to its current level of just less than one half.

In sum, forecasting models show that the most harmful effects of climate change will occur in the regions of the South, falling upon the poorest populations that are already considerably affected by lack of food and health security. It is, therefore not so much the existence of the greenhouse effect, but its intensification that is worrying.

Sustainability modelling   Over the course of the 1990s, sustainable development has gradually become one of the national and international fundamental principles guiding the formulation of most public policies. Because the concept of sustainable development demands multi-disciplinarity, an accommodation between hitherto distinct scientific logic, and harmonisation of the disciplines of ecology and economics, it is disrupting traditional academic boundaries. The three aspects of sustainable development, i.e. ecological, economic, and social political aspects express its interdisciplinary nature well (Gueneau et al, 1998).

The ecological aspect of sustainable development extends the issue of the industrial scale, which postulates the human needs that the economic system is required to satisfy. It proposes that nature places limits on industrialisation, and these need to be identified and respected. Its aim is to manage and optimise the use of natural capital instead of running it down.

The economic aspect of sustainable development relates to the current and future effects of the economy on the environment. Gueneau et al (1998) note that it raises the question of the choice, financing and improvement of industrial techniques in terms of natural resource utilisation. Sustainable development reconciles these two aspects by taking into consideration not just the conservation of nature, but the entire relationship between nature and human actions. Sustainable development is based on the synergy between man and the environment, and favours the technologies, knowledge and values that make for longevity. In addition, it advocates for an economic development process that takes long-term account of the basic ecological balances which support human, natural and plant life.

The social and political aspect of sustainable development is meant to turn development into an instrument of social cohesion and a process of political choice. This choice, first and foremost, must be for equity, both between generations and between States. In their concern for equity, current generations will preserve the development options of future generations and of different States, in both North and South. It is through this double imperative of equity that the environment and the economy must be reconciled (Gueneau et al, 1998).

The different strands of scientific thinking on the environment give priority to whatever corresponds to their perception of the relationship between man and nature. Not surprisingly, the two great disciplines, ecology and economics, have long been at odds in this area. Certain approaches deriving from these schools of thought still exercise an influence over ultra-liberals on the one side and conservationist environmentalists on the other.

The conservationist strand is strongest among urban populations with a yearning for nature and researchers in the nature sciences (e.g. biology, zoology and ecology). It specifically rejects the economic sphere, and advocates for a world in which nature would be inviolate and inviolable. From an ethical point of view, these standpoints, in their extreme forms, are open to criticism, since they confine themselves to seeking equity for non-humans. In fact, from a more general point of view, they might be judged to be particularly reductionist. This is because, the only criteria governing relations between the environment and society are ecological ones, all economic and social considerations being set aside.

The economist approach gives priority to the satisfaction and improvement of human activities. For instance, this position led it to refuse to attribute any value to natural resources, which were regarded as unlimited in the eighteenth century. Economic acts, however, necessarily have an ecological aspect, as they use, transform, trade and damage natural resources. In fact, economic growth in the nineteenth and twentieth centuries consumed enough natural resources to raise the question of scarcity. The quality of the environment has thus come to take on the attributes of a scarce, and hence, valuable commodity. This new situation has confronted the economic sciences with two major problems. First, there is no market price for environmental goods and services. Yet, according to economic theory, the scarcer a good is, the higher will be its price. Second, the market prices of goods and services do not accurately reflect the scarcity of the resources used to produce them.

Consequently, environmental economists have developed theories aimed at setting an economic value on environmental goods and services and re-establishing the 'normal' workings of the market. However, by drawing on the principles that govern neo-classical economic theory, these approaches have effectively ruled out any environmental regulation. The strand advocated for by environmentalist can take the form of either weak or strong sustainability modelling.

Weak sustainability is based on a rule for sharing capital between the generations. The argument here is that sustainability is assured if the stock of capital K, consisting of manufactured capital K_m, human capital K_h and natural capital K_n, is constant or increases in such a way as to ensure that potential well-being is maintained or rises over the course of time. For instance, $\delta K/\delta t = \delta(K_m + K_h + K_n) > 0$. Here, one or two components of capital (K_m, K_h, or K_n) may decline as long as this fall is compensated for by an increase in one or both of the other two components. As a result, the basic condition of growth in K is complied with. Consequently, the three components of K are perfect substitutes for one another.

This idea rests on the belief that while certain natural assets may be irreplaceable, most of them are of value only for the services they provide, and that they are not unique in being able to make these contributions. Non-sustainability arises, therefore, not when natural resources, such as fossil fuels, are consumed, but when the income withdrawn on this occasion is not reinvested (Gueneau et al, 1998). But the same capacity to produce goods and services, and thus well-being will be transmitted to future generations if, on the other hand, the effort is made to maintain the level of total capital stock.

Yet, this model is not without its limitations and therefore criticisms. For instance, the following most immediate questions inevitably arise: First, to what extent do the prices of the different types of capital reflect their value, and to what degree are they comparable? Second, since the model entails complete confidence in technical progress, can this alone enable new solutions to be found to replace lost natural capital? Third, even when the replacement of natural goods and services by material goods and services is technically feasible, can it always be countenanced from an ethical point of view?

An alternative model of strong sustainability has been developed. While it is based on the desire to preserve development options for the future as is the case for weak sustainability, it imposes three additional constraints. First, is the identification of critical natural capital that should not be tapped or replaced by productive capital or industrial products. This capital represents the natural conditions of existence for a human economy and should be preserved. Second, it demands that no inroads be made into cultural capital, which embraces three principles. For instance, natural resources are a form of capital that cannot be replaced by future generations; protection for them is based on the precautionary principle (preserving the minimum conditions that the biosphere needs to function); and natural beings and the biosphere have a value of their own. Third, it imposes limits on the maximum amounts of materials and energy that can be used for economic activity worldwide. This principle involves placing an absolute limit on the physical size of the human economy on earth. It implies a transition to an economy that is stationary in terms of its physical development (materials and energy mobilised) and redistributive in terms of development between North and South.

Gueneau et al (1998) note that strong sustainability recognises that certain types of environmental damage are irreversible. Account needs to be taken both of the harm that results from the disappearance of species (loss of bio-diversity), and the constraints of scale required to maintain the great planetary balances (greenhouse effect). This should be irrespective of how great the uncertainty about how much damage there may ultimately be. In addition, the idea of responsibility towards future generations represents the core of the ethical values.

Nonetheless, Gueneau et al (1998) have pointed out that the strong sustainability model also has its limitations. For instance, attempts to apply each of these principles have fared differently. The principle of compensating for any use of natural resources has in certain cases been put into practice, one example being the obligation for foresters to replant as many hectares as they clear. But, measures to enforce a maximum limit of exploitation for a given resource are more complex politically and practically. This is why the proposal that limiting developing countries' population growth should be at the top of the sustainable development agenda is far from being universally accepted.

Then there is the issue of measurement of wealth. There is often a temptation to measure development by economic growth alone when international economic comparisons is being made. Yet, this provides a picture only of changes in quantitative indicators of the economic wealth of a nation, gross domestic product (GDP) and gross national product (GNP). Of course, changes in these aggregates might provide a good index of the development of economic activities in a country. But, they neither say anything about the composition and distribution of income between different groups in society, nor tell us anything about the human wealth of a country (i.e., the quality of food, health services, the school and university system, and safety). In addition, these traditional economic indicators are as uninformative about the state of the environment as they are about cultural and social aspects. Strong growth in national income may mask unbridled consumption of natural resources and intolerable human exploitation (child labour, for example). From this perspective then, a good growth rate can conceal situations where natural resources risk being exhausted in the short- or medium-term and where under-investment in 'human capital' threatens economic activity (Gueneau et al, 1998).

Obviously, such measures cannot come even close enough to measuring sustainable development. Sustainable development is a complex process that encompasses not only the ability of a population to achieve long-term growth in wealth, but also its modes of thought and social organisation. It therefore combines a quantitative aspect, a qualitative aspect and, unquestionably, an intangible aspect as well. That is, if growth and development are linked, then the development process encompasses more than can be measured by growth alone. For this reason, numerous national and international programmes like those led by the UN Commission on Sustainable Development (UNCSD) have sought to produce indicators that take account of the different components of sustainable development. Currently, however, there is no harmonised system enabling one or more variables representing sustainable development to be compared internationally. In any case, the value of any such indicator would be open to doubt.

Similarly, the System of National Accounts (SNA) has limitations. It consists of all the accounts that States produce periodically in order to follow developments in their economies. These accounts are drawn up by all States on the same methodological basis, which was devised by the statistical division of the UN, enabling international comparisons to be drawn. However, the economic value of natural resources and their role in productive activities are not included in the SNA. In particular, expenditure on protecting or restoring the environment (defensive expenditure), such as the cost of anti-pollution systems, is accounted for as output, whence a paradoxical situation: the greater the damage, the heavier the expenditure, and the more wealth the public accounts show as being created. Furthermore, non-tradable or un-traded goods and services such as firewood or the planting of forests to protect catchment basins are not included. In addition, natural capital, such as forestry and fishery resources, is accounted for as revenue when it is consumed, when in reality a productive asset is being lost (Gueneau et al, 1998).

International trade Barker et al (1999) argue that economic globalisation is based on ever-increasing consumption, exploitation of resources, and waste-disposal problems. Therefore, it is intrinsically harmful to the environment. They believe that one of its most important elements, export-oriented production, is especially damaging as it directly increases global transport activity, fossil fuel use, refrigeration and packaging, while requiring very costly and ecologically damaging new infrastructures in the form of ports, airports, dams and canals. In addition, it accelerates conversion to industrial-style agriculture with corresponding increases in pesticides, water and air pollution, and biotechnology. These elements, combined with many other wasteful aspects of global trade, are also powerful contributors to the problems of global climate change, ozone depletion, loss of habitat, and unprecedented levels of pollution.

This unprecedented growth in international trade is having a twofold impact on the environment. Firstly, it is causing production processes to become more specialised (under the so-called international division of labour) and capital-intensive, and is thereby contributing to environmental damage. Secondly, it is making certain environmental problems more visible and turning them into more of an international issue.

Rising international trade and worsening environmental problems are stoking the debate between free traders and environmentalists. The former hold that international trade growth improves the efficiency of goods and services production and leads to rising wealth and collective well-being. The latter maintain that the way to improve the well-being of society is to protect the environment.

According to the theory of comparative advantage (see Chapter 2), if in an open economy with no trade restrictions, countries specialise in producing the goods and services for which they are most efficient by comparison with other countries, increased global well-being (understood as income) will automatically ensue. The liberal position is that these additional resources could for instance, be used to finance investment in environmental protection, encourage the spread of clean technologies and reduce poverty. Trade liberalisation would thus, be a very powerful engine of sustainable development. Gueneau et al (1998) point out that during the 1980s, large international institutions of a liberal bent such as the WTO, the OECD and the World Bank backed up this hypothesis by simple empirical observations. These organisations argued that at the macroeconomic level, pollution increases as a function of income per inhabitant up to a certain point, after which the relationship is reversed (an 'inverted U' curve). To strengthen this demonstration, these organisations emphasise that the existence of trade barriers has quite often led to natural resources within particular countries being over-exploited, at a much higher cost than would have been incurred had equivalent resources been imported. In particular, they cite the example of the environmental effects that the Common Agricultural Policy (CAP) has had in the EU, and cases where forest resources have been over-exploited in certain countries that levy high customs tariffs on untreated or processed timber.

But, this 'inverted U' has serious drawbacks. First, growth does not automatically feed through to environmental protection, which is primarily the result of political choices. Second, when the curve is at its peak, large quantities of pollutants are being emitted. At this stage, irreparable harm may already have been done, as some types of environmental damage are irreversible. Third, while the curve equates increased income with increased output, the measurement used for output does not take the state of the environment into account. And in these arguments, it must be noted that 'sustainable growth' is inversely related to pollution.

Gueneau et al (1998) argue that by its nature, international trade leads to spatial separation between the place of production (which is where environmental problems generally arise), and the place of consumption. This means that neither the harm caused when goods are produced nor the losses resulting from unsustainable use of resources are borne by the purchaser. There is the risk that trade will accentuate the separation between social costs (costs borne by the whole of society) and private costs. This implies that internationally, the externality aspect of environmental problems manifests itself in an acute form. This is why advocates of strong environmental regulation, led by environmental NGOs express concern about the environmental effects of free trade.

The argument goes further. For instance, that the international specialisation that results from the comparative advantage model tends to alter the volume and geographical distribution of production activities in accordance with the resources available in each country (capital, labour, and natural wealth). Moreover, in the case of primary resources (agriculture and mining products) it can consequently lead to the intensification of operating methods or to greater exploitation of untapped resources, not without effects on the quality of the environment. In addition, specialisation can sometimes lead to rich ecosystems or food crops being replaced by export crops. Yet it is developing countries that, impelled to specialise as part of structural adjustment policies, suffer the most severe social and environmental consequences (Gueneau et al, 1998).

In many developing countries, despite efforts to liberalise and specialise, constantly falling prices across the whole range of raw materials have led to increased production of export crops particularly on the most fertile soils. The end result has been a fall in the amount and quality of land given over to food production. This has exacerbated poverty and pressure on the environment, without thereby solving the debt problem or helping growth.

The freedom of financial flows means that companies can easily set up or relocate production units wherever wage and tax costs or environmental regulations are the least constrictive. Emerging countries could thus be tempted to apply the laxest possible social and environmental standards in order to attract such relocations (see Chapter 5). While this hypothesis has yet to be verified, it is certain that capital from unscrupulous companies is attracted to places where there is no movement in the direction of tighter social and environmental standards, and particularly where enforcement measures and penalties are weak.

The WTO shows a preference for voluntary International Standards Organisation (ISO) 14000 standards rather than national environmental labelling programmes, which can clearly have discriminating effects. On 2 February 1947, 25 countries set up an international body with responsibility for setting method and product standards, in order to facilitate trade. ISO is a world federation of national standards organisations. It draws up standards to which companies voluntarily subscribe in order to obtain approval for their exports more easily. Following the Rio Conference, a new committee was set up within ISO to draw up a series of environmental management standards, the ISO 14000 series. To obtain an ISO 14000 certificate, a company has to institute an environmental policy or strengthen its existing one. The information is sent to an ISO-approved certification body, which is usually a national standards agency. The methods for achieving the environmental objectives included in the policy must be implemented, inspected, then rectified if they are inadequate. It is on the basis of this objectives-methods-inspection-rectification system that certificates are awarded. The ISO standard is applied in the same way to an insurance company, a car manufacturer or a forestry company. Since its creation, ISO has been keen to facilitate international trade by formulating and harmonising production standards. Environmental NGOs, however, doubt the ability of these standards to improve environmental protection. They argue that ISO standards provide ambiguous support for the green trading strategies of companies, since they do not set any binding target for improvement. Moreover, numerous advertisements vaunt the merits of products that have obtained ISO certification, even though this does not entail any specifications regarding the environmental performance of companies. Theoretically, certificates cannot be used as eco-labels. In practice, however, there is no control over their use, since the certification bodies do not have the resources for this.

Globalisation and the North-South Equity Divide

Trade and Investment

Equity disparity A key characteristic of economic globalisation is the rapid growth in international trade that has been taking place since the Second World War. It has reached an extent where the value of trade in goods is increasing more rapidly than output and world income (the sum of gross domestic products). This increase has been most prominent in the services sector (transport, finance, telecommunications and tourism industries), which now accounts for a fifth of world trade.

Globalisation has also been characterised by accelerating financial flows particularly in the form of increased FDI and portfolio investment. In fact, as highlighted by the global trends in Chapter 3, FDI has been growing at a faster rate than international trade. Evidently, this tendency is partly due to the financial deregulation that became widespread since the mid-1980s, itself facilitated by technological innovations enabling information and funds to be transferred almost instantaneously. For instance, domestic stock market and banking activities have been liberalised almost everywhere, as have external capital movements.

The developed countries account for more than three quarters of world trade and world capital flows. While imports of consumer goods from developing countries are increasing at a moderate pace, the share of developing countries in world trade has increased more rapidly since the beginning of the 1990s. However, this particularly relates to the emerging economies in the dynamic regions (Asian and Latin American countries), which have had very rapid economic growth in the last three decades. These dynamic economies are also increasing their imports and are becoming increasingly integrated in the international economy. Consequently, uneven distribution of trade-related benefits has emerged from globalisation among the developed countries on the one hand, and integration between the developed countries and the dynamic developing countries on the other hand.

The global FDI trends discussed in Chapter 3 illustrated that although the share of the US investments abroad has diminished (a bit), the country remains the world's largest recipient of FDI. In addition, while the Netherlands, Germany and the United Kingdom have consolidated their position in the world, Japan and France have made significant breakthroughs. Evidently, although FDI flows were historically concentrated among industrialised countries, this tendency was reversed in the mid-1980s. However, FDI flows into developing countries are characterised, by a high degree of geographical concentration (mainly East Asia) implying that investment-related benefits are also unevenly distributed. Moreover, in so far as the Third World countries are concerned, it is arguable that most of the manufacturing FDI they receive, if any, is for access to protected domestic markets. Alternatively, it may be labour intensive in nature and take the form of sub-contracting agreements with core companies, where most of the value added is at the design, distribution or marketing stage.

Since these factors reflect the scale of wealth, they are indicative of the increasing divide between North and South. Not everyone has benefited equally from the increase in global wealth seen over the last few decades. While the developed economies integrate more and more rapidly, the least developed countries are becoming increasingly marginalised. This is mainly because they have neither the production and financial structures, nor the information structures that are now essential for integration in the globalised economy. East Asia is the only developing region that has proved capable of participating in the new global order being responsible for over one half of all the trade and investment flows in developing countries. Meanwhile, almost all of the African continent, a large part of Latin America and several Eastern and Central European countries are profiting little, if at all, from globalisation, and are falling further behind by the day. Inequality between countries has increased. The income gap between one fifth of the world's people living in the richest countries and one fifth in the poorest was 74 to 1 in 1997, up from 60 to 1 in 1990 and 30 to 1 in 1960. By the late 1990s, one fifth of the world's people living in the highest-income countries had:

- 86 per cent of world GDP, the bottom fifth just 1 per cent.
- 82 per cent of world export markets, the bottom fifth just 1 per cent.
- 68 per cent of foreign direct investment, the bottom fifth just 1 per cent.
- 74 per cent of world telephone lines, today's basic means of communication, the bottom fifth just 1.5 per cent (Gueneau et al, 1998).

More than 80 countries still have per capita incomes lower than they were a decade or more ago. While 40 countries have sustained average per capita income growth of more than 3 per cent a year since 1990, 55 countries, mostly in Sub-Saharan Africa, Eastern Europe and the CIS, have had declining per capita incomes. Therefore, there is little doubt that the failed growth of the last decades will continue if global opportunities are not shared better.

Many people are also missing out on employment opportunities. The global labour market is increasingly integrated for the highly skilled corporate executives, scientists, entertainers and the many others who form the global professional elite, with high mobility and wages. But the market for unskilled labour is highly restricted by national barriers.

This North-South divide is not confined between countries. Even within countries, inequality has been rising between regions. For example, disparities are widening in China between the export-oriented coastal regions and the inland regions. OECD countries, particularly, Sweden, the United Kingdom and the US also registered big increases in inequality between the affluent and the inner-city areas of the urban cities after the 1980s.

While the convergence theorists are optimistic, the past decade has shown increasing concentration of income, resources and wealth among people, corporations and countries. Moreover, as discussed in Chapter 5, the convergence theory has generally been rejected. The growing disparities in trade and investment shares are indicative of this.

Nonetheless, it is arguable that instead of all these trends being inevitable consequences of global economic integration, they have run ahead of global governance to share the benefits.

The inescapable power of the multinational The developments described above have been triggered, encouraged or closely followed by TNCs, which have developed in parallel with this trend towards globalisation and have been able to profit greatly from it. Operating chiefly in four key sectors (automobiles, oil, high technology and banking), TNCs most of which have their origins in the industrialised countries (although they have large networks of subsidiaries in other countries, including developing ones) account for almost all goods trading worldwide. They are also responsible for about three quarters of FDI, which is a driving force in their expansion.

TNCs bring with them management skills, technological know-how and access to international markets (see Chapter 5). But, they can also impact negatively on the development process of the host country. For example, a host country may seek new technologies while a foreign affiliate may wish to use mature technologies. Furthermore, a TNC may find it more efficient to close an affiliate, while a host country may want to preserve employment. Additionally, TNCs may seek stronger protection for intellectual property rights, while a host country may favour weak intellectual property rights to permit greater diffusion of technology (UNCTAD, 1999). Likewise, TNCs can use their transfer pricing to their own benefit, affecting the amount of profit reported in the host country, which in turn affects the tax revenue of the host country. Similarly, crowding-out may result from increases in host country interest rates caused by foreign firms' local borrowing under conditions of scarcity. In addition, TNCs can take-over local firms and relocate their R&D activities to the parent firm thus downgrading the potential for new technology in the host country. Alternatively, TNCs may not be willing to upgrade affiliated technological content as fast as host governments think desirable to stimulate local industrial deepening. In like manner, in a sub-contracting relationship, it is more often the case that supplying firms stay at the bottom of the technology ladder. This deters technological enhancement in the domestic firms. Likewise, the imported technology may be vintage and therefore, environmental-unfriendly. In fact, most TNCs' affiliates are not willing to pursue environmental-friendly policies in host developing countries unless they are put under considerable pressure. Moreover, the suppliers may lose market if wages rise and the affiliates (buyers) move to cheaper locations. Besides, the presence of TNCs in a host country may conflict with building strong national firms. For instance, TNCs may lower macroeconomic efficiency if they deliberately raise concentration levels, forcing competitors out of business through predatory practices, poaching skilled labour and R&D from local firms, or engaging in restrictive business practices which among other things deter technological development (UNCTAD, 1997a). Furthermore, national governments may be interested in protecting the environment, while TNCs address more importance to increasing profit margins. In addition, investors may pursue a deliberate strategy of shifting the location of their pollution-intensive production in response to lax environmental standards. Alternatively, developing countries may simply lack the resources and technical expertise to inspect, monitor and enforce appropriate environmental legislation.

The increase in the power and scope of TNCs has given rise to a new, global economy in which the capacity of nation-states to regulate their economies has been undermined by the 'hyper-mobility' of capital. Taken together, these characteristics give TNCs considerable weight in any negotiations with States, whether in the North or the South. They are thus equipped to influence the conduct of public policies, including environmental ones. This accounts for the active participation of TNCs in major international negotiations on the environment and development, and in discussions on voluntary codes of conduct drawn up with these very companies in mind. Because of their strategic capabilities, negotiations are often carried out in their favour.

Intellectual property rights (IPRs) were first raised as a multilateral trade issue in 1986 to crack down on counterfeit goods. The objective of the Trade-Related Aspects of Intellectual Property Rights (TRIPS) agreement is to protect the intellectual property (inventions, innovations and know-how) of WTO member countries. This is supposed to be achieved through the establishment, recognition and legal protection of IPRs. These rights, which are granted to private actors for their contribution to the development of new technologies, thus enabling them to control their innovation can take any of the following forms: patents, copyrights, registered trademarks, geographical information or trade secrets. For purposes of achieving its objectives in practice, the TRIPS agreement obliged WTO members to adopt legal protection tools by the year 2000 and extended the basic General Agreement of Tariff and Trade (GATT) rules to IPRs (i.e., principle of non-discrimination).

Environmental scientists estimate that 90 per cent of genetic information and traditional knowledge about species are to be found in developing countries. Around three quarters of the pharmaceutical products derived from plants are based on traditional indigenous knowledge. Unfortunately, while knowledge is the key to preserving biodiversity, it is not yet protected by the TRIPS agreement. Gueneau et al (1998) observe that the Convention on Biological Diversity (CBD) states, however, that the parties must preserve traditional knowledge in the interests of retaining biological diversity. It also stipulates that when the parties exploit these resources, they must share the benefits with those from whom they have obtained them. Similarly, the convention on desertification requires the parties to protect traditional knowledge and share the benefits obtained from its use in an equitable fashion. Remarkably however, no provision of this type was included in the TRIPS agreement. In addition, most local communities are often poorly informed or lack the means to acquire IPRs. Consequently, they are unable to protect their interests to an extent that their knowledge can be freely appropriated and exploited by multinationals, which then take their own legal protection measures. No wonder then, when the estimates by the UN suggest that the practice of biopiracy (i.e., exploiting traditional knowledge without any financial or other consideration) leads to an annual loss to developing countries of billions of dollars in unpaid royalties.

Liberalisation, privatisation and tighter intellectual property rights are shaping the path for the new technologies, and determining how they are used. But, the privatisation and concentration of technology are going too far. For instance, corporations define research agendas and tightly control their findings with patents, racing to lay claim to intellectual property under the rules set out in the agreement on TRIPS. Unfortunately, the reach of those rights now goes far beyond that into the ownership of life. In particular, new patent laws pay scant attention to the knowledge of indigenous people. In addition, these laws ignore cultural diversity in the way innovations are created and shared, and diversity in views on what can and should be owned, from plant varieties to human life. Furthermore, tighter property rights raise the price of technology transfer, blocking developing countries from the dynamic knowledge sectors. That is why the anti-globalisation activists are of the view that the TRIPS agreement will enable multinationals to dominate the global market even more easily. This will result in a silent theft of centuries of knowledge from some of the poorest communities in developing countries. No doubt, poor people and poor countries risk being pushed to the margin in this proprietary regime controlling the world's knowledge.

TNCs are globally restructuring the food and pharmaceutical industries in ways that are likely to further undermine the economies of the poorest countries dependent on trade in agricultural commodities. In addition, they are seeking to acquire recognition of TRIPS, which would give them ownership of any newly isolated genetic material used in their products, thus monopolising the future use of biodiversity. These TRIPS are threatening international markets and the use by peasant farmers the traditional, agricultural and pharmaceutical products in their countries. Similarly, they could threaten public access to plant genetic material held in the International Agricultural Research Centres. In a way then, the rules for trade and the rules for property rights have been written for the monopolies. This issue is bound to intensify as time goes by.

The implications of TNCs in the international division of labour are said to be unfavourable for the Third World. Anti-globalisation activists argue that although mobile capital may take advantage of cheap labour in the periphery, and thereby promote industrialisation, the character of this industrial development is not very desirable. It is based on low-level production and the super-exploitation of Third World workers, as States lower standards (wages and conditions) in order to attract foreign investment. Special areas, often called export-processing zones, have been established in parts of the Third World in order to attract foreign capital. Such attractions include low wages, minimal regulations and tax holidays. The result has been the growth of industrial employment but at the cost of low wages and poor working conditions, and in which the capacity of Third World states to regulate transnational corporate behaviour is severely undermined. For the developed countries, the results of globalisation are similarly unfavourable. For instance, capital has been relocated to lower-cost areas, which has led to de-industrialisation and unemployment. Moreover, since the imports have been increasing more than exports, their effect out weighs the employment-related benefits that have been generated.

In sum, corporate-led globalisation is creating two worlds, one gaining benefits from investment and trade, the other loosing out. In this system of win or loose out, it is estimated that almost two thirds of humanity has been left out or marginalised.

Environmental-related competition and trade barriers Some industrialists often argue against environmental policies on the grounds that they will impair competitiveness. Trade globalisation is reinforcing competition between States that are becoming more and more interdependent. In turn, increased competition limits the ability of States to implement environmental policies. For instance, a country that introduces an environmental policy obliging domestic companies to take appropriate measures to internalise external environmental effects is more vulnerable to competition from companies in foreign countries whose trade practices involve environmental dumping. Such policies, which do not incorporate protection for the environment into their production activities enable those foreign companies to supply products more cheaply.

Theoretically, this could encourage certain companies to move production to countries with lax environmental standards, otherwise known as 'pollution havens'. Indeed, companies never fail to brandish this threat when compulsory requirements are tightened. These results, of course, will vary between sectors, activities and countries. Labour, capital, technology, product differentiation, the nature and extent of international competition, the size of companies, the investment cycle, political stability and transport and communications infrastructure are just some of the key non-environmental factors that complicate assessments of the effects environmental policies are having on competitiveness and on the geographical location of companies. Sectors that are major polluters and big consumers of resources (the oil, chemical and paper industries, among others) are having to make particularly onerous changes, which it might be imagined would be detrimental to their competitiveness. However, those companies, which have a very strong presence on international markets, have the means to adapt to the new 'green' preferences of the market. For them, internalisation of external environmental effects can represent a commercial opportunity rather than a constraint.

In practice, it is small- and medium-sized enterprises that are the most affected by rigorous environmental measures, as they have smaller financial reserves and find it more difficult to exploit technical innovations and green demand. For obvious reasons, companies in developing countries may find it difficult to adapt when standards are laid down unilaterally by importing countries. Moreover, such policies sometimes force developing country exporters to change their production methods radically, and may even require them to introduce costly new products or techniques to comply with the standards in force in importing regions.

Currently, environmentalist NGOs and industrial lobbies in developed countries are exerting pressure on their governments to apply trade sanctions (taxes or embargoes on certain products) to countries that show themselves to be too lax about the environment. However, this trend worries developing countries, many of which are exporters of labour- and natural resource-intensive goods. They believe that developed countries all too often use tighter environmental, health or social standards as a way of protecting their markets against competition from foreign products. The upsurge in new trade barriers of this kind threatens to block the exports that are necessary to their growth (Gueneau et al, 1998). Arguably, this new protectionism will undermine the liberalisation efforts of multilateral trade negotiations. That is why advocates of free trade oppose the principle of trade retaliation measures based on environmental arguments. The encouraging news from their point of view is that rulings by GATT, and then by the WTO, on trade disputes relating to environmental matters have all inclined against protection measures.

Environmental policies influence the allocation of natural resources in an effort to ensure that these are used reasonably and sustainably. That is partly why they are instrumental in determining international trade flows. No wonder then that this interference disturbs the advocates of free trade, who believe that protection for the environment will inevitably give rise to a new form of protectionism, i.e. 'green' protectionism. Moreover, since the costs of environmental policies can be measured more quickly and easily than their benefits, they rush to the conclusion that these policies weaken the international competitiveness of States.

Gueneau et al (1998) have observed that voluntary agreements open to all products (both domestic and imported) on the sole condition that a set of specifications be complied with, are frequently proposed as an instrument for preserving natural resources without contravening free trade rules. Eco-labelling programmes have been particularly successful. The nature of these means that any company can participate in them freely, theoretically without trade discrimination. This implies that companies that do not participate in such programmes simply risk seeing their brand image suffer among environmentally aware consumers, to the advantage of other producers whose products are labelled.

In the past, eco-labelling programmes have mainly applied only to products that are not among the major exports of developing countries, and the criteria for inclusion have generally been based solely on the effects of consuming the product (and not on process and production methods). Therefore, they have not raised any real North-South trade problems. However, the recent extension of the eco-labelling programmes in developed countries to other sectors where developing countries are actual or potential exporters has sparked some problems. Gueneau et al (1998) note that these labelling programmes, which are based on the idea of a product life cycle include monitoring of the processes and methods used to make products, which differ depending on the socio-economic conditions and environmental preferences of countries. This implies that application of an eco-label to a product in a given country may result in implicit trade discrimination against similar imported products, insofar as labelling is based on criteria that reflect the environmental preferences of the country awarding the label. In addition, the choice of the criteria and product categories to be included in a national eco-labelling programme can be influenced by national producers so as to protect themselves against imports. This therefore, puts eco-labels in a position where they can act as a non-tariff barrier against imports or a barrier to market entry in the case of national industries.

Anti-globalisation activists also argue that developing country exporters that wish to qualify for the eco-labels devised by their trading partners, and thus maintain or increase their market share, are having to cope with growing costs. These are mostly imposed by limitations on the raw materials they can use in production processes and the need to employ modern technologies and monitoring procedures. For obvious reasons, the seriousness of these costs is inversely proportional to the production unit. This implies that the competitiveness of small and medium-sized enterprises, which make up so much of the industrial fabric in developing countries, is effectively affected by these measures.

The difficulty of internalisation arises from the need to compute the environmental costs incurred at each stage in the life cycle of a product (i.e., production, consumption and disposal), while the type, location and scale of the damage caused vary during these stages. The way environmental costs are evaluated depends on the collective preferences of each community. Thus, in the case of the basic commodities of which trade flows from the South to the North largely comprise, the demand for products to be environmentally sound will be stronger in the consumer countries of the North than in the producer countries of the South. Consequently, if country A wishes, for domestic political reasons, to give its environment greater protection than country B with which it trades, it cannot legitimately subject goods imported from that country to a tax proportional to the harm the production of these goods may have entailed for inhabitants of country B. The quality of the environment is a unilateral choice by country A, and does not provide a basis for extracting any compensation from countries that make different choices.

In any case, even if developing countries endeavour to internalise environmental costs, they lack the resources to bear the cost of international externalities connected with global common goods (i.e. the climate). Free trade-oriented NGOs also emphasize the risks that the creation of global reference standards poses to developing countries, many of which have neither the technology, nor the skills, nor the financial resources to comply with them. Developing country companies, particularly small ones, are badly informed and do not have the financial means to qualify for ISO 14000 standards. For these reasons, they could be marginalised in the process of international standard setting.

The Role of International Institutions

Free trade advocates argue that trade and investment are governed by increasingly complex rules that favour corporations over everyone else. And, the 'free market's' beneficiaries are increasingly few. Even 'consumers,' touted by free traders as the greatest beneficiaries, often find that goods produced in countries with exploited workers and lax environmental enforcement are not cheaper because large firms that dominate a market can keep prices high. The big losers have been workers whose wages and benefits are bargained down by mobile firms. Anti-globalisation advocates reject the traditional notion of 'protectionism'. They believe that the resultant effects of trade of many goods and services as well as foreign investment can be positive under the right terms and rules. Four organisations at the centre of trade and investment regulations are in particular scrutiny by anti-globalisation activists. These are the WTO, the World Bank, the IMF and the UN.

The World Trade Organisation Trade is good, but not when it is controlled by global corporations and trade rules, which favour them. Neither trade regulators nor the WTO have found a way of countering the destructive effects free trade imposes. Advocates of anti-globalisation argue that the most fundamental problem with the global trade order is the mandate of the governing institution, the WTO. Ironically, a debate was launched after World War II about the need for a global trade and investment institution that could help generate full employment and protect worker rights around the world. In addition, it was meant to help protect against what were then referred to as 'global cartels,' small groups of corporations that were gaining too much power in one sector. These broad-based goals where enshrined in a Havana Charter of a proposed new body, the International Trade Organisation (ITO). The US Senate raised objections to this broad mandate, and the ITO never opened its doors. Instead, governments created a smaller body whose mandate was centred on reducing tariffs on trade in manufactured goods, the GATT. This body, with its narrow trade expansion mandate, evolved into an institution that promoted corporate rights over the broader social agenda. Without a broader social and environmental mandate, increased trade after World War II benefited some but at the expense of many.

In 1994, the expansion of the GATT mandate into a much more powerful WTO deepened the imbalance. The WTO took on increased powers in areas unrelated to trade. Currently, in the absence of a world environment organisation, it falls to the WTO to rule on clashes between trade regulation and environmental regulation. Conflicts between trade and the environment made their appearance in the 1970s with the proliferation of unilateral trade measures taken to protect the environment, such as bans or restrictions on the import of products deemed dangerous to human health. Trade disputes which cannot be resolved by a bilateral agreement between the parties in conflict are brought before the dispute settlement body of the WTO. A panel of experts set up by this new body then make a ruling, which is crucial to an understanding of how far environmental considerations have been incorporated into the multilateral trading system. Alongside the objective of trade liberalisation, new agreements signed at the end of the trade negotiations extended the field of competence of the WTO to domains such as intellectual property rights, trade in services, sanitary and phytosanitary issues and trade-related investment. Other agreements, such as the Agreement on Technical Barriers to Trade (TBT) and the Agreement on Subsidies and Countervailing Measures, were strengthened. Certain provisions have implications for environmental protection. But, the WTO is not an environmental protection agency. Therefore, it plays no part in assessing national priorities or setting environmental standards. Obviously, these tasks will continue to be the responsibility of governments and of other intergovernmental bodies that are in a better position to accomplish them. Secondly, if CTE becomes aware of problems of co-ordination resulting from efforts to improve environmental protection, these must be settled in a way that does not contravene the principles of the multilateral trading system (MTS).

Moreover, the dominant model of economic globalisation enforced by the WTO that attempts to increase trade and investment at any costs is catastrophic for the environment, for working people, for small farmers and for cultural diversity. The WTO limits governments' ability to put controls on investment. In addition, it gained new powers to enforce its interpretation of trade and investment rules through sanctions, and to protect the so-called trade-related IPRs of corporations. With a series of rulings that negate national environmental legislation, the WTO has become a nightmare for environmentalists and has undermined democratic development around the world.

Consequently, while the free trade institution believes that the powers of the WTO should be strengthened, anti-globalisation activists believe that its powers should be scaled down. The latter argue that instead, accountability should be strengthened at the national and regional levels.

The World Bank and the International Monetary Fund The World Bank began with a lofty and worthwhile mandate to provide low interest, long-term loans to help rebuild a world destroyed by world war. It indeed could have done much more good than harm if it had been confined to this mandate. Anti-globalisation activists point out that instead, the Bank has evolved into a key purveyor of the corporate-led 'free trade and investment' development paradigm. In effect, it has become an institution that subsidises large energy and agribusiness corporations to break into new markets to an extent that these corporations have been the prime beneficiaries of hundreds of billions of dollars of low interest World Bank project loans. Other corporations have benefited from World Bank loans, by building roads, electrical grids, and power plants, which too often serve global corporations and not the local population (Barker et al, 1999).

Since 1980, the World Bank has also used its considerable leverage to press for the 'structural adjustment' of developing country policies towards privatisation, deregulation, and trade and investment liberalisation. This is aimed at remedying the high levels of indebtedness and restore growth in developing countries. The main objective of this liberal thinking is to encourage the countries where adjustment is taking place to specialise wherever they have a comparative advantage. In order to obtain foreign currency, developing countries have thus specialised yet further in the production of primary commodities. Even more seriously, certain countries have specialised for trade purposes in just a single commodity. This is the case for example with Uganda and Zambia, over three quarters of whose exports consist of coffee and copper respectively. Regional development banks have been set up for Latin America, Asia, Africa, and Europe and have largely copied this failed model.

Anti-globalisation activists argue that these institutions fail in part because they push the wrong development models and in part because they are simply too large to respond effectively to the needs of people on the ground. They have been promoting a development model that places a premium on maximum trade and investment. This model has been devastating for workers, the environment, equity, and financial stability. It is true that people in their individual capacities and small entrepreneurs often need loans. Yet, the World Bank and its regional affiliates are ill-equipped to meet these needs.

The World Bank is the main multilateral aid organisation (although some of the financing for sustainable development is allocated by UN organisations). However, since the beginning of the 1990s there has been a clear shift in its development policy. For instance, between 1986 and 1994, it financed 120 environment-linked projects, with total lending of US$ 9 billion. Nonetheless, certain NGOs are sceptical about how 'green' World Bank funding really is, since it is very difficult to isolate the strictly environmental component of projects. In respect of sustainable development, Gueneau et al (1998) have listed the following four main types of activity that the Bank finances:

- Helping member countries set priorities, strengthen institutions and formulate environmental policies and sustainable development strategies.
- Ensuring that the lending activities of the Bank take account of environmental concerns at every stage of project preparation, design and implementation.
- Helping member countries to take advantage of the complementarity that exists between anti-poverty measures and environmental protection: full understanding of demography, anti-poverty programmes, improvement of the position of women, decontamination plants and drinking water.
- Addressing international environmental problems through the Global Environment Facility (GEF).

An environmental project must be innovative and demonstrate the effectiveness of a particular method or technique in order to benefit from GEF financing. Other issues that may supplement the decision making include the contribution the project makes to developing human resources (education and training), and the procedures that are to be used for evaluating and disseminating the results. But, GEF is criticised for having neglected the developing countries by taking only developed country concerns into account when choosing its field of action. Anti-globalisation activists for instance argue that projects on desertification, for example, are mainly financed as and when they also have a bearing on global climate change. They also go further and contest the concept of instrumental cost (the additional cost involved in implementing sustainable development, calculated in relation to a reference situation showing what the country would 'normally' have spent to preserve its environment). From the viewpoint of developing countries, this notion is a means for sponsors to limit the financial contribution they make to the protection of the global environment.

The United Nations The trends of the past two decades have progressively weakened the UN system while infusing new powers into the IMF, the World Bank, and the WTO. Barker et al (1999) argue that the US government, after being the shepherd of the UN's creation in 1945, has largely undermined its efforts to carry out these functions since the advent of the Reagan administration in 1981. In particular, the Reagan administration systematically undermined UN agencies and threatened to cut off funds to stifle activity that was viewed as interfering in the market.

All this was done in the name of the free market and efficiency. These threats have continued under the different regimes.

The refusal of the US Congress to pay the full dues owed to the UN has created a permanent crisis atmosphere in what should be the most important and stable international body. While Exxon and General Motors, not to mention the World Bank and IMF, are flush with resources, the UN is starved from fulfilling its mandate. This is a tragic perversion of global priorities. This is not to suggest that the UN has been free of corruption and that resources have not been wasted.

Digital Disparity

With the costs of communications plummeting and innovative tools easier to use, people around the world have burst into conversation using the internet, mobile phones and fax machines. The fastest-growing communications tool ever, the internet had more than 140 million users in mid-1998, a number expected to pass 700 million by 2001 (Gueneau et al, 1998). But, there is a real risk in poor countries that the existing educational divide will be compounded by a digital divide. Around 80 per cent of the world's population has no access to reliable tele-communications, and nearly 50 countries have fewer than one telephone line per 100 people. It is estimated that there are more computers in New York, and more telephone lines in Manhattan than there are in the whole of the African continent. While more than half the people in Africa have never used a phone, international business is increasingly built on the rapid movement of information around the world.

There is evident inequality of internet access and exclusion not only worldwide, but even within societies of individual countries. For example, on the geography front, while Thailand has more cellular phones than Africa, South Asia, home to almost one quarter of the world's people, has a global share of less than 1 per cent of internet users. On the education front, estimates indicate that almost one third of internet users have at least a university degree, implying that education is a ticket to the network high society. From the income point of view, whereas it would take a person from a least developed country almost one half of their working life's income to buy a computer, it takes the average American just one month's wage. Even if computer prices fall to levels where they become easily affordable, there are other expenses for potential internet users. These include specialised cabling, advanced modems and online charges. In the gender and age categories, women make up the least percentage of users, while the under 30 year olds dominate the percentage of users. Moreover, the overwhelming proportion of internet activity takes place at work, and at academic institutions for the case of students. On the language front, while less that 10 per cent people worldwide speak English, English prevails in almost 80 per cent of all websites.

Evidently, those with income, education and, hence, literally connections have cheap and instantaneous access to information. The rest are left with uncertain, slow and costly access. When people in these two worlds live and compete side by side, the advantage of being connected will overpower the marginal and impoverished, cutting off their voices and concerns from the global conversation. This exclusivity is creating parallel worlds to an extent that the greater the expense of access to information, the higher the likelihood that larger portions of the world's poor in both the developed and developing countries will remain information poor. In fact, the information superhighway has by-passed most of the world's population and is likely to do so for the foreseeable future.

The Burden of Financing Development

Bilateral aid makes an absolutely essential contribution to the development of countries in the South, even though it is often used in the economic and strategic interests of donor countries. For instance, a great many countries make aid payments conditional on the beneficiary country purchasing goods and services from the donor country (tied aid). Around the world, development aid has helped to bring major projects to fruition over the last few decades. Thus, through the efforts of developing countries, supported by donors, around 1.4 billion more people gained access to clean water resources during the 1980s. The green revolution, which has helped to reduce malnutrition, has benefited greatly from international support for agronomic research, the development of new crop varieties, and irrigation among others. The impact of certain types of environmental damage is primarily local. These types of damage mobilise multilateral funds and political forces only to a very limited extent, even when they are regarded as serious. Efforts to combat such environmental problems are largely financed by bilateral development aid.

This explains why the new issues of international co-operation for sustainable development and the erosion of Official Development Assistance (ODA) are at the heart of North-South debates. Developing countries argue that the implementation of projects to protect or restore the global environment requires a level of technical, scientific and financial investment that they are not prepared to take upon themselves. They go further and remind developed countries of their historical responsibility for environmental damage, while reaffirming their desire to give priority to combating poverty and meeting basic needs. But, the actual fact is that many of them do not have sufficient access to resources other than aid and are putting pressure on developed countries to increase their financing. Donors on the other hand claim that beneficiary governments misappropriate funds, and in return are accused of meddling with internal issues of recipient countries.

Most bilateral and multilateral sponsors are attaching new green conditions to their development projects, which like all conditions attached to aid, have the following two aspects:
- To obtain the foreign financing, recipient countries should comply with environmental protection criteria.
- In return, the sponsors release additional resources to enable these criteria to be complied with (Gueneau et al, 1998).

The truth of the matter is that advances in international environmental law are multiplying the number of environmental measures that developing countries have to comply with. Moreover, stricter conditions on funding for environment-related development activities mean that sponsors have a determining role in environmental policy. Yet, beneficiary countries often see this not only as interference, but also perceive these new conditions as reducing their room for manoeuvre in the way they apply their own development policies. Hence, further North-South disagreements.

While the great bulk of the resources going to developing countries in the mid-1980s were composed of public financing, today the private sector is contributing a great deal more than the public sector to an extent so great that it seems possible that private aid may take over from public aid. After falling in the 1980s, private aid rose rapidly in the 1990s, suggesting that development financing is becoming more diverse. The cuts made by Development Assistance Committee (DAC) countries in the volume of ODA have affected bilateral funding more than multilateral funding, with multilateral aid remaining within a range of $17 to 19 billion since 1992 ($18 billion in 1997). While multilateral institutions are still the cornerstone of the international community's efforts to further development, the stagnation of national funding for the UN system and multilateral development banks is nonetheless worrying.

Private aid takes the form of loans and donations under market conditions financed by the private sector. These include FDI, international bank loans, obligatory borrowings, export credits, and bilateral or multilateral portfolio investments. However, the bulk of these flows goes to Latin America and Asia, to the detriment of Africa and the Middle East. The smallest and least developed countries have not yet succeeded in attracting this capital, which is a potential source of development financing. Furthermore, private resources do not as a rule go straight to certain essential sectors with priority needs, such as health and education.

Anti-globalisation activists argue that the countries disadvantaged by economic globalisation are often the ones that are the most heavily indebted. For instance, the debt service for the 41 heavily indebted poor countries amounted to $11.1 billion in 1996. These debts were contracted in the 1970s, being covered at that time by high demand for raw materials, which raised prices, and by low interest rates due to the 1973 oil crisis. These debts, denominated entirely in hard currencies, are still being repaid, while raw material prices are at rock bottom. The switching of demand into manufactured products means that any increase in raw material export volumes causes prices to fall. No wonder, these countries are facing depreciating terms-of-trade. Inevitably, debt servicing now takes up most of the profits from exports.

Gueneau et al (1998) argue that debt repayment programmes reduce yet further the funds available for education, social and health-care infrastructure and the environment. For example, countries in sub-Saharan Africa spend four times as much on debt servicing each year as on health and education, without thereby clearing their arrears. Lack of liquidity has led almost half of the most heavily indebted countries to sign up to structural adjustment plans in exchange for bank guarantees from the IMF.

Globalisation and Human Insecurity

One achievement of recent decades has been greater security for people in many countries and more political freedom and stability. But in the globalising world of shrinking time, shrinking space and disappearing borders, people are confronting new threats to human security, and sudden and hurtful disruptions in the pattern of daily life. For instance, governments have effectively transferred much of their sovereignty to the hands of global corporations for the past two decades. Yet, democracy flourishes when people organise to protect their communities and rights and hold their elected officials accountable. Other worrying developments include the dis-empowerment of the local communities, financial and economic insecurity, food security and food safety, job and income insecurity, health and cultural insecurity and criminal insecurity. This are highlighted below.

Dis-empowerment of the Local Communities

Barker et al (1999) point out that economic globalisation entails first, and foremost, de-localisation and dis-empowerment of communities and local economies. Evidently, a high percentage of people on the earth still survive through local, community-based activities including small scale farming, local markets, and local production for local consumption. For this reason, they have been able to remain directly in control of their economic and food security, while also maintaining the viability of local communities and culture. Even for the case of developed countries, most jobs have traditionally been connected to local economic production. Unfortunately, economic globalisation is rapidly dismantling this, strongly favouring economies based on export, with global corporations in control. This brings destruction of local livelihoods, local jobs, and community self-reliance.

Financial Volatility and Economic Insecurity

The 1997/98 financial turmoil in East Asia demonstrates the risks of global financial markets. Net capital flows to Indonesia, the Republic of Korea, Malaysia, the Philippines and Thailand rocketed remarkably in the 1990s. As turmoil hit market after market, these flows reversed overnight. Two important experiences were observed. First, the human impacts are severe and are likely to persist long after economic recovery. For example, bankruptcies spread, education and health budgets came under pressure, millions of jobs were lost, and all assets lost value. Meanwhile, as prices of essential commodities rose sharply, real wages fell sharply. In fact, one wonders whether the escalating social unrest, crime and violence are not an indication of an erosion of a previously well knit social fabric. While output growth, payment balances, interest rates and inflation may be returning to normal, human lives will take longer to recover.

Second, financial crises have become increasingly common with the spread and growth of global capital flows. They result from rapid build-ups and reversals of short-term capital flows and are likely to recur. More so, they are highly influenced by some person harbouring the name of a 'speculator'. More likely when national institutions regulating financial markets are not well developed, they are now recognised as systemic features of global capital markets. No single country can withstand their whims.

Food Security and Food Safety

Anti-globalisation activists argue that communities and nations are stable and secure when people have enough food, particularly when nations can provide their own food. People also deserve safe food, a commodity that is increasingly scarce as global agribusiness firms spread chemical- and biotech-intensive agriculture around the world. To make matters worse, global rules of trade now strongly favour the industrial agriculture model, rapidly destroying small-scale farmers who mainly produce staple foods for local consumption. Monopoly control of food and seeds among a small number of corporations now threatens millions of farmers and tens of millions of peoples' food security and safety. In sum then, globalised industrial agriculture is driving small farmers off their lands and replacing them with pesticide and machine intensive, mono-cultures producing luxury items for export, at great environmental and social cost (Barker et al, 1999).

Job and Income Insecurity

Countries and employers are having to adopt more flexible labour policies with more precarious work arrangements due to the pressures of global competition. People the world all over have experienced mergers and acquisitions, which have come with corporate restructuring and massive layoffs. Thus, dislocations from economic and corporate restructuring, and from dismantling the institutions of social protection, have meant greater insecurity in jobs and incomes.

Health Insecurity

The spread of primary healthcare practices such as the use of clean water, hygienic sanitation and the practice of simple re-hydration therapy for diarrhoea has saved hundreds of thousands of lives. But globalisation also poses risks. For instance, it has accelerated travel and migration, which in turn has had a dramatic effect on the spread of killer diseases including HIV/AIDS and TB. In Africa, most of the cases have their origins along the trans-African highway, which runs from Southern Africa, through Eastern and Central Africa to North Africa. And the epidemic is now spreading rapidly to new locations, including rural Asia, Eastern Europe and the CIS. With the dominant majority of the infected people living in developing countries, AIDS has become a poor person's disease, taking a heavy toll on life expectancy, and reversing the medical gains of recent decades. At present there is not enough medical research that benefits the poor. This is not only a human tragedy, but a developmental catastrophe as well.

Cultural Insecurity

Barker et al (1999) have pointed out that only a few decades ago, it was still possible to leave home and go somewhere else where the architecture was different, the landscape was different, and the language, lifestyle, dress, and values were different. Tens of thousands of communities around the world had perfected local resource management systems that worked, but that are being undermined by corporate-led globalisation. Cultural, biological, social, and economic diversity are central to a dignified, interesting, and healthy life. Globalisation has opened people's lives to culture and all its creativity, and to the flow of ideas and knowledge. But, the new culture carried by expanding global markets is disquieting. Today's flow of culture is unbalanced, heavily weighted in one direction, from rich countries to poor. To an extent that weightless goods, with high-knowledge rather than material content now make for some of the most dynamic sectors in today's most advanced economies. For example, the single largest export industry for the US is not aircraft or automobiles, but entertainment in form of films and music.

The expansion of global media networks and satellite communications technologies gives rise to a powerful new medium with a global reach. These networks bring Hollywood to remote villages. And the spread of global brands (i.e., Nike and Sony) is setting new social standards all over the globe. Such onslaughts of foreign culture puts cultural diversity at risk, and makes people fear losing their cultural identity. In fact, some anti-globalisation activists are of the view that this development represents a form of cultural imperialism (Barker et al, 1999).

Criminal Insecurity

Deregulated capital markets, advances in information and communications technology, and cheaper transport, have made the flow of capital and information not only easier, but also faster. Unfortunately, this is not restricted just for medical knowledge but for heroin, and not just for books and seeds but for dirty money and weapons as well. Consequently, criminals are reaping the benefits of globalisation. In particular, illicit trade in drugs, women, weapons, laundered money and even children is contributing to the violence and crime that threaten neighbourhoods around the world. The weapons trade specifically feeds street crime as well as civil strife. Among the chief communication channels is the internet, where such networked activities are almost untraceable.

At the root of all this is the growing influence of organised crime, rivalling multinational corporations as an economic power. Global crime groups can infiltrate politics, business and the police, and develop efficient networks, extending their reach deep and wide.

Globalisation has given new characteristics to national and international conflicts. Feeding these conflicts is the global traffic in weapons, involving new actors and blurring political and business interests. In the power vacuum of the post-cold war era, military companies and mercenary armies began offering training to governments and corporations. Accountable only to those who pay them, these hired military services pose a severe threat to human security (Gueneau et al, 1998).

The Ethical Dilemma

The revolution in communications technologies has created all sorts of new ethical dilemmas, just as technological change in medicine spurred interest in medical ethics in the 1970s. Because it is mainly businesses that develop and spread new technologies, businesses also tend to face the first questions about how to use them. So companies stumble into such questions as data protection and customer privacy. They know more than ever before about their customers' tastes, but few have a clear view on what uses of that knowledge are unethical.

Some of the most publicised debates about corporate ethics have been driven by globalisation. When companies operate abroad, they run up against all sorts of new moral issues. And one big problem is that ethical standards differ among countries.

In developing a formal ethics policy, companies usually begin by trying to sum up their philosophy in a code. Not surprisingly, codes are often too broad to capture the ethical issues that actually confront companies, which range from handling their own staff to big global questions of policy on the environment, bribery and human rights. Some companies use the internet to try to add precision to general injunctions.

As UNCTAD (1999) has rightly observed, unfortunately for developing countries, many issues often go unnoticed by the wider public and are not taken up by TNCs as long as they are not associated with sufficiently influential public pressure. This problem is amplified by the fact that most, if not all, corporate social responsibility deliberations are undertaken by the parent firms mostly based in developed countries. In addition, in terms of influence and recognition, developed country civil society groups excel most particularly because of the democratic rights they enjoy in their home countries. Moreover, differences in development and cultures imply a divergence between the requirements and interest of societies in the developed countries *vis-à-vis* those in the developing countries. Unsurprisingly then, issues of great concern to developing countries are not addressed when TNCs and civil society in the developed countries engage in debates over corporate social responsibility.

Conclusion

It is becoming increasingly recognised (at least by moderate anti-globalisation activists) that globalisation creates unprecedented new opportunities for sustainable development, poverty reduction, and faster progress in achieving the international development targets. However, its benefits have been unevenly spread. While living standards rise for many as a result of globalisation, many more live in extreme poverty, forced to make ends meet on a tiny economy. With wealth generally increasing but unevenly distributed, the disparities of development are affecting the state of the environment. The interdependence between economies also applies to the environment, as the consequences of damage spread from the local to the global level. For instance, trade liberalisation has led to increased production of goods and services that generate environmental damage. In addition, while the developed economies integrate more and more rapidly, the least developed countries are becoming increasingly marginalised. Furthermore, people are confronting new threats to human security, and sudden and hurtful disruptions in the pattern of daily life, dis-empowerment of the local communities, financial and economic insecurity, food security and food safety, job and income insecurity, health and cultural insecurity and criminal insecurity.

Instead of the acclaimed 'shrinking space, shrinking time and disappearing borders' effects of globalisation, there is in effect 'an incentive squeeze on the environment, a fiscal squeeze on public goods, and a time squeeze on care activities'. Thus, from the environmental perspective, globalisation leads to more environmental destruction. However, from the North-South equity-divide point of view, it causes more disparity within and between nations, and more marginalisation of people and countries. But, from the human insecurity viewpoint, globalisation engenders more violation of human rights, more instability of societies, more vulnerability of people, and more poverty and deprivation. Policies for rectifying this are discussed in Chapter 7.

5 FDI and Economic Growth: pro-globalisation views

Introduction

Economic growth is a process of change through time, which involves an interrelationship between economic, political and social factors. It can be envisaged as an almost uninterrupted increase year after year, in a country's per capita output. Thus, economic growth remains an urgent global need. Unsurprisingly, the development priorities of developing countries include income growth, rising investments and exports, creating more and better employment opportunities, and benefiting from technical progress. No wonder, developing countries are placed under considerable pressure to upgrade their resources and capabilities if they are to achieve these objectives.

Consequently, factors that have the potential to act as 'engines' of economic growth and hence, factors that may explain transition from an undeveloped economy to a developed economy have to be identified. Several factors have been hypothesised and empirically tested under several economic growth theories. These theories have evolved over time, beginning with the classical theory followed by the neo-classical theory and then the new or endogenous growth theory. However, the traditional factors that propel sustained economic growth have not changed over time. They include the generation and efficient allocation of the basic factors of production, capital and labour. In addition, they include the application of technology and the creation of skills and institutions traditionally otherwise referred to as technical progress. Instead, it is the global context for economic growth that has changed enormously over the past three decades. This change has affected not only the role of the engines of economic growth, but also the influence of government policies on the engines of economic growth. Technical progress can be achieved through several channels. For instance, it may be stimulated by investment that augments and improves the productivity of national physical resources. Alternatively, it can be driven by innovations, which not only improve the productivity of existing activities, but also create competitive advantages in new activities. Additionally, it can be promoted by development of labour skills, or investment in human skills. The most recent focus of accounting for economic growth embraces factors such as human resources development, which relate to the role of quality improvements in the labour-force of an economy, improvements that come about from better health, more education and greater access to training. It also comprises technological change, international trade and government policy. These factors not only determine how well each economy utilises its factor endowments, but also affect how flexibly and dynamically each country adjusts to changes in economic conditions.

Prior to the 1970s, FDI and, hence, TNCs were seen by developing economies as part of a problem to development, to be solved by minimising the role of TNCs. They were perceived by developing country politicians and development economist as an unnecessary evil that; made huge profits, imported obsolete technology, introduced unfavourable balance of payments, was a neo-colonial vehicle, milked the developing economies through transfer pricing, and introduced a dependencia syndrome which eroded their self-reliance. However, the past three decades have witnessed unprecedented and sustained high rates of economic growth most notably in the Asian NIEs, with substantial involvement of FDI. No doubt then, an awareness of the link between FDI and economic growth has been established. Moreover, many of the growth promoting factors identified by the endogenous growth theory have been hypothesised to form the foundation of the key positive spillover effects of FDI. For instance, FDI is said to stimulate economic growth through the creation of dynamic comparative advantages that lead to new technology transfers, capital formation, human resources development, expanded international trade, clean technologies and modern environmental management systems. In addition, TNCs are under considerable pressure to undertake social responsibility.

For this reason, national governments have recognised that TNCs can provide a package of external resources that can contribute to economic development. Therefore, it is not surprising that developing countries have changed attitude and are now considering FDI as part of the solution to their economic development. Subsequently, they have shifted from controlling and containing FDI to encouraging it. The growing importance and recognition of FDI is exemplified by the shift towards greater openness of national developing economies to FDI.

Nonetheless, it is essential to recognise the fact that the objectives of TNCs differ from those of host governments. For instance, whereas governments seek to spur national development, TNCs seek to enhance their own competitiveness moreover, in the international context. Consequently, although there may be considerable overlaps, there are also significant differences. In fact, FDI offers a mixture of positive and negative effects. It is then the task of the host country to disentangle these effects, and take measures that maximise the positives but minimise the negatives.

This chapter explores the views of the pro-globalisation school of thought but focuses on only the key element of globalisation, FDI. Nonetheless, some of the negative effects of FDI, and hence, globalisation are highlighted as and when appropriate. The chapter is divided into two sections, which explore both theoretical and empirical issues. The first section presents a brief discussion of the development of the growth theory starting with the classical theory through to the endogenous theory, and incorporates the role FDI is increasingly playing in the endogenous theory. The second section examines how FDI can influence the growth process of host developing countries through its contribution to their human resources development, new technology transfer, capital formation, international trade, environmental management and linkages.

An Introduction to Growth Theory

Theoretical Review

Classical growth theories   Classical economists (Adam Smith, 1776; Thomas Malthus, 1798; and David Ricardo, 1817) pioneered the earlier theories of economic growth. Later on, Ramsey (1928) initiated work on optimal savings, while Schumpeter (1934), Harrod (1939) and Domar (1947) made dynamic extensions of the Keynesian model. The classical models emphasised the importance of expanding the quantity of basic factors of production, i.e. capital, labour and land. Furthermore, they stressed the role of expanding markets in improving efficiency and productivity within an economy, and the role of demand and the multiplier effects from increases in investment, government consumption and exports. However, they held little hope for a nation to sustain its economic growth. No doubt, the general state of the economic characteristics at the time did not provide any indication of the possibility that development could be achieved in technology, particularly product and process innovation. For instance, Malthus (1798) predicted that the finite availability of land would limit any nation's development and that the natural equilibrium in labour wages would hover at subsistence levels because of the interaction of labour supply, agricultural production, and wage systems. He argued that low labour supplies would induce wage rises, which would in turn motivate workers to increase their numbers. Increases in the size of the population and labour pool would then put pressure on finite supplies of food, increase the costs of nourishment, and ultimately lead to decreases in wages because of increased competition for such employment.

Harrod (1939) and Domar's (1947) one sector models, and Mahalanobis's (1955) two sector model assumed that marginal capital-output ratios were constant, implying that the marginal product of capital did not decline. Thus, the growth rate was endogenous and depended on the rate of savings (investment) in such one-sector models and on the aggregate rate of investment and its allocation between sectors producing capital and consumer goods in the two sector models. Neumann (1945) pioneered work on balanced growth at a maximal rate. That is, growth in which outputs of all commodities grew at the same rate. His model characterised production technology by a finite set of constant-returns-to scale activities. The inputs were committed at the beginning of each discrete production period and the outputs emerged at the end. The model assumed that natural resources were inexhaustible and that there were no non-produced factors of production. The 'primary' version of the model characterised a vector of activity levels that enabled the maximum rate of balanced growth given that the outputs of each period were to be ploughed back as inputs in the next period. The 'dual' version was on the other hand characterised by a vector of commodity prices and an interest rate, whose properties meant that the value of output of each activity was no higher than the value of inputs inclusive of interest and that the interest rate was the lowest possible. Neumann made certain assumptions about technology and showed that the maximal growth rate of output of the 'primary' version was equal to the (minimal) interest rate of the 'dual' version. Furthermore, he showed that the usual complementary slackness relations obtained between the vector activity levels, prices, growth and interest rates.

In a nutshell, classical theory held that expanding the labour pools led to declines in the accumulation of capital per worker, lower worker productivity, and lower incomes per person, eventually causing stagnation or economic decline. Thus, it limited a nation's development and economic growth to its supply of land and labour and discounted any effects of technology improvements that create greater efficiencies. Naturally, this theory was proven incorrect by numerous scientific and technological discoveries, which provided for greater efficiencies in production and greater returns on inputs of land, capital and labour. For instance, the acceptance and popularity of birth control as a means of limiting population growth has been growing, and yet nations have continued to develop.

Neo-classical growth theories   Following the classical growth theories, focus changed to neo-classical growth models whose main thrust was to demonstrate that a growing economy is not inherently unstable (as had been suggested by the classical economist, Harrod). Many neo-classical economists including Tobin (1955), Solow (1956, 1957) and Denison (1985) researched aggregate production functions. Their models were characterised by some form of production function relating output to factor inputs, and the absence of an investment function so that investment was determined passively by savings. In the neo-classical framework, perfectly competitive conditions were assumed for both product and factor markets. Thus, factor prices adjusted freely to equilibrate (or 'clear') factor markets, and so were equal to the respective marginal products of the factors. In particular, the real wage maintained equilibrium in the labour market. Additionally, with a given technology, an economy would tend to grow with full employment, constrained only by the rate at which that ceiling was rising, i.e. by the rate of growth of labour. Production technology was assumed to exhibit constant returns to scale. Furthermore, in many, though not all models, smooth substitution between any two inputs with strictly diminishing marginal rates of substitution between any two inputs along an isoquant was also posited. In addition, the conditions ensuring the existence and uniqueness of steady state growth paths along which all inputs and outputs grew at the same rate were paramount to the analytical focus. The steady state growth rate was the exogenous rate of growth of the labour force in efficiency units, so that in the absence of (exogenous) labour-augmenting technical progress, output per worker was constant along the steady state.

Solow's (1956) view was, however, slightly different. He envisaged a possibility that a steady state need not exist, and that if one existed, it need not be unique. Thus, output per worker could grow indefinitely, even in the absence of labour-augmenting technical progress. Solow's model has basic features of a closed economy with comparative markets and a production technology exhibiting diminishing returns to capital and labour separately, and constant returns to all inputs jointly. In this model, population growth and propensity to save, which affect the per capita level of income, are only affected by exogenous factors. Exogenously determined technical progress is the only force accounting for growth in income per capita.

Thus, neo-classical models in general demonstrated the important contribution of technical progress to economic growth, over and above the contribution from expanding quantities of productive factors, and the role that can be played by elements such as improvements in the organisation of production. The question which arises is, 'what are the intrinsic factors of technical progress?'

Over the years, technical progress has been given a wide range of meanings and interpretations. Technical progress can be defined as the advancement of knowledge about methods of production. It propels the potential output obtainable from any input of 'physical' factors, or shrinks the inputs required to produce any quantity of output. In other words, it relates to an increase in productivity.

The term productivity on the other hand may be used to mean the ratio of some measure of output to input such as labour. When such a measure is used, however, the reasons for its increase may not be clear. It could be attributed for instance, to more efficient work practices or an increase in installed machinery, i.e. a larger capital input. Furthermore, an increase in the efficiency in the machinery through technical progress and innovation may also prompt productivity. The alternative meaning is embraced in the term *total factor productivity* (TFP), which refers to how output would change if all the factor inputs were maintained constant. This term is more meaningful since it embraces technical progress and changes in efficiency. It relates particularly to new technology, which comprises three elements. First is *product innovation*, which leads to new or upgraded products, or the improvement of quality. Second is *process innovation*, which spurs new and more efficient ways of production. Third, is the *stock of knowledge* both technical and managerial used in improving the efficiency of production and marketing. In other words then, TFP is a catch-all for those things that increase the joint efficiency of labour and capital, and can be measured as a component of output variation not explained by changes in the amount of capital and labour. The concept of TFP was first introduced in an article by Tibergen (1942) (Christensen et al, 1980). Several economists (Griliches, 1960; Denison, 1962; Domer, 1964; Christensen and

Jorgenson, 1969; Christensen et al, 1980; Krugman, 1994; Kim and Lau, 1992, 1994 and 1995; and Bende-Nabende et al, 2000a) have since made international comparisons of post-war patterns of aggregate economic growth. They have a common underlying theme of how productivity growth can be increased to enhance economic growth. Hence, the need for growth to be driven primarily by efficiency gains rather than by the rapid growth of factor inputs which, are subject to diminishing returns. The limitation of TFP, however, stems from the fact that since it is an unobservable variable, it is not directly measurable and therefore has to be estimated. The different methods and production functions that are used, therefore, heavily influence the results.

Technical progress often proceeds a number of distinct stages. The first is invention or discovery (often by a firm), which may be defined as the occurrence of new ideas. This often follows a process of commitment on R&D. Following this, is the process of adoption that constitutes innovation, which (innovation) can be defined as the commercial application of inventions for the first time. This is then followed by diffusion of the new knowledge to other firms, and imitation of the original innovation. Thus, it is only after the new ideal is successfully accepted, that the diffusion of knowledge and imitations then start playing an instrumental role in the technical progress process. No wonder then that Denison (1985) argued that the advance in knowledge is the biggest and most basic reason for the persistent long-term growth of output per unit of input. As knowledge relevant to production advances, the output that can be obtained from a given quantity of resources rises. He defined advances in knowledge to include advances in technological knowledge and advances in managerial knowledge. He extended advances in knowledge to comprise knowledge originating inside the country as well as that from abroad, and knowledge obtained in anyway - by organised research, by individual research workers and inventors, and by simple observations and experience. Knowledge obtained through an industrial or institutional espionage can also be added to this list.

Subsequently, technical progress may be visualised either as an upward shift of a production function whose augments are physical inputs, or as an inward shift of isoquants towards the origin. Such a shift may be due to innovations, education of the labour force or other factors. The shift representing technical progress may be incorporated in the production function as follows:

$$Y = f(K,L,t); \qquad f_t > 0 \tag{6.1}$$

where Y is output, K is capital stock, L is labour and t is time period. Owing to technical progress, Y increases with a passage of time even if K and L are constant. Thus in a way, t represents the stock of knowledge. Technical progress (which has been used to account for growth in growth-accounting models) is thus represented simply as an automatic, exogenous process, occurring independently of any economic variables.

Neo-classical economists introduced the concept of convergence in their models, which assumed diminishing returns to capital. It is worthwhile noting that there are two versions of the convergence theory. The stronger version postulates that if all economies had access to the same aggregate production function exhibiting constant returns to scale in capital and effective labour inputs, experienced the same rate of growth of labour force and labour-augmenting technical progress, and saved and invested the same share of output, they would grow at the same rate as effective labour. The weaker version, known as conditional convergence, allows for possible differences in steady states and initial level of labour-augmenting technical progress. Neo-classical economists hypothesised that poorer economies that have a lower initial level of capital stock per worker tend to have higher returns (marginal productivity) and higher growth rates, which eventually make them *catch-up* or *converge* with the richer economies in the long-run. That is, there exists a long-run tendency towards the equalisation of levels of per capita income or per worker product. Thus, the growth of developing countries could be rapid for a period of time, but would inevitably decelerate as the gap (with the developed countries) diminished.

The neo-classical assumption of diminishing returns to capital meant that the growth of output could not nearly be accounted for by the growth of inputs. Hence, the appearance of the large residual that was attributed to technical progress, which was an *exogenous* factor. Although efforts were made to decompose the residual into different elements, such as education, which had not been captured by the conventional measurement of factor inputs, the exogeneity of technical progress proved to be a major deficiency in neo-classical models.

Endogenous growth theory The deficiency in neo-classical models raised questions as to whether long-term per capita growth should actually be determined by an exogenous factor. Moreover, its depiction of a steady state exhibited no resemblance to the real world. For instance, development economists noted that middle-income countries tended to grow more rapidly than low-income countries. For example, in the late-1980s and early-1990s the dynamic economies of Southeast Asia experienced unprecedented high growth rates. Moreover, there was no tendency for their growth rates to decelerate. This empirical regularity sits uncomfortably with the catch-up or convergence hypothesis. Furthermore, there is no strong evidence to suggest the anticipated tendencies towards convergence in per capita incomes, contrary to what neo-classical growth and trade theories would have led one to think. So, were the initial per capita incomes of these economies so low that the measure of the period required for catch-up was more in terms of decades than years? In that event then, did it mean that neo-classical growth theory was after all unsatisfactory or perhaps even useless for understanding development? Unsurprisingly, a split developed between neo-classical growth theorists and development economists. Consequently, new researchers were prompted to develop models in which the key determinants of long-run growth are *endogenous* or explain the model. For this reason, the *new* or *endogenous* growth theory emerged. The term endogenous is used hereafter.

The key characteristic of the endogenous growth theory is the presence of some factor(s) whose accumulation is(are) not subject to diminishing returns. Hence, once growth starts, there is a continuous contribution to its perpetuation. Thus, the endogenous growth theory is accomplished through increasing scale economies in aggregate production. However, in assessing the role of increasing scale economies to growth, it may be useful to distinguish between generating sustained growth in output per head and endogenising the rate of growth. For instance consider the following production function:

$$Y = K^a L^b \qquad 0 < a, b < 1 \text{ and } a + b > 1 \qquad (6.2)$$

When labour is growing exogenously, at a rate of n, there exists a steady state (regardless of the savings rate) in which output grows at an exogenous rate of $n(a + b - 1)/(1 - a)$, where $1 - a > 0$. Thus, increasing scale economies together with a marginal product of capital strictly diminishes to zero (i.e., $0 < a < 1$) leads to sustained but exogenous growth. Therefore, increasing returns in themselves need not generate endogenous growth. On the other hand, constant returns to scale with marginal product of capital bounded away from zero at a sufficiently high positive number leads to endogenous and sustained growth. This is achieved (in some models) by introducing a factor other than physical capital (e.g., human capital or the stock of knowledge), which is not subject to inexorable returns. Consider for instance the following Cobb-Douglas production function:

$$Y_t = AK_t^a L_t^b \qquad 0 < a, b < 1 \qquad\qquad (6.3)$$

where A is a technology factor. Under the neo-classical production, A is assumed to be exogenously determined. The endogenous growth theory endogenises the technology factor (using human capital in this case) as follows:

$$A_t = BH_t^c \qquad 0 < c < 1 \qquad\qquad (6.4)$$

where H_t is the level of human capital stock. Thus, if H_t increases by 1 per cent, A_t is assumed to increase by c per cent. Substituting (6.4) into (6.3) gives:

$$Y_t = BK_t^a H_t^c L_t^b \qquad\qquad (6.5)$$

So what is the fundamental difference between neo-classical and the recent growth models? Take the following production function:

$$Y_t = A_t f(K_t, b_t L_t) \qquad\qquad (6.6)$$

where A_t ($A_0 \equiv 1$) is the disembodied technology factor (i.e., index of TFP), so that output at time t associated with any combination of capital stock and labour input efficiency units is A times the output at time zero associated with the same combination. Analogously, b_t (with $b_0 \equiv 1$) is the efficiency level of a unit of labour at time zero. Thus, the technical progress induced by increases in b_t is labour augmenting. It is easily seen that technical progress through A_t is Hicks-neutral, and that through b_t is Harrod-neutral (Srinivasan, 1995).

Individual scholars have endogenised technical progress in different ways. For instance, by relating productivity of workers operating newly produced equipment to the rate of growth of investment per worker, Kaldor and Mirrlees (1962) endogenised technical progress and hence, output growth rate. Arrow's (1962) 'leaning-by-doing' model also endogenised technical progress by postulating that growth results from a leaning process, which is itself a product of experience. The latter, in turn, is a function of cumulative gross investment so that the factor productivity was an increasing function of cumulated output of investment. In Uzawa's (1965) model, technical progress was endogenised by assuming that the rate of growth of labour-augmenting technical progress was a concave function of the ratio of labour employed (the only factor input) in the education sector.

Romer (1986) was the first expositor of this view in its modern form. He introduced an equilibrium model of technical change in which long-run growth is driven by the accumulation of knowledge by 'forward-looking, profit maximising agents'. He considered not only the accumulation of capital goods, but the accumulation of investment in knowledge as well. Investment in knowledge or R&D is assumed to be subject to diminishing returns, but the utilisation of such knowledge in production activity results in increasing returns (increasing marginal product). His argument was based on a consideration of an economy in which there are n identical firms. Each firm has a production function $Y_i = f(K_i, L_i, K)$ where K_i is the stock of capital or R&D employed by firm i, L_i is labour (or labour hours) and $K = \Sigma^n_{i=1} K_i$ is the industry level aggregate stock of knowledge. Although the choice of K is external to the firm, K is assumed to have a positive spillover effect on the output of each firm. He concluded that since it cannot be hidden from them, the investment in knowledge by one firm has a positive effect on the production possibilities of other firms through spillovers. It is these spillovers of knowledge (as a side effect of investment) across producers and external benefits from human capital that help avoid the tendency for diminishing returns to the accumulation of capital.

Lucas (1988) sought to formalism that leads to the thought about individual decisions to acquire knowledge, and about the consequences of these decisions for productivity. No doubt then that he formulated the theory of human capital to achieve this. He endogenised Harrod-neutral (i.e, labour augmenting) technical change through a mechanism of human capital accumulation otherwise known as the learning-by-doing effects of human capital. The theory of learning-by-doing states that the direct costs of manufacturing a unit of the good decline as the experience gained by the labour force increases. Lucas expanded Arrow's (1962) work by arguing that human capital accumulation is a social activity. The more educated workers interact with other educated people, the more new ideas come about which improve productivity efficiency. Therefore, human capital exerts two effects on the production process. One is the internal effect of the individual's human capital on his own productivity. The other is the external effect that no individual human capital accumulation decision can take into account. That is, people interact with others who are more educated in the production process and thereby learn-by-doing. For instance, if a worker of period t is endowed with b_t human capital, or skill, and one unit of labour, his labour endowment has to be allocated between accumulating skills and earning wage income. If he allocates the fraction α_t of his time in the current production sector and $1 - \alpha_t$ (where $0 \leq \alpha_t \leq 1$) in the learning sector (such as school or vocational training program), his future human capital can be increased by $\theta = b_t\delta(1 - \alpha_t)$. Evidently, there is a trade-off between current consumption and future physical capital. In fact, a person has a choice of either having a lower current α_t concomitant with a larger future human capital and thus a larger future stream of output or vice versa. Besides, there is an opportunity cost of time spent on skill acquisition, which is foregone income that could have been used for consumption or accumulation of physical capital. Lucas argued that neo-classical growth theory cannot account for observed differences in growth across countries and over time and for its evidently counterfactual prediction that international trade should induce rapid movements toward equality in capital-labour ratios and factor prices (Srinivasan, 1995). He asserted that the neo-classical model predicts a strong tendency to income equality and equality in growth rates in the absence of differences in pure technology and under the assumption of no factor mobility. Moreover, these tendencies can be observed within countries and perhaps within the wealthiest countries taken as a group, but which simply cannot be seen in the world at large. The permission of factor mobility powerfully re-enforces this prediction. He suggested that variation across countries in technology (which has been isolated by the neo-classical model) could potentially account for the wide differences in their income levels and growth rates. The differences in technology in this sense does not relate to knowledge in general, but is associated with knowledge of particular people or particular subcultures of people.

Grossman and Helpman (1991) formulated a model in which firms operating in imperfectly competitive markets undertook R&D and researched the dynamic spillover effects of export expansion. They observed that even if differences in levels of output and of consumption may exist, international spillovers of investment may provide over and above the effects of capital mobility and this is a strong reason for convergence of growth. It is through international communication of research ideas that scale economies are exploited and productivity of innovative activity is enhanced. They further argued that in an environment of a small country in which scientific and technological knowledge flows from abroad, trade generates an externality that coexists with the externality of domestic innovation, the latter leading to little innovation. Residents of the small country gain access to accumulated wisdom and new discoveries that are being made on an ongoing basis when they interact with agents in the outside world. The number of commercial interactions between the domestic and foreign agents influences the multitude of this factor. The extent of the spillover then increases with the volume of their bilateral trade.

Raut and Srinivasan's (1991) model endogenises growth and the process of shifts in production possibilities over time (i.e. technical change). Their model simply analyses the implications of assuming that technical change is influenced by population density in a world where fertility is endogenous. By assuming fertility to be endogenous, they exclude the possibility of aggregate growth being driven solely by exogenous labour force growth in the absence of technical change. Furthermore, by assuming that population density has an external effect (not perceived by individual agents) on the production process either through its negative congestion effect or through its positive effect in stimulating innovation and technical change, they make the change in production possibilities endogenously determined by fertility decisions of individual agents. For instance, they point out that the inducement of innovation largely depends upon the returns and risks to resources devoted to innovative activity and that there is no particular reason to suggest that pre-existing relative factor prices or endowments will necessarily tilt these returns toward search for technologies that save particular factors (Srinivasan, 1995).

Boserup (1991) and Simon's (1991) models assume that technical change in an economy is Hicks-neutral and that its rate is determined by the change in the size of the working population. In their production function:

$$Y_t = A(L_t)f(K_t, L_t) \qquad (6.7)$$

$A(L_t)$ is an externality for both consumers and firms. They introduce this externality in a model of overlapping generations in which a member of each generation lives through the three periods of: childhood (in the parent's household), a young person (working, having and raising children and accumulating capital) and an old person (retired, living off support from offsprings and from sale of accumulated capital). The model assumes that all people exhibit similar preferences during all the stages. Thus, people decide to have children for purposes of the support they expect to receive from them in the future. Production of a single commodity, which can be consumed or accumulated is organised in firms which buy capital from the retired and hire the young as workers. Markets for product, labour and capital are assumed to be competitive. Their models (Raut and Srinivasan, 1991; Boserup, 1991; and Simon, 1991) were criticised for not providing a complete theory of induced innovation on the grounds that having a large population is not a sufficient condition for generating growth. Hence, the need to examine the mechanism by which population density influences innovation.

As Balasubramanyam et al (1996) have observed, the endogenous growth theory for the most part explores the mainsprings of technical progress or the residual left unexplained in the neo-classical models. It postulates that human capital accumulation is one of the key factors that generates fast technical progress through learning-by-doing, or on-the-job training, as well as education. Its message in brief is that technical progress is accounted for by human capital formation and by spillover effects or externalities generated by investment in the production of knowledge. Its primary goal is to build models that can generate long-run growth in per capita income. Therefore, it complements the neo-classical models in explaining technical change. However, some of the endogenous growth theory models assigned a comparatively large role on only one or a few factors and either ignored the remaining factors or held them constant. These models also failed to make allowance for improvements in the quality of the labour force and so understand its contribution to economic growth.

The most recent focus attempts to ensure that the long-run growth rate of income not only depends upon the parameters of the production and utility functions, but also on other factors. These factors include the role of quality improvements in the labour force of an economy, improvements that come about from better health, more education and greater access to training (i.e. human resources development); technological change; international trade; and government policy (fiscal, monetary, trade and population). For instance, Phoeg and Tang (1992) have considered learning-by-doing, human capital, R&D and public infrastructure and even stressed the spillovers in some of these areas. The UNCTMD (1992) has considered all the above factors including investment in health. Barro (1991), Levin and Renelt (1992), Barro and Sala-i-Martin (1995), and Barro (1997) have investigated a variety of determinants of growth.

In summary, economic growth may be stimulated by a number of factors. For instance, it can be prompted by investment that augments and improves the productivity of national physical resources. Alternatively, it can be driven by innovation and technological change, which not only improves the productivity of existing activities, but also creates competitive advantages in new ones. Additionally, it can be influenced by development of labour skills, or investment in human resources. Furthermore, it can be induced by international trade, which allows exploitation of comparative advantages and development of new ones leading to efficient utilisation of domestic resources, economies of specialisation and participation in the international division of labour. Likewise, it can be propelled by different government policies. The discussion that follows, illustrates that these channels of economic growth also from the essential characteristics of the positive spillover effects of FDI.

FDI and economic growth in host developing countries The awareness of the link between FDI and economic growth in host developing countries has been propelled by the unprecedented and sustained high growth rates (for almost 30 years) most notably experienced by the Asian NIEs and the Southeast Asian economies in general, with substantial involvement of FDI. Moreover, many of the growth promoting factors identified by the endogenous growth theory have been hypothesised to form the foundation of the key positive spillover effects of FDI. FDI can stimulate economic growth through the creation of dynamic comparative advantages that lead to new technology transfers, capital formation, human resources development (i.e. spillover effects on domestic suppliers, research institutes, employment and training of more skilled personnel, and the introduction of new managerial and organisational techniques) and expanded international trade. Dynamism can take different forms, but its short-term is associated with moving up the next level of technological, skill and production complexity. However, its long-term does not only relate to the shift up the skill and technological scale in particular activities, but also encapsulates deepening the value added content of production activity and building the capacity to sustain such a shift across a range of tradable activities in response to changing world demand and technologies

(UNCTAD, 1999). Georgian and Weinhold (1992) have argued that FDI increases international integration and interdependence; facilitates the trade of goods, services and knowledge; and allows countries to specialise more effectively, thus increasing the benefits of comparative advantage based trade and economies of scale. It also increases productivity, widens the scope of competition, and spurs the economy of the host country. Furthermore, although debatable, UNCTAD (1999) suggests that TNCs often possess clean technologies and modern environmental management systems and can use them in all countries in which they operate. In addition, it argues that some TNCs are in the forefront of adopting high environmental standards at home and abroad. It has also recently emerged that TNCs are under increasing pressure to undertake social responsibility.

Therefore, it is not surprising that developing countries have changed attitude and are now considering FDI as part of the development solution. Subsequently, they have shifted from controlling and containing FDI to encouraging it. The growing importance and recognition of FDI is exemplified by the shift towards greater openness of national developing economies to FDI.

Nonetheless, it need not be emphasised that the objectives of TNCs differ from those of host governments. For instance, whereas governments seek to spur national development, TNCs seek to enhance their own competitiveness moreover, in the international context. Thus, their strategies are not devoted to the development of the host country. Subsequently, their needs and strategies may differ from the needs and objectives of the host country. In fact, FDI can have adverse effects on the host country's development. For this reason, not all FDI is always and automatically in the best interests of the host country. For example, a host country may seek new technologies while a foreign affiliate may wish to use mature technologies. Furthermore, a TNC may find it more efficient to close an affiliate, while a host country may want to preserve employment. Additionally, TNCs may seek stronger protection for intellectual property rights, while a host country may favour weak intellectual property rights to permit greater diffusion of technology (UNCTAD, 1999). Likewise, TNCs can use their transfer pricing to their own benefit, affecting the amount of profit reported in the host country, which in turn affects the tax revenue of the host country. Similarly, crowding-out may result from increases in host country interest rates caused by foreign firms' local borrowing under conditions of scarcity. In addition, TNCs can take-over local firms and relocate their R&D activities to the parent firm thus downgrading the potential for new technology in the host country. Alternatively, TNCs may not be willing to upgrade affiliated technological content as fast as host governments think desirable to stimulate local industrial deepening. In like manner, in a sub-contracting relationship, it is more often the case that supplying firms stay at the bottom of the technology ladder. This deters technological enhancement in the domestic firms. Moreover, the suppliers may lose market if wages rise and the affiliates (buyers) move to cheaper locations. Besides, the presence of TNCs in a host country may conflict with building strong national firms. For instance, TNCs may lower macroeconomic efficiency if they deliberately raise concentration levels, forcing competitors out of business through predatory practices, poaching skilled labour and R&D from local firms, or engaging in restrictive business practices which among other things deter technological development (UNCTAD, 1997a). Furthermore, national governments may be interested in protecting the environment, while TNCs address more importance to increasing profit margins. Consequently, although there may be considerable overlaps, there are also significant differences. Thus, FDI offers a mixture of positive and negative effects. It is then the task of the host country to disentangle these effects, and take measures that maximise the positives but minimise the negatives.

In light of the link that has been identified between FDI and economic growth, the discussion that follows focuses on the *positive* effects of FDI on the economic growth of host developing countries. Nonetheless, remarks are made about the negative effects as and when appropriate.

Empirical Review

Early theories of growth Any revival of growth theories also simultaneously revives its empirical analysis. As may be expected, empirical work on economic growth first concentrated on the classical and neo-classical models and then later shifted to the endogenous models. Empirical work on economic growth has increasingly emphasised the importance of technology and human capital while the stock of physical capital continues to play a large role as a component of economic growth for both developed and developing countries. For instance, most of the pioneering empirical work (Abramowitz, 1956; Solow, 1957; Denison, 1962; and Kuznets, 1966) focused mainly on growth accounting. That is, apportioning the observed long-run growth in real output between the growth of factor inputs and the growth of TFP. Most of the more recent work on the other hand (De Long, 1988; Barro, 1989; Dowrick and Nguyen, 1989; Jorgenson, 1990; and Barro and Sala-i-Martin, 1995) tests for convergence of an economy to a steady state.

The convergence theory has (in the author's opinion) been generally rejected. For instance, besides the contradicting facts discussed in the theory (i.e. queries by development economists), Barro and Sala-i-Martin (1995) found that the simple relationship between growth and the starting per capita income for a broad cross-section of countries does not reveal convergence except for the homogenous groups of economies such as the US states, regions of several European countries and prefectures of Japan. Fukuda and Toya (1995) also found that the starting level of per capita growth rates in East Asian countries have little correlation with the starting level of per capita product even after allowing for differences in the level of human capital. The convergence was found to be only conditional. For instance, convergence occurred when the relationship between growth rates and initial per capita position was examined while holding constant some significant variables that distinguish the countries. UNCTAD (1997b) observed that economic inequalities within countries remain large, and there is little sign of convergence in incomes across countries.

Recent empirical studies of growth have focused on the interrelationships among the various determinants of growth. Romer (1986) and Scott (1989) for instance, linked technological advance to capital accumulation. They suggested that advances in technology can make capital more productive and provide an incentive for new investment, or that technology is frequently in new plant and equipment and, therefore, enters an economy in the form of new capital. Researchers including Levin and Renelt (1992) found significant relationships between a variety of variables and growth rates. They observed: a positive and robust correlation between average growth rates and the share of investment in GDP; a positive and robust correlation between investment/GDP and trade/GDP; that exports and imports, and exports *plus* imports behaved in a similar way; and that trade policy if used concurrently with investment/GDP was not robust.

Several studies that have considered human capital as a factor of growth have provided varying results. For instance, Romer (1986) and Locus (1988) observed that human capital was a main source of increasing returns and divergence in growth rates between the developed and the developing countries. Barro (1991) found the initial level of human capital to be a significant determinant of economic growth, while Kryiacou (1991) found it to be insignificant. Kim and Lau (1992c), and Young (1993) found factor accumulation (human and physical capital) to account for most of the growth in East Asia. Young (1994) observed that the Republic of Korea's growth was due to shifts from low to high productive sectors, massive investments in human capital and increase in labour force (Srinivasan, 1995). Chou (1995) found human capital as one of the factors influencing production and, hence, growth in Taipei, China. Bende-Nabende's (1999) results showed a positive impact of human capital on growth in the ASEAN-5 (Indonesia, Malaysia, the Philippines, Singapore and Thailand) albeit statistically significant for only Malaysia. However, Wei's (1995) results revealed that the scale/average level of human capital did not appear to have contributed to China's cross-city differences in the industrial growth rates during 1980-90. A generalisation was made by Pyo (1995), who observed that developing countries, which used their human capital well were enabled to converge with developed countries, whereas other developing countries which did not effectively employ their human capital were unable to do so.

More research has been devoted to the role of international trade, particularly that of exports for various reasons, including economies of scale, efficiency of resource allocation and international knowledge spillovers. Studies that have investigated the role of exports in economic growth (Balassa, 1978; Krueger, 1980; Feder, 1982; and Edwards, 1992) have highlighted the positive role of exports on greater capacity utilisation, resource allocation according to comparative advantage, exploitation of scale economies, technological improvements, and efficient management in response to competitive pressure from abroad. Park (1988), and Fukuda and Toya (1995) observed that exports played a special role in the economic development of the East Asian countries, and that a higher export share tended to stimulate economic growth. Other researchers include Chen and Wong (1990) whose results suggested that export expansion led to scale enlargement and hence productivity growth, and Chou (1995) and Hsu (1995) who found a statistically significant correlation between export expansion and output growth in Taipei, China. Chou (1995) also empirically linked growth and trade, and agreed with Romer (1986) and Locus's (1988) findings that emphasise the importance of trade and human capital accumulation. He concluded that a small country can grow as fast as a large one by introducing international trade and improving human capital. Bende-Nabende (1999) found a statistically significant positive relationship between international trade and growth in Singapore and Thailand, an insignificant relationship for the Philippines, and a statistically significant but negative relationship for Indonesia and Malaysia. He attributed the results for Indonesia and Malaysia to possible mismanagement of the wealth derived from international trade. Other robust results include Wei's (1995) cross-city findings that suggested that the very high growth rates of the coastal cities in China could be explained entirely by their export performance and their attraction of FDI. However, Kormendi and Meguire (1985), and Levin and Renelt (1992) found export/GDP not to be explanatory for growth once the regression included other important variables.

Several empirical studies have investigated the role of physical capital and technological progress. Solow (1957) assumed Hicks-neutrality (on the basis of some evidence), and calculated the Hicks rate of progress (now the rate of factor augmentation) for the US private non-firm sector for every year between 1909 and 1949. He found an average rate of progress of 1.5 per cent per annum. Thus, he reports 'gross output per man-year doubled over the interval (1909-49), with 87.5 per cent of the increases attributable to technical change and the remaining 12.5 per cent to increased use of capital'. However, Jorgenson (1990) found that growth in inputs, rather than growth in total productivity, was the driving force behind the expansion of the US economy between 1947 and 1982. Kim and Lau (1992) advanced a new framework for analysis of productivity and technical progress, based on the direct econometric estimation of an aggregate meta-production function that does not require the traditionally maintained function (i.e. constant returns to scale, neutrality of technical progress and profit maximisation with competitive output markets). This new approach enabled the separate identification of both the degree of returns to scale and the rate of technical progress, and their biases, if any. The results revealed that even with the inclusion of human capital in the aggregate production function, technical progress remained the most important source of growth for the G-5 followed by capital, and human capital is relatively less significant. However, it was not possible to reject the assumption that all countries have the same underlying meta-production function of the transcendental logarithmic form. That is, traditional growth-accounting assumptions are all rejected. Boskin and Lau (1992a) attributed some of the growth in East Asia to their technological progress. However, Krugman's (1994) analysis revealed that while technical progress was the major source of growth for the G-5 (except Japan), the major source of Asian NIEs' growth was capital accumulation, and that over time, productivity efficiency for the NIEs dropped relative to the G-5. He concluded that nothing was left over after the factor contributions of capital and labour to growth were deducted from GDP growth so that there was no productivity growth in the NIEs. The hypothesis that technical progress is embodied in new investments and, therefore, affects the output of an economy only through the form of new capital goods was tested and rejected. However, although Bende-Nabende et al's (2000a) aggregated results supported Krugman's observations, their disaggregated results failed to concur with them. Instead, Bende-Nabende et al's disaggregated results revealed that Krugman's observations currently relate to the baby tiger economies. Thus, this led them to conclude that 'nothing was left over after the factor contributions of capital and TFP to growth were deducted from GDP growth so that there was no labour contribution in the Asian NIEs'. Other studies include De Long and Summers (1991) who found that machinery and equipment investment has a strong association with growth; and Barro (1991), and Magee, Brock and Young (1989) who provided evidence to support the theory that entrepreneurship is good for economic growth.

FDI and economic growth in host developing countries   Any researcher attempting to assess FDI's contribution in a developing country context is confronted by the question 'what does FDI offer?' Although most developing countries now consider FDI as an important resource for development, its economic effects are almost impossible to either predict or measure with precision. The impact of FDI and TNCs on a country depends on many factors. They include the role of the TNC in the economy, the sector in which FDI is undertaken, the type of investment, the links of the foreign affiliates with the host economy and the conditions in the host country (UNCTAD, 1995). These effects vary from country to country, by industry, and even by company and over periods of time. This is because government policy tends to have a strong influence on FDI. For instance, the effects of FDI in import-substituting industries may differ from those of export-oriented industries since the former targets mostly the limited domestic market, while the latter targets the larger international market. The latter is more likely to generate more employment and, therefore, spillovers due to the expected larger production capacity associated with the larger market. In addition, it is difficult to separate and quantify the TNCs' package of attributes since they are complex and vary from one host country to another. A scientific approach, which has 'a control measure' would be the most appropriate technique of measuring these effects. Thus, an assessment would be made on 'what would happen if a TNC did not undertake a particular investment' *vis-à-vis* 'what happens if the TNC undertakes a particular investment'. Unfortunately, for obvious reasons this method does not appeal to economic analysis. Consequently, the development effects of FDI end-up being assessed by one of the two general approaches, quantitative and qualitative analyses.

Quantitative analysis utilises econometric techniques by investigating the relationship between FDI and output. Obviously, it has to be supported by some form of hypothesis backed by economic theory. For instance, UNCTMD (1992) hypothesised that FDI can stimulate economic growth through the creation of dynamic comparative advantages that lead to new technology transfers, capital formation, human resources development and expanded international trade. Similarly, Georgian and Weinhold (1992) argued that FDI increases international integration and interdependence. Furthermore, it facilitates the trade of goods, services and knowledge, and allows countries to specialise more effectively, thus increasing the benefits of comparative advantage-based trade and economies of scale. Additionally, it increases productivity, widens the scope of competition, and spurs the economy of the host country. However, quantitative techniques often suffer from imprecise measurement of variables. The qualitative analysis is on the other hand survey-based and investigates particular aspects of TNCs' contributions without any major attempt of quantification. Qualitative analysis may suffer from selection bias.

Econometric analysis on the effects of FDI on economic growth still remains comparatively limited. However, research interest is mounting in this area and several scholars, individuals and institutions (UNCTMD, 1992; Wei, 1995; Balasubramanyam et al, 1996; Bende-Nabende et al, 1997a, 1997b and 2000b; Bende-Nabende and Ford, 1998; Bende-Nabende, 1999; and UNCTAD, 1999) have pioneered certain investigations. The conclusions of econometric analyses on the impact of FDI on economic growth still remain unclear. Some analyses show a positive impact of FDI on growth, while others show a negative impact. Gupta and Islam (1983) investigated aggregate capital flows (FDI plus debt) and found positive impacts on growth. They concluded that FDI makes a positive contribution towards the quantity of physical capital in developing countries and this quantitative contribution appears more significant in industries such as manufacturing that are crucial to growth and development (UNCTC, 1992). The UNCTMD's (1992) results on Taipei, China were statistically significant for FDI and its impact through employment, human skills and international trade. Wei's (1995) results suggested that by the late 1980s, the contribution to China's coastal cities' growth came mainly from FDI, but more in the form of technological or managerial spillovers across firms, rather than because of the magnitude of physical investment. Wei and Fan (1993), however, failed to find statistical support for the view that FDI alleviates the shortage of domestic savings or foreign exchange when they applied the test to China's 1988-90 city-level data. Balasubramanyam et al's (1996) most significant result related to the apparently significant role played by FDI-labour (including human capital) interactions in the growth process. Borensztein et al's (1995) regression on developing countries, revealed that although FDI impacted positively on output growth, its influence was stronger when it interacted with human capital. Mody and Wang (1997) also concluded that the education in China was more effective when it interacted with foreign knowledge. Bende-Nabende and Ford (1998) demonstrate a positive direct link between FDI and growth in Taiwan. However, Bende-Nabende (1999) found FDI for Indonesia, Malaysia and the Philippines to be positively related to growth, while that for Singapore and Thailand was negatively related. Specifically, the results revealed that FDI stimulated economic growth in the ASEAN-5 (Indonesia, Malaysia, the Philippines, Singapore and Thailand) most particularly through human capital and employment (human resources development). Similarly, the investigation by UNCTAD (1999) found FDI to exhibit either a positive or negative relationship with output depending on the variables it was entered with in the equation. Bende-Nabende et al's (2000b) results revealed a direct positive long-run relationship between FDI and output in Hong Kong, Japan, the Philippines, Thailand and Taiwan.

Evidence from the FDI related activities demonstrates that FDI plays an increasingly important role in the economic growth of the host developing countries, through its contribution in human resources development, technological transfer, capital formation and international trade. However, this mostly comes about as a spillover rather than as a direct effect. Most of the research on the impact of FDI-related activities on economic growth has been carried out by use of the survey-based qualitative analysis technique. Thus, any literature review (including the one presented hereafter) on the positive effects of FDI on the economic growth of developing countries has to draw extensively from findings generated by this approach.

FDI and Human Resources Development

Theoretical Review

Overview There is an economic argument that more workers stimulate economic growth. However, economic growth, is propelled by the quality, quantity and productivity of all inputs, i.e. physical capital, human capital, technology as well as number of workers. Thus, labour and human resources with skills are indispensable factors of production. If an increase in employment is accompanied by an increase in the quality of employment, and by investment in human skills and knowledge, it may result into an increase in value added per employee, leading to rising wages and improved conditions of work. Furthermore, employment creation and upgrading are important means for countries to achieve an equitable distribution of income and minimum standards of welfare for the people (UNCTAD, 1999).

The creation and diffusion of knowledge have become central to economic growth and development. Denison (1985) defined knowledge to include what is usually referred to as *technological knowledge*. That is, knowledge concerning the physical properties of things and how to make, combine, or use them in a physical science. He also included *managerial knowledge*. For instance, knowledge of business organisation and management techniques construed in the broadest sense. Similarly, UNCTAD (1999) defines knowledge to comprise not only technical knowledge (R&D, design and process engineering), but also knowledge of organisation, management and inter-firm and international relationship. Knowledge can originate inside the country as well as abroad. In addition, knowledge can be obtained in anyway, such as by organised research, by individual research workers and inventors, and by simple observations and experience. Knowledge obtained through an industrial or institutional espionage can also be added to this list. The importance of knowledge is not limited to modern or high-tech activities but pervades all sectors and industries (UNCTAD, 1999). Consequently, knowledge acquisition is a continuous process.

Human resource capacities can be categorised into *entrepreneurial*, *technological* and *managerial* capacities. The abilities to innovate, to identify opportunities, threats, weaknesses and strengths, and to take risks are embedded in entrepreneurial capabilities. The technological capability, which is closely linked to entrepreneurial capability includes the ability: to operate a plant or business; to create new productive capacity, to innovate or adopt, modify and improve methods and products; or to develop new ones. Factors which are embedded in managerial capabilities include: reasoning; analytical abilities such as the ability to plan, implement and evaluate projects; technical knowledge; theories and facts; values; attitudes and beliefs; organisation routines; and marketing skills (UN, 1992).

Human capital (i.e. knowledge be it entrepreneurial, technical or managerial), is human because it is embodied in individuals and is not 'general' since the owners move with it wherever they go. It is capital because it is a source of future satisfaction and/or future earnings. Schultz (1971) has observed that it can be acquired not as an asset purchased in a market but by means of investing in oneself.

Education and training, and health and nutrition Advances in knowledge and the diffusion of new ideas and objectives are necessary to remove economic backwardness and instil human abilities and motivations that are favourable to economic growth achievement (Chow, 1995). As economies grow and rising incomes create demand for new and improved products, improving the skill levels and knowledge base of the labour force is necessary for restructuring production towards higher value-added activities. This shift also allows higher wages and improved conditions of work. Thus, improving employment quality must be accompanied by the creation of higher-paid, more secure jobs with better working conditions and an improvement in the skill content of employment. Investment in human capital may boost the living standards of households by expanding employment opportunities, raising productivity, attracting capital investment, and increasing earning capital. Better education and training, and health and nutrition, also have value in their own right, enabling people to lead more fulfilling lives. While investment in general education and training creates the human capital necessary for raising the productivity by increasing the capability to accept and adopt new techniques and knowledge, improved health and nutrition increases the mental and physical productivity, and absorptive capacity for new knowledge of an individual (World Bank, 1995). The acquisition of skills by a worker not only increases productivity but, by increasing the average level of skills in the economy as a whole, has a spillover effect on the productivity of all the workers and therefore on the average level of skills in the economy as a whole (Lucas, 1988). Vocational training for instance, can lead to increased efficiency, profitability and wages in enterprises when the trained workers use their acquired skills effectively. Private investment in schooling has an external effect by causing growth in the stock of knowledge, which increases the effectiveness of time spent in school by the later cohorts (Stokey, 1991). Thus, human capital can be increased by devoting time to learning, but at the expense of the time devoted to work and leisure!

Individual productivity will be raised by the kind of education that gives skills that may later be transferred from job to job; and improves the ability to perform standard tasks, process and use information, and adopt new technologies and production practices. Such skills can be developed through learning-by-doing, on-the-job training and in formal training centres.

Since private vocational training capacity in developing countries is often weak and the efficiency of that provided by government agencies and ministries is questionable, these countries can partly access these capacities through imported technology and expatriate personnel. One of the most effective modes is FDI. Wei (1995) argues that FDI increasingly exposes local workers and firms to international management, and technical standards and know-how. It increases efficiency, not only of those firms that receive foreign investment or are under foreign management, but also of those domestic firms that interact with foreign-invested/managed firms through various channels. This transfer of knowledge and ideas has been termed the *spillover process*.

The spillover process is achieved in many ways. The spillover of knowledge and ideas is for instance, accomplished through informal meetings such as dinner table conversations and social gatherings (i.e. sports tournaments) of friends and/or family members who work in different firms. Other channels include formal business meetings, imitation of the management and/or marketing concepts of other firms (both foreign and local), and employees changing jobs. The spillover process need not be from foreign owned/managed to local firms alone. It can also be from local firms that do not receive foreign investment directly, but have links with foreign firms through the aforementioned channels to those that do not have any such links (Wei, 1995). Contact with firms with a higher level of efficiency enables the relatively backward ones to improve not only by copying or imitating, but also by inducing them to try harder. This spillover is closely associated with the spillover in the learning-by-doing concept where innovative working practices and inventions, which cannot be kept secret are observed and applied in a different working environment, which in turn is observed by others and similarly applied. It comes about through observation of other persons using certain techniques to perform certain tasks, using new tools or techniques arising from investment (in say construction) which have application in another sector (say services) or even as an industrial espionage (King and Robson, 1992). Young (1991) has observed that there are currently spillover effects in the development of knowledge across industries, with technical innovations originating in particular industries finding important applications, as well as instigating further technical change in other economic sectors. Therefore, productivity increases in each industry are not only a function of productive activity in that industry, but also the result of spillovers from learning-by-doing in other industries. This spillover is an extension of Lucas's (1988) external effect of human capital accumulation. Obviously, the spillovers are not confined to knowledge alone. They extend well into the other aforementioned spillover factors. For instance, the mere fact that an investment takes place means that jobs are created for the local people and that the employed people acquire skills by learning on the job. Moreover, the invested capital increases the capital stock of the host country, the capital machinery contains some form of new technology, and international trade is promoted through the initial importation of capital machinery and subsequent exports (if the investment is export-oriented). Furthermore, TNCs' backward linkages may stimulate the spillovers particularly into employment and technology with host country raw materials/components domestic suppliers. However, the extent to which this spillover process can be enhanced depends to some extent upon the degree of the linkages the TNCs have within the host country. Obviously, these activities do not form the initial objective of the TNCs, which is to enhance their competitiveness in the international context. Rather, they come about as by-products and, hence, spillovers of the investment. For instance, many forms of diffusion of technology are not priced or paid for in the markets. Rather, they are externalities that arise involuntarily or are deliberately undertaken to overcome information problems.

TNCs tend to be more aware than local firms of the benefits of training, and have well-developed routines, systems and materials for training. Whereas TNCs always undertake some minimal form of training to ensure that technologies in use are deployed efficiently, the decision to invest in more advanced forms of training depends on the returns they expect, their time horizon, and the extent of competition they are exposed to (UNCTAD, 1999). TNCs can contribute to skills generation by investing directly in training in their affiliates. They can also induce or support local firms through backward and forward linkages. The training provided by TNCs is tailored to meet the specific requirements of the enterprise within the different categories of employees and is dominated by the short period in-plant courses. The courses offered at their local centres may have a domestic content relevant to the participants of the region. TNCs that are involved in backward and forward linkages also provide another form of training in a form of help to business people in organising their production, and training of employees. This is aimed at raising the quality of their inputs in the case of backward linkages (particularly subcontractors), and after sales services in the case of forward linkages. In addition, they can influence local competitors or unrelated firms to emulate their practices. They can also instigate the government or industry associations to set up new training facilities. Furthermore, they can persuade training institutions from their home countries to set up similar establishments in host countries (UNCTAD, 1999).

The extent of skills deepening may be influenced by the development strategy of the host country, and may differ by sector, industry or even product line. For instance, affiliates in import-substituting regimes may not impart state-of-art skills. They may upgrade employee skills only slowly, as compared to affiliates in similar activities producing for more open markets. UNCTC (1989) observed that in service sector market-seeking FDI, foreign affiliates are particularly apt to reproduce abroad the factor proportions used in home countries, including the skill and capital intensities of their parent firm. This has implication for the quality of employment. Some TNCs may start with training employees in low skill categories and upgrading them as and when necessary. However, the degree of upgrading may be dictated by the capability of the host country skill base, and by the quality of the accompanying acquired factor endowments such as infrastructural facilities. Thus, the training requirements are highly dependent upon the level of the technology introduced *vis-à-vis* the capability of the human capital base and quality of infrastructure in the host country.

FDI can, therefore, stimulate human resources development through investment in education and training, and health and nutrition. This enhances the stock of human capital, and increases productivity of labour and other factors of production. Similarly, it improves entrepreneurial and managerial capabilities that enable the human agent to take better advantage of economic opportunities more effectively (UN, 1992). It also affects growth by affecting the incentives for schooling or other investments in human capital such as expected higher future earnings that are associated with further training or education.

Employment Employment is very important to economic growth because human capital deteriorates when it is left idle. Thus, unemployment impairs the skills that workers have acquired. Employment of the former unemployed and under-employed increases personal income, which can be used for the betterment of individuals and their families through personal investment. Employment also generates skills in a process of learning-by-doing and thus facilitates the diffusion of technology. Besides, cumulative experience increases the marginal contribution to cost reduction of an additional unit of output.

FDI contributes to economic growth directly by creating employment opportunities and indirectly through the creation of employment opportunities in other organisations. In addition, it contributes to economic growth qualitatively through changes in employment policies and practices in other organisations including those belonging to suppliers and/or consumers. This can take the form of creating wage equality for their members, and allowing greater access to employment for particular groups, including women and ethnic minority groups, who may experience discrimination in employment (UN, 1992). For instance, the fact that women are employed by foreign affiliates may exert some pressure on local firms to employ women where this was traditionally not the case. Likewise, domestic firms may be put under considerable pressure to upgrade working conditions to meet those of competing foreign firms. Some of the policies may be instituted through trade unions, which apparently have a positive effect conducive to higher efficiency and productivity. They provide workers with a collective voice and limit employer behaviour that is arbitrary, exploitative or retaliatory. In addition, they reduce turnover and promote stability in the work force by establishing grievance and arbitration procedure (World Bank, 1995).

Backward and forward linkages are among the principal channels whereby TNCs can indirectly contribute to employment generation. Indirect employment created by foreign affiliates in a host country can be large, significantly larger than that created directly where linkages to local producers are strong. Activities that involve a large number of input suppliers tend to generate substantial indirect employment. The importance of these effects has grown in recent years, following the trends towards a deeper international division of labour and a declining degree of vertical integration within the large TNCs. These firms have progressively focused on a smaller part of the value-added chain, relying increasingly on national and international outsourcing for technological, cost or flexibility reasons. Employment as a consequence, has been gradually 'externalised' (OECD, 1995). The extent of this indirect impact is however, strongly influenced by the capabilities of the domestic firms.

While FDI of all types involves employment in host countries, some FDI is motivated specifically by considerations directly related to the employment of skilled or unskilled labour. Resource-seeking and efficiency-seeking FDI in manufacturing and services is often made with the specific objective of accessing low-cost labour for labour-intensive production or taking advantage of relatively abundant supplies of educated and skilled labour. This has the potential to create employment. For market-seeking FDI, on the other hand, the availability and cost of labour or skilled human resources is not the main consideration of the choice of the investment location. Accordingly, most of the employment of labour necessary for host country production occurs in foreign affiliates. Countries with import-substitution regimes can stimulate employment especially when their markets are large. If investment is in green-field sites (new production facilities), it generates new demand for workers. Entry through mergers and acquisitions, on the other hand, not only does not create new demand for workers but may also lead to labour shedding.

Thus, the level of employment generated by TNCs depends upon the industry group, the production activity, the size of the TNC, the strategy of the TNC, the development strategy of the host country, the skill base of the host country and the capabilities of the domestic firms.

Empirical Review

Education and technical training Developing countries have realised the need to invest in human capital and have responded positively. For example, investment in human capital in East Asian economies has increased rapidly. Between 1965 and 1990 the gross primary school enrolment rate increased from 92 per cent to 102 per cent, and gross secondary enrolment grew from 27 per cent to 37 per cent (World Bank, 1995).

Whereas some researchers have held a view that in some cases TNCs in developing countries train the nationals of the host countries only at a low level of skill, which could prevent them from entering occupations with better career prospects in the technical or managerial fields, empirical evidence suggests the contrary. A number of TNCs provide training for their staff, most of which is for skilled workers including apprentices, highly specialised workers and technicians, and supervisory staff. For instance, over 100 workers are annually sent for training abroad by the Shell subsidiary in Nigeria. Some TNCs (e.g. Unilever, Metal Box and Locus Industries) have their own management training centres in their home countries. Others including Esso and Caterpillar prefer holding their training programmes at their overseas centres. For instance, Esso has training centres in Libya, Singapore and Indonesia (ILO, 1977).

In Asia, manpower training has become a major concern for Hong Kong's investment in China, but only the very large companies have training centres in Hong Kong and/or China. The mode of training differs with company size and the type of economic activity, but is more common in non-manufacturing companies. In the manufacturing sector, the workers of the subsidiaries of smaller companies are usually hired and trained in China to minimise costs. The senior staff of the parent company (managers, technicians and supervisors) is transferred to the subsidiary to provide on-the-job training to the local employees (Chen and Wong, 1995). In addition, the lack of sufficiently trained staff in China has prompted many Sino-foreign joint venture companies to initiate their own training schemes. This is due in part to China's gap in business education that has now become a huge canyon due to the demand created by a surge of private enterprises during the past decade. Increased competition on China has prompted many Sino-foreign joint ventures to teach functional skills including sales, marketing and accounting (Ritchie et al, 2001). Most companies use in-house training. However, care is taken to ensure effective translation of language and the correct interpretation of the specific cultural barriers that international training schemes may not transcend. United Biscuits has expanded its Shekou human resources department into a fully fledged training centre using expatriate staff to train the local trainers. Siemens has found that Chinese employees often need training in the methods and skills of general management and international business practice (Wilson, 1997). Many companies send staff to their company headquarters. Companies such as Henkel send their technical staff to Germany to teach them in areas of technical operation. This not only strengthens employees' technical knowledge, but also creates a stronger bond and understanding of company culture (Ritchie et al, 2001). Another method of ensuring a well-trained future management team is to sponsor employees or trainees through an MBA course. Cable and Wireless has initiated a scholarship programme to train students in finance, marketing and communication (Ritchie et al, 2001).

TNCs not only train their staff, and that of their suppliers and customers, but may also enter into training co-operation with local institutions. For example, the Esso-Exxon subsidiaries in Indonesia (Stanvac) and Singapore, and Shell-BP in Nigeria make financial contributions to universities and institutions, and/or award scholarship grants without requiring the holders to work for the company when they graduate. In Singapore, the Economic Development Board has collaborated with Tata, Brown-Boveri, Philips, Computerised Corporation and ASEA to establish and improve training centres and institutes. Other TNCs including Metal Box-India, Seimens-India, PUK-Ivorial-Ivory Coast, and Philips-Brazil, provide training for students from government institutions, and their company staff act as tutors. Staff members for Seimens-Brazil, Philips-Colombia, and Renault Safer-Ivory Coast, lecture at the respective country universities and provide consulting services as well. In Mexico, Ford provides equipment and counsel to the Ministry of Agriculture (World Bank, 1995).

TNCs have also been known to include basic education skills, training and literacy promotion in their training programmes when circumstances make it necessary. For instance, instruction in reading, writing and arithmetic is given to workers with little or no formal education in developing countries by Unilever and Mobil's developing country affiliates (ILO, 1981). Similarly, a study of Japanese affiliates in Brazil found that the introduction of total quality circles and just-in-time production methods required workers with above average skills. Where they could not find sufficient qualified workers, they invested in adult education and short courses in literacy, numeracy and group work techniques (Humphrey, 1993).

These investments alone may, however, not always lead to more rapid growth and may be misspent or remain idle if they are invested in the wrong people or invested in the wrong manner. Many African countries, for instance, in spite of expanding the education systems, and raising the average years of schooling of their labour force, have had little corresponding growth. What matters, therefore, is not the quantity, but the quality of education and training; and how effectively it can be employed for productive investment. Investment should, consequently, be made in training that improves skills of employees; develops their ability to adjust to changing technology; and meets growth requirement, replacements, retirements and departures from the enterprises. These will then collectively contribute to the economic growth of the host developing country.

Employment An understanding of actual employment implications of FDI in host developing countries has been curtailed by lack of relevant data. Empirical studies do not provide a consistent picture of the direct effects of FDI on employment and the focus has been on the static rather than the dynamic approach. Although most countries are both exporters and importers of FDI, the analysis is usually based either on outflows or inflows of FDI. It can, however, be assumed that this does not bring about much disparity for the host developing countries especially when analysed from the inflow point of view since most of them are currently primarily recipients rather than exporters of FDI.

The exact magnitude and trend of the importance of TNCs' employment in host developing countries is not known and different estimates give different figures. Most of the surveys carried out by the ILO are concentrated in the manufacturing sector, the service sector, which also employs a substantial number, being ignored. Pina (1981) estimated the number of people directly employed by TNCs in host developing countries in all economic sectors to have been 4 million in 1980. Direct employment in host developing countries was estimated at approximately 7 million in the mid-1980s (out of 22 million employed by TNCs outside their home countries) by the ILO (1994). Aaron and Andaya (1998) estimated direct employment in foreign affiliates in host developing countries to have been around 17 million and may be as high as 26 million in the mid- to late-1990s. UNCTAD (1999, Annex table A.IX.1.) estimates employment by US affiliates in host developing countries in 1996 to have been almost 2.7 million. About 1.5 million were in Latin America, 1 million in developing Asia, 0.7 million in Africa and 0.3 million in West Asia. It also estimates employment by Japanese affiliates in 1995 to have been almost 1.4 million. About 1.2 million were in developing Asia, 0.1 million in Latin America, 0.02 million in Africa and 0.01 million in West Asia.

The number of employees in foreign affiliates as a percentage of total number of employees in selected host countries is reported by UNCTAD (1999, Annex table A.I.7.). The statistics indicate that with the exception of Singapore and Sri Lanka (with 52 and 54.4 per cent respectively in 1996), foreign affiliates contribute less than 50 per cent of the total manufacturing employment in the selected countries. However, the percentage varies from country to country. For example, the contribution in percentage terms was 1.9 for Nepal in 1998, 3.2 for Turkey in 1990, 4.7 for Indonesia 1997, 13.4 for Brazil in 1995, 14.9 for Vietnam in 1995, 16 for Hong Kong in 1994, 17.9 for Mexico in 1993, 21.1 for Taiwan in 1995 and 43.7 for Malaysia in 1994. However, when a similar comparison is made across all industries, the percentages drop drastically in most cases to less that 10 per cent. In terms of direct employment then, TNCs account for a negligible share of the total work force in most host developing countries. This is highlighted by the UNTCMD's (1992) study, which concluded that the overall contribution of FDI to employment in host developing countries remains modest. This implies that there is potential for TNCs' direct employment contribution improvement. However, although almost impossible to measure, the share is certainly higher in relation to indirect employment via linkages.

With the growth of international production, the share of employment creation by TNCs' affiliates is growing. The growing importance of job creation by FDI is indicated by the ILO's survey which estimates, first that 67 per cent of the 5000 subsidiaries set up in host developing countries during 1951-75 were newly formed. Second, it estimates that 5 million of the 8 million jobs created by TNCs between 1985 and 1992 were in 1992, and by 1995, the number stood at 12 million, although the true number of those who owe their livelihood to TNCs may be twice that, given the prevalence of sub-contracting (UN, 1992). UNCTAD (1998) reports that employment in the top 50 developing country TNCs rose by 17 per cent per annum, roughly doubling between 1993 and 1996.

Employment creation in host developing countries has been partly attributed to the labour-intensive nature of the operations newly established by TNCs in these countries. The direct employment impact of TNCs is, however, virtually inconsequential in light of the large numbers of the poor who, often rural and either unemployed or under employed, have little if any prospect for working for a foreign affiliate. Since the 1980s, however, the dynamic NIEs of Asian and Latin America have attracted FDI and become more fully integrated in the international division of labour, with significant benefits in terms of the direct and indirect generation of new jobs. Others, including several in Africa, West Asia and Latin America, experienced a low growth or decline in employment in foreign affiliates (OECD, 1995). This gives an indication that labour abundant countries are likely to create more employment by following an outward-looking rather than inward-looking strategy. For instance, out of the 1,156,600 people employed by Japanese firms world-wide in 1989, slightly over one half (617,000) were in developing countries, and about three quarters of these (470,000) were concentrated in Asia (Ramstetter, 1993, Table 4) where outward-looking strategies were being pursued. Most of the African, West Asian and Latin American economies were either pursuing inward-looking policies, or had just started serious liberalisation of FDI policies at the time.

There have been arguments that while the share of employment in foreign affiliates of TNCs has been expanding in some countries, this growth may be attributable to a large extent to merger and acquisition activities, implying job acquisitions rather than generation of new jobs (OECD, 1995). The counter argument for this is that jobs from acquisitions are jobs *saved* from failing firms and this leads to a positive net change. For instance, Aho and Levinson's (1988) investigation on employment effects of US TNCs' investments in foreign countries indicated that acquisitions preserved employment that might have been lost otherwise. Little (1988) also concluded that FDI helped maintain total and manufacturing employment at higher levels than would have occurred otherwise. Other critics argue that FDI induces rationalisation of domestic firms and hence unemployment. Likewise, the counter argument for this is that, in the absence of FDI, competition from abroad and the loss of competitiveness by domestic firms would have had similar repercussions in terms of factory closures, since in many cases, firms have had to relocate part of their production simply in order to survive (OECD, 1995).

UNCTAD (1999) reports that affiliate employment tends to account for large shares of manufacturing-sector employment. This is particularly so in countries where export processing zones or similar special arrangements for export production are large relative to other industrial activity. The percentage share of foreign TNCs in manufacturing employment in developing countries varies from country to country. Estimates show a percentage share of 30-35 in Kenya (1975) and Zaire (1974) in Africa; 10-12 in Argentina (1970), 20 in Brazil (1970), and 28 in Colombia (1970) and Mexico (1970) in Latin America; and 33 in Malaysia (1970), 7 in the Philippines (1970), 32 in Singapore (1976/77), and 2 in Thailand (1975) in Southeast Asia (Pina, 1994, Table 3). In Thailand, one American computer disk-drive firm (Seagate) alone increased its Bangkok labour force from 5000 in 1986 to 20000 in 1988 (Lim and Pang, 1991); while in China, FDI related employment has rapidly grown in the manufacturing sector which employed about 6 million in 1993, up from close to zero in 1987 (OECD, 1995). UNCTAD's (1999, Annex table A.I.7.) recent statistics also demonstrate the manufacturing sectors' dominance in foreign affiliates' employment in host developing countries. Such percentages are, however, not meaningful unless they are accompanied by an assessment of the economic development contribution and the employment level of the manufacturing industry.

A change in the occupational structure of employment in TNCs took place in a number of developing countries between 1960 and 1977. An ILO survey of TNCs operating in Africa, Asia and Latin America shows a trend of a greater proportionate increase in the employment of high skill categories (managerial, technical and clerical and administrative staff) and a concurrent relative decrease in the production workers' category (Pina, 1994, Table 5). Another study of the same countries shows that the localisation of technical, professional and managerial staff has shown a considerable progress (Pina, 1994, Table 8). UNCTAD (1999) also cites an example from Siemens joint ventures in China. In 1992, there were roughly 800 employees including 50 expatriates in the company's joint ventures. By 1996, total employment had increased to 8070 and expatriates employed stood at 100, reducing the share of expatriates to local staff. This is in line with the host developing countries' desire for TNCs to train and employ local technical and managerial personnel, and the gradual replacement of expatriates by locals in the TNCs. However, it is worthwhile noting that this comes as a spillover. For instance, as a result of TNCs' economic interests to develop cheaper local skills to take over all local tasks.

The creation of linkages creates a multiplier effect in its own right by enhancing industrial growth, technological transfer, and job creation, besides strengthening national self-reliance of the host countries. In Singapore, a study of three TNCs revealed an employment multiplier factor of 1.2 in 1976 raising to 1.6 in 1980 (Lim and Fong, 1993, Appendix Table 1). That is, for every one employee of the TNC there were 0.2 and 0.6 employees created via linkages in 1976 and 1980 respectively. These multiplier effects are, however, very difficult to quantify due to the problem of having to trace all the jobs created indirectly. The process of sub-contracting, for instance, is often a multi-layered one, driven by buyers and suppliers at several production stages. In practice, therefore, indirect job creation ends up being severely underestimated.

TNCs not only provide employment but often offer good remuneration as well. Local firms in Ghana, Hong Kong and China have for instance reported that foreign subsidiaries poach their trained workers and the best graduates of the training schools by offering better remuneration and fringe benefits (ILO, 1994). A survey carried out on Australia, Austria, Canada, France, Norway, Sweden and the UK shows that the share of foreign TNC subsidiaries in the wage bill in all these countries exceeded their share in industrial employment (Franko, 1994, Table 3), indicating above average industrial wages and salaries, and hence productivity and profitability of these affiliates in these countries. One may of course argue that this may fuel inflation, but when looked at from another point of view, it sets a precedent for non underpayment of employees, especially the highly skilled ones who may have a choice of changing jobs.

The best example linking FDI and job creation for the discriminated groups has been cited by Foo and Lim (1988), and Lin (1986). The electronics industry in Malaysia employs women, including young single Moslem women who were traditionally not allowed to work. Although this has generated opposition from Islamic fundamentalists groups and critics who accuse TNCs for exploiting their Malaysian women workers, the women themselves have appreciated their employment. For rural Malay women in particular, it is likely that modern industrial wage jobs would have been unavailable without foreign investment in labour-intensive export manufacturing, and without the National Economic Policy's ethnic employment quota, since before these developments, the Malaysian industrial sector was dominated by urban Chinese enterprises, which employed mostly urban Chinese (Lim and Pang, 1991).

In summary, there is indeed evidence that FDI is playing an increasingly important role in the human resources development process of developing countries. However, the level of training and employment generated by TNCs depends upon the industry group, the production activity, the size of the TNC, the strategy of the TNC, the development strategy of the host country, the skill base of the host country, the capabilities of the domestic firms and above all the commitment of the host government.

FDI and New Technology Transfer

Theoretical Review

Technology has always been important to economic wellbeing. The current pace of technological change, and within it the role of information-based technologies is making technological revolution a focal point of economic growth. According to the theory of technological competence, the level of technological competence may affect a firm's market share through its influence on unit costs and/or product quality. Strong technological capacity lowers unit costs and improves quality or range. Consequently, it raises profit margins of advantaged firms relative to others in the same industry, or it enables them to enter a new market. Technology, therefore, propels the growth process in as far as it promotes the efficient use of resources.

Enos and Park (1988) have defined technology to consist of all knowledge utilised in, and stemming from, the design of a process, the design and procurement of the equipment that incorporates the process, the construction of the plant, the testing and start-up of the equipment, and its steady operation and improvement. According to the UN (1992), however, technology comprises four components. First is *product innovation,* which leads to the introduction of new or upgraded products, or the improvement of quality. It may be used to encourage consumption, and with rising incomes, consumer demand becomes more differentiated. This in turn may further stimulate product innovation. Second is *process innovation,* which spurs new and more efficient ways of production. It can dramatically cut the costs of production. As exemplified by the *e-com* application of information technology, some new technologies may open entirely new areas of activity. Consequently, activities with greater innovation potential, and hence high technology application may grow faster than those with less potential. Third is *capital* in the form of machinery/equipment and other forms of hardware embodied in physical goods. Finally is the *stock of knowledge* both technical and managerial used in production and marketing. This includes human skills, management methods, organisational structures and work routines for quality improvements, marketing, and process and product design.

It worthwhile noting that the current pace of technological change has also evolved the understanding of technology. For instance, the concept of technology transfer and diffusion is no longer as simplistic as it used to be. The idea of technologies being transferred 'embodied' in new equipment or in patents or blue prints, and their efficient use taken as given is becoming obsolete. The transfer and diffusion of new technologies can now be achieved amidst adoption of specific strategies on technology. These may include a strong base of absorptive capabilities and the needs of costly learning, organisation and managerial practices, and tacit knowledge. That is, all components of technology have to be addressed, moreover in a dynamic context. Without this, countries can remain at the bottom of the technology ladder where their competitive edge lies in the simple assembly or processing based on cheap labour. Besides, once the wages rise, they lose this competitive edge. Thus, the transfer and diffusion of new technologies is dynamic. Once a certain type of technology has been mastered, there is a necessity to move into more advanced technologies. Therefore, countries have to upgrade their own capabilities not only to remain competitive but also to have the capability of mastering the new technology. Moreover, as they enter into more advanced technologies, the application of the technologies may change. Obviously, it is an on-going process that requires continuous upgrading and deepening of all types of intellectual capital, as well as supporting networks and institutions. No doubt, it is a complex process under which each stage imposes its own new challenges. UNCTAD (1999) points out that importing and mastering technologies in developing countries is not as simple as originally envisaged. Technology is not sold like physical products, in fully embodied form; nor does it flow by osmosis when agents are exposed to more advanced systems of knowledge. It has important tacit elements that need effort to master. The process is incremental and path dependent. It often faces an uncertain environment where the skills, information, networks and credit needed are not readily available. Enterprises have to interact with other agents. All these features mean that technology development faces extensive co-ordination problems, externalities, missing markets and cumulative effects (UNCTAD, 1999).

Technology can promote and sustain economic growth by increasing factor productivity; introducing new high value added products and, therefore, the production of more high-tech manufactures *vis-à-vis* the primary product concentration particularly in the less advanced developing countries. Furthermore, it can change the composition of exports in favour of research intensive products with higher growth potential. In addition, it can provide an incentive for new investment.

Technology generation is concentrated in advanced industrial countries, and takes place mainly in large firms, which are typically, TNCs. These firms have strong strategic assets and the capability of investing in R&D. TNCs, therefore, both produce and transfer new technology from one county to another. They accomplish this through two channels. First, the technology may be internalised to affiliates under their own control. This takes the form of direct investment. Internalisation allows affiliates to have access to technologies generated by their parent firms. The extent of this is, however, influenced by the parent firm's strategy and the affiliate's capabilities. In general, foreign affiliates tend to be in the forefront of introducing new management and organisational techniques, quality management standards, training methods and marketing methods (UNCTAD, 1999). Second, the technology may be externalised to other firms. This may take the form of joint ventures, franchising, capital goods sales, licences, technical assistance, sub-contracting or original equipment manufacture. Furthermore, TNCs can play an instrumental role in providing 'entire' packages. That is, technology together with management, marketing and training. Moreover, where the technology involved is large-scale, foreign investors are able to mobilise the resources needed more efficiently than local firms.

Technology transfer is linked to the training process discussed earlier. Firms diffuse technology and skills to suppliers, customers and agencies, research institutes and universities, vocational training centres, financial intermediaries and infrastructure providers with which they have direct dealings. This is often through the vertical networks of information exchange and co-operation to facilitate production, planning and technology development. It is through training employees particularly the technicians and managers, staff of suppliers and customers, and the provision of after sales services for the end users that such transfer is effected. The transfer of R&D facilities to an overseas subsidiary, and importation and exportation of goods and services further aids the transfer of technology. FDI leads to access to technology particularly through imports of capital goods. No wonder, Quinn (1969) observed that the mere presence of a product in a particular country whether or not there is a subsidiary in that country may be a form of technology transfer. Wholly owned foreign affiliates and joint ventures export such technology through FDI. The firms maintain their competitive advantage by transferring their most recent technology to their affiliates, while selling or licensing older technology. For developing countries, therefore, FDI may be the only way to gain access to the latest or 'relatively' latest technology. In a vertical production system, technology can also be transferred to local suppliers and consumers. A supplier firm in a developing country that has a sub-contracting relationship with a foreign subsidiary can receive technical assistance to improve its product quality and production process or to undertake new product development (UN, 1992). FDI becomes an integral part of the growth process for the host countries involved as the TNCs upgrade their overseas affiliates from assembly-type operations to high-quality high value-added manufacturing sites. By doing so, it acts as a dynamic factor influencing comparative advantage.

Technology can be diffused to competing firms; to complementary and supplier firms in the same industry; to complementary and supplier firms in other industries; and even to unrelated firms in the same and other industries in the whole economy. The process of the diffusion of technology is, however, more difficult to carry out in developing countries than in the developed countries since many of the techniques may not be well suited to the developing countries due to shortage of skilled labour, capital and the necessary infrastructure. Also, there may be little incentive for the TNCs to adapt their products, production techniques, and marketing methods to the conditions present in developing economies. Likewise, developing countries may lack the necessary technical capability to effect the necessary adaptations themselves. The rate of technological transfer may depend on the rate at which individual firms substitute new techniques for old ones, the latter being dependent on the profitability of the technology, size of the firm and its liquidity (Mansfield, 1994).

It is through this technology transfer abroad that TNCs promote the diffusion of innovation. R&D that comes along with FDI induces competition which encourages local firms also to increase their R&D that would not otherwise have taken place in its absence. This may stimulate innovation in areas in which local companies have a competitive advantage. Where indigenous firms are weak, the entry of foreign TNCs may help them upgrade their production although the local establishment of fundamental R&D is unlikely (Cantwell, 1994). R&D activities may be located abroad either to take care of the local market or because of the immobile environmented conditions.

The introduction and/or development of new productive technologies in developing countries, either as a result of their transfer from the developed countries and/or local R&D efforts, and their eventual use in the production of existing and/or new goods also leads to rapid learning-by-doing.

The benefits from technology transfer by TNCs should not be taken for granted. Technology transfer by and the training efforts of TNCs may be looked at as contributing to economic growth if:

- They economise on the local scarce resources, thus directly or indirectly contributing to economic growth.
- They have an impact not only on GDP, but also on the livelihood and employment possibilities for the people.

- They form an integrated part of the host government's development planning process and strategies, and do not create 'technological enclaves' or 'regional imbalances' (Manson, 1994).

In a nutshell, the rate of international technology transfer may be higher, the greater is the technology gap between the source country and recipient country. However, a minimum level of technology in the recipient country is needed for it to be able to absorb the new technology. In addition, the rate at which new technology can be transferred to the recipient country through FDI, may depend on a number of other factors. For instance, the imported technology has to be concomitant with the host country's factor endowments. If the initial capabilities are low, then technological imports may fail to stimulate further learning. Without the right competitive incentives, firms do not invest in their capabilities. Without the efficient factor market and institutional support, they cannot go far. In sum, it is the role of the governments to arbitrate in the technology transfer process. For this reason, governments need to promote domestic capabilities, develop an integrated strategy, build the educational base, strengthen technological institutions, and encourage firms into export markets to test and advance their competitiveness.

Empirical Review

Although some developing countries have succeeded in building local technological capabilities, the transfer of technology from abroad remains the most important source of technology for most developing countries. TNCs have played an important role in the diffusion of technical innovation overseas by carrying it to the host countries. The transfer of diesel technology to India has for example been described by Baranson (1966) as one of the cases in which TNCs have played a role in the transfer of technology to developing countries.

Empirical evidence shows that technology transfer to developing countries has a beneficial impact on growth through increased productivity of factors of production. It improves the efficiency of labour-intensive processes of production, rather than promoting the development of technology-intensive sectors (Dunning, 1981). For instance, studies on selected developing economies in Asia reveal that their output growth rates ranged between 3 and 12.5 per cent; and apart from India (1970-80), the Philippines (1957-62) and Singapore (1972-80) with 0.2, 0, and -11.3 per cent contribution of factor productivity respectively, the contribution of all the other countries (including the ASEAN-5, Hong Kong, Taipei, China and the Republic of Korea) ranged from 15.4 per cent in the Philippines (1963-69) to 56.4 per cent in the Republic of Korea (1955-70) (UN, 1992, Table VI.1). Chudnovsky et al's (1997) study reveals that when TNCs took over several state-owned service utilities in Argentina and Brazil, the productivity of the utilities improved. The TNCs also made significant management changes, laying off excess staff, and introducing new management methods and computerisation. However, in contrast to productivity and quality, the TNCs gave little to promoting R&D activities in affiliates.

Lall (1995) and Ernst et al (1998a) have observed that some of the developing countries that succeeded in building up domestic technological capabilities (i.e. the Republic of Korea and Taiwan), did so by relying on externalised technology transfer. Their domestic firms often had long-term relations with TNCs in the form of sub-contracting or original equipment manufacture contracts. By encouraging the absorption of technologies in strong export-oriented setting, the respective governments forced local firms to develop and deepen their own technological base. With gradual upgrading, the firms realised that externalised technology was not sufficient. Thus, new technology had to be imported either by entering other arrangements or by developing their own R&D to imitate and build up foreign technologies. While the Korean governments intervened in the role played by the *chaebol*, the Taiwanese government made a direct intervention in the role played by its numerous SMEs.

The fact that within the manufacturing sector, R&D intensive industries have been the most rapidly growing exporters indicates that technology in developing countries promotes growth through improved export performance. For example, the rate of growth of imports into developed countries averaged 10 per cent for high R&D intensive industries, while that for low R&D intensive industries was only 5 per cent between 1980-87 (UNCTAD, 1989, Table 3). Data on Brazil, the Republic of Korea, Malaysia, Mexico, Singapore and Thailand confirms that foreign affiliates contribute to a change in the composition of exports in favour of more capital and technology intensive products. A rising share of FDI in technology-intensive industries has accompanied an increase of capital and technology intensive manufactured exports in these countries (UN, 1992).

Developing countries attract only marginal proportions of TNC affiliate research, and much of what they get relates to production, i.e. adaptation and technical support (UNCTAD, 1999). Nonetheless, in recent years,

TNCs have been relocating some of their strategic R&D in a number of developing countries that have built up the required innovative environment. The main incentives for these are access to highly qualified scientists and engineers (due to shortages in industrialised countries), cost differentials in research salaries, and rationalisation of operations. Countries in East and South Asia, and Brazil have been beneficiaries most particularly because they have provided the resources concomitant with the corresponding R&D activities. By contrast, countries that have not invested well enough in locational determinants of technology have not faired well. The majority of developing countries fall in this category. For example, UNCTAD (1999) reports that in India, many local firms remained technologically dependent on foreign technology and failed to develop internationally competitive capabilities over decades of such policy. The problem was exacerbated when government promoted local firms without simultaneously improving the skills or institutional base.

The best example for transfer of technology has been reported by Cyhn (1999) about Korea's Daewoo. Daewoo Electronics (DE) forms part of the Korean *chaebol* the Daewoo Group. DE entered an original equipment manufacturing arrangement with Japan's NEC in 1981. However, DE's prototype samples had many defects/deficiencies. For this reason, NEC enhanced DE's capabilities by providing a great deal of technological help. Today DE is a TNC with its own international brand and operates as one of the largest producers of television sets. Lateef (1997) and Taylor (1999) have reported another example in India's software industry. India is endowed with low-cost English-speaking labour. Citybank, Texas Instruments and Hewlett Packard established wholly owned export-oriented software writing subsidiaries respectively in 1985, 1986 and 1989. In addition to regulatory accommodation, the government of India developed a Software Technology Park of India Scheme in 1988. Here it provided infrastructure, buildings, electricity, telecommunication facilities and high-speed satellite links. In 1990-91 quantitative restrictions on imports of intermediate and capital goods for software exports were abolished. Texas Instruments and Hewlett Packard in particular participated in enhancing India's software writing by mobilising domestic capabilities in the Indian software industry. For this reason, currently the five largest software industries in India are domestically owned and have developed a reputation for reliable, high quality but cheap work. Others have managed to develop their own internationally acceptable brands.

Empirical findings by the OECD (1970) and Cooper (1971) indicated that the activities of TNCs contributed to the fast spread of technology from nation to nation. Although it is narrowing down in the dynamic economies of Asia and Latin America (as local firms from these economies enter partnership with foreign firms), the technological gap is so wide that TNCs find it exceedingly difficult to transfer many technologies to developing countries. Moreover, when they manage to effect a technological transplant, its effects often are restricted to narrow segments of the local economy. This is why some TNCs are forced to transfer what some economists have labelled *obsolete* technology, often embedded in the second hand machinery or equipment. There has been an argument about the *appropriateness* of such technology even by the poorest of the developing countries. The level of sophistication of technology imported by a host developing country should depict its level of development (probably indicated by its quality of infrastructure and human skills). When one considers the less advanced developing countries, the so-called obsolete technology may nevertheless still be new technology *vis-à-vis* what they have in stock. More significantly, such technology may be more appropriate in the sense that it improves resource allocation by efficiently utilising the relatively unskilled human capital, operating in a relatively underdeveloped infrastructure. Moreover, if the TNCs brought with them sophisticated technology, which the host countries cannot cope with (due to lack of the necessary skills and infrastructure), these economists would also criticise them for providing *inappropriate* technology. Such technology is even most likely to be capital-intensive and, therefore, equally likely to generate negative employment effects on the economy. Some least developed countries have, however, accepted this kind of technology as exemplified in Uganda's Minister for Finance and Economic Development reply to the National Resistance Council on matters arising from the 1992/93 Budget speech:

> '...some members have expressed concern on the removal of the ban on the importation of second hand machinery...besides, government has not banned importation of machinery for those who can afford it. The rational is to assist those investors that cannot afford new machinery but have identified usable machinery which can be utilised to economic advantage...New machinery in the world today is characterised by electronic guidance/computer controlled operations and robots. This is too advanced and inappropriate for our economy...' (Bende-Nabende, 1995).

The 'appropriateness' of technology is, therefore, *relative* and varies with the specific characteristics of the foreign parent firm, affiliate firm and host country. And, if a large portion of FDI is export-oriented, less old and more new machinery/equipment will be imported since the products will be targeted at the international market place and have to be of an acceptable quality to be competitive. UNCTAD (1999) reports that for countries that are part of export-oriented operations, internalisation transfer is very important to obtain mature as well as latest technology, depending on the product or market. Thus, what could rightly be said with respect to this issue is that TNCs have responded to specific characteristics of parent firms, affiliates and host countries. Technology transfer by TNCs reflects the strategy of the parent company and its assessment of what is appropriate to local capabilities not to mention the locational capabilities of the host country. Taking an example of the electronics industry in Malaysia, the TNCs placed their simplest assembly technologies and provided the training and information necessary to operate them. Over time, as wages rose, they started automating the technology. As skills rose, they upgraded the technological functions (UNCTAD, 1999). Otherwise, had suck costs been lower, they probably would have relocated production to lower wage countries. The locational advantages of most of the developing countries (e.g. efficient low-cost labour) provide opportunities for simple labour-intensive assembly type of processes, which are concentrated at the higher level of their value chain and which require less skills. Moreover, some of these TNCs merely relocate production from the most advanced developing economies to the less advanced ones as in the *flying-geese* concept. There may, however, be a case for individual countries, particularly those which host Japanese FDI and such cases should be considered individually. Evaluation of countries such as Singapore, which have invested heavily in creating skills and efficient labour markets shows that they have attracted high value-added and, therefore, skill-intensive TNC activities. The TNCs, therefore, respond to the current and/or future potential locational advantages, which form part of the host country's comparative advantage. Besides, if the investing firms have invested lots of money in R&D in order to develop such technology, it should not be expected that this source of their competitive advantage would be given away for free.

The successful transfer of technology depends on how government policy can facilitate the spillover process. It is this appropriateness and cost of the technology obtained by the host country that determines whether or not the recognised association between technology and economic growth is actually translated into net benefits. Thus, whereas the role of TNCs in transferring new technology is paramount, it can be significantly facilitated by certain conditions, which are highly influenced by government policy. These include promoting domestic capabilities, developing an integrated strategy, building and educational base, strengthening technological institutions, and encouraging firms into export markets to test and advance their competitiveness.

FDI and Domestic Capital Formation

Theoretical Review

Investment is a key stimulant of economic growth. Domestic capital formation (DCF) is the stock of physical capital that is used for further production. The endogenous growth theories postulate that when investment is taken in a broad sense, to include not only expenditures on capital goods but also expenditures on technology enhancement and human capital formation, there may well not exist diminishing returns to investment. Therefore, countries that devote a high proportion of output to investment may sustain more rapid growth than countries that invest less. Physical investment in equipment and machinery may lead to the acceleration of economic growth through the creation of technical and managerial skills, human capital and their externalities (Hamad, 1995).

In a closed economy, with no access to foreign savings, investment is financed solely from domestic savings. However, in an open economy investment is financed both through domestic savings and through foreign capital flows, including FDI. FDI may promote growth by increasing the quantity and improving the quality of the host country's stock of physical capital. The presence of FDI is expected to create competition that propels the efficiency of investment within the host country, and therefore the effectiveness of domestic investment. It increases the ratio of investment to GDP and the investment increases then translates into demand for goods and services of other sectors, via various multiplier and accelerator effects. This consequently prompts higher GDP growth rates. No doubt, sustained investment promotes sustained GDP growth rates and hence economic growth.

TNCs contribute to domestic savings generated through retained earnings, an amount that may be quite substantial, depending on the individual host developing country's wealth. Moreover, the retained or reinvested earnings can be viewed (based on residence principle and in the absence of transfer from abroad) not as an infusion of fresh capital from abroad, but as domestic savings (UNCTAD, 1999). The retained earnings together with internally generated savings, the savings of their parent and other affiliate branches which they obtain through inter-company borrowing, and revenue from the issue of capital can then be reinvested. Consequently, FDI has been seen as a source of funds which supplements domestic savings, and which might relieve the host developing countries from foreign exchange shortages. FDI is by definition funded from abroad. Therefore, little or no foreign exchange is desired for the capital equipment and machinery that are traditionally required in the initial investment stages, not to mention the components and parts that are often needed as inputs thereafter. Moreover, FDI is more stable than other capital flows since it is based on a longer-term view of the market, the growth potential and the structural characteristics of the host country. Thus, it is less prone to reversal than say bank lending and portfolio flows. TNCs create domestic employment opportunities and hence increase domestic savings through channels such as the institution of pension plans, direct deposits into savings accounts, and offering payroll deductions for purchasing insurance for their employees (UN, 1992). TNCs also stimulate investment through their purchases from local investors. In addition, they contribute to host government revenue directly via tax payments, and contractual fees, and indirectly through taxes paid by their employees and suppliers. Furthermore, FDI in tradable activities generates foreign exchange (export projects) or saves it (import-substituting projects). Besides, TNCs are capable of doing this more efficiently than the small domestic firms.

The distinctive feature between FDI and other financial flows is that FDI is capable of internalising foreign savings. That is, firms bringing these savings actually undertake investment. Thus, TNCs can affect investment in host countries directly through their own investment, and indirectly by affecting investment by host country firms (UNCTAD, 1999). The direct effect is transmitted instantly to domestic capital formation as discussed above. However, the indirect effect may occur either as crowding-out effects or crowding-in effects on domestic firms and other foreign affiliates. For the TNCs' investment to crowd-out investment by domestic firms, a one dollar investment increase by foreign affiliates should stimulate an increase of total investment in the host country by less than one dollar (multiplier effect is less than 1). However, if total host country investment increases by more than the increase in investment by foreign affiliates (multiplier effect is grater than 1), then it represents a crowding-in case. In the neutral case, any increase in the affiliate's investment is reflected in a dollar-for-dollar increase in total host country investment (multiplier effect is 1).

Crowding-out may result from increases in host country interest rates when foreign firms borrow locally under conditions of scarcity. The high interest rates then make borrowing unaffordable for domestic firms. Were the TNCs to finance their investment, instead from abroad, total investment in the host country could be higher by the amount of domestic investment not undertaken due to the high interest rates. Thus, this amount is crowded-out. However, since FDI is by definition financed from abroad, crowding-out may result from foreign firms out-competing domestic firms through the use of their superior firm specific assets. In this case, the foreign firms are not at the same level playing field with the domestic firms. Essentially, FDI in this case distorts the domestic enterprises from undertaking the learning process resulting into their incapability to compete with foreign affiliates. For this reason, there is a case for infant industry protection particularly in countries whose domestic enterprises are still in the lengthy learning process. Crowding-out can impart a long-term cost on the host economy. In particular, it disrupts the technological upgrading and deepening process and consequently, the technological capabilities of the host country. Nonetheless, crowding-out which forces only the inefficient domestic firms out of competition may be good for the host economy since it introduces dynamic competition and flexibility. In this context for instance, in the absence of this dynamic generating FDI, domestic firms would face stiff competition in the export markets.

Crowding-in takes place when investment by foreign affiliates stimulates new investment in the downstream or upstream production by other foreign or domestic producers or increases efficiency of financial intermediation (UNCTAD, 1999). The existence of backward and forward linkages to local firms plays an instrumental role in this case.

Accordingly, foreign affiliates that introduce new goods and services to a domestic economy are more likely to have favourable indirect effects on capital formation than foreign investors in areas where domestic production already exists. The former case generates positive effects because domestic producers may not have the know-how to undertake such production. In the latter case, foreign investment enters direct competition with domestic firms and takes away opportunities that were open to domestic entrepreneurs prior to foreign investment. In other words, FDI reduces domestic investment that would have been undertaken either immediately or in the future by domestic firms.

An important aspect of FDI is its commitment to the long-run. FDI involves much more stable and generally smaller amounts of capital than portfolio investment and credits. Besides that, they represent long-term, carefully selected investment projects that cannot be liquidated at short notice. Transaction costs involved are usually higher when an investor establishes an enterprise compared to the purchase of short-term bonds or options. This may explain its proven resilience during financial crises. In situations of international iliquidity, a country's consolidated financial system has short-term obligations in foreign currency in excess of foreign currency that the country has access on short notice. Under, such circumstances, FDI flows provide the only direct link between the domestic capital market in the host country and the world capital market at large. For instance, FDI flows to East Asian countries were remarkably stable during the 1997/98 financial crisis. In sharp contrast, portfolio equity and debt flows, as well as bank loans, dried up almost completely during the same period. The resilience of FDI to financial crises was also evident in the Mexican crisis of 1994 and the Latin America debt crisis of the early-1980s. This may reflect a unique characteristic of FDI, which is determined by considerations of ownership and control by multinationals of domestic activities, which are more long-term in nature, rather than by short-term fluctuations in the value of domestic currency and the availability of credit and liquidity. Furthermore, direct investment most often takes the form of equity capital, which, as opposed to debt creating instruments, imposes no obligations on the debtor to make fixed interest payments and to reimburse the principal at a determined date. A foreign investor may be unable or unwilling to liquidate his shares unless he can find a counterpart willing to buy them at the desired price. Finally and perhaps even more importantly, in the absence of perfectly fluid markets and substitutable financing instruments, direct investment can be expected to contribute to the financing of productive investment in a higher proportion than portfolio investment and credits, thereby enhancing the host country's capacity to assure the service of its debt through increased exports at a later stage.

Since capital formation is an important determinant of economic growth, FDI may also have a positive influence on economic growth when it increases both its quantity and quality in host developing countries.

Although FDI may be concentrated in relatively few industries, they may, however, be among the most important in terms of their contribution to economic growth.

Empirical Review

Empirical studies of inter-country differences in growth rates suggest that high growths are associated with high investment rates. Lewis (1984) and Stern (1989) have pointed out the importance of capital as a determinant of growth. However, it varies across countries over a period of time and is influenced by economic factors including the presence of other determinants of growth, non-economic factors such as the political and cultural framework within which the economic elements operate, and the development stage of the economy.

There is evidence linking economic growth to investment. The countries that have sustained high levels of economic growth are those that have experienced rapid increases in their stocks of physical and human capital. For instance, the East Asian economies significantly increased their investment/GDP ratio from an average 22 per cent in 1965 to 35 per cent in 1990 (World Bank, 1995). By the end of 1980, FDI had become the principle source of private foreign capital for the majority of developing countries. It accounted for 75 per cent of total long-term capital flows from private flows (excluding non-guaranteed credit and including FDI) to 93 capital importing developing countries during the period 1986 to 90, compared with 30 per cent during the period 1980 to 85 (UN, 1992). UNCTAD (1999) has observed that FDI flows increased in importance in the 1990s, becoming the single most important component of capital flows to developing countries. Their share in total flows doubled from 28 per cent in 1991 to 56 per cent in 1998.

The relationship between investment and economic growth has been captured by cross-country data comparing growth rates in GDP per worker with recent estimates of the accumulation of physical capital. The results exhibit a positive relationship between investment and growth in output per worker. The relationship is, however, not automatic, as exemplified by studies carried out on China, the former Soviet Union and Tanzania where investment amounted to over 20 per cent of GDP but growth was not as fast as expected (World Bank, 1995).

The ratio of FDI flows to domestic investment, an indicator of the significance of FDI in capital formation, has risen for most developing countries. The increase has been in all regions except West Asia, but more dramatic in East Asia and the Pacific, and since the mid-1970s, in Africa. UNCTAD (1999) reports that the importance of FDI relative to investment has consistently increased in all countries in the recent past. In the 1990s, this importance has become for the first time higher in developing countries and economies in transition than in developed countries. Furthermore, the ratio of FDI to total investment has increased consistently over time for all developing country regions and sub-regions (except West Asia). In the 1990s, the ratios in Africa, Latin America and the Caribbean, East and Southeast Asia were more than two times higher than in the 1980s. Aggregate FDI to developing countries accounted for 2, 3.5 and 7 per cent of for 1971-80, 1981-90 and 1991-97 respectively. The figures for these corresponding periods were 0.1, 2 and 4.5 per cent for North Africa; 3, 5 and 9 per cent for Sub-Sahara Africa; 3.2, 4.1 and 9.5 for Latin America and the Caribbean, 2.1, 3.4 and 7.2 for South, East and Southeast Asia; and 3.5 and 1 per cent for West Asia (UNCTAD, 1999, Figure VI.1). In spite of its rapidly growing importance, however, FDI still plays, on average, a modest role in domestic investment in all country groups, indicating perhaps potential for further growth in importance (UNCTAD, 1999).

The ratio of FDI stock to GDP, an indicator of the importance of the investments in relation to the size of the economy of the host country has also been rising over time. For instance, between 1986 and 1989, it was more than 20 per cent for Botswana, Seychelles, Singapore and Swaziland; and 15 to 20 per cent for Guatemala, Hong Kong and Papua New Guinea (UN, 1992, Annex tables 6 and 7, Table II.3 and Figure II.4). Between 1991 and 1997 the number of countries with a ratio of more than 20 per cent had increased to 19, while those with 15-20 per cent had increased to 16 (UNCTAD, 1999, Table VI.5). It is important, however, to interpret these ratios with caution. For instance, with respect to Africa, the ratio may reflect a drop in GDP rather than an increase in FDI flows.

The importance of FDI in stimulating the quality of new capital and thus increasing domestic capital formation is more significant in industries such as manufacturing which are crucial to development, and where local purchasing by TNCs provides a stimulant to local investment. For instance, high levels of capital formation in Singapore have been made possible both by the considerable domestic savings and by the flow of capital from abroad. Gross fixed capital formation increased steadily from 22 per cent of GDP in 1965, and after peaking at over 40 per cent of GDP in 1980, stood at 38 per cent in 1990. In the initial periods, the high investment rate was partly financed by foreign savings (GATT, 1992). Also, approximately a third, and in 1990 almost a half of the flows of FDI from the US to the developing countries took the form of reinvested earnings between 1982 and 1990. For Brazil and Mexico, reinvested earnings of TNCs between 1967 and 1989 accounted for between 15 to 90 per cent of the annual flows. Between 1989 and 1996, US foreign affiliates in developing countries invested one third more than the amount TNCs brought in as FDI (UNCTAD, 1999, Table VI.).

Direct tax payments by the foreign affiliates of the US based TNCs to foreign governments amounted to approximately $100 billion in 1989, equivalent to 10 per cent of their foreign sales. The contribution to individual countries, however, depends on their production capacities, tax rates and tax enforcement policies. For example, the share of tax by foreign affiliates of US TNCs, as a percentage of total government revenue of the host country was 0.2 for India, 0.4 for the Republic of Korea, 1.4 for Ecuador, 2.3 for Chile, 5.4 for the Philippines, 6.8 for Malaysia, 7.4 for Thailand, 12.2 for Peru, 12.9 for Trinidad and Tobago, and 15.5 for Guatemala in 1989 (UN, 1992, Table VI). TNCs' contributions to direct taxes can, however, be hampered by government policies such as those that grant tax exemptions.

Some studies have, however, shown that TNCs do not have a positive impact upon domestic savings in developing countries. For instance, Feldstein and Horioka (1980), Fieleke (1982), Dooley, Frankel and Mathieson (1987), Feldstein and Bachetta (1989), Wilkins (1989), Bayoumi (1990) and Tesar (1991) have suggested that foreign savings may not have been an important source of savings for both the developed and developing countries. They have also argued that capital formation is largely limited by domestic sources of savings. A study of TNCs by Schive (1993) on Taipei, China has revealed that FDI has not made a significant contribution to the total capital formation, except modestly in the manufacturing sector. Bende-Nabende et al (2000b) found that although FDI generated positive impulses on capital formation in the Philippines and Thailand, capital formation in turn impacted negatively on the Philippines' output and caused neutral effects on Thailand's output. Consequently, they concluded that spillovers were not attained via capital formation and attributed it to the possible crowding-out effects. Other studies have indicated that increases in foreign savings are accompanied by declines in domestic savings in developing countries. For example, Gupta and Islam (1983), and Rana and Dowling (1988) found that the regression coefficient of foreign savings on domestic savings was negative, but between zero and one, implying that foreign savings represented a net addition to national savings in host developing countries, while the flow of FDI had a positive relation (UN, 1992) - a contradictory result.

Studies that have investigated aggregate capital flows, i.e. FDI plus debt, such as that by Gupta and Islam (1983) have, however, found positive impacts on growth. They have shown that FDI inflows make a positive contribution towards the quantity of physical capital in developing countries and this quantitative contribution appears more significant in industries such as manufacturing that are crucial to growth and development (UN, 1992). Others include Koo (1985) who observed that the direct contribution of FDI to the economic growth of the Republic of Korea was significantly higher than the share of these firms in domestic investment would have suggested. Schive and Jenn-Hwa Tu (1991) found a statistically significant positive relationship between FDI and domestic investment, suggesting that the two respond to similar conditions within the host countries and are, therefore, complementary and not substitutes.

Chudnovsky et al (1996) observe that crowding-in took place in Argentina's telecommunications privatisation, where the development of domestic subcontractors was part and parcel of the privatisation agreement with the foreign investors. Riveros et al (1996), and Agosin and Benavente (1998) suggest that foreign investment in copper in Chile may have caused crowding-in effects. They argue that the national copper company (CODELCO), which is the largest copper mining enterprise in the world and operates with the state-of-the-art technology, was in a position to undertake investment in this sector. UNCTAD's (1999) results on developing countries show that neutral effects dominate while the number of crowding-in and crowding-out cases were equal. Out of the 12 Latin American countries included in the study, none was in the group for crowding-in effects and none of the 12 Asian countries was in for crowding-out effects. While neutral and crowding-in effects predominated in Asia, neutral and crowding-out effects prevailed in Latin America. African countries were found in all three groups.

It is therefore, evident that FDI contributes to host developing countries' domestic capital formation. However, its contribution currently remains marginal in most developing countries, perhaps demonstrating more potential for the future. Host developing countries may well exploit this future potential most particularly if they deepen their resource bases, thereby creating a more conducive environment capable of sustaining dynamic FDI activities.

FDI and International Trade

Theoretical Review

Countries engage in international trade for a variety of reasons. International trade contributes to economic growth through its beneficial impact on foreign exchange (exports), and on resource allocation resulting from specialisation. It helps to increase inputs to growth including natural resources, capital goods and technology by exchanging those goods and services that a country can produce efficiently for those the country either cannot produce, or can do so only at a relatively high cost as depicted by the comparative cost doctrine. Trade also induces growth by offering greater opportunities for economies of scale owing to an enlargement of the effective market and greater capacity utilisation due to additional external demand. Besides, the competition faced in the international markets for exports and in home markets through imports tends to force domestic producers to become more efficient, learn new technology and improve the skills of their employees. Therefore, it provides incentives for fostering more rapid technological change and better management in both tradable and non-tradable sectors, thus raising overall productivity and economic growth. FDI can enhance the level of competition in domestic markets and hence the economic efficiency to the benefit of the host country. By bringing new players able to challenge market positions of already established enterprises, FDI provides incentives for domestic enterprises to adjust in order to remain competitive. Participation of foreign investors on a national treatment basis in bids for concessions provides a guarantee that such concessions are granted on the best terms and conditions. Also, the faculty of domestic enterprises to borrow directly from foreign banks abroad exerts helpful pressure on domestic banks to reduce the cost of their services and extend the range of credits they offer. Similarly, the opportunity given to domestic enterprises to raise funds on international capital markets incites stock market institutions to improve the functioning and the attractiveness of local capital markets. There may be, however, situations where foreign investments reduce competition in the domestic market. In particular, if the investment is through the acquisition of a domestic producer by a foreign firm already exporting into that market, competition may be reduced through increased concentration. The presence of foreign firms in a domestic market may also complicate the task of the national competition authority, particularly if cartel activity is suspected, as information necessary to the investigation of a cartel is spread across the jurisdictions of several countries.

Higher growth of exports, in turn, permits a higher growth of imports for such purposes as procuring raw materials and capital equipment that sustain growth (UN, 1992). By participating in international trade, domestic firms take part in the international exchange of information necessary to acquaint themselves with perspectives on technical problems. To any country, especially the one with a free enterprise economic system, international trade is a means towards economic ends in terms of economic growth, stability and social equity. Increased trade for a country raises its GDP, which *ceteris paribus,* raises its per capita income. Increased per capita income induces a higher purchasing power or aggregate demand, which in turn propels the economic growth process.

Imports of intermediate and capital goods are crucial for domestic investment and economic growth. Competition in the domestic markets from imports may promote innovation, resulting in the introduction of technological improvements and product quality upgrading by domestic firms. Under such competition, some inefficient domestic firms may be forced out of business, resulting in increased productivity. While imports are expected to provide access to the technology and capital goods available in developed countries, exports help exploit the comparative advantage in resource development. Exports are also associated with positive learning effects that can be translated into product and process innovations. For instance, large scale exporting (and therefore production) allows workers and managers to continue taking on new tasks enabling sustained learning on-the-job (Locus, 1993). Moreover, exports generate the foreign exchange required to finance the import of goods and services. In the process, they help improve the balance-of-payments.

UNCTAD (1999) reports that export success among developing countries has been concentrated in a few countries. This is a consequence of the comparative advantage of most developing countries, which lies traditionally in primary commodities and unskilled-labour-intensive manufacturing. However, it is dynamic in the sense that as developing countries grow and accumulate capital skills over time, their wage rates rise and subsequently their competitive bases change. They are put under considerable pressure to upgrade their primary and labour-intensive exports into higher value-added items, and to move into new, more advanced, export-oriented activities, which require greater inputs of skill and technology. These objectives can be attained by either improving and deepening the capabilities of domestic enterprises, by tapping into TNC networks as conduits for trade, or by attracting FDI into export activities and upgrading these activities over time (UNCTAD, 1999).

Since developing countries face productivity, quality, financial and logistic constraints, it is not easy for them to launch new exports. For instance, the collection of information about consumer needs and designs or the requirements of industrial firms (where they are exporting intermediate products) is costly. Product distribution and marketing are also costly. Moreover, these problems rise with the technical complexity and differentiation of a product. In addition, the easiest market segments to enter involve simple production processes with low skill needs, no scale economies, standardised products and stable technologies. On the other hand, the most difficult market segments to enter involve complex processes with high learning and skill requirements, rapidly changing technologies, large scales of economies, branded products and after-sale service (UNCTAD, 1999). TNCs can help in this effort. Trading TNCs can boost exports of developing countries by providing marketing services, access to international distribution networks and assistance towards product design, quality standards, packaging, presentation, use of their brand name, and access to consumers. This assistance can be of critical importance particularly in those product groups in which host developing countries have comparative advantage in their manufacture, but lack a comparative advantage in marketing them abroad (Hall, 1991). TNCs' networks provide foreign affiliates and hence host developing countries privileged access to internal and external international markets. Domestic firms can in turn gain access to these markets by linking themselves to TNC networks through sub-contracting and other arrangements (UNCTAD, 1996).

UNCTAD (1999) has noted that TNCs themselves are large markets for internal transactions. Each TNC comprises a market in which three types of transactions take place: sales by the parent firm to its foreign affiliates, sales by foreign affiliates to their parent firms, and sales between affiliates in different countries. Domestic firms can also access these markets by linking themselves to the affiliate companies. However, this intra-firm trade tends to increase with an increase in technological content. Therefore, countries that have or can establish more complex technology intensive industries and activities have a higher potential of accruing benefits from such linkages. Nonetheless, those countries that can only attract FDI in low-skill manufacturing activities and therefore, may not benefit from these linkages can take advantage of the trading networks built up through inter-firm agreements of various kinds.

Only two decades ago, services were deemed non-tradable by nature. However, recent technological advances in telecommunications and computer-communications links have enhanced the tradability of information-intensive services. Unsurprisingly then, the potential for exporting services across borders is increasing. Because of the complexity involved with the service sector, FDI remains the predominant mode of delivering them to foreign markets. TNCs can provide certain sophisticated business services that are not available locally but are necessary for efficient domestic production by both foreign affiliates and local firms. These include banking, insurance, advanced data processing, and telecommunication services (UN, 1992). Moreover, domestic firms may be able to acquire access to the internal and external service markets of the TNCs as they take advantage of the liberalised trade system. The provision of such services is, however, highly dependent among other things, on the quality of infrastructure and human resources available in the host developing country.

The net contribution of foreign investment to the host country's balance of payments could become negative over time if profits are systematically repatriated abroad rather than reinvested locally, or if foreign-controlled enterprises display a greater propensity to source abroad than domestic firms. For any given investment project, once the affiliate is profitable, repatriated profits may in the long run exceed initial inflows of equity capital. The retained earnings of the affiliate will usually sustain the investment. Based on this notion of the investment cycle of a foreign investment project, it has been argued that FDI may lead to a deterioration in the balance of payments position of the host country over time. Such reasoning is flawed for several reasons. First, FDI also affects the balance of payments through the trade account, with net exports from the affiliate potentially offsetting net capital outflows. In the short term and depending on the sector, an investment is likely to be accompanied by an increase in imports of capital goods from the home country as the investor establishes a production facility. In the longer term, however, the investor is likely to begin to export from the host country, provided host country policies are such that the affiliate is able to compete with producers elsewhere. The net effect on the balance of payments from these offsetting current and capital accounting flows is difficult to determine *a priori*. There might be future problems, however, when the foreign direct investor buys firms in the non-tradable sectors. Second, the experience of an individual investment project is not the full story. FDI is a continuous process: as some older investors begin to repatriate profits, new arrivals inject additional equity capital into the host economy and existing investors expand their presence through retained earnings. Both forms of investment are recorded as capital inflows in the balance of payments. Third, more important than the actual direct effect of inward investment on the balance of payments is the long-term indirect benefit derived from transfer of technology and know-how to domestic producers. These transfers improve the overall ability of the host country to export and hence allow the economy to sustain greater inflows of foreign capital over time. To focus only on the direct impact on the balance of payments of individual investments misses these important indirect gains to be derived from inward investment (Ribeiro, 2000).

FDI, therefore, stimulates international trade by providing opportunities to expand and improve the production of goods and services. For the host developing countries where production is cheaper, and the skill base and infrastructure are adequate, it is efficient to relocate production from the developed countries particularly in the later stages of the product life cycle when technology related to production becomes standardised and readily available in most countries. Such FDI creates exports of finished products to the investing countries and third-party countries, as well as imports of parts and components from investing countries. Thus, the TNCs involved in FDI are influential in terms of determining the volume, direction and composition of a substantial and increasing proportion of international trade. FDI facilitates higher growth rates by raising the demand for domestically produced goods through host country exports, easing supply constraints of both host and home economies through imports, and facilitating a dynamic learning process (UN, 1992).

Empirical Review

Overview Most empirical international trade analyses have been carried out independent of investment, centred on the descriptive literature that observes trends, and the interrelationship between trade and FDI. In addition, they have been analysed in the concept of balance-of-payments. Trade was regarded as a major determinant of the growth of countries in the nineteenth century and early twentieth century, owing to favourable demand conditions. For example, it was the tremendous expansion of Western Europe's, and especially the UK's demand for foodstuffs and raw materials that provided the basic inducement for the development of its major trading partners, the US, Canada, Argentina, and Australia (UN, 1992). Experience of individual countries, e.g. the Asian NIEs, also associates trade and growth, particularly between trade in manufactured products and growth in manufacturing output.

Exports The role played by exports in the economic growth process cannot be emphasised. Nurkse (1961) found evidence that trade played a crucial role in world economic growth, particularly in the 1950s and 1960s, when world trade in manufactured products grew in real terms at an annual average rate of 9 per cent while world manufactured output rose at 7 per cent. The Asian NIEs increased their shares of world trade in manufactured products between 1973 and 1988 from 4 to 10 per cent. Michalopoulos and Jay (1973), Krueger (1978), Balassa (1978), Feder (1982), Balassa (1985), Chen and Wong (1990), and Park (1992) also observed that developing countries with higher than average export growth tended to experience higher than average growth in their output. Rhee, Ross-Larson and Pursell (1984) found a positive correlation between export expansion and growth of factor productivity in the Republic of Korea. They observed that the export imperative necessitated improvements in product standards and acquisitions of greater expertise in production and marketing techniques (UN, 1992).

The importance of TNCs in the growth of exports in developing countries is usually illustrated in terms of the percentage share in total manufactured exports of affiliates in manufactured exports. However, this is not necessary an indicator of the importance of these affiliates to the developing countries. Studies of Mexico have shown that foreign firms played an important role in the growth of non-oil exports, increasing their share from a 22 per cent in 1983 to 53 per cent in 1987. In the same period, their share in total exports from the export sector rose from 34 to 65 per cent (Nunez, 1993, Table 5). Most of this has been attributed to Mexico's *Maquiladora* 85 per cent of which are located near the US border, specialising in automobile equipment and accessories, electrical and electronic machinery, appliances, and materials and accessories. UNCTAD's (1999, Annex table, A.I.8.) individual country statistics illustrate that exports of foreign affiliates as a percentage of total exports in all industry sectors were 3.4 for India in 1991, 18.2 for Mexico in 1993, 26.8 for Taiwan in 1995 and 36.1 for China in 1997. With the exception of Taiwan, these percentages increase when only the primary and secondary sectors are considered. For instance, exports of foreign affiliates as a percentage of total exports in the primary and secondary sectors were 3.5 for India in 1991, 16.4 for Taiwan in 1995, 21.1 for Mexico in 1993, 35.4 for Hong Kong in 1997, 40.9 for China in 1997, 51 for Malaysia in 1994 and 60.6 for Singapore in 1996.

The hypothesis that FDI generates more home country exports than it replaces, in the initial stages, has been supported by a number of empirical studies including those by Bergsten (1978), Donges and Juhl (1979), Lipsey and Weiss (1984), Milton (1984), and Arnaud-Ameller (1985). This positive impact has three major determinants, which are linked to technology. First, investment is partly financed in kind through purchases of plant and equipment, and intermediates from home countries. Second, there is a considerable size of deliveries of capital goods, raw materials and intermediates from parent companies to their foreign affiliates in the initial process of production. Finally, during its 'follow-the-leader' and 'follow-up' effects, investment makes competitors and suppliers follow the producers to the host country (Langhammer, 1989). These factors facilitate the transfer of technology from the developed to the developing countries as discussed earlier.

Studies of South Asia have shown that foreign firms export a higher proportion of their output than their local counterparts. Chia (1985) and Lim (1988) have observed a high significance of this in Singapore where the domestic enterprise is still not well established in manufacturing. Similar observations, although less significant, have been reported by Ranis and Schive (1985) for Taipei, China; Koo (1985) for the Republic of Korea; and Sibunruang and Brimble (1987) for Thailand.

According to a study by UNCTAD (1994), the proportion of export sales in total sales by US and Japanese firms increased in the developing countries from 22 to 33.1 per cent and 32.8 to 39.2 per cent respectively between 1982 and 1989. That for Japanese affiliates grew from 8.2 to 15.2 in Africa, 33.6 to 40.2 in Asia and the Pacific, and 18.6 to 23.9 per cent in Latin America and the Caribbean. This probably reflects the shift from import-substitution to export-promotion policies by the developing countries. Individual country data also confirms that by the mid- and late-1980s, foreign affiliates came to account for significant proportions of exports, particularly in the manufacturing sector. For instance, over 50 per cent of the manufactured exports in Malaysia, the Philippines and Sri Lanka, almost 90 per cent in Singapore, 58 per cent in Mexico, and 46 per cent in Paraguay were accounted for by foreign affiliates (World Bank, 1995). The trend shows an increasing share of foreign affiliates in developing countries' exports since the late 1970s.

The study of Lall and Streeten on Jamaica, Kenya, India, Colombia and Malaysia has, however, revealed that 'trans-nationality' does not appear to have been an important aid to exporting (Hood and Young, 1993). This indicates that the influence of TNCs on export growth may be dictated by the host government's policies. For instance, exports cannot be expected to play a significant role in the economic growth process of an economy that pursues an import-substituting policy since production is targeted at the local domestic market under such a policy.

UNCTAD (1999) has observed a statistical relationship between 1995 FDI and manufactured exports across 52 countries, suggesting a significant positive relationship between FDI flows and export performance as well as between FDI inflows and the technological sophistication of exports. The relationship is stronger for developing countries than developed countries and in high-technology activities than low-technology activities. The data thus suggests that there is a correlation between FDI and export dynamism in the developing world, at least in a cross-section sense.

Imports Disaggregated data on the role of TNCs in the import of capital goods by developing countries are not available. Agosin and Esfahani (1991) have observed that imports are a significant factor in explaining the growth performance in developing countries. Such imports are unsurprisingly in intermediate and capital goods crucial for domestic investment and output growth. Data on imports of capital goods by affiliates of US TNCs in developing countries shows that they accounted for 5.2 to 6.3 per cent of capital goods imports by developing countries between 1982 and 1989; 4.7 to 5 per cent in Asia and the Pacific, and 9 to 11.1 in Latin America and the Caribbean (UN, 1992, Table VIII. 6). Wells (1978) also attributed the growth of local textile industry in Hong Kong to the imports of new machinery from foreign-based TNCs. This growing value provides an indication of the role played by TNCs in the imports to meet local production. This role is, however, only beneficial to the host developing country insofar as the value added locally is substantial.

Thus, the role FDI is playing in developing countries' international trade is paramount. Nonetheless, it can be strengthened by either improving and deepening the capabilities of domestic enterprises, by tapping into TNC networks as conduits for trade, or by attracting FDI into export activities and upgrading these activities over time.

FDI and Environmental Protection and Social Responsibility

Theoretical Review

Environmental protection The environment comprises the four gifts of nature: land, water, air and living organisms. The former three are basic necessities for the survival of all living things, be it animals or plants. Unsurprisingly then, environmental protection has of recent become a factor of interest to all nations, both developed and developing. No wonder, since the 1992 Earth Summit in Rio de Janeiro, heads of states nowadays gather together on an annual basis to discuss environmental issues.

It has become apparent that in the absence of appropriate action, economic growth can on the one hand be the key factor that downgrades the environment. On the other hand, economic development offers new opportunities for environmental protection by increasing and diffusing more advanced environmental technologies and management systems (UNCTAD, 1999). Although moral and regulatory imperatives were the traditional principle drivers of environmental responsibilities, non-government organisations (NGOs) have of recent played the dominant role. Through the NGOs' vigilantism, national governments have come to realise the need to protect the environment, and not to treat environmental damage as part of a price paid for development as was the case traditionally. Consequently, other stakeholders have joined arms in addressing environmental issues. These include, consumer groups, local communities, shareholders of companies and even employees of companies. National governments have responded by increasing stringency in environmental regulation. Thus, it is becoming accepted that environmental protection and economic growth should be attained simultaneously, and both the public and private sectors are becoming increasingly active in addressing environmental issues.

This aside, environmental protection still remains a challenging issue most particularly in developing countries. For instance, policy makers in developing countries may be desperate to achieve projected economic growth rates and securing FDI, and in the process accept to undertake environmentally risky activities. In addition, investors may pursue a deliberate strategy of shifting the location of their pollution-intensive production in response to lax environmental standards. Likewise, the imported technology may be vintage and therefore, environmental-unfriendly. Alternatively, developing countries may simply lack the resources and technical expertise to inspect, monitor and enforce appropriate environmental legislation. In this case, TNCs can be called upon to bridge the resource gap.

TNCs have at their disposal strong strategic assets and capabilities. For instance, they have sufficient resources to research and apply new techniques of environmental management, and also new techniques of production. In addition, they have not only the experience of handling environmental problems, but also the ability to respond and adapt to change. Because most TNCs originate from the developed countries, the parent firms are already under considerable pressure to innovate environmental-friendly technology. Thus, even if their affiliates may be at liberty to use environmental-unfriendly least-cost strategies in developing countries, this can be reversed if the respective host governments demand for environmental-friendly technologies similar to those used by parent firms. Indeed, where there are commercial benefits to being environmental-friendly, the use of clean technology may spur domestic consumers to acquire such knowledge (UNCTAD, 1999). There is also a linkage component in environmental issues. For instance, TNCs have the capability and advantage in assisting their suppliers to upgrade their environmental management systems and their consumers to change their consumption habits.

Nonetheless, issues pertaining to environmental downgrading are still far from being resolved. Most TNCs' affiliates are not willing to pursue environmental-friendly policies in host developing countries unless they are put under considerable pressure. As incomes rise, demand for a better environment and pollution abatement inevitably increases. Developing countries have to recognise environmental policy challenges, capacity development for environmental monitoring, and more rigorous control of environmental damage arising from economic activity. Since environmental downgrading tends to be greater in low-productivity operations utilising vintage technology and hence insufficient factor inputs, it implies that there is much scope for firms operating in developing countries to improve their environmental performance. This can be achieved through the adoption of corporate strategies that promote the development and mastery of technological processes. The challenge for both TNCs and national governments is to devise ways in which the transfer of environmentally sound management practices and clean technologies in domestic industry can be encouraged.

Social responsibility   Following the footsteps of the environmental protection campaign, the issue of social responsibility has emerged as a major concern to the aforementioned stakeholders. Thus, pressure is mounting such that expectations related to TNCs are undergoing unusually rapid change, reflecting societies' changing social and cultural mores. Social responsibility obliges firms to go beyond what countries require individually, and beyond what agreements prescribe internationally. It incorporates standards of behaviour that may be expected, but are not required, under society's legal status. Thus, social responsibility requires that TNCs go beyond the law instead of taking advantage of loopholes in the regulations, and governance failures of the law-making or enforcing institutions in the country. This can be taken as an expected voluntary 'and yet compulsory' contribution (or repayment) by the TNCs to any social-economic disruptions that could threaten the privatisation, deregulation and liberalisation frameworks, which countries may have undertaken for the sake of luring TNCs into their economies. Corporate social responsibility that extends beyond legal mandates can help meet societal expectations in the absence of statutory devices. Such conduct may be particularly important to meeting societal needs in host developing countries where legal regimes may be absent or underdeveloped in areas related to certain TNC conduct. However, there are occasions when the requirements of civil activists may conflict with those of the host country. In this case, actions by TNCs, whether on their own initiative or as a response to pressure from civil society groups, can be viewed by the host country as unwelcome and unjustified external interference in its internal affairs (UNCTAD, 1999).

UNCTAD (1999) points out that TNCs have become more capable, proximate and aware actors whose activities can create causal links to societal outcomes in multiple countries and cultures. Thus, TNCs can be called upon to use their expanded capabilities to prevent or to rectify offensive conditions even in countries in which a firm has played no causal role in their creation.

Because of its voluntary nature, the scope of corporate responsibility is currently conceptually unbound. The current key issues relate to human rights, the environment and workers' rights. Thus, companies are socially responsible for both the direct and indirect negative effects imparted upon the respective stakeholders through their operations. The negative effects can take on any form including employment downscaling, environmental pollution, technology transfer, local labour-force training, promotion of local entrepreneurship and creation of linkages. Thus, negatively affected groups are expected to ask or make protests to companies causing these impacts to take measures to prevent, reduce or rectify such consequences, or otherwise to internalise costs resulting from their activities (UNCTAD, 1999).

Civil society groups have increased their focus on devising monitoring and public reporting programmes that can add enforcement aspects to the implementation of voluntary social responsibility codes. The advantage of the voluntary *vis-à-vis* legally binding codes is that the former are sometimes more efficient and cost-effective to address technically complex and rapidly changing business operations. Otherwise, negotiating new international legal regulations can be a cumbersome, time-consuming process that can yield results that may be already overtaken by technological or managerial change the day an instrument enters into force (UNCTAD, 1999).

As UNCTAD (1999) has rightly observed, unfortunately for developing countries, many issues often go unnoticed by the wider public and are not taken up by TNCs as long as they are not associated with sufficiently influential public pressure. This problem is amplified by the fact that most, if not all, corporate social responsibility deliberations are undertaken by the parent firms mostly based in developed countries. In addition, in terms of influence and recognition, developed country civil society groups excel most particularly because of the democratic rights they enjoy in their home countries. Moreover, differences in development and cultures imply a divergence between the requirements and interest of societies in the developed countries *vis-à-vis* those in the developing countries. Unsurprisingly then, issues of great concern to developing countries are not addressed when TNCs and civil society in the developed countries engage in debates over corporate social responsibility. The good news is that, on a few, but now increasing number of occasions, civil society activists in the TNCs' home countries have mounted pressure on grounds related to the firm's operations in other countries, including developing countries. Furthermore, developing country organisations that represent various elements of civil society are growing both in number and capabilities, and are expanding their ties with similar organisations in other countries

(UNCTAD, 1999). Nonetheless, a lot more pressure needs to be imparted on TNCs if any significant results are to be accrued from this approach.

Empirical Review

Environmental protection Most of the debate on environmental issues has been rhetorical rather than empirical. Recently, some researchers (Whalley, 1991; Perroni and Wigle, 1994; Grossman and Krueger, 1992; and Lee and Roland-Holst, 1997) pioneered investigations of the linkages between trade, growth and the environment. Their essays indicate that the available evidence does not substantiate the fears of extensive environmental degradation brought about by free trade. The link between trade and pollution appears to arise primarily from the expansion of aggregate output rather than new patterns of international specialisation.

However, Lee and Roland-Holst (1997) found an implicit domestic pollution abatement in trade between Japan and Indonesia. Japan imports goods that are pollution-intensive in their production phase from Indonesia. Moreover, it appears that Indonesia specialises in production activities that release substantial effluents, and implicitly export pollution services to the rest of the world, especially the industrialised countries (Beghin et al, 1998). Could Indonesia's industry have attracted foreign investment that was lured by lax pollution regulations? Beghin et al's (1998) study on Mexico found that trade expansion alone occasions significant environmental damage in only a few sectors such as energy. They also found no evidence to suggest that Mexico would specialise in dirty industrial activities. They argued that labour-intensive specialisation under free trade translates into less pollution-intensive aggregate output. Moreover, increasing outward orientation by Mexico induces a combination of contraction and expansion of pollution activities whose aggregate net is almost neutral to the environment in terms of the average pollution intensity of GDP.

Empirical investigations on the environmental impact of FDI still remain inconclusive. The 'pollution haven' hypothesis (i.e. shift of investment to lax pollution regulation locations) has been tested by correlating FDI outflows with environmental standards. The results (Repetto, 1998; Eskeland and Horrison, 1997; and Warhurst and Bridge 1997) found no econometric support that TNCs direct their investments to countries with lax pollution standards. However, a qualitative study, examining specific company decisions has found support for this hypothesis in Costa Rica, Mexico, India, Indonesia, Papua New Guinea and the Philippines (WWF, 1998 and 1999a). Warhurst's (1999) study on Australia, Bolivia, Brazil, Chile, Papua New Guinea, Peru, Russia, South Africa and the US found that clean-technology suppliers did not export old, obsolete, polluting technology to developing countries. Instead, they worked intensively to train the recipients to manage and monitor their newly acquired technologies and environmental management systems. Moreover, as an incentive to optimise this learning process, suppliers allowed recipients to keep the benefits accruing from modifications and harness the enhancement capacities for comparative advantage. A study of the Chilean pulp and paper industry by Herbert-Copley (1998) revealed that foreign owned and joint venture firms were more likely to have formal environmental policy, and to have designated a specific individual to take responsibility for environmental matters at plant level. In addition, they were also more likely to have pursued international certification. This is an indication of more active pursuit of incremental improvements in environmental performance in foreign affiliates relative to domestic firms. TNCs have assisted their suppliers in the form of technical workshops, training courses and International Organisation for Standardisation 14000 certification. Intel, for example, insists that its suppliers conform to its rigorous in-house environmental standards. Hewlett-Packard also has a product stewardship programme that embraces the design, manufacture, distribution, use, take-back, disassembly, reuse, recycling and ultimate disposal of constituent parts and materials of all its affiliates and suppliers (UNCTAD, 1999). However, the global involvement of TNCs in deepening the spillovers in environmental-friendly technologies sill remains to be seen.

TNCs affiliates' environmental-friendly policies differ between countries, affiliates, and industry. In general, affiliates in host developing countries still lag behind their parent countries. For instance, Shell's environmental policy in Nigeria is environment-unfriendly. Although some local communities have attempted to put some pressure on Shell, the situation has been worsened by the Nigerian government's negative attitude. Therefore, unless host developing countries take the initiative and support local communities and NGOs by instituting policies that can pressurise TNCs' affiliates into taking responsibility for environmental protection, the environmental spillovers will remain theoretical.

In sum, the main environmental opportunities associated with FDI arise from the fact that FDI promotes higher incomes, which could lead to higher levels of investment in pollution prevention and control facilities. There is also the possibility of tapping into the better technologies, information, management systems, and training programs that foreign investors often have at their disposal. Finally, FDI offers the potential to link the economic fates of the developing and developed countries on those environmental issues likely to affect both groups. The main environmental risks associated with FDI would on the other hand arise from two areas. First, higher incomes associated with FDI-induced growth may not 'pull' environmental quality along with it fast enough, implying reduced environmental quality in certain countries, for certain pollutants, over potentially long time periods. Even where the link between higher incomes and improved environmental quality is a positive one, this link may not turn out to be strong enough to prevent absolute degradations in environmental quality from occurring. Second, there is the possibility that competitive pressures may tempt some companies or countries to engage in a 'race to the bottom' in environmental standards. There will certainly be individual companies and sectors that will be 'losers' in the economic restructuring likely to accompany expanded FDI flows. Firms whose economic position seems to have worsened may well blame FDI for this, and seek political intervention to protect the *status quo*. They may also cite lower environmental standards in host countries as one reason that their enterprises have become non-competitive. Nevertheless, the fears of the 'race to the bottom' in environmental standards, based on the idea of 'pollution havens', may be generally unfounded. On the other hand, this conclusion may not hold in specific cases, especially where the firms involved produce undifferentiated products (and where small cost differences make a significant difference to their profitability), or where the countries involved are under-capitalised and fast-growing. There has been vigorous debate about the 'race to the bottom' in environmental standards resulting from competition between countries, and also among regions within a country, to attract FDI. The so-called pollution haven hypothesis implies that competitive forces would push FDI away from countries with high environmental standards, or pull it towards those with low standards. Conversely, the notion of pollution halos suggests that FDI might promote the establishment of higher environmental standards through technology transfer effects or via existing management practices within multinational or other firms. Overall, there does not appear to be evidence corroborating the pollution haven hypothesis. On the other hand, there are some studies that are consistent with the pollution haven hypothesis (Ribeiro, 2000).

Social responsibility The number, range, co-ordination and activism among civil society groups on issues relating to TNCs' social responsibility has been expanding in the recent past. UNCTAD (1999) has observed that although some groups organise around very specific products (e.g. tobacco and nuclear energy), most activism focuses on a relatively small set of major issue themes. These are then exemplified and addressed in terms of specific products, companies or events. Some of the most vigilant groups are Greenpeace, which is primarily concerned with environmental issues, Amnesty International and Human Rights Watch whose prime interests relate to human rights, and individual country Labour Unions, which focus on workers' rights. The International Labour Organisation also in a way plays the role of civil vigilantism.

Examples of the campaigns by civil group include the criticism of the shoe giants, Nike and Reebok against abusive working conditions in foreign plants most particularly in Asia, which produce for them under subcontracting arrangements. Likewise, England's football club, Manchester United has received similar calls regarding the production of its football kits. In addition, following social responsibility concerns surrounding the marketing of breast-milk substitutes (infant formula), a code was developed by the WHO and implemented by pharmaceutical associations. There are often times when the objectives of the civil society groups are to interfere with the internal activities of particular government regimes. A best example for this is the case of the former apartheid regime in South Africa. However, it is evident that the success of civil groups is highly influenced by the degree of vigilantism, the level of host country involvement and probably the importance of the host country in the international economic relationships. The case for Rover presents a good example. During early 2000, BMW the then owners of the Rover car brand decided to get rid of it because of its market unattractiveness. Venture capitalists, Alchemy were BMW's favourite buyers. However, Alchemy's strategy was to whittle down Rover to a small specialist sports car producer, with loss of many thousands of jobs. The other options included either selling Rover to the Birmingham based Phoenix consortium which would retain most of the workforce, or closing down the main plant in Longbridge and of course render all the workforce redundant. Eventually, a deal was made with the Phoenix consortium, but only after significant pressure from the government, the labour unions, the workers and the local communities in Birmingham. If Britain had not been a developed country, there is a real possibility that BMW would not have honoured its social responsibility.

In America there is now a veritable ethics industry, complete with consultancies, conferences, journals and 'corporate conscience' awards. Accountancy firms such as PricewaterhouseCoopers offer to 'audit' the ethical performance of companies. Corporate-ethics officers, who barely existed a decade ago, have become *de rigueur*, at least for big companies. The Ethics Officer Association, which began with a dozen members in 1992, has over 650 today. As many as one in five big firms has a full-time office devoted to the subject.

Outside America, few companies have an ethics bureaucracy. In Germany, for example, workers' councils often deal with issues such as sexual equality, race relations and workers' rights, all of which might be seen as ethical issues in America.

In developing a formal ethics policy, companies usually begin by trying to sum up their philosophy in a code. Not surprisingly, codes are often too broad to capture the ethical issues that actually confront companies, which range from handling their own staff to big global questions of policy on the environment, bribery and human rights. Some companies use the internet to try to add precision to general injunctions. Boeing, for instance, tries to guide staff through the whole gamut of moral quandaries, offering an online quiz (with answers) on how to deal with everything from staff who fiddle their expenses on business trips to suppliers who ask for kickbacks.

The ethical issues that actually create most problems in companies often seem rather mundane to outsiders. An example is when a company has to decide whether to sack an employee who is productive but naughty or, when the boss lies to you subordinates. Issues such as trust and human relations become harder to handle as companies intrude into the lives of their employees. A company with thousands of employees in Southeast Asia has been firing employees who have AIDS, but giving them no explanation. It now wonders whether this is ethical. Several companies scan their employees' e-mail for unpleasant or disloyal material, or test them to see if they have been taking drugs. Is that right? Even more complicated are issues driven by conflicts of interest. For instance, if a company is spinning off a booming e-commerce division, which employees should be allowed on to the lucrative 'friends-and-family' list of share buyers?

Indeed, the revolution in communications technologies has created all sorts of new ethical dilemmas, just as technological change in medicine spurred interest in medical ethics in the 1970s. Because it is mainly businesses that develop and spread new technologies, businesses also tend to face the first questions about how to use them. So companies stumble into such questions as data protection and customer privacy. They know more than ever before about their customers' tastes, but few have a clear view on what uses of that knowledge are unethical.

Some of the most publicised debates about corporate ethics have been driven by globalisation. When companies operate abroad, they run up against all sorts of new moral issues. And one big problem is that ethical standards differ among countries.

Many companies first confronted the moral dilemmas of globalisation when they had to decide whether to meet only local environmental standards, even if these were lower than ones back home. This debate came to public attention with the Bhopal disaster in 1984, when an explosion at a Union Carbide plant in India killed at least 8,000 people. Most large multinationals now have global minimum standards for health, safety and the environment.

BP Amoco thinks it better to stay in the venture and try to raise standards. But Shell claims to have withdrawn from one joint venture because it was dissatisfied with its partner's approach. Most companies rarely talk about these cases, creating the suspicion that such withdrawals are rare.

Bribery and corruption have also been thorny issues. American companies have been bound since 1977 by the Foreign Corrupt Practices Act. Now all OECD countries have agreed to a convention to end bribery. But many companies turn a blind eye when intermediaries make such payments. Only a few, such as Motorola, have accounting systems that try to spot kickbacks by noting differences between what the customer pays and what a vendor receives.

Human rights are a newer and trickier problem. Shell has written a primer on the subject, in consultation with Amnesty International. It agonises over such issues as what companies should do if they have a large investment in a country where human rights deteriorate; and whether companies should operate in countries that forbid outsiders to scrutinise their record on human rights. The answer is 'yes, but only if the company takes no advantage of such secrecy and is a 'force for good'.

Stung by attacks on their behaviour in the past, companies such as Shell and Nike have begun to see it as part of their corporate mission to raise standards not just within their company, but in the countries where they work. Nike would like its factories to be places where workers' health actually improves, through better education and care, and where the status of women is raised. Such ideals would have sounded familiar to some businessmen of the nineteenth century. Quaker companies such as Cadbury and Rowntree, for instance, were founded on the principle that a company should improve its workers' health and education. In today's more cynical and competitive world, though, corporate virtue no longer seems a goal in its own right.

When, in the late 1980s, companies devoted lots of effort to worrying about the environment, they told themselves that being clean and green was also a route to being profitable. In the same way, they now hope that virtue will bring financial, as well as spiritual, rewards. Environmental controls can, for instance, often be installed more cheaply than companies expect.

There may still be two good reasons for companies to worry about their ethical reputation. One is anticipation: bad behaviour, once it stirs up a public fuss, may provoke legislation that companies will find more irksome than self-restraint. The other, more crucial, is trust. A company that is not trusted by its employees, partners and customers will suffer. In an electronic world, where businesses are geographically far from their customers, a reputation for trust may become even more important. Ultimately, though, companies may have to accept that virtue is sometimes its own reward. One of the eternal truths of morality has been that the bad do not always do badly and the good do not always do well.

Since social responsibility is still largely voluntary, many individual companies adopt their own codes of conduct that address these issues, sometimes drawing on an industry code or a set of international business principals. Alternatively, companies in the same industry get together and draw an industry code along the same principals. No doubt, these codes are often reactive, sparked by instances in perceived misconduct by a firm or others in the industry. The firms often take action so as to minimise the risk of potential consumer boycotts or other commercial sanctions, damage to its product brand and negative talk about company.

Linkages

The foregoing literature illustrates that although FDI spillovers may impact directly on the economic growth of host developing countries, their indirect effect via linkages should not be underestimated. The spillovers via forward and backward linkages can only be significant and successful insofar as the conditions in the host country are favourable for the formation of these linkages. Some countries have provided such a conducive environment. For example, a case study of FDI in Singapore concluded that foreign firms had successfully stimulated local suppliers to become effective exporters. In addition, a substantial number of spin-offs had been generated as employees of TNCs became successful entrepreneurs, and often became suppliers to their former employers (Lim and Pang, 1991). Likewise, a survey of 63 large foreign affiliates operating in Mexico revealed that almost two thirds of the foreign affiliates sub-contracted locally, and of those firms nearly one third sub-contracted more than 25 per cent of their total product value (UN, 1992).

Empirical literature on linkages has been confined to backward linkages. Some of these linkages are a result of government policy, which requires firms to buy certain proportions of input from local sources (local content) particularly under the protective import-substitution policy. In spite of this, studies by Mason (1967), Thoburn (1973), UNCTAD (1975), Vaitos (1976), Daftary and Borghey (1976), and Jo (1976) have revealed that TNCs buy relatively few inputs within the less-industrialised host countries due to technological backwardness, small-scale, high-cost, poor quality, or unreliability. However, they may be forced or persuaded to increase local content by the more advanced countries (Mansfield, 1994). This may be mainly due to the fact that apart from mineral/extractive investment, most of the TNC linked production in the developing countries is mostly that of assembly type, which requires the use of unskilled labour. The training linkage, however, demands the availability of suppliers of inputs such as components and parts, which require the use of skilled labour for the vertical production process. There are, however, more opportunities for creation of linkages for export-oriented TNCs especially through sub-contracting. More efficiency, beneficial to host countries, is associated with such firms since they require producing goods capable of competing in the world markets. It is under these circumstances that technical assistance is rendered by the TNCs. Unilever has, for example, instructed firms in developing countries on the manufacture of high-quality chemicals, and pharmaceutical companies have helped firms in developing countries with the fabrication of dosage forms (ILO, 1994). The best example of forward linkage is in the computer industry where IBM has transferred a considerable amount of important technology by training potential users, providing software, and servicing computer installations in various countries (Mansfield, 1994).

Local procurement has been on the increase in the Republic of Korea and Taipei, China. Local procurement, however, tends to be affected by several factors. Statistics show that between 1981 and 1988, local procurement by Japanese affiliates in Asia decreased in all the other manufacturing sectors apart from wood and pulp, and chemicals, but increased in Latin America in all manufacturing sectors except transport equipment (Lim and Pang, 1991). This suggests a locational advantage inducing a local procurement shift from Asia to Latin America. In other countries such as Indonesia and Malaysia, however, local procurement has been a result of government pressure for TNCs to increase local content. This has not strengthened the technical, managerial and financial linkages of TNCs with their subcontractors. Export processing zones have also proved to be barriers, as TNCs must cross borders in order to source locally. Moreover, they may prefer to source in neighbouring countries due to the absence of a strong entrepreneurship class. Lim and Pang (1991) have attributed the low level of linkages in the more developed, developing economies of East Asia to the regional development. The regional integration of the electronics industry in East and Southeast Asia for example, means that plants in the new locations of ASEAN already have established suppliers (including affiliates) in the neighbouring countries of Singapore, Malaysia and Hong Kong where higher skills are available. Moreover, since export-oriented firms have to be internationally competitive, this means that inputs of the right quality must be available at world prices. The less developed countries may not have the potential to produce high quality components and parts given the comparatively less skilled human resources and less experienced manufactures they have, especially in the high-tech industry.

This evidence suggests that if FDI spillovers are to be derived from linkages, then the process of linkage should be allowed to develop naturally without any serious host government interference. However, government may intervene through deepening the resource base. The final impact may vary over time and depends to a great extent on the modalities of an FDI project, the sector of the investment and the conditions of the home and host countries.

Observations and Conclusion

The evidence from the forgoing review highlights the role of the spillover effects of FDI. Thus, it justifies the presumption that FDI is playing an increasingly important role in the economic growth of host developing countries, through its contribution in human resources development, technological transfer, capital formation, international trade and environmental protection, although this mostly comes about as a spillover rather than a direct effect. The review demonstrates that the factors through which the spillover effects of FDI act to bring about economic growth are inter-linked, complementary and cannot possibly be discussed separately. The interaction is such that gains in one factor may stimulate improvement in one or more of the others, thus magnifying the stimulus or forming a *synergy*. For example, the growth of exports can serve as an important source of employment creation when they stimulate domestic production in a multiplied way. This leads to acquisition of skills through learning-by-doing. International trade can accelerate human capital accumulation by expanding and diversifying the production frontier. The export of manufactured goods, and import of capital machinery/equipment and intermediate goods result from the acquisition and hence, transfer of relatively widespread technologies. The transfer of technology is, however, only made possible through the diffusion of knowledge via training and on-the-job progressive learning. Introduction of new technology also leads to production of new products and hence rapid learning-by-doing, leading to cumulative experience which increases the marginal contribution to cost reduction of an additional unit of output. Physical investment in equipment and machinery may lead to the acceleration of growth through the creation of technical and managerial skills, and access to new technology, which in turn is made possible by the fact that these people are actually employed by the TNCs. Moreover, human skills and imports (which form part of international trade) are a form of technology in their individual capacities.

FDI is becoming important in relation to world-wide investment, output, trade, technology and capital flows, and TNCs are playing an *increasingly* important role in the economic growth of developing countries. Although most developing countries now consider FDI as an important resource for development, its economic effects are almost impossible to either predict or measure with precision. The impact of FDI and TNCs on a country depends on many factors. They include the role of the TNC in the economy, the sector in which FDI is undertaken, the type of investment, the links of the foreign affiliates with the host economy and the conditions in the host country (UNCTAD, 1995). These effects vary from country to country, by industry, even by company and over periods of time. This is because government policy tends to have a strong influence on FDI. For instance, the effects of FDI in import-substituting industries may differ from those of export-oriented industries since the former targets mostly the limited domestic market, while the latter targets the larger international market. The latter is more likely to generate more employment and, therefore, spillovers due to the expected larger production capacity associated with the larger market. In addition, it is difficult to separate and quantify the TNCs' package of attributes since they are complex and vary from one host country to another. For obvious reasons, a scientific quantification assessment does not appeal to economic analysis. Consequently, the development effects of FDI end-up being assessed by one of the two general approaches, quantitative and qualitative analyses.

It emerges that FDI also has its negative effects, which may reduce the rate of economic growth of a given host developing economy. It is these negative effects that are weighed against the positive effects to produce a *net* effect. FDI therefore, *ceteris paribus*, imparts a *net* positive impact on the factors that determine the growth process of a host developing country insofar as it influences the quality and quantity of new capital formation, the transfer of hard and soft technology, the development of human resources, the expansion of trade opportunities and the protection of the environment. It need not be emphasised that these *net* benefits if any, do not directly arise from the mere presence of FDI in the economy because the foreign subsidiaries are efficient, but arise from the spillovers that can occur when TNCs cannot capture all quasi-rents due to their productive assets. However, the net effect can highly be influenced by government policy. Thus, to promote FDI related development of their own countries, governments need to institute policies that are capable of maximising the positive contribution that FDI can make to development, and minimising any negative effects it may generate. A summary of the positive spillover effects is presented in Table 5.1.

It has become increasingly recognised that there are many different paths to economic growth. Thus, FDI is by no means the only mode of achieving economic growth. Instead, it is one of the options that may complement the economic growth process if skilfully planned and implemented. Japan for instance, prohibited FDI and relied solely on organic growth and its story is a success miracle. Similarly, the Republic of Korea's initial development had a low reliance on FDI. Domestic firms can also be exposed to international management and technical standards and know-how through foreign trade in the absence of FDI. For instance, exporting firms can learn new ideas about marketing, design and technology from interacting with buyers in the world market. This knowledge later spills over to the other domestic firms, while technological diffusion is achieved through imitation of imports. This is how Western Europe, the US, Canada, Australia, and New Zealand managed to derive their economic growths from international trade during the nineteenth century and the first half of the twentieth century. The transfer can also be effected through licensing agreements with foreigners covering patents, trade-marks, franchising, and technical assistance. Countries can also achieve economic growth through the investment of foreign capital in the form of commercial loans and aid, and the possession and exploration of natural resources, i.e. precious metals and minerals. However, for the developing countries, FDI is a potential current channel through which they can stimulate their economic growth rates. It is worthwhile noting that the role of FDI in countries' processes and efforts to meet development objectives can differ greatly across countries, depending particularly on the nature of the country and its government policy. For example, Malaysia, Singapore and Thailand planned to rely substantially on FDI, integrating the economy into TNC production networks and promoting competitiveness by upgrading within these networks. However, Hong Kong's policy was to leave resource allocation largely to market forces, while providing infrastructure and governance (UNCTAD, 1999).

Although low-cost labour remains a source of competitive advantage particularly for developing countries, its importance is diminishing. Likewise, the importance of natural resources is diminishing as their substitutes are developed. Instead, TNCs are increasingly seeking world-class infrastructure, skilled and productive labour, innovatory capacities and an agglomeration of efficient suppliers, competitors, support institutions and services. In addition, large domestic markets remain a powerful magnet for investors. In fact, low-cost labour does not provide a base for sustainable development since rising incomes erode the comparative edge it provides. Thus, low-cost labour is only a beginning point for luring FDI and consequently generating static economic benefits. Therefore, developing countries can attain sustained economic growth, through the exploitation of TNCs' dynamic competitive advantages. Consequently, they have to set-up a resource base that can facilitate their progressive shifts up the levels of technological complexity. This involves instituting plans for deepening the content of export activity and building the human capital and macroeconomic capacity to sustain such a shift across a range of tradable activities in response to changing world demand

Table 5.1   A summary of some of the positive spillover effects of FDI activities on host developing countries

Activity	Positive Spillover Effects
Human Resources Development	
Education and Training	* Raises productivity by increasing
* Vocational and in-plant training	capability to accept and adopt new technology and knowledge
* Training rendered to personnel in linkage activities	* Increases productivity and average level of skills of country
* Training by staff in government institutions	* Facilitates diffusion of technology
* Awarding scholarships	* Facilitates the transfer of foreign management methods and worker
* Financial contributions to education institutions	discipline
* Consultancy services	* Promotes entrepreneurship
* Promoting basic education skills - literacy promotion - instructions in reading, writing and arithmetic	
Health and Nutrition	* Raises productivity by increasing
* Investment in health and nutrition activities	mental and physical productivity and absorption capacity for new knowledge
Employment	
* Employment of former unemployed and underemployed	* Increases personal income
* Indirect employment creation in other organisations	* Generates skills in the process of learning-by-doing
* Localisation of technical and managerial staff	* Facilitates the diffusion of technology through the process of learning-by-doing
* Changes in employment policies and practices in other organisations	* Creates wage equality for members
	* Allows greater access to employment for discriminated groups, i.e. women and ethnic minority groups

Table 5.1 cont.

Activity	Positive Spillover Effects
New Technology Transfer * Transfer of most recent technology to affiliates * Importation of new capital goods and equipment * Introduction of R&D in overseas subsidiaries * Selling or licensing old technology * Technical assistance rendered to suppliers and consumers in linkage activities	* Improves efficiency of labour-intensive processes *Transfers technology to host country * Improves product quality and range; and production process and hence factor productivity by lowering unit costs * Changes composition of exports in favour of research intensive products by introducing new high tech, high value added products * Provides an incentive for new investment by acting as a dynamic factor of comparative advantage * Induces competition, encouraging local firms to increase R&D and therefore innovation

Capital Formation
* Investing - Retained earnings
        - Inter-company loans
        - Equity
* Payment of taxes, contractual fees, etc.
* Tax payment by employees
* Indirect contribution through linkage activities
  - Tax payment by suppliers
	* Increases quality and quantity of host country's stock of physical capital
	* Increases ratio of investment/GDP
	* Increases competition and therefore efficiency of investment
	* Reduces host country's foreign exchange strain
	* Increases domestic savings from employees through institution of pension funds, direct deposits into savings account, and payroll deduction for purchasing insurance
	* Stimulates local investment by buying locally

Table 5.1 cont.

Activity	Positive Spillover Effects

International Trade
* Involvement in international trade
  - Imports of parts and components from investing countries
  - Exports of finished products to investing countries and third-country market
* Provision of marketing, distribution, product design, quality standards, packaging, presentation, brand name use, etc., services
	* Increases international trade by providing opportunities to expand and improve production of goods and services
	* Increases demand for host country's products
	* Eases supply constraints of host country
	*Improves balance of payments
	* Increases competition and hence promotes innovation and product quality
	* Facilitates the process of transfer of technology
	* Exposes exporting firms to international techniques in marketing, processing and other information

Environmental Protection * Research in clean technologies * Introduction of modern environmental management systems * Adoption of high environmental standards	* Exposes domestic firms to new technologies and modern environmental management systems
Social Responsibility * Adoption of beyond the law responsibility	* Meets societal needs related to certain TNCs' conduct * Addresses technically complex and rapidly changing business operations

and technologies. This is made more challenging by the current unprecedented and accelerating pace of technological change, whose developments they have to keep pace with. The policy issues that may lead to this achievement are considered in Chapter 7.

6 Regional Integration, FDI and Economic Growth: pro-globalisation views

Introduction

Co-operation between nations in its simplest form of bilateral agreements dates back to when States started trading with each other. With time, different types of co-operation began to emerge as the States and the global environment became more complex and more organised. International co-operation among nations is mainly dictated by economic, historical, political, social, cultural, religious, and geographic factors. The Organisation for Economic Co-operation and Development (OECD), the G-8, and the Organisation of Petroleum Exporting Countries (OPEC) are basic examples of economic oriented co-operations. The Commonwealth and the Francophone states give an example of co-operations linked by historical and political factors. The Nordic Councils and Anglo links are examples of co-operation based on social/cultural lines, while the Islamic States form one group based on religious lines.

In the post-World War II period, the developed countries came to realise that the task of economic reconstruction and expansion could be achieved more smoothly through co-operation among governments. One channel was to form an economic integration through market agreements among nations in geographical proximity to each other. In addition, although it was not precisely understood at the time, regional economic integration can generate economic advantages capable of acting as strong determinants of FDI.

Therefore, the American program of European aid under the 'Marshall Plan' served to stimulate discussion and study of the possibility of a customs union in Western Europe. One of the conditions on which American aid was being granted was that the beneficiary countries pursue economic recovery through self-help on a collaborative basis. The US government therefore encouraged political as well as economic unification of Western Europe, in part or in whole. As part of this program, a customs union, small or large, partial or complete was given a steady encouragement. Of course, as the tensions with the Soviet Union and the Eastern Bloc grew, America also saw a policy of trade co-operation between Western European countries and others as part of an international strategy for the containment of Communism. The Marshall Plan and American requirements for the internal liberalisation of Western Europe were all part of this strategy. In the presentation of their case for the receipt of American aid, the participating European countries bound themselves collectively to abolish as soon as possible the abnormal restrictions, which at the time hampered their mutual trade. They also directed their efforts towards a sound and balanced multilateral trading system based on the principles, which had guided the farmers of the Draft Charter for an International Trade Organisation (ITO).

The past decades have, therefore, seen a surge in regional trade arrangements involving developed countries formed along these lines. This has increased developing countries' interest in similar arrangements based on the expectations of benefits such as economies of scale that may result from market size, market growth and tariff-discrimination, which act as additional incentives to lure FDI into the region thus accelerating industrialisation and economic growth. A brief background to the development of, membership of, and objectives for the formation of the respective regional economic blocs is presented in the Appendix.

The customs union (used in this chapter in a general context, to stand for the different regional economic integration schemes) theory has attracted controversy since Viner presented it, with some authors offering support and others criticism. These theoretically focused arguments are, however, beyond the scope of this book. Instead, the objective of this chapter is to explore the link between the customs union theory and the theory of international production, which has either direct or indirect implications for the ongoing globalisation process. For instance, it seeks to establish whether a customs union generates any specific effects that can then act as determinants of FDI, and if so, under what circumstances it can do so. That is, it explores how a customs union affects the locational advantages of the economic bloc, and how it can influence firms' investment decisions based upon their firm specific and internalisation advantages. In addition, it addresses the issues regarding in the event of a customs union generating effects that attract FDI, what effects FDI would in turn impart on a customs union.

The chapter is divided into three sections. The first section establishes the theoretical link between the two theories in the developed and developing economic blocs, while the second section contains a comparative review of empirical findings. Observations and concluding remarks are presented in the third section.

A Theoretical Review

Overview

The link between regionalism and FDI is a fairly new phenomenon. Even if FDI started in the early 1960s, its impact only began to be felt in the 1970s when the term MNE or TNC became a household word in political, social and economic circles (Van den Bulcke, 1993). The dynamic effects of regionalism improve the competitive advantages of firms located within the customs union. For example, trade liberalisation lowers trade costs and improves the competitiveness of home country firms. This then prompts higher rates of capacity utilisation in the export sector and stimulates further investment. By expanding market size and creating opportunities for scale economies, high levels of innovation activity can be stimulated by allowing firms to sustain larger R&D expenditures. Increased innovative activity provides the route for the accumulation of ownership advantages that firms could not have obtained if they had continued to operate within the limited domestic (national) markets (Kindleberger, 1993). However, firms from outside the customs union can strategically plan and also exploit these advantages.

Regionalised FDI is, therefore, a strategic response of firms coping with changes in relative competitiveness, locational advantages and organisational forms brought about through the realignment of tariffs, increase in market size and market growth after the formation of a customs union. The removal of tariff barriers in a customs union (both internal and external), creates the confidence that these barriers will not be re-erected in the future. This increased certainty of access to foreign markets stimulates both international trade and investment. Investment does not only increase due to reduced uncertainty, increasing savings and possible inflow of foreign capital, but also gets allocated in a more efficient way through what is now famously known as *the international division of labour*. The combined activities of the domestic and foreign firms eventually stimulate the economic growth of the customs union.

Regionalism is, therefore, supposed to lead to three major integration effects namely, *tariff-discrimination, market size* and *market growth* which, in their individual and collective capacities have implications for the theory of international production.

Regionalism as a Determinant of FDI Inflows

Types of investment responses The earlier theory of international trade assumes that trade and investment are substitutes. More recent studies have, however, identified a weak theoretical inter-link between the theory of international economic integration and the theory of international production. The actual link is rather complex and varies with the form of integration attempted. For instance, Yannopoulos (1990) who argued that trade and investment are not necessarily substitutes, developed this link by examining how various effects on costs, competitiveness, market size and market growth stemming from the realignment of tariffs within customs unions affects the determinants of FDI that have been identified by the theory of international production. He suggested that the combined result of the static and dynamic effects of regionalism enhances the locational advantages of production based inside a trading bloc. Consequently, by generating these advantages, the formation of a customs union affects the firm's choice of strategy in servicing foreign markets. The dynamic effects of regionalism improve the ownership advantages of firms located inside the customs union through market expansion and creation of opportunities for scale economies, which they could not have attained if they had continued to operate within the boundaries of fragmented, smaller markets. Such a tendency stimulates investment within the customs union.

Each of the static and dynamic effects of regionalism can be linked with the likely strategic responses of firms engaged in international production. For instance, Kindleberger (1966) suggested that FDI is a strategic response of TNCs to the *investment-creation* and *investment-diversion* phenomenon, which are in direct relation to the static trade-creation and trade-diversion effects without their welfare implications. Investment-creation (the surge of inward FDI from non-member countries) is a strategic response by firms to trade-diversion. Investment-diversion (reorganisation of production within the union, i.e. shifting investment from one member state to another) is on the other hand a strategic response to trade-creation (Yannopoulos, 1990).

There are four types of investment responses. These are, defensive import-substituting, reorganisational, offensive import-substituting and rationalisation investments. Each of them may respond to movements in economic integration via the effects of such integration on the locational and organisational decisions of firms.

Defensive import-substituting investment (*tariff-jumping* investment) is a response to the trade-diversion effects of regionalism resulting from locational advantages generated by the tariff realignment process and represents a firm's response to maintaining its market share (UNTCMD, 1993). These 'tariff-jumping' investments are often based on product differentiation and tend to be substitutes for trade. This concept has been investigated by Molle (1990) who has argued that if host country H operates trade impediments, firms from partner country P that want to export to country H need a comparative advantage superior to the level of the tariff equivalent of country H's trade barrier. Such an advantage may be based on firm-specific intangible assets. Exporting firms of country P who judge their advantage real but inferior to the tariff, and firms of country P unwilling to have their profit margin taxed away by the tariff will consider setting up production in country H. This necessitates a direct investment by firms from country P in country H, and facilitates the ability of firms from country P to serve markets in country H. Heitger and Stehn (1990) have also observed that the system of efficient protection is one of the most important factors explaining the increases in investment within customs unions. Trading partners within the customs union are forced to protect domestic producers by various tariff and non-tariff barriers when exports from outside the customs union boom. These tariffs eventually reach a critical level, at which it becomes increasingly favourable for foreign firms to substitute FDI for exports. With the formation of a customs union, special interest groups could still seek additional external trade barriers and if successful, would lead to additional external FDI by third country firms. For instance, local firms losing comparative advantages may increase political and economic pressure by asking for additional protection, which eventually leads to an increased external protection and a shift in location-specific advantages. Regionalism, therefore, results in a reduction of internal tariff and non-tariff barriers, and the supply of, as well as the demand for protection shifts to an increase of external trade barriers. This leads to further incentives for other third-country firms to change their strategy of internationalisation towards the establishment of subsidiaries within the customs union. These incentives are stronger the more successful the customs union is in liberalising trade.

Reorganisational investment (*optimum location seeking* investment) results from the pressures generated by trade-creation effects, which encourage reallocation in accordance with member states' comparative advantages (UNTCMD, 1993). Thus, it relates to the regrouping of production facilities in fewer locations where more favourable costs are found. Firms following a strategy of growing through product specialisation may opt for operations in several markets, wanting to export to foreign markets from their current base. However, this may not always prove the optimum solution, as production in other areas may be less costly. Within the customs union area, a location is chosen for each plant that is optimum in view of the prevailing market costs and taxes. These 'optimum location seeking' investments often take advantage of the international division of labour and are facilitated by a larger integrated market.

Offensive import-substitution investment (*market seeking* investment) is a result of growth enhancing and market augmenting effects of regionalism that looks at investment whose motivation is to take advantage of growing demand and the opening up of new markets. The dynamic effects of regionalism lead to the expansion of the barrier-free market within which the firm operates. It is this increased market and growth potential that often act as determinants for this type of investment. A firm's response to this kind of investment depends on whether or not it was operating in the market prior to the integration process. If it was operating in the market, then it tries to increase its market share by pursuing vigorous FDI and marketing activities. However, if it was not operating in the market, then it pursues a deliberate FDI strategy of getting into the market as a new entrant.

Rationalisation investment (*efficiency seeking* investment) results from improvement in the costs of production through enhanced efficiency (Yannopoulos, 1990). These efficiency gains are more often static (resulting from mass production) than dynamic (resulting from new innovative technology). Cantwell (1987) identified a shift away from the import-substitution types of FDI towards rationalised investments, which cannot be treated individually but are part of a globally integrated network of affiliates, and suggested that the two can coexist in most sectors. He argued that the formation of a customs union and consequent reduction of tariffs increases the incentives to organise an international division of labour in which productive activity in each country becomes more highly specialised. The existence of an economically integrated region strengthens the trend towards a joint determination of production decisions in different countries by TNCs operating within the region since they tend to move closer to a regionally integrated strategy in their regional activities.

In a nutshell, defensive import-substituting investment is essentially trade replacing in nature. Rationalisation and reorganisation investments are on the other hand likely to be complementary to trade, and may encourage both inter-industry trade (more likely in the case of rationalised investment) or intra-industry trade (more likely in the case of reorganisation investment). Offensive import-substituting investment is unlikely to reduce existing trade, but may restrict opportunities for trade expansion (UNTCMD, 1993). The dynamic effects of regionalism imply that production costs in locations in a customs union fall in the medium- to long-run making those locations better places for international sourcing by TNCs. The elimination of internal tariff and non-tariff barriers leads to more opportunities for reorganisation, rationalisation and offensive import-substituting investment, and relatively fewer opportunities for defensive import-substituting investment. These investment responses are summarised in Table 6.1.

The level of FDI into a region, as well as its distribution is consequently affected by the type of strategy pursued, and by other factors which affect the strategies in their own capacities. For instance, reorganisation investment which presupposes the presence of TNCs inside the trading blocs before economic integration may not lead to increased investment. Rather, it may reduce it by redistributing the existing investment in a more efficient manner, hence forcing the most inefficient firms out of business. The level of defensive import-substitution investment depends on whether it is made in response to trade-diversion or trade-suppression effects. The former case leads to the location of the investment in the partner country other than that whose source of supply from the rest of the world has become cost effective. The latter case prompts investment location inside the member state that experiences a shift in the source of its import supplies. Similarly, the effects of cost-reduction on reorganisation or rationalisation investment depend on the location of production facilities prior to the formation of the customs union. If the TNC was supplying the customs union market by exports from outside production locations, then there will be rationalisation investment as scale economies associated with integration lead to lower production costs. However, if production facilities are inside the customs union, then there will be reorganisation investment

Table 6.1   Foreign direct investment responses to regionalism

Effect of Regionalism	Investment Response

* *External tariff realignment*
  - Generates locational advantages -
freer movement of goods and services
  - Leads to trade-diversion
  - Intra-regional trade more attractive
than extra-regional trade
	* *Defensive import-substituting*
	investment (tariff-jumping)
	  - Replace exports with FDI
	(substitutes trade)
	  - Need to maintain market
	share and profitability by
	avoiding external tariffs

* *Internal tariff and non-tariff*
realignment
  - New configuration of locational
advantages among members of the
region
  - Leads to trade-creation
	* *Reorganisation investment*
	(optimum location seeking)
	  - Complementary to trade
	  - Adjust existing investments
	in region to reflect intra-regional
	trade
	  - Locate investment in
	accordance with comparative
	advantages of member countries

* *Internal tariff and non-tariff*
realignment
  - Reduces transaction costs (cost
reduction)
* *Market expansion*
  - Introduces scale economies and
hence efficiency gains
	* *Rationalised investment*
	(efficiency seeking)
	  - Complementary to trade
	  - Increase value-adding
	activities within region
	  - Reduce physical number of
	investments and replace them
	with fewer but larger and more
	efficient investments

* *Internal tariff and non-tariff*
  realignment
* *Market expansion*
* *Demand growth*
* *Technical progress*
  - *Encouraging innovation and*
competition
	* *Offensive import-substituting*
	investment (market seeking)
	  - Replace exports with FDI
	(substitutes trade)
	  - Increase market share if
	operating in region
	  - Enter market if not operating
	in region

with concentration in fewer plants. Overall, the removal of market fragmentation and the stimulus of growth from the dynamic effects of regionalism open up new opportunities for TNCs with strong ownership advantages and internalisation opportunities (UNTCMD, 1993).

Regionalism, therefore, creates additional locational attractions to the customs union market and makes potential rents to be realised from ownership advantages of investors, so that higher investment takes place. Such investment may have been diverted elsewhere in the absence of the customs union. The major forces behind these locational advantages being tariff-discrimination, market size and market growth. Regionalism does not necessarily provide assurance that TNCs that are subject to external national jurisdiction will not have differing objectives and aims from those of the regional integration. A customs union's own external tariff encourages its own firms to invest within the customs union, while elimination of import duties within the customs union encourages them to distribute these activities in the most economic way. When the tariffs are linked with corporate integration, then it may not only lead to a more efficient allocation of resources but also to concentration of economic power and promotion of oligopolistic and/or anti-competitive behaviour, which may work against the goals of regionalism.

The Economic Effects of FDI and Regionalism

The enlargement of the internal market brought about by regionalism may bring economic advantages besides those of more efficient allocation of production and consumption between countries on the basis of costs of production of commodities before its formation. For instance, it may bring about more widespread and effective competition between firms and industries, eliminating monopolistic distortions of the economy (Johnson, 1964). Competition may increase both the efficiency and specialisation of production. The additional protective effect of a common external tariff, together with the strengthening of union competition, and lessening of structural distortion all work positively to promote the growth of investment. The removal of internal tariffs, the imposition of a common external tariff, and the harmonisation of other relevant policies such as fiscal incentives, might often be expected to favour smaller and peripheral countries which were previously the least attractive to foreign investment (due to their market size and growth) when they become the least-cost locations within the customs union. However, because of agglomeration economies and the freer movement of factor resources, there is also reason to suppose that economic activity would become more concentrated in established areas if factor products can move freely. Regionalism could increase the average rate of growth of the member economies, since the larger size of the internal market available to individual industries may both make it safer for the individual firms to invest resources and effort in the introduction of innovations and the deliberate pursuit of expansion. In addition, it would put increased competitive pressure on individual firms to exploit whatever opportunities they have for expanding their share of the market and their absolute level of sales.

The economic implications of investment have been summarised by Kokko (1994) who has theorised that a single market affects investment and growth via an increase in competition. Tougher competition leads to higher efficiency. Higher efficiency means, *ceteris paribus,* that the return to investment increases. Higher returns to investment encourage more investments, which should lead to a permanently higher investment ratio. Membership to an regional economic integration scheme means that firms can presume that the increase in returns to investment is permanent. A higher investment ratio can result in a permanently sustainable growth effect.

FDI and Regionalism in Developing Countries

Most of the existing literature on developing countries has concentrated on issues concerning regionalism rather than the link between the two theories. One of the most powerful arguments for regionalism among developing countries put forward by economists (i.e. Brown, 1961; and El Agraa, 1981) is that the size of the country-product market very often is insufficient to allow minimum optimum scale plants. The important benefits which developing countries seek through regionalism arise from the exploitation of economies of scale. The domestic markets of most developing countries are so small that the manufacture of many items for the home market alone is not practicable, even under heavy protection. Nor is it practicable to plan for exporting these items to the open market, at least in the crucial early period after the establishment of a new industry. By integrating their markets, developing countries are able to overcome this difficulty. Furthermore, by moving into industries in which economies of scale are important, they can increase productivity of their resources engaged in manufacturing and put to work the additional resources in manufacturing.

The advantages derived from both specialisation of production and enlargement of markets depend upon more trade and greater freedom of trade, since inside a very large and rich country the necessary enlargement of markets can be achieved within national boundaries. For a group of countries which are relatively poor or in which income per head is low and for that reason markets are small, the necessary enlargement of markets involves the crossing of national frontiers and, hence, some element of international co-operation (Arndt and Garnaut, 1979).

The orthodox analysis of the customs union has been criticised for disregarding factors that cause special problems of regionalism in developing countries. These include the determination in operational terms of the appropriate scope and direction of regional trade, development and specialisation; the issue of equity in the distribution of benefits; and *policy towards FDI and TNCs*. El-Agraa (1981) has, for example, argued that the conditions laid down under the traditional customs union theory are most unlikely to be satisfied in the majority of developing nations. Moreover, most of the effects of such integration are bound to be trade diverting, since most developing countries seek to industrialise. As the inadequate size of their individual markets makes development of industry in developing countries very limited, there is, therefore, good reason for increasing market size so as to encourage optimum plant installations and thus the need for regionalism. When it comes to external economies, there is much more scope for them and absolute need for them for development purposes in the developing countries than in the developed world since a pool of skilled labour, provision of technology and infrastructure are the basic necessities of industry, and they are lacking.

However, other researchers including Cooper and Massell (1965) have suggested that the principle objective of regionalism among developing countries is to foster industrial development and guide such development along more economic lines. There is, therefore, a justification of political and economic protection in order for these countries to alter their terms-of-trade, increase domestic employment, raise revenue and foster local industry.

A majority of developing countries have pre-union protection, suggesting that free trade is not viewed as desirable. Moreover, complete liberalisation of all trade may not be politically acceptable as it may lead to polarisation of industrial growth in certain countries and uneven distribution of the benefits of co-operation popularly known as the *backwash effect*. Such liberalisation may also not yield quick results, in the face of rigidities in national economies, scarcity of entrepreneurs, inadequate infrastructure and difficulties in financing very large projects.

This means that regionalism among developing countries in the early post-war period was considered primarily as a way of extending the policy of import-substitution on a regional scale. This approach is subject to serious limitations resulting from the establishment of inefficient plants and industries (Balassa and Stoutjesdijk, 1976). Regionalism in developing countries, therefore, does not seem to benefit from increased competition and rationalisation of existing productive activities. Rather, the benefits accrue from the introduction of new activities and/or from production-deepening. Since such integration activities are new, the productive, technological and institutional infrastructure of the countries concerned is not likely to be ready to meet the demands of their implementation. Instead, the corresponding strategic production inputs are likely to be found captive within the corporate integration structure of the TNCs. Consequently, the TNCs are the actors most likely to be called to fulfil this role, thus creating a novel and more complex structure of dependence of host countries on foreign firms (UNCTAD, 1993). However, the discussion presented in the previous chapter provided evidence that this *dependencia* school of thought has been proved to be wrong.

In regional economic blocs of developing countries, the concepts of defensive import-substitution, reorganisation, rationalisation and offensive import-substitution investments are still relevant although to a very limited extent, with those possessing the import-substitution component being more relevant. This is due partly to the limited number of investments in these economies prior to integration *vis-à-vis* the developed countries and, hence, the limited need to reorganise or rationalise them. It is also partly due to the fact that much as integration has taken place, the new combined market in most cases has still remained dynamically small by TNCs' standards. However, rationalisation investment is relevant with respect to the global economy in that TNCs from outside the union can target it as a centre for sourcing, and assembling components and parts. The empirical comparative review that follows highlights some of these issues.

An Empirical Comparative Review

Overview

When assessing regionalism effects on inflows of FDI, it is necessary to first verify whether or not an increase actually did occur following the integration. Second, it is important to establish whether or not the increase if any is indeed wholly, partly, or not at all attributable to the regionalism effects. Finally, there is need to ascertain how firms reacted, particularly when the increase was due to the regionalism effects.

The analysis of the effects of regionalism on the inflows of FDI should in principle test three hypothesises resulting from the three regionalism effects, i.e. market size, market growth and tariff-discrimination. Under market size, it is hypothesised that once a market attains a size that permits local production to realise effectively economies of scale then, *ceteris paribus,* the level of the FDI in that market is likely to be closely related to its size. Similarly, it is hypothesised that FDI is expected to be related to the rate at which the market expands. The tariff-discrimination hypothesis is based on the presumption that a common external tariff represents an increased restraint on trade and thus encourages defensive FDI in the customs union, while the freedom of internal trade facilitates its distribution.

Empirical studies have revealed that regionalism has led to a surge in inward FDI and have attributed this mainly to either the response to enlarged market opportunities and tariff-discrimination among other reasons for the developed blocs. FDI is, however, a response to outsourcing and cheap factor endowments for the less developed blocs. These responses, however, vary from bloc to bloc and among the investment host countries. There is evidence to suggest that the formation of the EEC led the member countries to attract an increasing share of FDI particularly from the US. Similarly, empirical evidence suggests that the formation of NAFTA promoted FDI activities mostly from Europe and Japan within the region, particularly, in Mexico. However, the formation of economic blocs in the developing countries has had little, if any, impact on FDI inflows. These effects are reviewed below.

Developed Country Economic Blocs

Western Europe - FDI from the US Much of the earlier work on the impact of the formation of the EEC on FDI was concerned with assessing trends and, hence, the locational patterns of the flow of FDI from the US to the EEC. Most of the studies have focused on the inflows of US FDI due to the fact that data on these flows are more readily available and reliable than those from any other sources. The difficulty with the established empirical literature on the EEC, like any economic bloc, arises from the separation of the integration-induced effects from other developments that were either raising the locational advantages of the EEC members (e.g. the period of German reconstruction) or strengthening the ownership-specific advantages of non-EEC (particularly the US) firms (UNCTAD, 1993).

Empirical studies on the effects of regionalism on the flow of FDI into the EEC have been inconclusive. The earlier studies found no evidence to support the hypothesis that regionalism led to an increase in the inflows of FDI. For instance, Mikesell (1967) argued that, while tariff advantages and relative low costs in the EEC may have constituted favourable and permissive factors for the establishment of US enterprises in the community, they were not sufficient to explain the surge in the US FDI in the community. The later studies have, however, shown that the surge of FDI from the US into the EEC in the late 1950s and early 1960s was in response to enlarged market opportunities and growth in incomes of the EEC rather than tariff barriers to American exports. Furthermore, they have suggested that Japanese investment in the EEC, although still small by the standards of US TNCs, has been rising rapidly, and has been attributed mainly to the response to trade barriers against Japanese imports, and in some cases (such as the motor vehicle industry) to the establishment of co-operative arrangements with European firms. In general, the results from these later studies have collectively indicated that FDI inflows responded to two of the three regionalism effects, i.e. market size, and tariff-discrimination, the results for market growth being inconclusive.

Scaperlanda (1967), for instance, analysed the EEC and US FDI for the period 1951-64 and observed that since 1959 the European area experienced both absolute and relative insignificant increases in the US FDI flows. The results show that the EEC's share of the US FDI increased by 0.549 per cent points whereas non-EEC Europe's share increased by only 0.278 per cent points annually during the 1951-58 period. By contrast, however, the 1951-64 coefficients indicate that over the entire period, there was no significant difference, an indication that the EEC did not attract a larger share of US FDI since its first tariff reduction. Scaperlanda and Mauer (1969) also came to the same conclusion after finding only the market size hypothesis statistically significant. Goldberg's (1972) results were on the other hand inconclusive, and only significant at the 10 per cent level for the tariff-discrimination variable in manufacturing FDI (UNTCMD, 1993). This led to the conclusion that the general assumption that the creation of the EEC would cause a reallocation of international investment was not supported by empirical data. It was also concluded that there was an indication that factors such as familiarity with the country in which investment is to be located, international differences in the application of technology, and the financial liquidity to fund the foreign investment, outweighed the influence of the creation of the common market on the pattern of international investments.

Wallis (1968), however, pointed out that Scaperlanda's regression covering the whole period of study contained both 'before' and 'after' effects that weighted the scales in favour of the 'no-change' hypothesis by ignoring the 1959-64 regression. He eliminated this by dividing it into two periods (1951-58 and 1959-64), and after regressing, the results showed an increase in the annual growth of 0.73 and 2.7 percentage points before and after 1958 respectively. His findings have been supported by Schmitz (1970), and Schmitz and Bieri (1972) (UNTCMD, 1993). Studies by Dunning (1972) and Balassa (1976) have also provided evidence to the effect that the formation of the EEC was accomplished by an increased inflow of the US investment.

A tariff-discrimination proxy variable has been used in all studies attempting to measure regionalism effects. There has, however, been an inconsistency in the choice of the variable. For instance, Scaperlanda and Mauer (1969) used the exports of the US to the EEC divided by the exports of the member States of the EEC to one another. Goldberg (1972) replaced the numerator of the above ratio by world exports to the EEC, while Schmitz and Bieri (1972) used the EEC share of total US exports. Other researchers have used other proxy variables or employed a dummy variable. Consequently, their results have differed. Among the studies that have attributed FDI inflows to tariff-discrimination include, Clark, Wilson and Bradey (1969) who further suggested that the elimination of import duties within the EC encouraged FDI to be distributed in the most economic way. Schmitz and Bieri (1972), and Lunn (1980) found that all the three effects of regionalism were statistically significant determinants of FDI in the EEC but based their conclusions on the tariff-discrimination results alone. Dunning and Robson (1987) argued that FDI was a result of the additional protective effect of common external tariff together with the possible strengthening of European (*vis-à-vis* US and Japanese) competition, and the lessening of structural distortions which all worked positively to promote the growth of such investment. Scaperlanda and Balough (1983) provided more empirical support for the hypothesis that the formation of the EEC and the process of regionalism had a definite influence on the locational patterns of the US FDI. Their dummy-variable approach overcame the deficiency of using trade data for the tariff-discrimination proxy variable that could be affected by the degree of substitutability between FDI and trade flows. However, Mayers (1985) pointed out that such a dummy variable incorporates the effects both of the relative movement of extra and intra EEC tariffs (the tariff-discrimination proper) and of the decrease of the common external tariff from its levels in 1956. The result, therefore, probably owes more to the internal *trade-creation* of lowering barriers to intra-EEC trade than to the *trade-diversion* of the increasing difference between the common external tariff and internal tariff levels (UNTCMD, 1993).

The market size hypothesis has been consistently verified for US FDI in the EEC by Bandera and White (1968), Scaperlanda and Mauer (1969), Schmitz and Bieri (1972), Lunn (1980), and Scaperlanda and Balough (1983). Bandera and White (1968) have also attributed income growth of the unified EEC as a main reason for changing locational patterns of the US FDI in the EEC. This is in line with Balassa's (1976) conclusion that the formation of the EEC resulted into increased investment, which was undertaken to exploit the possibilities for scale economies (resulting from increased market size) giving a further boost to economic growth in the member countries, and enabling them to maintain the rates of growth attained during the post-World War II reconstruction period.

The results for the market growth hypothesis have, however, been inconsistent. For example, Scaperlanda and Mauer's (1969) results were never significant and at times wrongly signed. In addition, Schmitz and Bieri's (1972) results were negatively (sometimes significantly) related to growth rates for 1952 to 1958, but positively related for 1959 to 1966. Furthermore, Lunn (1980) found the growth rate in the most recent year (Y_t - Y_{t-1}) to be significantly positively related to US FDI in the EEC, but that lagged one year (Y_t - Y_{t-2}) to be significantly negatively related (UNCTC, 1992). Studies by Goldberg (1972) found a positive relationship between US FDI flows and the rate of growth of the EEC market when absolute market size was omitted. Scaperlanda and Mauer (1969), and Lunn (1980) have, however, argued that this test is probably miss-specified since the statistical relevance of the level of GNP is substantially verified elsewhere. These results indicate that whereas FDI tends to be strongly related to the level of GNP and its underlying growth, it does not react consistently to short-term changes in the rates of GNP growth.

Western Europe - Non-EEC and non-US FDI   Some researchers have investigated determinants of FDI from countries other than the US. For example, Heitger and Stehn (1990) attempted to identify the determinants of Japanese FDI in Europe and observed that the European system of protection was one of the most important factors explaining the increases in such investment. They observed that trading partners within the EC were forced to protect domestic producers by various tariff and non-tariff barriers when exports from outside the EC boomed. These tariffs eventually reached a critical level, at which it became increasingly favourable for foreign firms to substitute FDI for exports. Balasubramanyam and Greenaway (1992) also argued that Japanese FDI was for 'tariff jumping', i.e. to ensure a continued market presence before more restricted access was imposed. They also noted that the single market programme altered locational characteristics and locational advantages of the EC, offering a lure to Japanese investors with pronounced ownership advantages centring on organisational and managerial skills, consequently stimulating an increase in FDI in the EC over and above what would have occurred without the single market programme. A study by Dunning (1986), however, found market factors to be the overwhelming basic motivation for Japanese investors in the UK. That is, Japanese investment was primarily to supply the UK market, as a point of entry into the EC, and as a part of an integrated European or world-wide product mandate. Results from a study by the EC Secretariat (1992) on the flow of FDI from Israel into the community showed that in the period under study (1984-87 and 1988-91) it increased by over 500 per cent from $94m to $262m and attributed it to Dunning's 'market seeking' FDI.

North America   The North American market is dominated by the US market which is the world's leading source of demand for goods and services and whose population has considerable discretionary income to spend. For instance, in 1993 the US' GDP of about $6260 billion was almost equal to the EC(12)'s GDP of about $6280 billion! In the 1980s domestic production failed to match demand and this gave foreign companies an opportunity to enter the market. Economic explanations have focused on either the market structure that producers face, or on the technical side of production as central elements in explaining FDI. The explanations have, however, changed since the proposal and consequent formation of NAFTA.

As NAFTA is still a relatively new economic bloc, there have been few empirical studies and most of those that have been carried out have focused on the FDI flows to CAFTA and the US. Empirical studies suggest that in preparation for the enlarged market, TNCs engaged in manufacturing activities undertook major restructuring, particularly in their automobile plants by increasingly utilising their Mexican affiliates to supply the US markets. For example, Volkswagen decided that from 1990, the successor to the Golf and Jetta models would be exported exclusively to the US from its Mexican plant. Nissan also announced that, from the summer of 1992, the company would ship 200,000 engines a year to the US from its Mexican subsidiary, while Zenith Electronics Corporation announced that it would close down its manufacturing facilities in Taipei, China and move the production to Mexico. Other companies including Hoechst, a Germany company announced its intentions of investing $800 million in a Mexican petrochemical plant; Mercedes-Benz considered building an assembly line for luxury cars; and other German companies planned to invest $600 million in the tourism industry. Electronic companies including IBM, Hewlett Packard, RCA, and Thomas also geared their Mexican plants production sites to the supply of the North American market (UN, 1992). However, a study by Krajewski, Bank and Yu (1994) suggested that the North American regional market was a centre point in the strategic outlook of many firms rather than NAFTA itself. The survey revealed that the majority of the firms had adopted or were considering to adopt a North American (US and Canada) focus in their corporate strategy, and restructure by integrating business operations into continental operations and rationalisation of production capacity.

The reason responsible for the growing Japanese FDI in the US was investigated by Georgion and Weinhold (1992) who suggested that the primary factor was to gain accessibility to the vast and diverse US market. However, Fukushima and Kwan (1995) argued that the primary factor was trade barrier-circumventing, and market and technology accessing. Non-NAFTA firms (particularly from Japan and Europe) attempted to get access to the US market by investing in Mexico. The strategy behind investing in Mexico tended to stem from the desire to attain competitive advantage through the use of the relatively low labour costs in Mexico, and access to tariff free movement of merchandise within NAFTA and particularly to the US. Kehoe (1995) on the other hand attributed the surge of FDI to Mexico in the late 1980s and early 1990s to the 1989 regulatory changes. For instance, following the 1989 change in regulations, the Foreign Investment Commission granted automatic approval for investment projects in 'unrestricted industries' in cases that met guidelines designed to promote foreign trade and to create jobs outside of the major industrial areas of Mexico City, Guadalajara, and Monterrey. The decisions by non-NAFTA firms were made in light of the anticipation of the formation of NAFTA, which would be expected to create a large market and introduce tariff-discrimination measures upon its formation.

Studies that have been based on CAFTA include that by Thompson (1994), who investigated the impact of CAFTA on investment in Canadian manufacturing industries. His investigation was based on the investment theory, which states that an increase in the expected profits of a firm should lead to an increase in investment spending. He addressed the issue of whether there is a relationship between the stock market reaction to the news that a free trade area had been reached, on subsequent patterns of investment spending. The results show that fabricated metal products, chemicals and electric equipment industries increased their share of total investment spending by more than 20 per cent while the paper industry had an actual investment during the free trade area period 127 per cent greater than the predicted level. Overall, the results provide some weak evidence that the free trade area had an impact on investment patterns in the Canadian manufacturing industries. This weak relationship is attributed to the fact that the actual consequences of the free trade area were not as important as initially expected, or that the impact of the free trade area on investment was obscured by the impact of other changes in economic conditions during the period under investigation.

It is also not surprising that little research has been carried out on the effects of NAFTA on intra-NAFTA investment. There is evidence to the effect that the formation NAFTA led Mexican firms to increase investment in the US in industries in which they enjoyed comparative advantages. For example, conglomerates like Vitro (glass) and Cemex (cement) built production plants in the US in order to expand into the market (UN, 1994). Hummels and Stern's (1994) study on the pattern of FDI in NAFTA has, however, revealed that the US FDI in Canada, and Central and Latin America has been decreasing markedly in relative importance and increasing significantly in Western Europe and Asia/Oceania. Similarly, inward FDI to the US was dominated by Western Europe whereas the US (with a share of 63.4 per cent in 1991) was by far the largest source of FDI to Canada and Mexico. This indicated that Canada and Mexico had a much larger stake in NAFTA than did the US whose interests appeared more closely tied to the other major countries/regions in the multilateral trading regime. The little impact of NAFTA on intra FDI flows may stem from the fact that the US already had established trading relationships with Canada through CAFTA, and with Mexico through bilateral agreements, and Canada and Mexico had little interests in each other (*vis-à-vis* the US). These factors often tend to be underestimated.

The evidence indicates that there was actually some change in FDI flows and, hence, investments prior to and after the formation of NAFTA and CAFTA. The US has always been a difficult market for foreign firms to operate from partly because of its high quality requirements and high costs of production. However, it is apparent that even if the formation of NAFTA increased the size of the market, most TNCs' interests were focused on the US market more than NAFTA. This should not be surprising especially when it is brought to light that the US population of about 258 million was about two and a half times the combined Canadian and Mexican population of about 120 million. Additionally, its purchasing power when GDP is used as an aggregate measure was almost 90 per cent that of NAFTA in 1993. For instance, in 1993, the US's GDP was about $6260 billion, while Canada and Mexico's were $477 and $343 billion respectively. By investing in Mexico, the firms concerned were taking a defensive strategy that would enable them jump NAFTA's external tariffs on non-NAFTA goods, as well as have access to cheap production costs and facilities such as the *maquiladoras* that could enable them to gain competitive advantage when selling in the US market. The effects of Canada and Mexico, much as they also had large and growing market sizes, therefore, tended to be of secondary importance.

Developing Country Economic Blocs

Comparatively little research has been carried out on the effect of regionalism on FDI flows to the developing country economic blocs in Asia, Latin America and Africa *vis-à-vis* Europe. This is probably due to data limitations and lack of interest on the side of the researchers.

Asia Empirical studies on FDI flows into the ASEAN do not provide much evidence that directly links the formation of the APTA to changes in FDI inflows. Studies based on econometric techniques include Tang (1993) and Bende-Nabende (1999). Tang's study has revealed that the APTA has not led to a higher level of investment and factor productivity growth among the member countries. This is presumably due to the lower level of integration frame work, such as the preferential trade area. By contrast, Bende-Nabende's (1999) study revealed that FDI responded to the formation of APTA to the advantage of the more developed member countries, and disadvantage of the less developed member countries. For instance, the results suggested that the formation of the APTA imparted a negative FDI influence on the less developed Indonesia and the Philippines and a positive FDI influence on the more developed Malaysia, Singapore and Thailand. This led to the conclusion that when a regional economic integration scheme is undertaken among countries with different levels of economic development, investment may be relocated to the more developed countries in the economic bloc probably because of the comparatively superior locational advantages they offer. Furthermore, the results demonstrated that there was a time lag before these impacts were realised. In addition, they suggested that the location and/or relocation of international production in the region was influenced mainly by the availability of relatively low production costs and the quality of human skills and infrastructure, and was facilitated by a positive liberalisation policy over and above other factors. There was also an indication that once per capita income levels are low or high, their growth rates may be less relevant to the FDI decisions and, hence, not positively related. On the other hand, per capita growth rates of moderate income levels as indicators of future market potential may be relatively important. Furthermore, FDI responded to market size only in the presence of a large population and/or high per capita income. Overall however, the results suggested that the influence of positive liberalisation policy, infrastructure, quality human skills, and cheap factor endowments outweighed that of the formation of the APTA in attracting FDI.

The majority of the studies which have been undertaken to establish the determinants of FDI in ASEAN have been based on the descriptive survey type of work and have come to almost the same conclusions. Some researchers have focused on locational factors within ASEAN. For example, Rana (1985) attributed FDI flows into the ASEAN countries, to their individual dynamic growth rates of GDP; abundance of petroleum and other natural resources (Indonesia and Malaysia); relatively large domestic markets (Indonesia, the Philippines and Thailand); favourable conditions for the manufacturing of export production; infrastructure; and investment policies such as incentives, regulations, tax benefits and investment insurance. Riedel (1991) has attributed Japanese investment in the ASEAN economies to the advantage they offer in terms of low-cost labour for export manufacturing and because of the abundance of natural resources especially in Indonesia and Malaysia. Fong (1995) has observed that FDI in Singapore has been driven in part by expanding opportunities in the region and strongly supporting government policy. Aquino and Bolanos (1995) have argued that FDI in the Philippines, has been affected by political instability and that its flow was low until the restoration of democratic institutions in 1986 improved business confidence. Hill and Lindsey (1987) identified the market growth potential, proximity to markets, trade restraints and transaction costs as additional determinants of FDI in the Philippines. Saad (1995) has suggested that the investment law introduced by Indonesia in 1967 stimulated FDI flows, leading the US to invest more in oil; and Japan, the UK, Germany, and the Netherlands to invest in non-oil manufacturing. The success of the ASEAN countries in attracting FDI from this point of view can, therefore, be attributed to a combination of factors that can be summarised into political, social and economic stability; buoyant economies with rapidly growing domestic markets; favourable factor endowments, particularly natural resources and labour supply in the ASEAN-4 (Indonesia, Malaysia, the Philippines and Thailand) and human resources and infrastructure in Singapore; and development-oriented governments with sound macroeconomic and pro-FDI policies.

Other studies have focused on factors originating from outside the ASEAN. For instance, Yue (1991) attributed FDI inflows to the rapidly rising labour and land costs in the Asian NIEs, leading to the loss in comparative advantage and thus the pressure to relocate labour and land-intensive industries. He also suggested the environmental pressure to relocate polluting industries, and the need to secure market shares in the Asian developing countries where market access was threatened by measures to support import-substitution. The FDI inflows from the Asian NIEs, has been facilitated by geographical proximity and capitalises on favourable factor endowments, circumventing protectionist measures of developed countries, and exploiting ownership advantages. Fukushima and Kwan (1995) have also argued that the enormous change in the competitive conditions for Japanese firms caused by the sharp appreciation of the yen, and rising domestic demand on top of the above factors, stimulated

Japanese FDI flows to Southeast Asia.

Recent studies have focused on the ASEAN's growing market and its role in the international division of labour. For instance, studies in the automobile industry in Thailand indicate that Thailand's growing domestic market and increased parts manufacturing skills have made it attractive as a large-scale parts manufacturing base, especially for Japanese firms. Another study by Fong (1995) in the electronics industry in Singapore has revealed that all the large firms (AIWA, Hitachi, JVC, Matsushita, Sanyo and Sony) have upgraded their operations by bringing in high value added products and phasing out or relocating labour-intensive assembly operations to sister plants in the ASEAN-4. This has been attributed to the *billiard-ball* shift style of FDI and not to regionalism.

Alun (1988) had earlier attributed the slow progress of the ASEAN integration to the heterogeneity of its economies which results from the increasing differences in their economic growth rates, while Riedel (1991) argued that it is a result of the strict rule-of-origin restrictions, since each country maintains its own separate tariff schedule. The formation of the APTA, therefore, seems to have contributed only indirectly through its influence on regional stability which in turn contributed to certainty in decision making in the public and private sector.

Latin America A research of CACM has suggested that the process of regionalism turned out to be the factor that was perhaps most responsible for the significant increase in FDI, especially in the manufacturing sector. For example, US FDI which was reported to be $206m in 1929 and $350m in 1959, jumped to $879m in 1969. These flows of FDI have been attributed to: preserving an existing market, previously supplied through exports, basically from the parent firm (i.e. defensive import-substitution investment); the desire to counter and modify the initial plans established by the UN Economic Commission for Latin America with respect to the mechanisms by which regionalism should be pursued; and the urgent need to change the content of the US business presence in Latin America by incorporating considerations of economic development as part of their objectives (UNCTAD, 1993). The Rosenthal Report, aimed at establishing among other things to what extent the integration programme contributed to the economic development of Central America as a whole, and each country as an individual, however, concluded that there is no evidence to suggest that regionalism directly affected total private investment in any of the member countries. A study by Torrisi (1985) on the other hand revealed that market size was significantly related to FDI flows to Colombia in the period 1958 to 1980, whilst market growth was positively signed but not significant. A test for regionalism using a dummy variable gave persistently insignificant results. The likely interpretation of this result is that whilst expectations of market growth through regionalism should encourage FDI in principle, in practice the explicit aspects of the Andean common market (especially the phased divestment elements of Decision 24 which sets a comprehensive package of the rules for the entry and operation of foreign-owned business in the Andean Pact: for example, any foreign investment project must be approved by the 'competent national authority'; and there are rules requiring partial fade-out of ownership after fifteen years) repelled investors (UNCTC, 1992). A study by the UNCTC (1983) has, however, revealed that since the formation of the Andean Pact, FDI flows to member countries including Colombia increased, in some cases significantly, despite opinions expressed to the contrary and qualifications concerning yearly fluctuations. National policies such as those of Chile and Peru proved far more important factors in determining FDI flows than regional regulations. The growth rate of US manufacturing investment in the member countries was higher after the Pact's establishment than before, and TNCs from other countries increased their investment at an even higher rate than the US firms (UNCTAD, 1993).

Africa Most studies on FDI flows to Sub-Sahara Africa (SSA) have not been carried out on a regional basis but on English-speaking Africa (ESA) as a whole. Bennell (1994) attributed the flow of FDI to SSA in the 1980s to the improvement in the investment climate for TNCs. These included the introduction of new investment codes that swept many of the restrictions and impediments that had previously seriously limited FDI, and replaced them with a variety of investment incentives and guarantees. British Corporate investment comprised between 50 and 80 per cent of all manufacturing FDI in each ESA country. Its annual investment for all ESA averaged $85m between 1980 and 1987, and grew to $149m between 1988 and 1992, an increase of nearly 60 per cent. FDI flows, however, declined drastically since mid-1994 following the TNCs' divestments in ESA. Bennell's survey revealed that by mid-1994, there were only 65 British companies with equity stakes in 233 manufacturing enterprises out of the original 90 companies which had 336 equity involvements in manufacturing in 1989. One half of the 1989 parent companies had divested, 28 (31.1 per cent) completely and 20 (22.2 per cent) partially. The divestments were concentrated in Kenya, Nigeria and Zimbabwe where two thirds British equity involvements were located. He further pointed out that one third of the companies with manufacturing equity involvement in ESA in the late 1970s had divested in the 1980s. The main reason for divestment was economic - the unacceptable low levels of productivity due mainly to shortages of foreign exchange, inability or delay to remit profits to parent companies, and profitability undermined by currency devaluations. The economic advantages of the region appeared not to be sufficient to attract larger flows of new investment. Political stability coupled with fundamental market and cost considerations also played a role. The reasons for FDI flows in ESA, therefore, tended to be independent of regionalism.

Agodo's (1978) study of 33 US companies in 20 African countries, found that the lower cost of African labour and effective protection did not have a significant stimulating effect on FDI, but that the presence of development planning was positively and significantly related to FDI although it was suggested that the effect was not that direct. Rather it was the organised economic environment that it created and the positive economic climate that frequently was associated with it. Other studies have been carried out on developing countries in general. Root and Ahmed (1979), and Schneider and Frey (1985) for example, found the rate of growth of GDP to be a determining factor of the attractiveness of developing countries for FDI, whilst absolute GDP was not, indicating that once income levels are very low, the small differences between them may be less relevant to FDI decisions, whilst current growth rates as indicators of potential may be relatively important. Agodo (1978), and Root and Ahmed's (1979) results indicated primary infrastructure to be a significant determinant of FDI. Root and Ahmed (1979), and Schneider and Frey (1985) also found per capita income to be a major determinant (UNCTC, 1992).

Observations

One evident weakness with the econometric analysis in the above investigations particularly with respect to the EEC/EC is the use and emphasis of one variable, tariff-discrimination, as a sole representative of regionalism effects. For example, Schmitz and Bieri (1972), and Lunn (1980) in spite of including the market size and market growth variables in the analysis, have based their regionalism conclusions on only the tariff-discrimination results. The theoretical literature discussed earlier, however, suggests that regionalism leads to three effects (tariff-discrimination, market size and market growth) all of which have to be addressed in any attempt to establish its impact on FDI flows. In this way, the researcher may find the most significant/prominent of the three determinants. Treating the other two variables as independent of the implications of regionalism, is a disregard to the rational of the theory of economic integration. The most immediate fact is that, to the very least, regionalism leads to a *static* market size increase due to the simple fact that it results into a combined single larger market. The fortunate thing is that since some of the studies included the variables that represent the other two factors even if they did not consider them in their conclusions, an independent analyst can still draw the conclusions based on them.

Nonetheless, caution has to be exercised when interpreting the results, first, because tariff-discrimination may not be independent of market size and market growth. Investors may 'jump' tariffs because of their desire to have access or continued access to a market that may be growing or is anticipated to grow in the near future. This implies that tariff-discrimination in the presence of a static or a negatively growing small market may have no positive impact on FDI inflows. Second, whereas market size is directly associated with regionalism, market growth does not necessary follow suit. Third, there are other determinants of FDI that are independent of regionalism whose impact should in principle be isolated from the regionalism effects but can not because it is not practically possible. It would be more interesting to look at these variables independently and obtain an indication of their relative influence and/or importance. Fourth, regionalism can lead to reorganisational and/or rationalised investment without necessarily increasing its level.

In the EEC, the FDI determinants can be categorised into the offensive response to market size for US firms and defensive response to tariff-discrimination for other non-EEC firms, although there is an overlap between the two categories. These responses are not surprising particularly when consideration is made on the operations of the firms before regionalism took place. The US firms which already operated in the market prior to the establishment of the common market naturally had to offensively increase their market shares, while the other non-EEC firms had to get access to the market before the tariff-discrimination came into effect. In NAFTA, the FDI determinants are also the emerging market size and tariff-discrimination, but access to the US and/or the North American market as an individual market tends to be a very strong factor as well. As

Table 6.2   FDI determinants and investment responses to economic integration blocs

Level of Economic Development	Level of Economic Integration	
	High	Low
High	*FDI Determinant* * market size * tariff-discrimination * individual country specific characteristics *Types of Investments* - Defensive import-substitution - Offensive import-substitution - Reorganisation - Rationalisation	*FDI Determinant* * individual country specific characteristics *Types of Investments* - Offensive import-substitution - Rationalisation
Low	*FDI Determinant* * market growth * tariff-discrimination * individual country specific characteristics *Types of Investments* - Defensive import-substitution - Offensive import-substitution - Rationalisation	*FDI Determinant* * individual country specific characteristics *Types of Investments* - Offensive import-substitution - Rationalisation

for the APTA, there is almost conclusive evidence that the individual country characteristics have played an overwhelming role to an extent that regionalism effects tend to have had no impact at all. The limited results for CACM show a mixture of regionalism effects and country-specific characteristics as determinants of FDI, while those for the other developing regions have attributed only country specific characteristics to FDI flows. Further analysis of the empirical evidence leads to conclusions that have implications for the level of economic development, the level of economic integration, the regionalism effects, the type of investment, and the role of regionalism in developing countries. These are briefly highlighted below and summarised in Table 6.2.

Level of economic development The empirical evidence indicates a positive link between regionalism and FDI inflows particularly in the more developed economic blocs, i.e. the EEC and NAFTA. This correlation, however, tends to decrease with the decreasing level of economic development of the economic blocs. Therefore, the higher the level of economic development of the economic bloc, *ceteris paribus,* the higher is the positive impact of the regionalism effects on FDI inflows.

Level of economic integration The link between regionalism and FDI inflows tends to be strengthened by the level of economic integration. There is an indication that the economic blocs based on the higher level integration schemes (from the level of a free trade area upwards) are more likely to draw more FDI than those based on the lower level integration schemes (from the level of a preferential trade area downwards). This may be due to the fact that whereas there is an approach towards a common internal tariff for the case of a preferential trade area, there is a further approach towards a common internal and external tariff as well for the higher level integration schemes, which tends to play a bigger role in attracting FDI. The higher the level of economic integration, therefore, the higher is the positive impact of the regionalism effects on FDI inflows.

The regionalism effects The regionalism effects as determinants of FDI are more prominent in the more developed and/or high-level economic blocs although they may differ in combination. However, they are less significant in the less developed and/or lower level economic blocs. For example, market size and tariff-discrimination are prominent, while market growth is less significant in the more developed and high-level economic blocs. Market growth and tariff-discrimination are prominent, while market size is less significant in the less developed but high-level integration economic blocs. However, the individual country locational advantages are the principal determinants in both the developed and the less developed low-level integration economic blocs. This suggests that once regional income levels are high, current market size as an indicator for current demand is a necessary locational determinant of FDI inflows. But, when regional income levels are low, the current growth rate of the market as an indicator of its future potential demand is the necessary locational determinant of FDI inflows. That is, in developed economic blocs, FDI does not seem to react to short-term changes in the rates of GNP/GDP growth as it does in developing economic blocs/countries.

Impact on type of investment The combination of the level of economic integration and economic development also affects investment responses. For instance, whereas the developed high-level economic integration blocs tend to attract all the four types of investments, the developing high-level integration blocs mostly attract the defensive and offensive import-substitution investment. The low-level economic integration blocs on the other hand mostly attract the offensive import-substitution investment.

The role of regionalism in developing countries The review also reveals that apart from CACM, the empirical investigation of the determinants of FDI in developing countries and/or economic blocs has mostly focused on the individual country characteristics, ignoring the role, if any, of regionalism. Those for the APTA although fairly conclusive, have mostly been based on the descriptive and, hence, qualitative type of analysis. In order to confirm the impact of regionalism in developing country economic blocs, there is a necessity to link the qualitative evidence to findings from quantitative investigations. This requires econometric investigations of hypotheses based on the impacts of the regionalism effects on FDI inflows.

Conclusion

Regionalism is supposed to lead to three major integration effects, tariff-discrimination, market size and market growth which, in their individual and collective capacities have implications for the theory of international production. These effects in turn lead to four types of investment responses, i.e., defensive import-substituting, reorganisational, offensive import-substituting and rationalisation investments. Each of them may respond to movements in economic integration via the effects of such integration on the locational and organisational decisions of firms.

Customs unions among developing countries have been put forward as a strategy to strengthen industries in developing countries. In most cases, the markets in individual developing countries are too small to take advantage of economies of scale, which are necessary in order to reach efficient production levels. A customs union with a bigger 'domestic market' can solve this problem. A major problem for customs unions among developing countries is to ensure that all individual member countries benefit equally from the formation of the customs union. If some of the countries are more developed than others, it could easily mean that the more developed countries get all the benefits. Even where the countries are at the same level, problems may arise if market mechanisms, which are supposed to guarantee the establishment of new companies do not work. If there are no private entrepreneurs who can take advantage of the new potentials, the public authorities must intervene to help set up new businesses. This calls for political agreement about where the companies should be located. As each country will look after its own interests and therefore would prefer to have as many production units as possible, experience shows that political disagreements can easily occur.

Empirical studies have revealed that regionalism has led to a surge in inward FDI and have attributed this mainly to either the response to enlarged market opportunities and tariff-discrimination among other reasons for the developed blocs. FDI is, however, a response to outsourcing and cheap factor endowments for the less developed blocs. These responses, however, vary from bloc to bloc and among the investment host countries. There is evidence to suggest that the formation of the EEC led the member countries to attract an increasing share of FDI particularly from the US. Similarly, empirical evidence suggests that the formation of NAFTA promoted FDI activities mostly from Europe and Japan within the region, particularly, in Mexico. However, the formation of economic blocs in the developing countries has had little, if any, impact on FDI inflows. Further analysis of the empirical evidence leads to conclusions that have implications for the level of economic development, the level of economic integration, the regionalism effects, the type of investment, and the role of regionalism in developing countries.

One factor that is often overlooked is the factor of free trade within the customs union. Therefore, for as long as the number of regional economic blocs continue to grow the world all over, regionalism presents the only formula of free trade at least among selected countries, and therefore the beginning phase of a free trade paradigm. This is explored further in Chapter 7, under 'the role of regional economic integration'.

7 Policy Considerations

Introduction

This era of globalisation is opening many opportunities for millions of people around the world through increased trade, new technologies, foreign investments, expanding media and internet connections, and fuelling economic growth and human advances. There is more wealth and technology, and more commitment to a global community than ever before. All this offers enormous potential to continue the unprecedented progress of the twentieth century and eradicate poverty in the twenty-first century. The growing interdependence of people's lives calls for shared values and a shared commitment to the human development of all people. Global markets, global technology, global ideas and global solidarity can enrich the lives of people everywhere, greatly expanding their choices.

Yet, it is also evident that these agents of advancement are also the same instruments for potential environmental derailment, increased North-South divide, growing human insecurity and consequently potential stimulants of unsustainable development, particularly, in the developing countries.

Usually, government policies on FDI need to counter two sets of market failures. The first arises from information or co-ordination failures in the investment process, which can lead a country to attract insufficient FDI, or, the wrong quality of FDI. The second arises when private interests of investors diverge from the economic interests of host countries. This can lead FDI to have negative impacts on development, or it may lead to positive, but static benefits that are not sustainable over time. Private and social interests may, of course, diverge from any investment, local or foreign. Policies are then needed to remove the divergence for all investors. However, some divergence may be specific to foreign investment. While TNCs offer the potential for developing countries to access capital, technology, management techniques and external markets, this does not necessarily mean that simply opening up to FDI is the best way of obtaining or benefiting from them. The occurrence of the aforementioned market failures means that governments may have to intervene in the process of attracting FDI with measures to promote FDI generally or

216

measures to promote specific types of FDI. Furthermore, the complexity of the FDI package means that governments face trade-offs between different benefits and objectives. For instance, they may have to choose between investments that offer short as opposed to long-term benefits. The former may lead to static gains, but not necessarily to dynamic ones. FDI may differ from local investment because the locus of decision-making and sources of competitiveness in the former lie abroad, because TNCs pursue regional or global competitiveness-enhancing strategies, or because foreign investors are less committed to host economies and are relatively mobile. Thus, the case for intervening with FDI policies may have a sound economic basis. In addition, countries consider that foreign ownership has to be controlled on non-economic grounds, i.e. to keep cultural or strategic activities in national hands. Consequently, the role of FDI in countries' processes and efforts to meet development objectives can differ greatly across countries, depending on the nature of the economy and the government.

This implies that there is no ideal universal strategy on FDI. Any strategy has to suit the particular conditions of a country at any particular time, and evolve as the country's needs and its competitive position in the world change. Increasingly, it also has to take into account the fact that international investment agreements set parameters for domestic policy making. Governments of developing countries need to ensure, therefore, that such agreements do leave them the policy space they require to pursue their development strategies. Formulating and implementing an effective strategy requires above all a development vision, coherence and co-ordination. It also requires the ability to decide on trade-offs between different objectives of development. In a typical structure of policy making, this requires the FDI strategy-making body to be placed near the head of government so that a strategic view of national needs and priorities can be formed and enforced (Ribeiro, 2000).

Whereas it is now widely recognised that globalisation can engender both positive and negative effects on the growth process, the focus on positive effects has often overshadowed the negative effects. This has been particularly true in the case of FDI. Consultants, from UNCTAD for example, have in the recent past offered comprehensive packages of information on which policies and strategies developing countries should undertake in order to maximise the stimulation of FDI inflows. However, extensive specific policies and strategies on how to eliminate or at least minimise the negative effects of FDI are often overlooked. Yet, it is this maximisation of the positive effects compounded with the minimisation of the negative effects that eventually lead to sustained development.

This chapter is meant to correct this 'traditional' trend, which has occurred in the past either by design or accident. The first section concentrates on policy issues relating to the positive effects of a key factor of globalisation. It focuses on how developing countries can maximise the benefits generated by the positive spillovers of FDI and therefore engender their economic growth rates. In the second section focus shifts to policy issues that relate to how the negative globalisation effects can be contained, so that the economic growth is translated into sustainable development.

Policies for Maximising the Positive Effects of Globalisation

Overview

The foregoing chapters have highlighted the fact that FDI can indeed complement the economic growth enhancing factors of developing countries. In addition, they have presented evidence indicating that the more advanced developing countries are doing comparatively well in translating FDI spillovers into economic growth. In view of this, this chapter concentrates on policy issues that relate to FDI. Its objective is to explore policy issues that a given developing country can pursue including lessons, if any, which it can learn from any country that has been comparatively more successful than it in attracting FDI and in maximising the positive FDI spillovers.

Although the discussion focuses on policy issues pertaining to developing countries in general, in most cases it relates to the less advanced developing countries. It is worthwhile noting that the phrase 'developing countries' is in most cases adopted in this chapter not in a true economic definitional sense, but merely to represent countries at a lower level of economic development than the OECD countries, including the least developed countries. In addition, it is instructive to first highlight the current state of affairs of developing countries.

The economic situation of most less advanced developing countries (48 of which are in an economic definition group of 'least developed countries') has continued to deteriorate, with virtually all major economic indicators reflecting poor performance. Among the many reasons given for this poor performance, UNCTAD (1994) identified the problem of relying on export of primary commodities, and particularly on agriculture. Additional factors include civil unrest, wars and hence mounting social problems. Poor economic performance causes a vicious circle of problems including poor nutrition, increased mortality, lower school enrolment ratios, and lower productivity. These factors then jointly impact directly on the human development conditions and disrupt the country's development, which is based on the capacity to work and, hence, to be productive.

Two issues are of critical significance to developing countries namely, political stability and corruption. Developing countries continue to be characterised by armed conflicts both within and between individual countries. For this reason, the largest share of the already small budgets is allocated to defence, leaving the economic growth-enhancing sectors grounded. Then there is the chronic problem of corruption, which is now almost institutionalised. These require immediate reversal.

The literature review demonstrated that FDI facilitates the economic growth process of developing countries most particularly, through its positive spillover effects. Therefore, FDI is a justified channel through which economic growth can be pursued. However, this can only be effective within certain policy bounds. To begin with, developing countries require to make the environment conducive for FDI and this involves a great effort of liberalisation of the FDI regime. Nonetheless, there is need to safeguard against liberalisation that promotes economic devastation or technological stagnation.

The most effective means of improving economic performance and, hence, revitalising economic growth in developing countries is through industrialisation. However, it is almost impossible to undergo industrial growth without a significant rise in the level of literacy and skills, which help to stimulate productivity. Therefore, policies should be directed at mobilising resources particularly human capital and utilising them efficiently. Unfortunately, developing countries under-fund and provide poor quality services in these sectors. For example, they have low budget expenditure ratios in national budgets, and low absolute levels of funding. Hence, adequate finances, competent management and skilled personnel for primary education are essential in the short-run. In the medium- to long-run, however, middle level and higher education, and better health facilities have to be planned for.

Technology was, and still is, transferred through the movement of men and goods in developing countries. It flows across economies in many ways, disembodied and embodied. The rapid changes in information technology, and the abilities needed for technology transfer have become more varied and skill-intensive. The necessary conditions and factors of useful application cannot, however, be transferred from one place to another, implying that the mere transfer of knowledge and know-how does not by itself ensure successful application. Consequently, necessary conditions are required to capture and diffuse technology, otherwise it slips away. These include the need to strengthen the scientific and technological capacities, and to restructure the existing patterns of international scientific and technological relations. For these reasons, there is a necessity to link the world of technical education to the world of practical work.

The infrastructural services in developing countries have remained comparatively poor and inefficient and consequently deterred the inflow of FDI. But, infrastructure plays an instrumental role by facilitating the production and distribution of goods and services. Therefore, governments require to improve their countries' competitive edges by putting more emphasis on infrastructural development and treating them as necessary conditions for the enhancement of the profitability of business enterprises.

The capacity of developing countries to have sustainable growth also depends on the nature of its trade links with the rest of the world. In addition, sustained economic growth increasingly calls for not only the application of new technology, but also a shift in the production structure from low- to high-technology activities. Unfortunately, most of the developing countries' export bases remain concentrated in natural resource-based products. Therefore, there is a necessity to diversify the export base through the identification of the most competitive industries and stimulation of Small and Medium Sized Enterprises (SMEs). Furthermore, it is instrumental to build a dynamic comparative advantage, whose short-term focus is to move up the next level of technological complexity. Its long-run strategy would then be to deepen the content of export activity and to build the capacity to sustain such a shift across a range of activities in response to the changing world demand and technologies. An institutional environment conducive to exporting can complement the above strategies.

Developing countries' weak economic performance and less sound macroeconomic control have hindered large capital inflows. This situation needs to be reversed by implementing macroeconomic policies that lead to the stability of the currencies in real terms and, therefore, promote the competitiveness of production and, hence, confidence of investors.

A regional economic integration scheme among proximate developing countries, if based on an economic rather than a political foundation, can contribute towards introducing peace and political stability, inducing economic stability, creating a larger resource base, and creating a large economic bargaining unit. It can also lead to maintaining lower relative wage rates, facilitating joint project development, creating a complementary manufacturing region and, hence, attracting FDI and consequently stimulating the growth process. The sections that follow discuss these issues in detail.

Political Stability and Corruption Culture

Political stability Developing countries continue to be characterised by armed conflicts both within and between individual countries. For this reason, the largest share of the already small budgets is allocated to defence, leaving the economic growth-enhancing sectors grounded. There may be several reasons for armed conflict between two or more developing countries. However, in many cases, the persons involved have had hidden agendas of externalising internal problems, accruing economic benefits or attaining political power/authority/influence. Externalising internal problems often comes about when the incumbent leader senses public or military unease or instability within the country, significant enough to undermine leadership creditability. The strategy then is to divert attention elsewhere, in this case by entering armed conflict with another country. The other two cases are straightforward in the sense that they relate to generating wealth or raising one's magnitude of 'political power'. Angola, Namibia, Rwanda, Uganda and Zimbabwe's involvement in Congo can for instance to some extent be linked to the mineral wealth in the disputed area. Nonetheless, it also has a blend of the other two factors. Similarly, Namibia, Sudan and Sierra Leone's internal conflicts are linked to mineral wealth. Likewise, the economic reason can be extended to Liberia's involvement with one of the conflicting parties in Sierra Leone. However, some conflicts including those experienced by the Philippines, Indonesia, China, Israel, Palestine, Eritrea/Ethiopia, Rwanda and Burundi relate more to the desire by the ethnic groups to establish their own sovereign states, or rather self-governance. Therefore, they are often a 'perpetuation' of historical conflicts. The reason for most of the internal conflicts can be summarised into 'selfish' interests. Although, the leaders of the warring factions often claim they take-up arms in the national interest, this is not the case. What they fight for is power, and personal power at that. The simple solution for developing countries is to resolve conflicts at round table discussions, and not through armed confrontations. Moreover, they have to do so by themselves without the expectation of much assistance from the developed countries, which have their own strategic agendas. For instance, the West argues that Africans should solve their problems. No wonder then that they for example stood aside and watched the genocide committed in Cambodia and Rwanda, and are merely watching the other conflicts in Africa. In contrast, the response to the conflict in the former Yugoslavia and in the Middle East (Israel/Palestine and Iraq/Kuwait), particularly on the side of the US was not only swift, but its presence there is now perpetual. Of course one could likewise argue that the Yugoslav problem was a European issue, while the Middle East problem is for the Arabs to sort out. Therefore, following their 'norm' of argument, there is no justification for the US to intervene. Obviously, the fundamental factor is that while Eastern Europe and the Middle East are of strategic importance to the West, particularly to the US, Africa is of little significance. Worse still, when the dictatorial regimes they support collapse, they are very fast to offer safe custody to the ousted leaders. Such was the case when the West kept friendly relations with Zaire's heavy-handed ruler Mobutu Sese Seko, and eventually offered him safe passage to Belgium after the collapse of his regime. Developing country governments must bear in mind the fact that on top of the other negative effects it causes on their economies, political instability erodes the foreign investors' confidence in the host country, and therefore deters FDI.

The developed countries also have a role to play here since in most cases they act as supply sources (directly or indirectly) of the destructive heavy artillery used in most of the aforementioned conflicts. In fact, one may wonder whether some developed countries do not indeed pursue deliberate strategies of destabilising certain developing countries. Alternatively, this comes as a by-product of the developed countries' desire to promote their own interest (i.e. international trade) irrespective of the consequences on the developing countries. This is exemplifies by the controversial British arms sells to Iraq, China, Indonesia and Sierra Leon. Moreover, the so-called commissions of enquiry have acted as convenient channels to silence the critics. Likewise, one can confidently argue that the current problems in East Timor were in effect engineered by the British when they advised Indonesia to colonise those Islands a few decades ago, allegedly to avoid Russia 'communising' them.

Corruption culture   The irony in developing countries is that when a typical village person ('villager') is found guilty of stealing for instance chicken worth $1 to $5, (s)he may face mob justice death. By contrast, high-ranking civil servants and politicians get away with stealing millions of dollars from their respective government departments. Moreover, should they be found out, then the word changes from 'stealing' to 'embezzling'. The political fall out in early-2001 in Peru, Indonesia and the Philippines, and the bitterness expressed by the citizens of other developing countries exemplifies this. Despite this, events in developing countries continue to amaze onlookers. For example, in Uganda, one person alleged to have embezzled for several years was instead given a promotion amidst a public outcry to investigate how he amassed his wealth in such a short time. In addition, at the time of writing (2001), there is an unnecessarily expensive commission of enquiry in the purchase of military helicopters. It has emerged that the *second hand* helicopters were bought for close to $300,000 but sold to the government for over $9 million! The two most immediate questions that arise here are (*i*) why should government pass through a third party in order to purchase (classified) helicopters? (*ii*) doesn't any one in the ministry of defence (including military officers and even the president himself) know roughly how much a military helicopter should cost? A disgruntled Ugandan resident in Canada writes:

...'The Ssebutinde Report on corruption in police has among its recommendations that, 'all officers named must be investigated, and explanations of how they amassed their wealth in excess of their income, made.' I believe that is the single most important recommendation of the report. So important that it should be applied across the board, not only on police officers. A universal audit of wealth for all prominent Ugandans is needed to separate ill-gotten from hard-earned wealth. As a starting point, we could use 1986. Let President Museveni, Maj. Gen. Salim Saleh, cabinet ministers, senior army officers (especially those who have 'served' in the Democratic Republic of the Congo), officers of Uganda Revenue Authority, Airport Immigration Officers, among others, all account for how they earned their wealth. In particular, they should account for the part in excess of legitimate income, as well as the difference between what it was in 1986 to the present. I am in no way defending corrupt police officers; I simply feel the same yard stick applied against them should be used on all others of equal merit'...(name withheld).

Developing countries' leaders should stop playing the hypocrite and lead by example. Persecute the thieves, and make sure those found guilty repay what they have stolen. By doing so, not only will the money end-up in the good causes but, corruption in the FDI enhancing institutions will also gradually diminish.

Liberalisation

Liberalisation of policy consists of many factors. They include ownership policies, taxes/subsidies (including tariffs and transfer payments), convertibility of currency (including limits on dividends and royalties and fees), price controls, and performance requirements (such as export, local content and foreign exchange balancing abilities). Unfortunately, it is beyond the scope of this book to unbundle all these policies and assess their individual impacts on FDI flows to individual developing countries. Consequently, liberalisation of policy is analysed as a bundle of all these factors. General policy considerations are, therefore, presented. FDI regime policy liberalisation should cover three major areas, namely entry requirements, operational conditions, and incentives and legal framework.

It is apparent that positive improvement in policies, regulations and administrative practices as seen by foreign investors is a move towards improving the host country's investment climate. Since factors relating to FDI keep changing with time, it follows that the general investment climate needs constant and consistent improvement for better FDI performance. It is evident from the review that a number of developing countries have come to realise the development benefits of FDI and have responded by liberalising their policies through the institution of new investment laws particularly since the end of the 1980s and the beginning of the 1990s. For example, most developing countries have made a move to improve the investment climate by permitting free transfer of profits and repatriation of capital, providing other incentives to attract FDI, and setting up 'one-stop' investment centres. In addition, the reduction of obstacles to FDI inflows is being complemented, at the national level by the strengthening of standards of treatment of foreign affiliates. These may include legal protection, national treatment, fair and equitable treatment and most-favoured-nation treatment. Many of the restrictions that remain are supposed to safeguard the host country from FDI's potential negative influences. However, there are still some problems. For instance, the FDI trends presented in Chapter 3 demonstrate that FDI particularly in the less advanced developing countries has not responded to liberalisation in the manner their governments had anticipated. Perhaps their expectations have been too high and have been based on a myopic assumption that there is no competition from elsewhere, forgetting that because the less advanced developing countries are not the most favourable locations for FDI, they have to compete with other host countries, including OECD countries, in attracting FDI. In particular, the current image of most developing countries of Africa is associated with civil unrest, war, poverty, diseases and mounting social problems. Subsequently, they are not even listed for consideration by TNCs, let alone make it to the short list when it comes to locational decisions for FDI, despite offering a number of investment incentives. This has raised the question of what additional measures are required to remedy the situation.

Entry requirements Of the various activities of one-stop shops, or other organisations designed to deal with foreign investors, the screening function generally receives the most attention. Screening may be used to decide which foreign investments should be allowed to enter the country. Alternatively, for countries that offer incentives, screening may be used to decide which investment projects qualify for these incentives. A government may, of course, elect not to carry out screening. Instead, it can allow all (or no) foreign investors to enter, or it can grant incentives to all (or no) investors. The rationale for screening is to protect the country from investors who might pursue projects that would be injurious to the economy or from wasting incentives on projects that are not the most beneficial or the most needed (Ribeiro, 2000).

To the governments of most developing countries, the case for screening seems so compelling that few governments are completely open to foreign investment. Most have some mechanism to admit foreign investors selectively or to exercise some choice in allocating incentives. Countries vary widely, however, in the stringency of their entry regulations. Most have general laws or regulations that prohibit foreign investment in certain industries, such as the distributive trade, local transportation, and utilities. Others prohibit substantial foreign ownership of firms or industries that are critical to the nation's defence. Some countries have only general rules in place, others have an active policy of screening each investment (although the applicable criteria governing the decisions that are made may not be at all transparent) (Ribeiro, 2000).

The project-by-project approach to screening seems, on the surface, to be more appealing to a country, given that reliance on general laws might allow the entry of damaging investments. The strongest case for the project-by-project approach is made by countries with tariff and other protection against competition. But even though their governments have relied on screening to reject harmful projects, the skimpy data that exist (largely from one study and considerable casual evidence) suggest that such screening has not been very effective. Indeed, in some cases, it seems that harmful projects have about the same chance of passing through the screen as beneficial ones (Ribeiro, 2000).

Most developing countries have already established 'one-stop shops' which facilitate the processing and approval of investment proposals. Studies by UNCTAD (1995) have, however, revealed that these agencies are not only costly, but have also instead become 'additional' stop points, on a route that still involves a range of government departments often with different perceptions of a given project. Moreover, some of them go beyond the initial objectives, such as screening for compliance with legal requirements or incentive qualification and screening potential investments for financial viability. This is a major mistake. FDI is by definition financed from abroad, implying that foreign firms that go to developing countries take investment capital along with them. Besides having their own capital, it is of no administrative concern to such agencies whether the potential investments are financially viable since it is the firms themselves that suffer losses should the investments not be financially viable.

Investors need to take rapid investment decisions while the money is still available since in most cases there is competition elsewhere from alternative equally fruitful investment ventures. These agencies should, therefore, focus on improving the speed of the investment approval process rather than concentrating on screening and, hence, slowing it. It may prove more productive if they set a target time within which investment approvals should be made, periodically evaluate it by comparing it with actual performance times, and consequently revise/reset it to achieve an optimum performance. The efficiency of processing investment approvals, if good, will earn them credit from the investors and probably even draw in more investment since it will be judged comparatively with the performance of the investment agencies elsewhere. Thus, the efficiency and efficacy of the administrative system that impinges on the entry and operation of TNCs can influence the inflows of FDI. Alternatively, screening and authorisation requirements can be replaced by simple registration on the basis of minimum and generally-applicable requirements. However, for purposes of minimising the negative effects of FDI, there may be a case for screening to continue in specific strategic industries, especially in sensitive activities, or where FDI entry takes place through mergers and acquisitions.

The other problem results from the 'political' appointments of 'loyal partisans' to the top positions in such agencies, who are non-representative of the ministries that they are meant to represent and who are incompetent in handling the technical matters that may arise. This results in all sorts of problems including inefficiency and corruption. Amalgamating party politics with any process such as the FDI process, that acts, as an engine of economic growth can prove counter productive. Hence, the need to make appointments on merit and strictly avoid this kind of cronyism.

Operational conditions Liberalisation is considered to be effective when perceived as positive from the TNCs' point of view. If developing countries want to benefit from the spillover effects of FDI, then they should not only set strategies and conditions for attracting as much of it as possible, but also find the best ways of capturing the spillover effects. Introducing and imposing the at times restrictive *performance requirements* such as the requirement to create and maintain a certain number and type of jobs, to achieve export targets, or to meet a given local content level can prove counter productive. That is, liberalisation that embraces all policy categories can be countered by tightening performance requirements. Developing countries can attain these same objectives through human skills development, the promotion of SMEs, and export diversification. Nonetheless, some countries are relaxing some operational requirements including, restrictions on the entry of professional and managerial personnel subject to emigration law requirements.

Foreign firms want to maximise their profits and this can partly be achieved by keeping production costs, particularly wages, as low as possible. For a given foreign firm, employees from its parent or other foreign country cost it dearly due to the remuneration and additional incentives they demand. As exemplified by Singapore, under normal circumstances, if the host country has well qualified managerial and technical personnel, then the foreign firms do not hesitate to employ them since they are less expensive. This arises from the differentials in wage rates and the currency exchange rates between the host developing countries and the major investing countries. Similarly, due to transport and time related costs, if there exists local firms that can produce the right quality production inputs including components and parts needed for the final assembly process, or any other inputs required for the production process, then the investors prefer to procure them locally instead of importing them from parent or third countries. Likewise, in the presence of small markets, that are characteristic of developing countries, which are not large enough to provide opportunity for scale economies, the investors automatically target the external market and, hence, produce for export in order to reap the benefits of scale economies. Therefore, there is indeed no necessity to put emphasis on these restrictive performance policies. However, it does no harm if developing countries propose a periodic package of rewards to those firms that attain an outstanding performance in exports, local employment, and local content so that other firms which are satisfied with the way they operate without such rewards continue to do so. Alternatively, they can introduce competitions in which interested firms can register and participate.

In this context, it is more important for developing countries to create other conditions that are capable of increasing employment opportunities, exports and local content. Furthermore, they should provide operational conditions that make production competitive and profitable in the global market place and to allow the process of linkage to develop naturally. These conditions are discussed in the later sections of this chapter.

Each country has industries, which it regards as strategic due to various sensitive reasons including the industries' contribution to GDP. However, for developing countries, such industries are few. For this reason, it is more logical for developing countries to provide short negative lists in which foreign investors cannot participate, instead of long positive lists where private investment is allowed. Moreover, such lists should be with respect to government and, hence, public investment and not give local private investment special status. For instance, the negative list may contain properly defined highly protected industries where the government intends to hold a 100 per cent stake. In this respect, it is more appropriate to introduce a national status treatment (discussed under incentives) for foreign investors. Governments can then help local investors (particularly the SMEs) in other ways such as those discussed under diversification.

Some developing countries have still got deregulation wrong by maintaining barriers allegedly in the 'national interest' in areas which are key determinants of FDI inflows. For instance, most developing countries still maintain the operation of departments such as water and sewerage, electricity power generation and supply, and telecommunication services as public utilities often under the names of parastatals. These parastatals, besides being a source of corruption within the investment machinery, are marred with inefficiency and, hence, very little profitability, if any. Moreover, instead of having a progressive improvement that can lead to the attraction of FDI, they are associated with progressive deterioration and consequently form no base in the determination of FDI inflows. These utilities should be run efficiently so that they generate spillover effects of attracting FDI. At the very least, governments should allow joint ventures either between foreign investors and local enterprises; foreign investors and governments; or foreign investors, local investors and governments. Alternatively, they may as well consider management contracts or even unrestricted privatisation.

Incentives and legal framework An appreciation of the benefits that FDI can bring, have resulted in most countries actively seeking FDI, often with the use of *incentives*. As competition for FDI intensifies, potential host governments find it increasingly difficult to offer less favourable conditions for foreign investment than those offered by competing nations. Investment incentives can be classified into:

- *Financial incentives*, involving the provision of funds directly to the foreign investor by the host government, for example, in the form of investment grants and subsidised credits.
- *Fiscal incentives*, designed to reduce the overall tax burden for a foreign investor. To this category belong such items as tax holidays, and exemptions from import duties on raw materials, intermediate inputs and capital goods.
- *Indirect incentives*, designed to enhance the profitability of FDI in various indirect ways. For example, the government may provide land and designated infrastructure at less-than-commercial prices. Or it may grant the foreign firm a privileged market position, in the form of preferential access to government contracts, a monopoly position, a closing of the market for further entry, protection from import competition or special regulatory treatment (Ribeiro, 2000).

Nonetheless, one can pose the following question. What are the deeper reasons responsible for investment incentives? The arguments for this can be broadly grouped into four categories (adopted from Ribeiro, 2000):

- *Distributional considerations* Investment incentives transfer part of the value of FDI-related spillovers from the host countries to TNCs. The more intense the competition among potential hosts, the greater is the proportion of potential gains, which are transferred to the TNCs. If the *total* stock of FDI available for investment in a region is largely insensitive to the amount of incentives being offered, host countries may find themselves providing incentives that simply neutralise other countries' incentives, without actually increasing the amount of FDI they obtain. Such incentives are nothing more than a transfer of income from these countries to the investing firms.

- *Knowledge considerations* Arguments in favour of incentives rely heavily on the assumption that governments have detailed knowledge of the value/size of the positive externalities associated with each FDI project. In practice, it would be an almost impossible task to calculate these effects with any accuracy, even with the aid of well-trained specialists. In reality, getting drawn into competitive bidding for an FDI project is like sending government officials to an auction to bid on an item whose actual value to the country is largely a mystery. As the winning host country generally is the one with the most (over-) optimistic assessment of the project's value to the country, incentive competition can give rise to over-bidding, the so-called 'winner's curse'. If a country offers $200 million in incentives to obtain an FDI project that brings $150 million in total benefits, the country as a whole is $50 million worse off with the FDI.

- *Political economy considerations* Lack of knowledge is not the only reason that can lead a government to offer an amount of incentives that exceeds the benefits of the FDI. The benefits from a particular FDI project are likely to accrue to certain groups within the economy (for example, to a particular region or to workers fortunate enough to get jobs with the affiliate), while the costs of the investment incentives are likely to be spread more equally across the society. This different incidence of benefits and costs among groups in the host country opens the door for politically influential special interest groups to lobby the government to provide investment incentives which primarily benefit them, but which are largely paid for by other groups. The previously mentioned knowledge limitations simply open this door even wider.

- *Introducing new distortions* The discussion has assumed that the cost to a host country of providing a million dollars worth of incentives is just a million dollars. This is overly optimistic. Financial incentives must be financed, and taxes create their own inefficiencies. Fiscal incentives are no better, and non-pecuniary (indirect) incentives can be even worse. For example, granting a monopoly position to a foreign firm allows the host government to escape direct budgetary outlays by shifting the cost onto consumers in the form of higher than necessary prices. Developing countries, in particular, may for budgetary or balance-of-payment reasons feel compelled to utilise highly distorting incentives, such as monopoly rights and guarantees against import competition to foreign investment projects. In contrast, developed countries with 'deeper pockets' may offer straightforward financial grants with less distorting effects. This asymmetry puts developing countries at an extra disadvantage when competing for FDI, beyond a simple lack of deep pockets. Once the realities of using investment incentives to compete for FDI are taken into account, one may be tempted to conclude that the world economy (and the vast majority of individual countries) would be better off with a multilateral agreement that included limitations on the use of investment incentives. Such incentives are no different from any other kind of subsidy program and, as with most other kinds of subsidies, developed countries (and in this case the largest developing countries) can out-spend the vast majority of other countries. Under very stringent conditions, investment incentives can correct for market imperfections. But the reality is that the necessary knowledge is missing, the programs are very vulnerable to political capture by special interest groups, and there is considerable scope not only for introducing new distortions, but also for redistributing income in a regressive way. The latter effect is a particular concern since developing countries as a group are net recipients of FDI. A country's attractiveness to FDI is quite closely linked to the degree of transparency of their policies. The more transparent are the policies, the more attractive the country concerned is to foreign investors (Ribeiro, 2000).

Most developing countries have attempted to provide investment codes that mainly comprise a tax related comprehensive investment-incentive system for private investment. Such schemes are, however, counter productive especially when there is conflict between different government departments, and therefore end up as a form of 'giving with one hand and taking with the other'. For example, a tax concession may be provided in an incentive code (prepared by the investment agency) in order to offset the negative effect of unusually high tax rates (put forward by the Finance Ministry/Treasury Department) that would escalate production costs.

In view of this, giving foreign firms *national status* treatment may act as a better incentive for foreign investors than tax related incentives. A development oriented government endeavours to promote productivity, industrialisation and international trade by providing any possible assistance to its local industry and thus its local investors. Therefore, its tax rates and any other requirements ought to be fair even from the point of view of the investors. That is, such a government does not penalise *the goose that lays the golden egg*. If the foreign investors are given the same treatment, then it amounts to regarding them as *geese that lay golden eggs* and subjecting them to similar conditions. For instance, developing country governments can introduce similar investment codes governing both local and foreign private investment. This treatment may also act as a control measure within the investment mechanism since no party can blame government for favouring the other. It may then bring about more collaboration between the local and foreign investors, create linkages and, hence, promote the spillover process in a more natural way. UNCTAD (1999) reports that during their liberalisation processes, many host countries have adopted FDI-specific laws that spell out the main features of their FDI regimes. As the global economic environment changes, these laws have been adopted to reflect policy changes. For this reason, there has been a move towards treating foreign investors in a similar manner to domestic companies.

Nonetheless, there may be situations that provide a strong case for giving incentives. In this case, it is essential that the host country first carefully weighs the benefits and costs for offering such incentives before choosing the most appropriate incentives. For instance, whereas financial incentives are given up-front irrespective of whether the investment project will be fully realised, fiscal incentives only come into play once the project is successful. The rule of the thumb is to safe guard against engaging a financial incentive-competition race towards the sky, a fiscal incentive-competition towards zero or a policy-competition race towards the bottom (UNCTAD, 1999). Moreover, incentives may play a significant role in luring specific investments if they are target-oriented. For example, a strategy targeting specific technology could offer foreign investment incentives to projects whose products or processes are new to the country. Alternatively, they can offer incentives to existing investors to move into more complex technologies and where appropriate, to increase or upgrade the technological R&D undertaken locally. In relation to incentives, UNCTAD (1999) has suggested the development of industrial parks (as public or private utilities) with high quality infrastructure to attract high technology investors. These parks can either be general or for specific technologies as was the case of India's Software Technology Park reported in Chapter 5.

The progress of attracting FDI particularly into the less advanced developing countries has been slow and may continue to be slow. Hence, the need for a vigorous promotion activity. Foreign investors can only learn about potential investment opportunities and the associated incentives through promotion activities. In addition, promotion helps improve the image of the potential host country as a favourable location for FDI projects. Furthermore, it puts the country on the map and hence, in a position to be short-listed. Therefore, increased marketing strategies aimed at attracting FDI in potential principle home countries and in other centres of investment financing has to be taken as an ongoing strategy. Investment promotion is defined to include certain marketing activities through which governments try to attract foreign direct investors. Promotion excludes the granting of incentives to foreign investors, the screening of foreign investment, and negotiation with foreign investors, even though many of the organisations responsible for conducting investment promotion activities may also conduct these other activities. Investment promotion includes the following activities: advertising, direct mailing, investment seminars, investment missions, participation in trade shows and exhibitions, distribution of literature, one-to-one direct marketing efforts, preparation of itineraries for visits of prospective investors, matching prospective investors with local partners, acquiring permits and approvals from various government departments, preparing project proposals, conducting feasibility studies, and providing services to the investor after projects have become operational.

Promotion involves the provision of precise information on economic data, industry profile, lists and descriptions of potential joint venture partners, privatisation programmes, suppliers, legal framework, investment incentives, and administrative procedures providing information to potential investors. It is also responsible for creating an attractive image of the country as a place to invest, and providing services to prospective investors. Although attracting foreign investment requires efforts in many areas, promotion techniques provide an important mechanism for communicating all these efforts to potential investors.

Promotion efforts are the result of competition by governments in the effort to attract FDI. This competition is not entirely new. What is new is its aggressiveness and intensity. Competition for FDI has also increased because of the entry of new players. Developing countries that traditionally, because of their large domestic markets or significant reserves of natural resources, did not think it necessary to compete for foreign investment have begun to compete seriously for export-oriented investment. This phenomenon appears to be the result of, among other things, changes in the international economic environment that have characterised the period of the late-1970s and the 1980s. During this period, raw material prices seemed more unstable than usual. At the same time, import-substituting policies seemed to be running out of steam. As a result, an increasing number of developing countries eschewed resource-driven and import-oriented growth strategies in favour of growth strategies that emphasised the export of manufactured goods. Further, during the same period, industrial countries became even more active as they began to court not only firms from other industrial countries but also firms from developing countries that were beginning to spawn their own multinational enterprises (Ribeiro, 2000).

The rationale for public programs to promote FDI in developing countries is built on the need to overcome the effects of the market imperfections on investment decisions. For example, it is thought that information about investment opportunities in unfamiliar environments is either unavailable to outside investors, or may be too difficult to find under normal circumstances. It is also sometimes thought that the factors constraining FDI are particularly acute for smaller firms in industrial countries because they have less capacity than larger firms to search for information. Smaller firms also may have less experience with international business and thus may be more prone to overestimate risk in foreign environments. The need for investment promotion is bolstered by what is known about investment decision processes. Studies of foreign investment decisions show that even the largest firms do not systematically search the environment for investment opportunities. Rather, such a search is often a response to problems from the external environment. While firms follow strategies that can include foreign involvement, these strategies are usually shaped within a narrow range of options. As a result, some foreign investors tend to exhibit follow-the-leader behaviour. That is, they respond to the actions of competitors rather than acting as independent decision-makers searching the whole environment for the best investment opportunities. In these circumstances, promotional activities may have an impact on a firm's decisions.

With trade liberalisation becoming increasingly popular and new attitudes toward foreign investment taking hold across much of the world, the approaches governments use to attract, screen, service, and monitor foreign investment are undergoing change. Thus experience is necessary and it shows that investment promotion requires functional expertise in certain key areas. National circumstances can guide the degree of emphasis these functions should receive relative to one another and how that emphasis might change over time. To one degree or another, however, each of the key functions is present when investment promotion is conducted according to international best-practice standards. The key functions of investment promotion include the following:

- *Image-building* It is the function of creating the perception of a country as an attractive site for international investment. Activities commonly associated with image building include focused advertising, public relations events, and the generation of favourable news stories by cultivating journalists.
- *Information* A key function of any investment promotion agency is to gather and distribute the information that prospective investors need to evaluate the attractiveness of a country as an investment site. Potential investors will require accurate answers to questions across a wide range of topics, including current macro-economic data, domestic laws and regulations pertaining to investing and conducting business, the local costs of land, labour, energy and other factors of production, and information pertaining to specific business sectors.
- *Investor facilitation* It refers to the range of services provided in a host country which can assist an investor in analysing investment decisions, establishing a business, and maintaining it in good standing.
- *Policy feedback* Investment promotion generates market-based information on a country's strengths and weaknesses relative to other investment locations. Governments can use this information to adjust, maintain or strengthen competitiveness.
- *Investment generation* It entails targeting specific companies and persuading them to choose your country as an investment site (Ribeiro, 2000).

A promotion agency that engages in investment generation may need to employ senior and more experienced staff members. In most cases, the necessary level of expertise already exist in the industrial community and in other parts of government. A collaboration with all parties could be used by the investment promotion agency to draw on their inputs. In other cases, part-time consultants rather than full-time staff can most effectively provide technical expertise. A good strategy provides a frame of reference and a program of work for the investment promotion agency. In developing an investment promotion strategy, it is necessary to determine the short- and long-term objectives of investment promotion and to find the appropriate balance between investment promotion activities, taking into account important factors such as the investment environment, the comparative advantages of the country, and global developments and recognising that these factors change over time. The development of a strategy also entails understanding what to promote, where to promote, and how to tailor and time the message to achieve maximum impact. Effective promotion should go beyond simply 'marketing a country', into co-ordinating the supply of a country's immobile assets with the specific needs of targeted investors. This addresses potential failures in markets and institutions (for skills, technical services or infrastructure) in relation to the specific needs of new activities targeted via FDI.

A developing country may not be able to meet, without special effort, such needs, particularly in activities with advanced skill and technology requirements. The attraction of FDI into such industries can be greatly helped if a host government discovers the needs of TNCs and takes steps to cater them. The information and skill needs of such co-ordination and targeting exceed those of investment promotion *per se*, requiring investment promotion agencies to have detailed knowledge of the technologies involved (skill, logistical, infra-structural, supply and institutional needs), as well as of the strategies of the relevant TNCs. This way, the first steps could be the following:

- A survey of existing and potential investors to get their views on the FDI environment in a given country and the comparative advantages of that country.
- Development of a recommended strategic mix of investment promotion activities, taking into account the quality of the business environment, the country's overall development objectives (if articulated, factor endowments, and investors' perceptions).
- Identification of the key sectors that may be candidates for targeted promotion.
- Making clear distinction needs in promotion between different categories of FDI. For instance between location-specific investment, which is restricted to a particular location (e.g. to get access to natural resources or the acquisition of a specific company) and mobile investment (in establishing plants or expansion projects), which can locate in any one of numerous countries.
- Recognising alongside unprecedented growth in the volume of FDI, the changing pattern of FDI driven by globalisation and the impact of technology, e.g. new sectors.
- Establishing meaningful relationships with identified target sectors and companies and providing strategic solutions to such companies.

Closely linked to incentives and promotion is the idea of targeting. Investment promotion is like selling a product. Product marketing entails targeting specific market segments. Likewise, investment-attraction programmes should target specific types of investors in accordance to the factor endowments the host country possesses. This initially requires some research to identify the best candidates. The first step is to analyse the trends of investment in either the host country or in a country with identical locational advantages. This gives a clue to the fastest growing type of investment *vis-à-vis* the host country's factor endowments. The host country can then utilise the locational advantages it possesses as strategic tools for the promotion of that specific type of investment. In this respect, a regional grouping may be good for targeting complementary intra-industry activity. For instance, the Toyota automobile networks in Southeast Asia involve the production of petrol engines and stamped parts in Indonesia; diesel engines and electrical equipment in the Philippines; transmission parts in Thailand; and steering parts and electrical equipment in Malaysia, while co-ordination is undertaken in Singapore. Embassies, high profile magazines, web sites and international organisations including UNCTAD can be used to provide the information required by potential investors.

As discussed earlier, most developing countries only started the liberalisation process in the late-1980s and early-1990s. Their legal infrastructure is, therefore, in its 'infant' stage. Such an infrastructure consists of policies involving issues such as private ownership and transfer of property, technology and industry property protection, assessment and payment of taxes, and foreign exchange dealings. The more advanced economies have already passed through several stages of this legislation. The most practical method for a given developing country is to appoint a team of experts in this area who can analyse what has been done in countries that have been more successful in attracting FDI inflows. It can then take on board (with some adjustments if need be) only what is good and relevant to the host country's investment environment. Otherwise, developing countries (most particularly the less developed ones) will continue to be disadvantaged in this area particularly during the bargaining process with foreign investors. For example, when it comes to the question of the transfer of technology, ignorance and often lack of bargaining power has often led to the holders of the technology to include many restrictive clauses, which inhibit the full benefits accruing to the recipient country. Abdel Rahman (1979) has rightly suggested that such negotiations should be held by a group of competent people in order to import the type of technology that is capable of strengthening the local technological base in a country. Such technology should be in line with the technological capability of the country that arises from the possession of assets such as trained personnel at all levels, especially technicians, research equipment and institutes, libraries and reference facilities, scientific and technological publications and discussion forums, pilot and semi-industrial plants, patents and technology transfer rules and regulations, design and consulting services, and appropriate financing and management capacities (Abdel Rahman, 1979). It may also be worthwhile if developing countries maximise the participation of local consultants in engineering contracts to develop basic process capabilities. However, a balance of legal know-how is essential for purposes of avoiding potential future conflicts. Thus, it is important that host developing countries get proper legal advice particularly during negotiations, in which they are often legally disadvantaged. Such advice can be sought from international organisations such as the World Bank, or even from the investing TNCs themselves. Developing countries should revise and introduce more transparent legislation from time to time, avoiding conflict with existing laws as much as possible. UNCTAD (1999) argues that the key to attracting FDI is not only to design appropriate regulatory framework, but also to have timely reviews and constant monitoring of the results, and the ability to change policies and adapt them to new circumstances. One way is through investment policy reviews undertaken by UNCTAD. Moreover, consultation with the relevant stakeholders is crucial before any changes are implemented. No doubt, this requires a strong national commitment, and a strong administrative infrastructure and skill base, able to select technologies, target and bargain with TNCs, and handle incentives efficiently.

Investment agencies   Of course, the discussion of screening, promotion, incentives and legal framework would be incomplete without examining some issues pertaining to the organisations responsible for the formulation and implementation of the policies.

A host governments' side of relations with foreign direct investors in general consists of a the following steps (adopted from Ribeiro, 2000).

- Attracting FDI through a marketing mix of product, promotional, and pricing strategies.
- Screening foreign investment proposals to identify those that are desirable and deserve support.

- Monitoring foreign investment to ensure that the investment conforms to expectations.
- Intervening in FDI if the operations can be made more favourable.

Therefore the following four important features need consideration when formulating agencies:

- The joint involvement of the private sector where possible (e.g. on promoting missions, in meeting new investors and on agency boards where such exist, etc.) seen as beneficial.
- The creation of the one-stop-shop agency insofar as possible.
- The need to have focused strategies in investment promotion aimed at relevant target sectors and companies with good prospects for high-value added products.
- Ensuring that agency staff have the necessary business and sectoral skills to be competent discussion partners with potential investors.

Indeed, one of the most widely recommended and widely instituted changes has been the move to some kind of 'one-stop shop' approach to the management of a government's relations with foreign investors. The one-stop shop takes various forms in practice. The expectation that typically lies behind such a title, however, is that a single organisation in a country is to have responsibility for conducting or co-ordinating various matters related to the entry or supervision of foreign investment. Thus, a would-be foreign investor would have to deal only with this one organisation to obtain all the permits needed to invest in the country. One organisation with responsibility for all investment matters could achieve several goals. In its evaluation of proposed investments, such an organisation could weigh rationally all the advantages and disadvantages of a proposed investment because of its broad perspective and its ability to assemble expertise on a variety of matters in one place. In addition, it could capture the learning benefits to be derived from frequent negotiations with foreign investors. Finally, and usually most important, such an organisation could reach decisions relatively quickly and predictably because only one entity would be involved. Speed and predictability of decisions are thought to be important elements in a program designed to encourage foreign investment. The advantages of one-stop organisations are also believed to extend to other government activities during an investment's life, such as promoting the investment, providing services to investors, and monitoring investment projects.

Nonetheless, it has to be recognised that one-stop organisations are not without downsides. For instance, they may lack the industry expertise that an industry-specific agency could provide, as well as the functional expertise of a line ministry. The national oil-company, for example, is likely to know the oil industry better than any one-stop investment authority. Similarly, a country's department of revenue is the agency most likely to be conversant with the intricacies of corporate taxation. Nevertheless, for the management of most categories of foreign investment in a country, the advantages of these one-stop organisations seem to outweigh any disadvantages.

The first step for most countries that have made the decision to open their borders to foreign investment is to set up an agency to attract potential investors. And while significant intellectual resources have been dedicated to understanding management and decision making systems in multinational enterprises, there is only diffuse knowledge of the activities promotion agencies perform and how they should be organised. There are three basic types of organisations: a government agency dependent on a Ministry, an independent government agency, or a private agency.

Most of the times, the central issue that host governments face in carrying out their investment promotion efforts relates to the nature of the institutional framework that will execute these efforts. In principle, there are two ways to structure an investment promotion agency. The first option is for a government to carry out investment promotion itself (directly as a part of its administrative structure), but this approach has the disadvantage that the government organisation may be unable to acquire the skills required to manage the activity properly. The required skills may reside in the private sector and attracting them to the public sector may prove difficult, especially with the salary constraints typical of the public sector. Another option is the creation of a 'quasi-governmental' organisation. This involves an independent agency, funded (in total or to a large degree) by the government but separated from the government ministries and public financial institutions. This separation would create the image of an independent organisation that is dedicated to serving the interests of investors. An alternative approach is for the government to delegate the management of investment promotion activities to the private sector. This approach often has the disadvantage that the private sector may not execute effectively those related activities, which are traditionally government responsibilities.

Regardless of the approach that is chosen, there will be management issues with respect to how the inherent disadvantages of either approach are to be overcome. In an attempt to overcome these disadvantages, governments may search for the organisational approaches that combine most effectively, the skills and resources of both the public and private sector. The effort in the development/strengthening of an institution capable of carrying out an investment promotion strategy should then focus on two aspects namely, the institutional framework of the agency, and its internal structure and capacity. An 'ideal' investment agency will adhere to the following critical issues:

- Act like top-class commercial service businesses, with a highly professional and efficient approach.
- Act as development agency by seeking not just to undertake promotion but to improve the wider environment for investors while liasing and instigating change with relevant authorities, and by displaying innovation in seeking investment in new emerging sectors.
- Have the mandate and resources to undertake work.
- Be central to national industry policy.
- Recognise a clear 'best practice' agency model. Key elements of this 'best practice' model include having a clear service management system which spells out the service they offer, target segment, and delivery method; uses customised marketing to target clients; pursues FDI in all elements of the value chain; roots FDI through linkage with local suppliers; achieves a high volume of repeat investment; and is focused also on opportunities in new sectors such as e-commerce, software, biotechnology and multimedia.

It may be difficult to staff a promotion agency with appropriate people. Nonetheless, the agency must successfully interact with government, if it is to be of service to investors when they are implementing their projects and if it is to influence policy and the bureaucracy. On the other hand, it must have people who are oriented toward sales. These kinds of marketing people are rare in the public sector and they earn high salaries in the private sector.

Infrastructure

Excellent telecommunication, transport and other facilities such as water, gas, and electricity services which facilitate the production and distribution process of goods and services need to run efficiently in order to facilitate the competitiveness of and for FDI in the global economy. Unfortunately for developing countries, these facilities are often included in the negative list and are, therefore, run as public monopolies. Unsurprisingly, they are inefficient and unproductive, not to mention the corruption riddled within them. To make it even more ironical, the political leaders know of the existence of corruption but take no major steps to combat it! Such is the case in Uganda according to the following extract:

> '...Museveni said the Asians had continued to bribe government officials thereby entrenching a culture of corruption. 'You're the ones letting us down in the battle against corruption because you're the ones who pay the bribes.' He said the Uganda Investment Authority, Uganda Electricity Board, Uganda Posts and Telecommunication, Immigration and Land Offices were rackets of thieves who are crafty enough to hide the deals from him..' (Bende-Nabende, 1995).

Infrastructure is an economic activity, which requires to be competitive and, hence, to operate efficiently. Since the local private sector often lacks the financial, technical and management capabilities for operating such facilities, they ought to be open to foreign companies either through full privatisation, foreign/government joint ventures, foreign/local/government joint ventures or through other schemes such as management contracts.

Of course, there may be a danger of turning a public monopoly into a private monopoly. However, such a danger may be overcome by creating conditions for competitive entry and regulations that hinder the creation of market imperfections. For instance, these utilities can be privatised in such a way that they operate on a divisional level basis, such as regions or districts depending on the most convenient and economical administrative unit at hand.

With respect to telecommunications, the World Bank (1995) observed that governments traditionally held on to the provision of telecommunication services on the grounds that the fixed costs of establishing an operational network were too high for the private sector (mainly local) to handle. However, new technologies and falling costs in telecommunications equipment have greatly increased contestability in this industry. Therefore, governments are finding it increasingly difficult to enforce regulatory barriers to entry. Moreover, developing countries with the minimum necessary telecommunications infrastructure can now leapfrog stages of development by adopting new technologies, such as cellular telephony.

However, it is worthwhile noting that foreign investors will not just automatically participate in any privatisation. In order to design an attractive privatisation program, developing country governments have to take into consideration investor concerns. Political commitment, business orientation, and transparency are fundamental principles of any successful privatisation program. Only if every element of the process, from the design of the general political, legal, and institutional framework down to every single step in the actual sales procedure is based on these principles, can a government expect strong participation by foreign investors.

Human Resources Development

The empirical review highlighted cases where the spillover process was found to be highest via the 'human factor', suggesting that emphasis be put on human resources development in order to increase the economic growth process. Thus, in an ever-changing competitive environment, one of the most important assets for a nation is undoubtedly human skills at all levels. Moreover, a skilled labour-force acts as one of the main determinants of technology transfer and diffusion. Therefore, any country that wants to sustain its development process has to develop a productive and efficient workforce, which is flexible and adaptable to the changing technology. Unfortunately, the workforce in most developing countries is short on technical skills. Moreover, those few people with technical skills that could set the industrialisation process rolling have been forced to look for 'green pastures' elsewhere because of the poor remuneration, and the unstable political and economic conditions their countries offer. To make matters worse, the industrialisation process may start off by utilising an unskilled labour force and then gradually graduates into employing a technically skilled labour-force. However, the supply side of the developing countries is not in a position to cope since it is not science oriented and government funding remains low. Therefore, there is justification for the need to re-plan and refocus the direction of the human resources development process in developing countries. Consequently, there are two important areas that should be examined when considering human skills development, namely pre-employment and post-employment skills development.

Pre-employment skills development   UNCTAD (1994) reported that whereas primary schooling in other developing countries was close to being universally provided, by 1991 only Botswana, Cape Verde and Togo had universal school enrolment among the less advanced developing countries. In problem-ridden countries such as Ethiopia, Mali, Niger, and Rwanda, up to 70 per cent of the children did not attend school. Enrolment ratios have

244 Globalisation, FDI, Regional Integration and Sustainable Development

remained low and when they rise, they do so at a rate lower than the population growth, indicating a potentially persistent problem of illiteracy in the years to come. The situation is worse at secondary school level where enrolment ratios are as low as 4 per cent in the less developed developing countries such as Malawi, and The United Republic of Tanzania. A UNESCO (1993) report concluded that as a whole, the less advanced developing countries' enrolment ratios were half those for the other developing countries and even declined slightly between the late-1980s and early-1990s. The picture is grimmer at the tertiary level where enrolment ratios average at a low 2 per cent and are even lower than 1 per cent for a number of countries. The 1991 figures for government budget expenditure devoted to education on average ranged between 2 and 8 as a percentage of Gross National Product. UNESCO statistics also show that the level of enrolment in private secondary schools has been growing, indicating that there is a high level of demand for secondary schooling which governments are not keeping abreast with. The private sector involvement is only marginal although significant at the primary level.

The current education curriculum in most developing countries focuses on an area that produces a human skills base that is unemployable. For example, UNESCO statistics show that the current university enrolment in most developing countries stands at an average of about 30 per cent for science oriented courses at the first and second degree level although the actual levels vary from country to country. Emphasis is put on arts subjects probably because the unit costs are much lower since equipment and laboratories are hardly essential. At the end of its training process, such a labour force finds itself unemployable. It then joins the 'army' of the unemployed, gets frustrated and, hence, blames government for not creating jobs. No doubt, it forms a potential 'elite guerrilla warfare force' and, hence, a potential threat to the peace of the nation and stability of the government of the day should such an opportunity arise. Then there is the problem of the brain drain. Abdel Rahman (1979) has observed that a developing country attempts to build a strong and qualified 'human base' of highly educated personnel in the different branches of science and technology. But, once qualified, many fail to find jobs corresponding to their training. The level of remuneration and availability of equipment and facilities are such that they are lured back to their sophisticated training grounds abroad or shift to administrative or other professions including politics for which their sophisticated training is unnecessary. Those who stay at the universities and local research institutes are forced to lower the standards of their scientific activities. This process erodes the country's limited precious resources.

Vocational training provides an opportunity for individuals to enhance productivity and disseminate newer technologies. It is capable of enhancing the formal and informal sectors and can be implemented on-the-job or be school based. The provision of technical and vocational training modifies peoples' attitudes towards work, promotes links between theoretical technical education and the world of practical work. Therefore, it provides a strong link between technical institutions and practising enterprises. However, due to various reasons, this programme is currently underdeveloped in most developing countries. For example, the industry and business communities may in principle want to benefit from the national research and development centres, but then find them inadequate to handle the current jobs of designing an industrial process, or building infrastructural services such as large dams and bridges. Business and industry invariably play safe by seeking the experience of international experts and firms. By-passed in this way time after time, the national institutes never gain enough experience to mature and end up by becoming incompetent for even their own economic industrial community (Abdel Rahman, 1979).

In view of these shortcomings, four major policy considerations can be explored. These are, the curriculum, vocational training, school enrolment and governments' funding, and employment opportunities.

The product life cycles of scientific techniques and innovations are becoming shorter and are now likely to become obsolete more rapidly. The implication here is that the curriculum should in general focus on the 'dynamic' ability to access and apply knowledge and technology, rather than only on some particular 'static' (replaceable) state-of-the-art. A special effort is therefore, required to expand and improve the teaching of sciences and technology at all levels by laying greater emphasis on the understanding of scientific concepts, observations, experiments and guidance towards the solution of practical problems (Abdel Rahman, 1979). Moreover, the content of the curriculum should be dynamic in the sense that the science and technology teaching is in keeping with the latest advances in scientific research and technological innovation and takes into account the characteristics of the local environment.

Human skills development begins with driving away illiteracy and, hence, giving a key to the ability to benefit from the accumulated wealth of knowledge and know-how. Thus, the enhancement of literacy and numeracy at the lower-primary level is paramount. Further improvement in education particularly in terms of strengthening the foundation in mathematics and science is then crucial from mid-primary level onwards. Increasing emphasis on technical areas is of relevance at the secondary and tertiary levels. In a nutshell, a special effort is required to expand and improve the teaching of sciences and technology at all levels. During this process, greater emphasis may be put on the understanding of scientific concepts, observations, experiments and guidance towards the solution of practical problems. Consequently, the curriculum should consistently develop to ensure that the focus on specialist areas needed for the country's technology thrust is maintained. A strong national commitment, a strong administrative infrastructure and skill base are the basic ingredients for the achievement of this strategy.

Industrial training can spearhead and complement the industrialisation drive. Therefore, it is essential for investment promotion and economic growth. Linking educational policies and employment policies through vocational training can strengthen the liaison between technical education and the world of work. For example, technical students could be required to work in industries during their vocations preferably under close supervision of the teaching staff.

If education in developing countries is eventually left to the private sector, then only the privileged few, who have the capability to finance it will benefit from it. Therefore, it is essential that respective governments make an effort and increase the levels of budget contributions to this sector. Since their financial handicaps mean that they cannot possibly afford to provide free education for all at all levels, the following recommendations need consideration. The *primary education* level constitutes low unit costs. Developing countries should in principle be capable of affording to finance it. This level of education should, therefore, be made *compulsory* and *free for all*. Uganda has for example undertaken this under the Universal Primary Education (UPE) programme. There is no doubt that UPE is a brilliant idea. However, instead of fulfilling its objectives, the politicians use it as a political weapon for attaining cheap popularity. For instance, it is inconceivable how the pupils can benefit from this programme when class numbers increase to challenging levels of 100 or more, all under the instruction of one teacher! To put this into context, the Ministry of Education regulations recommend one teacher for every 27 pupils. The teachers therefore, end-up by lecturing, and not teaching, and indeed lecturing to infants! In fact, as one headmistress pointed out when interviewed by a British Broadcasting Corporation corresponded, instead of laying the foundation for literacy at the primary level, UPE is in effect a potential ingredient for promoting *illiteracy*! She rightly attributed this to the practical impossibility for a single teacher to conduct an effective supervision in writing and numeracy under such circumstances. No doubt, then that she concluded that UPE is instead effectively developing a 'bomb' of unemployment resulting from lack of basic education, which is bound to explode any time! Moreover, when it comes to accommodation, those students who are lucky get cramped in classrooms that were originally designed to accommodate 40 pupils. The unlucky ones find themselves using tree sheds as substitute classrooms, which are unfortunately prone to weather disruptions. Then there are side factors including sitting arrangements, which range from crowding on small desks, using stones as substitutes for desks, or even sitting on dusty floors that are characteristically infested by jiggers. For the poverty ridden in the rural areas, there is nothing better than seeing notorious children away from home for most of the week, more so on free education. Consequently, there is no better government regime than the one promoting this programme. However, those who have had some exposure on the requirements of education and who have financial capability, have realised the hidden 'taboos' associated with the programme. Unsurprisingly then, they opt for private schools. So, the government plays the quantity game at the expense of quality. Surprisingly enough, even the donor agencies including Britain's Department for International Development, join in this quantity game by unreservedly showing their gratitude on how 'well' their money is being spent! The end result is that a brilliant idea ends-up as a joke. One wonders what will happen when this UPE 'reserve army' qualifies to advance to the secondary level. Converting an idea into tangible results requires proper planning, funding, and most preferably a pilot project and should not be driven by cheap politics.

The unit costs increase with an increasing level of education, thus making it more difficult to finance. In order to encourage mathematics and sciences (often perceived to be difficult by the majority of students) for reasons discussed above, it is logical to make them *compulsory* and *free for all* students for the initial years at *secondary* (probably 2 years). Free education can then be offered to those students *capable* and *willing* to continue pursuing them as core subjects from then onwards. The other students can then only be subsidised by government. However, this also necessitates increasing the funding for the associated facilities such as the laboratories and equipment not to mention the teachers who provide the instruction. The secondary level policy can also be implemented at the *tertiary* level. However, in addition, loans that have to be paid back at a certain time after qualification can be arranged for those students in the paying group. *Vocational training* needs to be promoted at all costs. Therefore, it should be *free for all*. Countries facing financial constraints can seek official development assistance grants to alleviate the problem.

In addition, governments can initiate public-private training partnerships to complement publicly-funded or TNC based training. The idea of whether managers are born or whether they are taught has divided specialists in human resources management. However, given the growing complexity of the global business environment, a modern manager may require a blend of both assets. In view of this, developing countries should encourage management courses by initiating Business Schools. The private sector, including TNCs can be called upon to undertake these programmes if resources curtail the public sector's participation.

Of what value is it for a government to spend so much on educating an individual who, upon completing the formal education process, seeks green pastures elsewhere or becomes a potential threat to its political stability? A mechanism for improving *employment opportunities and conditions* and, hence, retaining the skilled labour force is required to combat the brain drain. First and foremost, developing countries should provide the green pastures within their countries themselves by offering competitive salaries. After all, in the absence of the local skilled manpower, they often employ expatriate staff who may not even be well conversant with the country specific characteristics. Moreover, they pay them far more than they could have spent on the local staff. However, the long-term solution lies in the curriculum which should be designed to create a labour force that is employable, and also in the stimulation of both local and foreign investment which should provide the employment base for the labour force. In the field of technology for example, governments can follow the example Kwami (1983) has reported on Ghana. That is, by encouraging and assisting the education institutions to establish consultancy centres, thus forming a type of technical transfer. Such a centre can then collaborate with all departments of the institution concerned to keep the outside community, particularly the business community, informed of their resources and expertise and to help them to develop technologies of use to the nation as a whole. They can then co-ordinate the consultancies by channelling the outside requests to the relevant departments. Of course, to be able to achieve this, they have to indulge in collecting, organising and disseminating information about the technical, research and training facilities in the country. In sum then, governments should reform research institutions and induce them to sell their services to international standards. In this way, the specialists involved can earn not only money for the institution, but also an extra income for themselves over and above the official salary.

Governments can also improve the financial conditions of academicians by recommending and/or appointing them as members of Board of Directors of the various institutions. Here they can then offer their expertise, skills and knowledge in terms of professional advice and earn a wage in return. They can also be allowed to attend international seminars and conferences from which they can draw some allowances. These extra official incomes from here and there can then raise morale and consequently act as 'retaining' incentives.

Because of political persecution and poor remuneration, all developing countries have a number of skilled personnel abroad. It is important to have a policy directed at convincing these people to get back home. However, this depends upon the provision of good labour policies, good remuneration, and a politically and economically stable environment. Some countries are already making an effort towards combating the brain drain problem. For example, a Return and Reintegration of Qualified African Nationals (RQUAN) Program has been designed and developed by the International Organisation for Migration in co-operation and with funding from participating OECD countries. Countries in other continents have similar arrangements, comprising a total of 61 countries by 31 May 1998. RQUAN for example, promotes the return and long-term reintegration to or relocation within Africa of trained and experienced African nationals by encouraging them to take up key positions of employment or to enter self-employment. It is, therefore, advisable for non-member countries to join and take full advantage of this programme.

Post-employment skills development   There is a tendency for firms in developing countries to over-invest in equipment and under-invest in skills development. But companies require workers to keep abreast with the latest technology in order to remain competitive and productive. Subsequently, as economies become more industrialised, there is need to retrain workers more frequently over their employment life cycles as their performance becomes more dependent on the availability of new technology. Thus, skills upgrading and retraining of the workforce has to be undertaken as an ongoing exercise to update and enhance the skills of employees.

But, developing countries face a constraint on the quality and relevance of the training of their workforce. For instance, the working population is in most cases not prepared to be receptive to technological change. This can be achieved through the in-house training, which can partially compensate for the shortcomings of the formal education system in preparing workers to use technology. Alternatively, manpower development units and staff skills development programmes can be established. Thus, companies can be encouraged to train their staff and upgrade their skills over their employment life cycle. Industrial training with the long-term aim of developing a core skilled workforce for future potential investors and providing assurance of the country's technical capability would be the principle objective in this instance.

In order to improve literacy and numeracy for all, adult education is also important. Adult literacy education enables compensation to be made for certain social-economic and social-cultural disadvantages. This programme can be designed in such a way that besides improving the literacy and numeracy of the older population, it also aims at eroding the negative perceptions from the older cohort and population as a whole. After all, they are looked upon as the 'granary' of knowledge in the informal arena and, hence, have a strong influence on the community.

Skills are an infrastructure in a way and require long-term planning. Therefore, investment in human skills, particularly in the formal sector requires patience. Its duration may take up to twenty or more years depending on what type of skills are being developed, for what purpose they are being developed and, hence, the intensity and technicality of the training. This is reflected in Chan Chin Bock's (Singapore's Economic Development Board Chairman 1972-1974) following statement:

> '... One of Singapore's 1992 (sunrise) industries will be the state-of-the-art computer disk drives. We produce more than $5 billion worth hard disks a year and have earned the reputation of being the world's largest exporter of it. But do you know when we started training skills for such work? 1972 - almost twenty years ago!' (Singapore Economic Development Board, 1996).

In summary, learning is a never ending process. What seems to matter is the quality of education and training, and how effectively it can be employed for productive investment. Investment should, therefore, be made in training that improves skills of employees; develops their ability to adjust to changing technology; and meets growth requirement, replacements, retirements and departures from the enterprises. These will then collectively stimulate economic growth.

Export Production Diversification

The World Bank (1995) reported a rising output share of services, a decline of manufacturing in developed countries and associated decline of imports of industrial raw materials from developing countries. It suggested that much as technology is developing at a very fast rate and international trade is making trade in services a lot easier, FDI remains the main mode of supplying foreign markets. As trade dominance shifts from the manufacturing sector to the services sector in the developed countries, these shifts imply increasing opportunity for export of traditional manufactures by developing countries. After all, industrialised countries are creating more room in the markets for these goods to imports from developing countries.

As stated earlier, heavy dependence on primary commodities is one important reason for the slow growth of developing countries' exports and of their economies in general. Needless to say, there is not only a need but also a chance for these countries to embark on programmes to transform and diversify their economies from those, which rely on natural resources (extractive, or processing type of investment) into modern industrial economies which are internationally oriented.

Expansion of exports requires the development of supply capacities and diversification into production and exports of manufactures, which in turn necessitate increased investment and imports. However, resources are scarce and not all industries possess the same linkages and externalities. UNCTAD (1994) proposed the need for establishing clear criteria in selecting those industries destined for development, upgrading and export expansion particularly where, as in developing countries, the initial industrial base is very small. To achieve this, governments have to provide an institutional environment conducive for exporting. This may involve the provision of trade-related physical and institutional infrastructure including transport and telecommunications, standardised bureaus, efficient procedure for implementing customs procedures, and access to export finance and insurance. The strategy is therefore highly influenced by the national capabilities, government policy and the extent of the TNCs' participation.

Such a program requires a strong backing of the individual countries. Some countries have initiated such programmes but failed to supportively follow them up. The National Resistance Movement government of Uganda, for example, embarked on an agricultural oriented campaign to diversify into what it called 'non-traditional' cash crops in the late-1980s. This included the production of products such as beans, maize and other cereals, traditionally renown for subsistence and, hence, domestic consumption. When the people took up the call and produced far in excess of domestic consumption, the government had not laid any logistics to facilitate the purchase and exporting of these products. The local private sector was also not prepared since it thought that the government had it all planned. The produce remained in the granaries and deteriorated, much to the joy of rodents, and the campaign, therefore, lost meaning.

A diversification programme needs proper planning. If the countries do not know how to transform and start industrialisation, then help can be sought from experts abroad, including the UN (UNIDO and UNCTAD), to tailor a plan for an individual country bearing in mind all its economic and social characteristics. Diversification involves stimulating new free enterprise industries, which are efficient. To begin with, since developing countries have massive unemployment problems, the most immediate strategy should be to stimulate labour-intensive industries with export potential in accordance with their sources of comparative advantages. Productivity and consequent economic growth will then be promoted through gradual upgrading and through the learning-by-doing knowledge spillovers.

The import-substitution industrialisation strategy which the more advanced developing countries pursued in the mid-twentieth century is, however, not appropriate for the less advanced developing countries since their markets are too small to make it viable. Export promotion in developing countries with little technical and managerial know-how and financial handicaps can be accelerated by investment promotion and industry development. The latter requires a comprehensive package of development assistance programmes to help local enterprises to expand and upgrade. It can be achieved through incentives such as financing schemes particularly targeted at SMEs. These schemes can include low investment loans for SMEs for equipment and upgrading programmes. This alone is, however, not sufficient. There is further need for co-ordination at all levels. This can be achieved for example, by organising workshops bringing together relevant government agencies, academia and private sector organisations to brainstorm the issues of SMEs. In addition, it may involve creating a body with responsibility for establishing SMEs, examining their problems and needs, and eventually helping them to evolve into efficient, well managed, technically competent and professionally operated utilities. This co-ordination has two advantages. First, it places both TNCs and SMEs in the industrial policy-making process. Second, it creates a direct link between the public sector and the private sector. Eventually, it may lead to the initiation of training programmes for domestic companies aimed at upgrading their product quality and productivity. The main objective of such a scheme is to encourage SMEs to provide support services for TNCs, establishing linkages and, hence, integrating into the value chain of the international division of labour. Thus, support has to be given to local domestic exporters and encourage efficient supplier networks. It should also encourage TNCs to upgrade local functions, promote conditions that promote subcontracting, and promote technology alliances between domestic firms and TNCs. There is no better way of deepening linkages than by raising the capabilities of potential suppliers. In addition, the promotion of SMEs neutralises the long-term vulnerability of relying on FDI alone. The long-run objective is that the SMEs develop into large enterprises capable of pursuing foreign investment ventures elsewhere. Additionally, developing countries should institute policies aimed at enhancing exports through upgrading and make sure that they upgrade their sources of comparative advantages on a continuous basis. This will assist in reducing trade deficits and balance of payments problems. Other export-oriented strategies that can be pursued include targeting FDI conducive to export competitiveness and upgrading. This involves providing information to the promotion department in areas where potential exists. UNCTAD (1999) suggests that a special effort could be made to draw FDI into industries in which the host country has a revealed comparative advantage. That is, where its exports of a product are growing faster than exports of that product world-wide.

There is no doubt that the external environment has influenced and will continue to influence the growth prospects of developing countries, although in a less favourable way particularly in Africa. For instance, the commodity boom is not as good as it was during the early-1970s, and the entrepreneurial capability has remained low in most developing countries apart from in Asia (to a small extent). Policies should change accordingly, be flexible and take advantage of any factors that result from the external environment such as the growth of the OECD countries that results in increased demand and, hence, international trade.

Even if the above recommendation stresses the need for developing countries to take advantage of the shift of investment from the manufacturing to the services sectors in the more developed countries, it should not be taken primarily and exclusively as if they must follow the 'footsteps' of the more developed countries' development process. Developing countries with comparative advantages in the service sector, particularly the tourism industry, can also take advantage of the current focus and exploit the benefits that may accrue from this industry by treating it as a special 'niche'. That is, they should allow niches within the service sector to also take over from the primary and secondary sectors. They can also attract FDI into natural resource processing and induce a greater value added in resource-based exports. In fact, developing countries should try as much as possible to avoid exporting raw materials, which are then processed in developed countries and resold to them at a multiple price. For example, instead of exporting raw hardwood timber, why not produce plywood, furniture and floor tiles? Likewise, instead of exporting iron and copper ore, why not export steel bars, copper pipers, and copper wire? Surely, the type of technology required for these activities should be fairly standard and therefore affordable. Besides creating more wealth, this strategy leads to both increased domestic value added and to considerable technology transfer. UNCTAD (1997c) reports that there is a risk of converting valuable natural resources into less valuable finished products. However, if this is the case, then developing countries should make provisions for processing the raw materials for domestic consumption and make sure that the raw materials that are exported are not re-imported in a processed form. This was originally a colonial strategy, which repressed local manufacturing so that processed goods were bought from the colonial masters. It should not be allowed to continue.

Foreign Exchange Rates and Macroeconomic Controls

Owing to developing countries' weaker economic performance and less sound macroeconomic response to large capital inflows, the likelihood of the capital inflows is still quite low for these economies. The fleeing of both physical and human capital can only be averted if confidence exists in domestic markets. Such performance will depend on the effectiveness of their policies in maintaining macroeconomic stability, encouraging domestic savings and investment, and providing an incentive structure that promotes competitiveness and attracts FDI. This involves providing investors and exporters with a stable financial environment reflected by low inflation, and low variability in inflation and real exchange rates, thereby protecting external competitiveness. There is also need to improve budget deficits, current account deficits, private capital inflows, government consumption, national savings and investment. The good news is that the problem of transferring/repatriating funds has so far been overcome by many developing countries through the establishment of open market Foreign Exchange Bureaus where currencies are freely transacted. However, countries may reserve the right to impose temporal exchange control restrictions in the event of balance-of-payments crises.

Moreover, lessons can be learnt from the 1997/98 Southeast Asian financial crisis, which originated in Thailand. This is how it developed. The indigenous population initially dominated Thailand's labour force. However, the recent rises in labour costs forced it to rely increasingly on immigrant cheap labour. Evidently, Thailand came to the end of the easy stage of export-orientation and started losing competitiveness. Having benefited from the flying-geese model of development, it failed to upgrade its activities including infrastructure, education and R&D in order to keep abreast with it. Thus, in a nutshell, government policy was limited in its involvement in upgrading its created assets. Moreover, it found itself locked between two strong competitors. At the upper end was Malaysia with a superior infrastructure, while at the lower end were several countries including China, Indonesia and Indochina whose relative wage rates were more competitive. This together with the over valued baht prompted the loss of competitiveness to the neighbouring less developed countries. Inadequate upgrading made it highly vulnerable to interruptions of capital inflows. As a consequence, the inflows started slumping, exports decreased and its trade deficit increased, maximising the risk of serious balance of payments problem and a sharp slow down in growth.

Furthermore, Thailand has not relied exclusively on foreign capital since its domestic investment has remained strong for a long time. However, its degree of reliance increased as time went by. Its persistent high growth rate lured investment worth billions of dollars even in the unsustainable real estate industry. No doubt, there was strong need for more liberal policies particularly in the financial sector. The liberalisation of foreign exchange controls since 1991 and the promotion of overseas corporate bond issues, encouraged speculative movement of capital. Financial liberalisation increased domestic lending and eventually slipped over from the financing of safe and productive investments to risky speculative assets. Furthermore, the liberalisation of the financial sector gave the private sector access to large amounts of cheap foreign capital. This put excess risks on banks followed by wide spread defaults and hence bankruptcy. Moreover, as the indigenous firms grew and became foreign investors themselves, their activities became less transparent and more difficult to monitor leading to problems of over-borrowing, over-investment and indulgence in risky financial operations. This then led to a very rapid expansion of the inflow of short-term 'hot money'. As a consequence, Thailand's short-term debts started exceeding its short-term foreign reserves. This was made worse when the government at first took no action to regulate matters, and further when it squandered more of the country's foreign exchange reserves in a misguided attempt to defend the over valued baht. Domestic interest rates were increased to slow down the economy and improve external payments by attracting additional capital inflows and expanding bank liquidity and further lending. However, the loans became non-performing and the banks were weakened further. Further, in July 1997 the government abandoned baht's exchange rate peg to the dollar by devaluing its currency. Between May and September 1997, the baht and Thai asset prices had lost about 50 per cent of their original value. When investors realised this, they lost confidence in the economy and gradually started withdrawing their investment. The investment withdrawal eventually developed into a stampede, which the local banks could not cope with without defaulting. Even when the IMF made provision of emergency funds, this did not solve the problem but encouraged the stampede particularly when the IMF insisted that dozens of financial institutions be closed. Other creditors then withdrew their savings. The stampede then spread to the neighbouring countries. Thus, prudential limits on bank lending, capital adequacy requirements were improperly enforced since financial liberalisation meant abandoning the necessary checks.

Because of the aforementioned factors, developing countries need to provide effective prudential regulation and supervision of the banking system. Even this may not be sufficient. There is further need to create instruments to restrict and/or monitor the level of capital inflows in order to contain their impact on macroeconomic and monetary conditions.

The Role of Regional Economic Integration

Most of the economic blocs comprising developing countries have been established with a major focus on political than economic considerations. Political differences have occasionally triggered off misunderstandings that have been so bad as to bring about de-integration, as was the case for the EACM in 1978. Regionalism among developing countries can only be of economic significance if its foundation is based more upon economic than political arrangements. Nonetheless, a 'political will' is instrumental for its survival.

The low share of intra-regional trade in these blocs, however, indicates that the capacity to progress towards a viable economic integration is quite low. Because of their poor economic performances, developing countries have very low per capita incomes and, hence, market sizes, low financial bases, low technological capacities and capabilities, poor infrastructure, and lack of a comprehensively skilled labour-force. Earlier observation revealed that the economic benefits, which developing countries can accrue from the regionalism effects are minimal most particularly because of their low per capita incomes. The short-run recommendation would therefore, be to discourage any attempts towards such collaboration. Needless to say, it is the long-run benefits that are at stake. Time will come when developing countries' markets will grow. Moreover, there are some advantages that can be derived even at this level. Thus, it is worthwhile laying the foundation sooner than later. Besides, as illustrated below, there indeed are reasons why regional economic integration can be useful to developing countries. These include scale economies, macroeconomic and political stability, bargaining power, technology transfer, wage inflation, investment relocation, joint project development and investment targeting.

Scale economies This is no doubt the oldest argument. Developing countries' markets are often too small to realise scale economies. The combined market size of a regional bloc may create a market capable of realising scale economies for particular goods and services. Consequently, FDI can be attracted, when the TNCs look at the whole region as a single unit and not as individual segments as before. The combined skilled labour base can also then be equally capable of attracting FDI.

Macroeconomic stability Macroeconomic stability is critical to the continued success of any development strategy. Regional economic integration can help support stable macroeconomic policies. Real-financial links pertinent to regional economic integration agreements require stable macro-economic policies if the agreements are to function smoothly. In order to ensure a stable partnership, countries must share information, co-operate in advocating stable fiscal and monetary policies, and engage in strong 'peer pressure' against unstable policies (Plummer, 1997). In most advanced regional agreements, countries find that they must focus on non-traditional areas affecting trade and investment, including competition policy and government procurement if they are to advance economic integration. These 'non-border' measures force a stronger market-orientation, inject more microeconomic competition by reducing the power of domestic monopolies or 'rent-seeking', and place constraints on government spending through, for example the abolition of export subsidies and restrictions on industrial policies (Plummer, 1997). Furthermore, the influence of special interest groups seeking protection may diminish, leading to more openness in the trading and investment environments. As these policies exacerbate transparency problems and make micro and macro reform difficult, they are often the greatest culprits when instability and/or economic stagnation is in evidence in developing countries. Thus, such forced macroeconomic stability could be highly beneficial to the economic development strategies of participating countries (Plummer, 1997).

Political stability If properly planned, regionalism may contribute to the political stability which, is a baseline requirement for FDI activities in any given country/region. In an economic bloc, a member country would reconsider antagonising another member country because of the possible combined repercussions of the other member countries. For instance, since guerrilla war activities against a given country are often launched in neighbouring countries whose relationship with the target country is not good, this could be minimised under an integration scheme. Regional economic blocs are, therefore, good for the consolidation of peace. Economic co-operation in Southeast Asia was for example, seen as an important vehicle for political stability goals in the region. To the extent that regional economic integration agreements add to the political stability of the region, they do service to economic development in general and the goal of policy reform in particular, even if the agreements have very weak substance to them (Plummer, 1997).

Bargaining power The combined effort of regional economic integration can improve the member countries' bargaining and manipulative power with both the TNCs and other regions or countries. This then gives developing countries an opportunity to not only use their country specific characteristics to attract the offensive import-substitution and rationalisation type of investment, but also to use the regionalism effects, i.e. market growth, and tariff-discrimination to attract the defensive import-substitution investment.

Technology transfer and FDI Regional economic integration accords can promote FDI inflows through reductions in transaction costs, and in doing so, they are able to establish an attractive business environment within which TNCs can easily benefit from the vertical division of labour. In addition, member countries will, at the margin, gain more technology transfer, in view of the greater technological gap. Moreover, formal regional integration agreements can help in creating a strong underlying framework for the protection of intellectual property and put pressure on the implementation of associated laws. This further strengthens the attractiveness of the environment in which the TNCs like to operate. Furthermore, a regional economic bloc can be used by the member countries in jointly devising means to import appropriate technologies.

Wage inflation Wage inflation can also be held back under regionalism by a wide use of intra-regional labour flows, thus keeping the relative wage rates lower than the other competitive countries and, therefore, attracting FDI.

Relocation of production Even if the relocation of production can still be implemented in the absence of regionalism, its presence would facilitate such relocation since it would imply that there are fewer obstacles to be overcome. Similarly, even if regionalism would make the more developed member countries to benefit from the FDI inflows at the expense of the less developed member countries as Bende-Nabende's (1999) results suggested in the case for the ASEAN-5 after the formation of the APTA, the less developed member countries would *ceteris paribus* benefit in the long-run through the relocation of production under the flying-geese concept. However, this requires the presence of at least two relatively developed countries, one to act as the 'lead goose' (such is the case of Japan in Asia and the US in America) and the other to act as the 'support goose' (such is the case of the NIEs of Asia and America). The lead goose, in the course of its own development process, constantly develops new industries and passes on to the next-tier countries those in which it has lost competitive advantage. Bearing in mind that most of the relocation of production takes place on a regional basis, it would require these countries to either be within the organisation or be geographic neighbours. It is evident that Africa is still disadvantaged on this basis. For instance, South Africa (the 'lead goose') has more Anglo-economic links than Afro-economic links. However, the Asian and American developing countries could respectively benefit from spillovers from Japan and US. Of course, the shortcomings of the role of South Africa as a development engine for the sub-Saharan African region have to be appreciated. The economic circumstances behind the growth of the Southeast Asian countries for instance vary considerably from those of Africa. To begin with, South Africa has to contribute to capital formation of the neighbouring host countries through FDI. Although this has started happening, the future extent of its operations might be quite limited. This is because South Africa itself has serious unemployment problems to address, and these will take quite a while to solve. In addition, an untapped reservoir of labour in South Africa suggests that the potential for labour-intensive production in that country has not been exhausted. Therefore, any deliberate attempt to restructure by relocating production to the neighbouring countries can come under strong opposition. Moreover, compared to the lead geese in other regions, South Africa's innovation capabilities are comparatively lower. However, its relatively rich endowment of human capital is conducive to the development of new industries, which could gradually replace those that are based primarily on an abundant supply of cheap labour. Specifically, this flying-geese model is workable if the countries are at different levels of development; have the ability to restructure; posses sufficient demand and markets; have market verification of restructured industries through internationally competitive exports; posses enabling framework for the transmission of TNC assets; and have a favourable investment climate (UNCTAD, 1997). UNCTAD (1997) observes that of these conditions, only the first is satisfactorily met by the Southern Africa region. However, although there is a move towards containing the other factors, most of the conditions necessary for the initiation of intra-regional restructuring are still far from being in place.

Joint project development   There is the potential for collaboration in project development and implementation, which would be too expensive to be undertaken by individual countries. Together they can plan projects involving foreign private investors such as improving infrastructural facilities, in transportation, telecommunication, common investment negotiation and promotion for the whole region.

Investment targeting A regional grouping may be good for targeting complementary intra-industry activity. This has for instance, been successfully achieved by Toyota in Southeast Asia. Toyota's automobile networks in Southeast Asia involve the production of petrol engines and stamped parts in Indonesia; diesel engines and electrical equipment in the Philippines; transmissions in Thailand; and steering parts and electrical equipment in Malaysia, while co-ordination is undertaken in Singapore.

A step towards free trade Of course supporters of multilateral trade and investment (MTI) may disagree with such protectionism. For instance, the World Trade Organisation (WTO) is advocating for multilateral trade. This is a good idea, albeit only theoretically. For example, MTI would reduce transaction costs to TNCs resulting in greater supply of 'investible funds' or lower costs of FDI or both. The agreement would also reduce uncertainty that is typically a major component of investors' risks. Since the agreement would also most likely include elements that can be seen as 'prudential regulations', it would certainly reduce the volatility of capital flows. Moreover, MTI would be an important instrument towards avoiding unilateral restrictions against each country's exports. Last but not least, since MTI would also include a dispute settlement mechanism, it would give weaker and smaller countries a better chance to protect their rights. Nonetheless, it comes at a time when Europe is pursuing further integration and when America intends to extend its integration with Central America and eventually South America. Thus, whereas the Western countries want to generate benefits from regionalism, they evidently want to intimidate developing countries through such international organisations, which often act as their 'mouth-pieces'. For instance, whereas the US is against the Asian countries forming a free trade area, the idea becomes palatable when the possibility of an APEC free trade area in which it would be a member is envisaged, no doubt demonstrating the US' selfish interests. Furthermore, the WTO is rather fragile since the 1999 Seattle Ministerial Meeting failed to launch the anticipated Millennium Round. In large measure, this failure was due to the US insistence on labour and environmental standards which developing countries, in particular Brazil and India, felt would deprive them of their comparative advantage, as well as infringing on their national sovereignty. In addition, larger developing countries (i.e., Brazil, Indian and Indonesia) have been reluctant about services sector liberalisation under the General Agreement of Tariffs and Trade (GATT) because they fear that industrial countries with well developed services sectors, will hinder them from building up their own equivalent services.

Strictly speaking, regional trade co-operation is a breach of the idea of multilateral removal of trade barriers, and is against the principle of non-discrimination. But, who first breached this principle? The significant exemption to the principle of the most favoured nation clause in the GATT rules was Article XXIV of 1947, which allowed countries to form regional arrangements in the form of customs unions and free trade areas. Such regional trade arrangements meant that a given country could discriminate in favour of member countries and against non-member countries. This is a clear breach of the most favoured nation clause, which states that if one country is given preferential treatment, then other member countries of the WTO are entitled to similar treatment. The main reason for the introduction of this exemption to the GATT rules was a need to ease the European reconstruction through a gradual phasing out of protective trade barriers within Europe, but without obliging European countries to liberalise to the same extent *vis-à-vis* the US. The US supported the enactment of this exemption because of the opportunity afforded to build up Western European regional co-operation, which America had favoured. Most important, was the US' strategic and political agenda. For instance, an integrated Western Europe would prove a stronger partner and ally against the Eastern bloc. A condition of receiving Marshall Plan aid was for Western Europe countries to start the abolition of import restrictions between themselves. Although Article XXIV was originally tailored for Western Europe, the general acceptance of regional trade associations by GATT was based on the recognition that closer co-operation between neighbouring countries would be of value in its own right. In addition, such co-operation would be hard to establish under the principle of a single-tiered global most favoured nation clause.

Generally speaking, it is easier to liberalise trade when economic conditions are good. If, however, economic problems arise, then those forces that seek to solve them by protective measures gain greater influence in the formulation of economic policy. For instance, when a recession increases unemployment, the most immediate measure is to shield domestic industries in the hope of creating jobs. This generates a negative impact on the outside world, which in turn resorts to increased protectionism. From this point of view, it is then arguable that developing countries, characterised with increasing debt and balance of payments problems, are comparatively in an economic crisis. If an economic crisis in Western Europe warranted a tailored exemption from most favoured nation clause, then there is no reason why developing countries should not similarly have a tailored exemption under their current economic hardships.

The theory of free trade presupposes the fulfilment of certain assumptions of imperfect competition. These theories include assumptions of scale economies and enterprise specialisation, and of the existence of external economies. If these assumptions are not fulfilled, then protectionism can become an option. That is, normatively applied, these theories clearly demonstrate that there are advantages of intervening, either in form of industrial or trade policy measures. The most notable example is that provided by the argument that it is necessary to protect infant industries by means of import duties. These measures can be made in order to realise scale economies or to achieve external economies.

In fact, rather than being a stumbling block to multilateralism, outward-looking regionalism is an effective stepping-stone towards non-discriminatory global trade. Thus, regional trade arrangements may be seen as a step in the direction of increased global free trade. Needless to say, this may only be true if there is a general lowering of trade protection between the different regional blocs.

Channel of economic growth A major mistake developing countries make is that of trying to emulate European regionalism very fast without first considering the repercussions. For instance, there is this ambitious programme of COMESA that is aimed at an integration towards a fully developed common market extending from Egypt in the north to Lesotho on the south. It happens at the time when on one hand some of its members such as Botswana, Lesotho, Swaziland and the Republic of South Africa are still strongly committed to SACU, and SADC, while on the other hand Kenya, the Republic of Tanzania and Uganda are trying to forget their old differences and revitalise the EACM. This definitely implies that there is a difference in priority. For instance, the 'hidden' reason behind Kenya's pursuit for the revival of the EACM is its rivalry with South Africa. For example, Kenya's industry is losing its Ugandan and Tanzanian market shares to South African products. Thus, a common external tariff could help alleviate this. What would be more realistic is for the establishment of two independent economic blocs independently (i.e. the EACM and

SADC), making sure that they operate efficiently, and then developing trade links between them before finally merging them.

Policies for Minimising the Negative Effects of Globalisation

Overview

In this section, focus now changes to sustainable development-oriented policies and strategies that can be undertaken by both the developed and developing countries to protect the environment, reduce the North-South equity divide and minimise human insecurity.

The Brundtland Report (1987) recommends a new approach to development. An approach which gives developing countries a larger role and greater benefits; and which maintains the balance between economic growth and the ecosystem, so that natural resources can support growth over the long-term. It emphasises the need to revive economic growth, particularly in developing countries, as well as on the qualitative aspects of growth. It proposes that growth should involve lower energy consumption, more equitable sharing of its benefits, and satisfaction of the essential needs of developing countries. Therefore, there is a need to understand and propose new governance structures and mechanisms at the global and local levels, encompassing political and social needs of the State, social movements and NGOs, grassroots movements, the media, multinationals, organised citizens, the science community and religious movements, among others.

Globalisation should be managed properly so that it does not become merely the survival of the biggest, and the most powerful. The current means of management is via global trade rules. If these rules are fair and transparent for all, not just the most vociferous or historically influential, then globalisation can become a road to prosperity for many. Thus, if the interconnected world is to work for everyone, not only should effective multilateral trade rules be applied for open trade, but the international rules countries play by should also be fair.

Social policies and national governance are more relevant today to make globalisation work for human development and to protect people against its new threats. Therefore, new policies are needed to tackle the negative effects. For instance, the world needs market policies that protect elite labour, and promote job-creating growth, invest in workers' skills, promote labour rights and make informal work more productive and remunerative. Policies should support national cultures, not by shutting out imports but by supporting local culture, arts and artists. All countries need to rethink their social policies for redistribution, for safety nets and for the universal provision of social services. In a nutshell, what is required is an approach that combines human development and poverty eradication with social protection.

Thus, even to the extreme anti-globalisation activists, while some vigilantism may still be required, the way forward in the globalising world should not be to try to prevent change. Rather, it should be about looking for reform that will improve life in the country and provide support for those who are losing out. Anti-globalisation activists' involvement should now shift away from confrontation to dialogue. It is time to change from being anti-establishment to being proactive.

Although the topics are not mutually exclusive, the policy considerations more or less follow the format presented in Chapter 4. For instance, policy issues are examined under environmental, North-South equity divide and human insecurity sub-topics. The exception is that the role of international institutions is elevated to a major sub-topic. Some of the policy issues discussed have been adopted from Gueneau et al's (1998) 'Globalisation and Sustainable Development: 12 fact sheets'; and from Barker et al's (1999) 'Alternatives to Economic Globalization: A Preliminary Report'.

Environmental Issues

Company-specific environmental policy instruments   The dominant concern in the globalisation debate is not just about economic flows. It is about preserving biodiversity, addressing the ethics of patents on life, ensuring access to health care and respecting other cultures' forms of ownership. It also goes further to address the growing technological gap between the knowledge-driven global economy and the rest trapped in its shadows.

While organisations of a liberal cast still give international trade a leading role in environmental protection, they recognise the need for environmental policies to accompany trade liberalisation. Producer countries, like the international community, have an interest in seeing international trade play a positive role in the conservation of resources and in having in place market conditions that enable environmental costs to be taken into account.

Environmental degradation (acid rain, global warming and ozone depletion) has transboundary consequences, particularly for poor people and nations. Such emergencies demand global action, with initiatives building on the progress at the global conferences in Kyoto and Buenos Aires, and on proposals for tradable permits and clean development mechanisms.

The potential of the new technologies for human development and poverty eradication should be tapped. For instance, intellectual property rights under the TRIPS agreement need comprehensive review to redress their perverse effects undermining food security, indigenous knowledge, biosafety and access to health care.

Multilateral negotiations on the environment is one way through which the different perceptions these societies have of the environment and the priorities they set themselves are expressed. While the proliferation of international meetings has spread awareness of the worldwide scale of environmental problems, a number of developing countries still think that the environment is essentially a problem for which the countries of the North are responsible. Instead, they are more concerned by the concentration of technical and financial resources in the North, and the fear that their own environmental problems (i.e., desertification and access to drinking water) and especially their development problems (i.e., food security and health) will be neglected as efforts are concentrated on the global problems to which the North gives priority. From the developing countries' viewpoint then, combating poverty is the most important step that can be taken towards halting the damage being done to the environment (Gueneau et al, 1998).

Regardless of who is to be blamed for the current environmental problems, the best way forward is for both the developing countries and the developed countries to accept that indeed a problem exists and should be addressed. The three policy instruments namely, *economic*, *regulatory* and *voluntary* that can be used to moderate the problem are discussed below.

Economic instruments give individuals and companies an incentive to behave in a way that does not affect the environment. They act directly upon costs and prices in order to establish market trading conditions where these conditions are incomplete or absent.

The first instrument is 'the polluter-pays principle' under the taxes and fees scheme. Adopted by OECD in 1972, it states that 'the polluter should bear the expenses of carrying out the measures (introduced by the public authorities) to ensure that the environment is left in an acceptable state'. It may prove necessary to pay polluter countries to adopt good environmental practices in cases when pollution crosses frontiers. This is the case with acid rain, whose effects on biological diversity, the health of forests and the acidification of lakes are felt beyond the borders of the emitter country. Similarly, river pollution can have harmful effects in countries situated downstream (Gueneau et al, 1998). In such cases, solutions have to be sought through co-operation between the country producing the pollution and the country suffering from it, the latter agreeing to finance part of the clean-up effort. In this latter instance, the polluter-pays principle becomes the 'victim-pays (contributes) principle'.

These taxes or fees penalise practices or ways of using a good that has a detrimental effect on the community. They seek to correct market mechanisms that do not reflect social costs in their entirety, or otherwise enable external effects to be internalised. Taxes or fees can be used at different stages of polluting production processes. The most common sort are levied against polluting emissions (air, water and noise). Others include usage fees covering the cost of collection and treatment services; and taxes on polluting products at the manufacturing, consumption and disposal stages. Examples are taxes on fertilisers, pesticides and batteries, and environmental taxes on energy.

Gueneau et al (1998) point out that taxes and fees have the advantage of increasing the production costs of polluters, who thereby have an incentive to curtail or halt polluting practices. With the exception of instances where they are so high as to discourage the offender altogether from following polluting practices, taxes and fees generally lead to a rise in tax receipts. Nonetheless, they also have a number of drawbacks. For instance, while this principle has been widely accepted by Governments and aid organisations, its generality implies that it does not always enable the most appropriate and most profitable measure to be chosen. For example, the fact that pollution may cross national boundaries makes it difficult to identify, let alone to monitor the polluters. Moreover, it is almost impossible to 'allocate' the level of pollution to individual businesses, and difficult to establish the optimum level of pollution. Particular care has to be taken to ensure that taxes and fees do not have adverse effects on the competitiveness of small businesses. The worst scenario, however, is when they are transferred to the consumers.

The second instrument involves subsidies, which in contrast with taxes and fees, are aimed at promoting consumption of products and services that do not harm the environment. For example, subsidies for commercial fuels other than wood and charcoal for heating and cooking use, subsidies for renewable energy (wind and solar energy), and subsidies for fertilisers to discourage extensive agriculture practices that threaten ecosystems. The obvious problem with subsidies is not only the burden they impose on the public purse, but also the misappropriation and abuse opportunities they create. In fact, in some countries they are just another way of squandering what are already very limited tax resources.

Nonetheless, amalgamating taxes with subsidies sometimes proves effective. In this case, the revenue from taxes levied on polluting firms can be paid out to companies that choose to invest in environmentally sound practices. Competition thus induces the former to change their practices to bring them into conformity with the environmental regulations in force.

The third instrument, which relates to the allocation of global quotas of pollution rights is aimed at spreading efforts to combat pollution among different actors while enabling the public authorities to maintain a global cap on polluting emissions. This cap takes the form of a set number of individual transferable emission rights. The public authority distributes the rights either by sharing them out between the companies concerned on the basis of what they produce, or by putting them up for auction or for sale at a fixed price. Each enterprise is thus authorised to pollute up to the maximum represented by the sum total of the rights it holds. Any additional pollution is penalised, unless the company purchases new pollution rights from another, 'cleaner' company, i.e. one that has not used up all its pollution rights. Thus, in any given area, increased emissions by one producer can be made up for by a reduction in the emissions of another one, through the mechanism of permit trading (Gueneau et al, 1998). This approach can, however, be impaired when the 'clean' companies refuse to sell their right. For example, when the developing countries refused to sell their pollution quotas to the US, it culminated into a conflict, which eventually led to the Kyoto declaration being undermined.

Regulatory instruments comprise a system of penalties aimed at enforcing environmental quality objectives set by the public authorities. They may set a limit on the quantity of pollutants that producers can emit, or require them to adopt non-polluting systems of production. For these rules to be effective, compliance should be rigorously enforced so that those who contravene the rules are subjected to criminal penalties.

Gueneau et al (1998) have listed four specific regulatory rules that can be implemented. First, are environmental quality rules, which set general quality objectives, based on the capacity of the environment (e.g. maximum carbon dioxide content in the atmosphere). Second, are emission rules that set a maximum authorised level of polluting discharges in a given place. An example is a limit on vehicle noise emissions. Third, are product rules, which specify the characteristics of a product. For example, lead content of petrol. Lastly, are rules on production processes. These specify the technical production methods to be used and the anti-pollution systems to be installed.

Since they do not lead to externalities being internalised in the production process, regulatory instruments are criticised for neglecting the economic component. The four cited by Gueneau et al (1998) are as follows: First, regulatory measures are the outcome of a political decision-making process that is not governed either by a desire to achieve the optimum economic solution or by scientific considerations. Often, they are arrived at by tacit agreement between the Government and polluting industrialists. Second, environmental damage is maintained at exactly the level the rules allow. For instance, concerned above all to preserve competitiveness, companies make no effort to lower their pollution level below the regulatory limit. Third, all users are obliged to make reductions in the same way and to the same extent. Thus, a ban on car use is more costly to taxi drivers and others who earn their living on the road than to those for whom private car use is not an essential part of work, and who can switch to another form of transport. Fourth, in certain cities, for example, rules on vehicle use are undermined by registration fraud. In general however, the regulatory approach can also be curtailed by the aforementioned monitoring problems.

Voluntary approaches are presented as a third generation of environmental policy instruments. They lay emphasis on negotiation, compromise and voluntary agreement between economic sectors and the public authorities, and sometimes NGOs. These mainly fall under three categories. The first one is a unilateral undertaking by a company thereby involving its shareholders, its customers, its employees and the public at large in the implementation of a self-regulatory environmental programme. Thus, it takes the form of a company code of conduct, which can be manifested in its mission statement. The second alternative is a negotiated environmental contract between the public authority and the company, setting out the environmental objectives to be achieved, and a timetable for attaining them. In return for this undertaking by the firm, the public authorities undertake to exempt it from domestic legislation. For instance, they may stop enforcing compliance with any general legislation, and only retain enforcement concomitant with the terms of the contract. Under the third alternative, the terms of reference to which companies can subscribe voluntarily in exchange for accreditation or specific labelling of the products they sell are drawn up by the public authorities. The terms of reference may relate either to environmental performance (an emissions reduction objective, for example) or to the technology or production procedures used. These mechanisms include systems of environmental labelling otherwise referred to as eco-labels.

Because of its voluntary nature, the scope of corporate responsibility is currently conceptually unbound. The current key issues relate to human rights, the environment and workers' rights. Thus, companies are socially responsible for both the direct and indirect negative effects imparted upon the respective stakeholders through their operations. The negative effects can take on any form including employment downscaling, environmental pollution, technology transfer, local labour-force training, promotion of local entrepreneurship and creation of linkages. Thus, negatively affected groups are expected to ask or make protests to companies causing these impacts to take measures to prevent, reduce or rectify such consequences, or otherwise to internalise costs resulting from their activities (UNCTAD, 1999).

Civil society groups have increased their focus on devising monitoring and public reporting programmes that can add enforcement aspects to the implementation of voluntary social responsibility codes. The advantage of the voluntary *vis-à-vis* legally binding codes is that the former are sometimes more efficient and cost-effective to address technically complex and rapidly changing business operations. Otherwise, negotiating new international legal regulations can be a cumbersome, time-consuming process that can yield results that may be already overtaken by technological or managerial change the day an instrument enters into force (UNCTAD, 1999).

By involving firms in the political planning process, these approaches not only give company heads greater incentives to achieve environmental objectives, but also enable environmental progress to be achieved more rapidly. Moreover, consumers are given a chance to choose products made by companies that can be seen to be making a voluntary effort to protect the environment. Companies that show willingness are rewarded by growing 'green' demand.

Gueneau et al (1998) argue that these instruments do not work against the logic of the market, and they appear ultimately to place fewer demands on the public authorities than certain traditional tools. Nonetheless, their effectiveness depends partly on how the public authorities act. They need to ensure that negotiations are democratic by seeing that the broadest possible range of actors (companies, consumers and associations) is represented. In addition, they have to be on their guard against the strategies of polluters wishing to pass on their costs to society. The public authorities also need to be aware of the problems of competitiveness that may arise for SMEs, as the voluntary approach entails a fixed cost that may be proportionally higher for them than for large firms. Green marketing may be seen by big companies as an aggressive sales strategy that smaller and less financially powerful companies cannot match.

International environmental policy instruments   International law governing relations between States is the main tool for promoting sustainable development worldwide. Gueneau et al (1998) argue that the provisions of international law should not only establish fundamental principles and rules of conduct, but also create frameworks of co-operation. This enables States to jointly determine their common interests and the sectoral policies needed to preserve them. These policies are then expressed in the form of economic instruments, obligations of trade measures and rights enshrined in multilateral agreements. Ultimately, private regulation initiatives tend to develop on an international scale.

Bilateral rules enshrine the duty of States not to cause damage to the environment beyond their own territory, to co-operate and to inform other States about any pollution or any risk. However, the multilateral approach, which is of very long standing, has been greatly strengthened in three successive stages starting in the 1970s. In the first instance, it was greatly developed to deal with sectoral environmental protection problems, the effects of which were supposed to be felt particularly at the local level. These include for instance, protection for the sea, continental waters and the atmosphere, and conservation of wild flora and fauna. A further stage in the development of international environmental law was marked at the end of the 1970s following growing awareness of the need for transversal rules for substances that were potentially damaging to the environment at every stage in their life cycle (production, transportation, commercialisation and disposal). In these areas, recourse has often been made to codes of conduct or non-binding directives drawn up by the branches of industry concerned. The drawing up of real laws, of a preventive nature, to deal with global problems such as the need to safeguard the ozone layer, preserve biodiversity and combat the greenhouse effect formed the milestone of the beginning of the final stage. In each sector or transversal field, a proliferation of international treaties is developing (Gueneau et al, 1998).

Consequently, the idea behind international environmental law is not so much to harmonise national rules, but rather to prepare the instruments needed to protect interests deemed common to all humanity. It has gradually adapted to the different environmental challenges, transcending the old framework of inter-State responsibilities, through the creation of true global management instruments, most of them economic.

Despite the progress that has been made in terms of both quality and quantity, though, there are still major difficulties in applying international environmental law. According to Gueneau et al (1998), the greatest obstacle to the implementation of international environmental law derives from the economic disparities between States. In particular, what may appear to one Government as merely an administrative formality may be an insurmountable task to another. Merely participating in international negotiations to conclude an MEA can sometimes be a problem. Since MEAs are voluntary agreements that only apply to signatory countries, certain countries can refuse to sign-up, and opt to go it alone. By doing so, they avoid the obligations and constraints dictated by the agreement and at the same time gain certain economic advantages. For instance, they can benefit from a short-term competitive advantage in energy costs since signatory countries are obliged to implement costly policies to reduce the greenhouse effect. In addition, the architecture of the international legal system is also a source of difficulties. Different environmental agreements, be they bilateral or multilateral, are co-ordinated with one another. But, conflicts of authority can still arise in the absence of any ultimate governance, which would require some sort of world environmental organisation. More broadly, there are serious problems of compatibility between MEAs and other international legal provisions, such as the multilateral trade rules of the WTO, particularly in view of the fact that the legal texts that set up the WTO make no reference to the precautionary principle. Recourse to trade instruments on the basis of an MEA can also lead to conflicts with the WTO rules. Lastly, the fact that treaties are in many cases not binding makes it difficult to apply and consolidate them even as the good intentions expressed by States accumulate. Moreover, international regulations are often judged to be ineffective because of their rigidity and the wide scope for evasion and abuse even when they do include legally binding provisions. Liberals criticise them for placing restrictions on the free working of markets. Nonetheless, this position is tending to weaken as economic instruments are increasingly incorporated into MEAs. Indeed, whether they take the form of taxes, subsidies, eco-labels or negotiable permits, the proper functioning of economic mechanisms can only be guaranteed by the legal instrument from which they derive (Gueneau et al, 1998).

Trade policy instruments Many MEAs provide for trade measures, which essentially have the following three objectives:
* To secure a total or partial ban on trade in products obtained from endangered species, such as ivory or skin and fur products (as with the Convention on International Trade in Endangered Species of Wild Fauna and Flora).
* To penalise or prohibit international movements of polluting or dangerous products (as with the Bamako Convention).
* To provide purchaser countries with information as to whether a traded product is 'environmentally sound' or harmful (Gueneau et al, 1998).

The measures employed to achieve the first two objectives include trade embargoes, and import or export permits and quotas. Those employed for the third objective on the other hand include prior informed consent procedures (i.e., regarding the hazardousness of a product being traded), and eco-labelling procedures for a product manufactured in accordance with specifications previously negotiated multilaterally. Unfortunately, the *eco-labelling* instrument is not included in the provisions of any MEA. For it to be applicable, it would require the parties to an MEA to establish sustainability criteria and indicators that companies in the signatory countries would have to comply with to obtain an eco-label for the products they sold. In most cases, negotiations stall when it comes to defining sustainable practices. It is partly for this reason that international convention on the protection of forests has yet to yield any fruits. In effect, eco-labelling is currently being developed primarily at the national and regional levels, raising problems of international competition. Nonetheless, international non-governmental initiatives are now emerging from alliances between industrial groups, environmental movements and social organisations to certify that environmentally sensitive economic activities are being managed sustainably. The *ISO 14000 standards* approach on the other hand finds less favour among States and international organisations than the one developed by the ISO. The ISO 14000 comes in response to the pressure applied by an ever-growing body of consumers who want to be informed about the environmental quality of products, without having to pay a great deal more for them. This tool also enables companies to improve their environmental performance, and to comply more easily with national environmental legislation. The characteristic features of the ISO 14000 standards apply exclusively to systems for assessing procedures and do not oblige producers to meet any environmental performance criteria in excess of minimum legal requirements (Gueneau et al, 1998).

Measurement of wealth   Created in the early 1990s, indicators of sustainability have been developed as another way of responding to the need for environmental information in political and economic circles, and among the public at large. This approach made a strong comeback at the beginning of the 1990s largely because it had the backing of certain international organisations despite being criticised in the 1970s for being incomplete and static, and then abandoned in favour of accounting methods. The objective of green GDP, a strictly macroeconomic approach to environmental accounting is to adapt the SNA by adding a number of elements to it. These include the cost of environmental damage and depletion of stocks of natural resources, environmental management costs, and the value of environmental services. In this way, by treating the consumption, depletion and reconstitution of natural resources as so many types of intermediate consumption, the value added by production can be reduced and GDP figures corrected for damage to the environment (known as green GDP), can be calculated. This method was applied for the first time at the end of the 1980s by the World Resources Institute, which evaluated the disappearance of Indonesian forests in order to include this in figures for net domestic product. However, this demonstration, which was widely covered by the media, was more valuable as a way of alerting environmentalists and economists to the failings of the SNA than as a contribution to the development of a macroeconomic indicator representative of the sustainability of the Indonesian economy. Costa Rica undertook a similar exercise more recently, giving rise to a great deal of debate. A consensus has finally been reached. For instance, it is now being accepted that environmental accounting efforts should concentrate more on the establishment of accounts that can be used to support sectoral decision-making than on the calculation of green GDP. Nonetheless, the intrinsic characteristics of the environment, which is essentially non-tradable has exposed certain discrepancies in SNA adjustments and green GDP calculations (Gueneau et al, 1998).

Gueneau et al (1998) have observed that the satellite accounts approach supplements the economic information appearing in the SNA without altering it. It is used in a number of countries to provide detailed accounting information on a particular activity, such as research, education, transport, social protection or the environment. In this last area, satellite accounts serve to put into perspective the efforts being made by a country to protect the environment. They combine physical data from statistics on the state of the environment and natural resources with the information available from the main body of national accounts, such as expenditure on restoring the environment or the costs of environmental damage. Consequently, they extend the analytical capabilities of the SNA in selected areas. Unfortunately, they do not change the traditional macroeconomic indicators (GDP and GNP) at all, and consequently do not correct their failings.

The most promising uses of environmental accounts are not so much at the macroeconomic level, where the practical applications of these accounts are poorly defined and major problems of methodology remain. Rather, it is at the sectoral level, where demand for such instruments reflects precise needs, such as water or forestry management. The different names used in environmental accounting (satellite accounts, natural heritage accounts and natural resource accounts) do not reflect major differences of principle. These three accounting tools serve the same purposes. However, creating such accounts entails an effort to bring structure and coherence to data on the environment, and to integrate and organise information. By showing the state of natural resources and environments, and the way these change as they are subjected to the pressures of human activity, they provide the kind of knowledge about the environment that is needed for effective management. These accounts provide a picture of the major trends in environmental change and the impact of sectoral economic activities on flows and stocks of resources (and vice versa). Environmental accounts collect together basic data that can be used to produce indicators of sustainability, such as data on the intensiveness of forest use (Gueneau et al, 1998). Therefore, they contribute towards the production of sustainable development policies.

The Role of International Institutions

While multilateral agreements and international human rights regimes hold only national governments accountable, national governance holds all actors accountable within national borders. But, these are being overtaken by the rising importance of supranational global actors (TNCs) and international institutions (IMF, World Bank, WTO and Bank for International Settlements). It is partly for this reason that poor countries and poor people have little influence and little voice in today's global policy-making forums. For instance, whereas developing countries are a majority of the WTO's members, its discussions can be dominated by the concerns of older, richer members. The most influential is the G-8, whose members control the Bretton Woods institutions through voting rights, and the UN Security Council by occupying three of the five permanent seats. Moreover, although there have been many efforts to develop collective third world positions through such bodies as the G-15, the G-24 and the G-77, there is no developing country body equivalent to the G-8 or OECD, with similar levels of resources, consultation and policy co-ordination. Consequently, a feeling that their voices are not being heard can frustrate poorer countries. In fact, half of the least-developed countries have no representation at the WTO headquarters in Geneva.

An essential aspect of global governance, as of national governance, is responsibility to people through equity, justice and choice enlargement for all. Therefore, needed are standards and norms that set limits and define responsibilities for all actors. Some of the key institutions of global governance needed for the twenty-first century include, a stronger, broader and more coherent UN to provide a forum for global leadership with equity and human concerns; and a global central bank and lender of last resort. In addition, there is need for a WTO that advocates for both free and fair international trade, with a mandate extending to global competition policy with antitrust provisions. Furthermore, the global era requires a code of conduct for TNCs, a world environment agency, a world investment trust with re-distributive functions, and an international criminal court with a broader mandate for human rights. Even before these long-term changes are initiated or achieved, many actions could be taken in the short-run. For instance, a great deal more work is needed on how to strengthen national labour laws and enforcement of existing laws through national, regional, and global mechanisms. From this point of view then, the principle of subsidiarity, that decision-making should start with strong local institutions and then work up toward regional, national, and global institutions, still requires effective global implementation.

The World Trade Organisation   Rather than responding to the ineffectiveness of the trade rules with the scrapping of the WTO, as proposed by some (extreme?) anti-globalisation activists, the better option is to retain the WTO but ensure that the trade rules work for all. But without a rules-based trading system, the powerful countries can bully the rest not least by striking mutual deals, which exclude poorer countries. The WTO needs reform, which enables more effective participation in the WTO and international trading system by developing countries. Hence, the need for an open and rules-based international trading system, equitable trade rules, and an effective voice for developing countries. In addition, there should be a continuing reduction in barriers to trade, both in developed and developing countries, and work to improve the capacity of developing countries to take advantage of new trade opportunities. Furthermore, there is need for the WTO to commit itself, with the rest of the international community, to achieving the International Development Targets. This would be a powerful signal of its commitment to poverty reduction and sustainable development, and acknowledgement that trade is not an end in itself.

The United Nations Although there is now a special body dealing with the subject, the governance of sustainable development within the UN system is complicated by the existence of numerous UN agencies that take a close or passing interest in environmental and development issues. These include the Food and Agricultural Organisation (FAO), the UN Development Programme (UNDP) and the WHO. In addition, there are regional programmes and organisations, not to mention the secretariats of the international conventions on climate change and desertification.

Two fundamental issues need to be addressed. First, rather than engage in embarrassing conflicts, there should be more co-operation between UN organisations. Second, the weight of influence given to the UN organisations should be comparable to that given to the international economic institutions. More generally, there is the need for in-depth reorganisation of the institutional architecture of sustainable development. It is partly for this reason that a number of political actors have put forward the idea of a superstructure, a World Environment Organisation (WEO), as a sort of counterpart to the WTO.

The Commission on Sustainable Development The main function of the CSD is to promote and evaluate implementation of Agenda 21 by strengthening co-operation between States and institutions in all areas. The CSD has concentrated on a number of priority issues including sustainability criteria for development, financial resources and mechanisms, education, science and technology transfers for environmental ends, and decision-making structures and the role of the main actors concerned with the environment.

Since its foundation, the CSD has played an important role in creating a common basis for action between developed and developing countries. Most of these countries have set up a national commission for sustainable development and drawn up national strategies. The CSD has also provided a forum for discussion in which NGOs, and to an ever greater extent companies, have a strong presence. Nonetheless, it currently suffers from two failings. On the one hand, it does not have the real power it needs to enforce the agreements entered into at the Rio Conference. On the other hand, it is basically composed of ministries of the environment from member States. Gueneau et al (1998) argue that if the CSD is to be a place where international policy is really made, its working agenda will also have to include economic issues, and it will need to be able to involve ministers of finance. By taking a stronger position on economic policy, the CSD could provide an institutional basis upon which consensus over policy co-ordination and harmonisation of minimum standards could be built.

International economic organisations Gueneau et al (1998) have observed that in parallel with the changes going on within the UN system, economic organisations, foremost among them the World Bank, are planning to reorganise their activities to take account of the sustainable development principle. However, they are poorly prepared to deal with this new issue. In particular, these attempts at reorientation have been highly criticised so far, specifically by ecologists, who often describe as 'window dressing' the way in which these organisations take environmental matters into consideration. Nonetheless, more and more interest is being shown in the idea of establishing international environmental standards that would enable the governance challenges posed by international trade rules and competitive pressures to be identified. For instance, there have been proposals to set up a single multilateral body to deal with international environmental and sustainable development issues. The first relates to co-ordination of the use of economic and financial instruments. As discussed earlier, fiscal and economic instruments are being used more and more to apply environmental agreements. The effectiveness of these instruments would undoubtedly be enhanced if the institutions involved shared their experience with one another. This was the substance of a proposal by UN Environment Programme (UNEP), whose project to set up an intergovernmental panel on the use of economic instruments provided for by conventions unfortunately failed to arouse the interest of the international community. The second relates to integrating the private sector and civil society. Even though a great deal of progress has been made in bringing together NGOs and the private sector in the international decision-making process, NGOs still point to democratic failings, in respect of legal recourse for example. For instance, the idea of giving a central role to the International Court of Justice by creating an Environmental Division has not come to anything. Other proposals include the introduction of an international environmental mediation function, which could enable NGOs to take action to enforce MEA compliance by States. Another proposal is for the creation of international networks with competence over a limited number of issues of worldwide importance, which would bring together representatives of civil society, the private sector and Governments. Such transversal networks could be used to counter institutional inertia.

While international institutions have opened up to NGOs, what is most striking, is the way the great international economic organisations have gradually opened up to civil society. The UN, for example, has granted several hundreds of them observer status in international debates. The positions of NGOs generally seem to be less dogmatic now than they were in previous decades. Consequently, many NGOs have moved from a strictly anti-establishment position to a proactive one. Taken together, these components of civil society are playing a more and more important role in drawing attention to environmental problems and putting them on national and international agendas. Their influence has been brought clearly to light by their participation in several UN conferences. But, this is still not enough. Therefore, NGOs should be given more status in these organisations.

The Kyoto negotiations only reinforced the division between North and South over strategies for combating the greenhouse effect. At previous Conferences of Parties, it was agreed that developing countries did not have to accept binding commitments because it was the industrialised countries that were historically responsible for greenhouse gas emissions. At Kyoto, the US went back on this position. This aroused categorical opposition from developing countries, which believe that rich countries ought to show the way in reducing emissions. However, Gueneau et al

(1998) argue that it seems to be indispensable for countries such as China, India and Brazil, whose contributions to the greenhouse effect are increasing, to enter the agreement. Besides, they have every interest in doing so, both for economic reasons and to improve their development models. For this to happen, though, their participation needs to be under conditions that take due account of their core development requirements.

The North-South Equity Divide

Trade and investment All countries need strong and coherent policies for managing their integration into the rapidly changing global economy. Therefore, narrowing the gaps between rich and poor and the extremes between countries should become explicit global goals.

In order to negotiate more favourable provisions in multilateral agreements, poor and small countries need to pursue active participation in the global dialogues on multilateral agreements from their development to negotiations and then implementation. Poor and small countries can gain from collective action to link negotiations on intellectual property rights with rights to emit carbon into the atmosphere, and to link environmental assets, like rain forests, to negotiations on trade, debt and investment. They can also gain in negotiations by pooling resources for policy analysis and developing common negotiating positions. Since regional collective action is a first step in this direction, this is where the role of regional integration could play a paramount role in increasing their bargaining power. Therefore, they should utilise regional solidarity and regional institutions to develop common positions for negotiations. In addition, it would help to maintain policies and practices consistent with economic and financial stability. Furthermore, a regional support fund such as that for financial stability proposed in 1997 would help in crises.

In addition, the West should institute a pro-development negotiating position in a new Trade Round, including substantial cuts in high tariffs and in trade-distorting subsidies, especially to sectors such as agriculture and fisheries, which are important to developing countries. Western Europe should recognise that its CAP is an unfair barrier to the access of developing countries to their markets. Therefore, the recent European Commission proposal which would allow all exports from least developed countries into the EU duty free, except for arms should be implemented.

As consumers reasonably press for more information and higher standards to protect labour and the environment, developing country exporters find it hard to keep up with the proliferation of regulations and standards. They fear the 'process standards' on labour, animal welfare or the environment, may be used to keep their products out of developed country markets. While there is need to promote core labour, environmental, social and health standards, the West should deliver information and quality to consumers while still enabling developing countries to export and grow their way out of poverty. Standards should not be used to lock developing countries' products out of their markets.

Official development assistance Developing countries need help to make their emerging industries conform to global environmental agreements and objectives (such as on emissions of greenhouse gases) as well as their own national priorities for sustainable development. While protecting the fragile resources of the planet, and the people who depend on them, makes globalisation work, richer countries cannot expect developing countries to do this alone. They have to make sure that aid does what it's supposed to do. That is, not only to reduce poverty by strengthening the arm of the poor, but also to create conditions to attract inward investment and boost economic growth. Donor countries should stop tying aid only to suppliers. In addition, they should work to ensure that aid is more effective and is focused on low income. Aid from developed nations needs to dovetail with realistic strategies to reduce poverty, designed and led by developing countries themselves.

In sum, stronger international action is needed to support growth and accelerate human development in marginalised countries. This requires reversing the decline in flows of ODA, down by almost a fifth in real terms since 1992. Even without increasing resources, ODA can be targeted more to the countries in greatest need, and to achieving key human development goals.

Debt relief Currently, debt payments cripple the ability of many developing countries to invest in development. For several highly indebted poor countries, then, development is dependent on concerted international action to reduce what they owe. Tentatively, the member States of the Paris Club (the main public sector creditors) have cancelled some debts, most of them owed by low-income countries. Conversion solutions for reducing developing country debt were also put forward at the end of the 1980s, including proposals to establish a 'debt for nature' trade-off mechanism (Gueneau et al, 1998).

Debt relief for the heavily indebted poor countries whose debt payments have been squeezing spending on education and health should be given priority. Gueneau et al (1998) recommend that any resolution to this crisis should include an expansion of the resources available, and the countries eligible, for bilateral and multilateral debt relief. Moreover, this relief should not be conditioned on IMF and World Bank structural adjustment programs and it should allow countries to dedicate sufficient resources to health care, education, social services, and environmental protection. The IMF should enforce Article 6 of its charter, which highlights the need for it to oversee capital controls, not capital account liberalisation, and to end structural adjustment. In addition, the IMF need only retain minimal capability as lender of last resort, and gather and publish international economic data. Furthermore, decision-making by the IMF board needs greater transparency and accountability. This could be fulfilled, in part, by introducing greater democracy in voting and publicly releasing all information about its operations.

In addition, regional, national and local agendas should be drawn. At the regional level, regional funds should be created outside IMF control to ensure a quick response to crises while maintaining regional sensibilities and interests. At the national level, the rules and institutions of the global economy should allow maximum space for national government policy making to regulate the amount, pace and direction of capital movements. National governments should set regulations and incentives on cross-border transactions so as to eliminate capital flows that are entirely speculative (e.g. gambling on market fluctuations as differentiated from hedging risk) and can undermine the real economy. National governments should strive to reduce the volatility that has characterised exchange rates since the collapse of the Bretton Woods arrangements in the early-1970s. Any international regime should reinforce the ability of governments to maintain this stability. At the local level, local and national regulations and taxes should be structured in such a way so as to encourage local investment and control of local capital. Local education initiatives should also inform citizens about the power of using their assets (Gueneau et al, 1998).

Transinational corporations   TNCs influence the lives and welfare of billions of people, yet their accountability is limited to their shareholders, with their influence on national and international policy-making kept behind the scenes. If they were brought into the structures of global governance, their positions would become more transparent, and their social responsibilities subject to greater public accountability. Greater public accountability and more transparency would make their operations more democratic and increase their credibility.

A multilateral code of conduct needs to be developed for TNCs. Today, they are held to codes of conduct only for what national legislation requires on the social and environmental impact of their operations. True, they have in recent years taken up voluntary codes of ethical conduct. But multinationals are too important for their conduct to be left to voluntary and self-generated standards.

The Human Development Report 1994 proposed a world antimonopoly authority to monitor and implement competition rules for the global market. That authority could be included in the mandate of the WTO but with representation from both the developed and developing countries, and also with representatives of civil society and private financial and corporate actors. A joint World Bank-UN task force should be set up to investigate global inequalities and suggest policies and actions on how they can be narrowed over the next two or three decades. The task force should report to the UN Economic and Social Council and to the World Bank Development Committee.

Digital disparity Communications networks can foster great advances in health and education. They can also empower small players. For instance, the previously unheard voices of NGOs helped halt the secretive OECD negotiations for the Multilateral Agreement on Investment, called for corporate accountability and created support for marginal communities. Barriers of size, time and distance are coming down for small businesses, for governments of poor countries, and for remote academics and specialists. Information and communications technology can also open a fast track to knowledge-based growth. This is exemplified by India's software exports, Ireland's computing services and the Eastern Caribbean's data processing.

The governance of global communications especially the internet should be broadened to embrace the interests of developing countries in decisions on internet protocols, taxation, domain name allocation and telephone costs. Public investments are needed in technologies for the needs of poor people and poor countries, in everything from seeds to computers. An international programme should be launched to support this. New funds should be raised to ensure that the information revolution leads to human development. New sources of financing for the global technology revolution could be investigated, to ensure that it is truly global and that its potential for poverty eradication is mobilised. A 'bit' tax and a patent tax could raise funds from those who already have access to technology, with the proceeds used to extend the benefits to all. In addition, more connectivity can be achieved not by just individual ownership, but by setting up telecommunications and computer hardware, and focusing on group and, hence community access. Furthermore, more capacity can be realised by building human skills for the knowledge society, and more content by putting local views, news, culture and commerce on the Web. Likewise, more creativity can be seized by adapting technology to local needs and opportunities, more collaboration by developing Internet governance to accommodate diverse national needs, and more cash by finding innovative ways to fund the knowledge society everywhere. The challenge is to connect more people from the world's poorest countries with the benefits of the new globalisation. Nonetheless, this depends on political will, and on governments and people across the world.

Human Insecurity

Financial volatility   The financial crisis in East Asia spot-lighted the inadequacies of national and global governance in managing economic and financial integration. All countries are affected by the swings of the world economy, particularly if they have opened their economies. While countries need to manage their vulnerabilities to these swings, international action is needed to manage and prevent financial instability. Policy should focus on liberalising the capital account more carefully, with less international pressure and greater flexibility for countries to decide on the pace and phasing based on their institutional capacities. Financial institutions should also be subjected to greater transparency and accountability. Developing countries need to strengthen the legal and regulatory institutions in their financial sectors. Macroeconomic management should be integrated with social policies to reduce the impact of financial turmoil on the economy and to minimise the social costs. There is need for strengthening international action to regulate and supervise banking systems, building on the provisions of the G-10 in requiring greater transparent. Since people feel the real losses and risks from financial crises, a parallel funding mechanism should be established to protect them and their rights to development. This can be achieved by establishing an international lender of last resort for people to complement financial packages.

The rules and institutions of global finance should seek to reduce instability in global financial markets. They should discourage all speculation and encourage long-term investment in the real economy in a form that supports local economic activity, sustainability, equity, and poverty reduction. In addition, they should allow maximum space for national governments to set exchange rate policy, regulate capital movements, and eliminate speculative activity. Governments should not absorb the losses caused by private actors' bad decisions. The rules and institutions of the global economy should seek to decrease private speculative flows while increasing those public flows that support sustainable and equitable activities. In addition, the governments of the world's major currencies should levy a tax on certain international transactions so as to discourage speculative and herd behaviour in international capital flows.

Criminal security   One of the biggest barriers to development is armed conflict. Its threat to investment, stability and security destroys the conditions for growth. Stronger global co-operation and action are needed to address the growing problems beyond the scope of national governments. The fight against global crime requires national police to take co-operative action as rapidly as the crime syndicates do. Dismantling bank secrecy and providing witness protection for foreign investigations would dramatically improve the effectiveness of the global fight against global crime.

International efforts should be stepped up to regulate the trade in small arms. In addition, a licensing system to control arms brokers and traffickers should be introduced, and tighter controls implemented internationally through the UN conference on small arms.

Health security   More global action is required to address HIV/AIDS, which is penetrating borders everywhere. Developed countries should work with developing countries and international organisations to help strengthen the international effort to tackle HIV/AIDS. They should seek to increase public and private expenditure on research for development, and the provision of new public health care units. Efforts should be directed at disseminating the benefits of research from developed to developing countries, providing medicines and preventive measures at reasonable cost in developing countries, and strengthening public health systems in the developing world.

Food safety and food security Gueneau et al (1998) have rightly recommended that any new rules of trade should recognise that food production for local communities should be at the top of a hierarchy of values in agriculture. Local self-reliance in food production, and the assurance of healthful, safe foods should be considered basic human rights. Shorter distances and reduced reliance on expensive inputs, which should be shipped over long distances, are key objectives of a new food system paradigm.

Conclusion

This era of globalisation is opening many opportunities for millions of people around the world. Increased trade, new technologies, foreign investments, expanding media and Internet connections are fuelling economic growth and human advance. All this offers enormous potential to eradicate poverty in the twenty-first century, to continue the unprecedented progress in the twentieth century. There is more wealth and technology, and more commitment to a global community than ever before. Global markets, global technology, global ideas and global solidarity can enrich the lives of people everywhere, greatly expanding their choices. The growing interdependence of people's lives calls for shared values and a shared commitment to the human development of all people.

The post-cold war world of the 1990s has sped progress in defining such values in adopting human rights and in setting development goals in the UN conferences on environment, population, social development, women and human settlements. But today's globalisation is being driven by market expansion, opening national borders to trade, capital, information outpacing governance of these markets and their repercussions for people. More progress has been made in norms, standards, policies and institutions for open global markets than for people and their rights. And a new commitment is needed to the ethics of universalism set out in the Universal Declaration of Human Rights.

Gueneau et al (1998) note that competitive markets may be the best guarantee of efficiency, but not necessarily of equity; and liberalisation and privatisation can be a step to competitive markets, but not a guarantee of them. And markets are neither the first nor the last word in human development. Many activities and goods that are critical to human development are provided outside the market. But, they are being squeezed by the pressures of global competition. There is a fiscal squeeze on public goods, a time squeeze on care activities and an incentive squeeze on the environment. When the market goes too far in dominating social and political outcomes, the opportunities and rewards of globalisation spread unequally and inequitably, concentrating power and wealth in a select group of people, nations and corporations, marginalising the others. When the market gets out of hand, the instabilities show up in boom and bust economies, as in the financial crisis in East Asia and its worldwide repercussions, cutting global output by an estimated \$2 trillion in 1998-2000. When the profit motives of market players get out of hand, they challenge people's ethics, and sacrifice respect for justice and human rights.

But because globalisation offers both positive and negative effects, its challenge in the new century is not to stop the expansion of global markets. Rather it is to find the rules and institutions for stronger governance local, national, regional and global to preserve the advantages of global markets and competition. Additionally, it is to provide enough space for human, community and environmental resources to ensure that globalisation works for people, not just for profits.

That is why the policy recommendations presented in the foregoing discussion are based on the understanding that for developing countries, which are characterised with vicious circles of problems, FDI as a channel of economic growth is of particular relevance. However, in order to get maximum benefits from its positive spillover effects, governments have to employ several tools. These may include tax incentives and grants; provision of industrial estates, export processing zones, and other infrastructure; and simplification of the bureaucratic procedures facing potential investors. In addition, they may negotiate bilateral tax, trade, and investment treaties with countries from wherever investments might come. Further, governments recognise the importance of political stability, realistic exchange rates, and rapid growth in attracting foreign investment. Therefore, they may attempt to create a favourable environment by guaranteeing repatriation of profits, assuring access to imported components, and promising not to expropriate property without compensation. In addition they may pursue strategies aimed at creating an employable human base founded mainly on scientific and technical norms and continuing to develop it through its useful employment life cycle; upgrading infrastructural services; diversifying and upgrading the export production base through the identification of the most competitive industries and stimulation of SMEs; implementing macroeconomic policies that lead to the stability of the currency, promote the competitiveness of productions and, hence, the confidence of investors; and if possible, establishing regional integration schemes based more on an economic than a political foundation to counter some of their shortcomings.

The message in brief is that if developing countries are to benefit from this channel of economic growth, their governments should first and foremost endeavour to integrate into the value chain of the international division of labour. They need to treat their countries as if they are 'products', which they are developing and want to market. This involves the pursuance of all sorts of strategies in the development, promotion and marketing arenas implying that the whole process requires a *strategic management approach* since there are other 'products' in the market place some of which are already superior, which they have to compete with. In addition, developing countries require to set-up a resource base that can facilitate their progressive shifts up the levels of technological complexity. This involves instituting flexible plans for deepening the content of export activity and building the human capital and macroeconomic capacity to sustain such a shift across a range of tradable activities in response to the rapidly changing world demand and technologies.

But that is not the end of the story. The economic effects generated through the aforementioned strategies have to be managed in such a way that they induce sustainable development for all. Specifically, globalisation should be managed so that it leads to economic growth, to less violation of human rights, less disparity within and between nations, less marginalisation of people and countries, less instability of societies, less vulnerability of people, less environmental destruction, and less poverty and deprivation. Hence, besides engendering economic issues, it should also address issues pertaining to ethics, equity, inclusion, human security, sustainability and development. In other words, economic issues should be amalgamated with ecological, and social and political issues so that the debate goes beyond examining just economic growth, to exploring issues in terms of sustainable development for all. To achieve this, the benefits of economic growth should be shared equitably, so that the increasing interdependence arising from globalisation should work for all people, and not just for profits. Additionally, the environment should be treated as a scarce resource so that some of the benefits derived from economic growth are utilised in its preservation. Thus, while sustainable economic growth combined with environmental protection should lead to sustainability, sustainable economic growth coupled with less poverty deprivation should result into development.

8 Conclusion

Overview

While the 'extreme' strand of the anti-globalisation activists may disagree, the 'globalisation institution' has come to stay (for a while at least). Characterised by 'shrinking space, shrinking time and disappearing borders' this era of globalisation is opening many opportunities for millions of people around the world through increased trade, new technologies, foreign investments, expanding media and internet connections, and fuelling economic growth and human advances. These have resulted from breakthroughs in communications technologies and biotechnology, and led to integration of global markets, global technology, global ideas and global solidarity. There is more wealth and technology, and more commitment to a global community than ever before. All this offers enormous potential to continue the unprecedented progress of the twentieth century and eradicate poverty in the twenty-first century.

Unfortunately, however, the agents of globalisation are also the same instruments for potential environmental derailment, increased North-South equity divide, growing human insecurity and consequently potential stimulants of unsustainable development, particularly, in the developing countries. Specifically, globalisation may lead to more violation of human rights, more disparity within and between nations, more marginalisation of people and countries, more instability of societies, more vulnerability of people, more environmental destruction, and more poverty and deprivation. Thanks to the vigilante civil groups, which have played and continue playing an instrumental role in raising those issues that were otherwise being ignored or overlooked by governments, international institutions and TNCs.

Evidently, the views of the moderate anti-globalisation activists and those of the moderate pro-globalisation advocates appear to be converging. For instance, while the former group perceives globalisation as a potential hazard, it recognises that globalisation can generate some good effects. Likewise, while the latter group is biased to the positiveness of globalisation, it has started appreciating the negative effects it may

290

engineer. Arguably, putting an entire blame on the globalisation process can be equated to the renowned 'politics is a dirty game' phrase. Yet, politics as an institution is not dirty at all! Instead, it is the people and their often unregulated 'tricks' that are indeed dirty. Likewise, there is no apparent problem with the 'globalisation institution'. Instead, it is the inappropriateness or lack of policies within the globalisation framework, which cause the potential hazards to the well-being of mankind and the environment.

It is almost impossible to realise sustainable development in the absence of economic growth. For instance, diverting resources to environmental preservation becomes an unassailable task in the absence of economic growth. Similarly, distribution of wealth becomes a problem when there is none to be shared. But, there is sufficient evidence to suggest that through its agents, especially FDI, the globalisation process can engender sustainable economic growth. For this reason, the globalisation institution should be embraced and encouraged. Therefore, there should be a vigorous pursuance of policies that enable the globalisation process to stimulate the economic growth process, particularly, of developing countries. At the same time, the potential for the negative effects of globalisation is eminent. However, rather than abandon the globalisation institution on these grounds, the better option is to pursue policies that can translate the benefits generated from the growth process engendered by the globalisation process into sustainable development. Such policies should for instance, lead to a reduction of: environmental destruction, violation of human rights, disparity within and between nations, marginalisation of people and countries, instability of societies, vulnerability of people, and poverty and deprivation. Put simply, the globalisation institution requires the simultaneous pursuance of policies capable of maximising the positive effects of globalisation, and eliminating or minimising its negative effects.

From this point of view then, there are some serious implications for the anti-globalisation NGOs. While some vigilantism may still be required, the way forward in the globalising world should not be to try to prevent change. Rather, civil activists should look for reform that will improve life in the country and provide support for those who are losing out. Anti-globalisation activists' involvement should now shift away from confrontation to dialogue. It is time to change from being anti-establishment to being proactive. But this also means that the global institutions should accept, embrace and start liasing with civil activists' groups.

Maximising the Globalisation Benefits

It has become increasingly recognised that there are many different paths that countries can pursue in order to generate economic growth. Japan for instance, prohibited FDI and relied on organic growth, and its story is a success miracle. Similarly, the Republic of Korea's initial development had a low reliance on FDI. Domestic firms can also be exposed to international management and technical standards and know-how through foreign trade in the absence of FDI. For instance, exporting firms can learn new ideas about marketing, design and technology from interacting with buyers in the world markets. This knowledge later spills over to the other domestic firms. Technological diffusion can on the other hand be achieved through imitation of imports. This is how Western Europe, the US, Canada, Australia, and New Zealand managed to derive their economic growths from international trade during the nineteenth century and during the first half of the twentieth century. Technology transfers can also be effected through licensing agreements with foreign firms covering patents, trademarks, franchising, and technical assistance. Countries can also achieve economic growth through the investment of foreign capital in the form of commercial loans and aid, and the possession and exploration of natural and acquired resources.

Thus, FDI is one of the options that may complement the economic growth process if properly planned and implemented. In fact, FDI is a potential current channel through which developing countries can both stimulate and sustain their economic growth rates. For instance, the evidence from the forgoing review justifies the presumption that FDI is playing an increasingly important role in the economic growth of host developing countries, through its contribution in human resources development, technological transfer, capital formation, international trade and environmental protection. However, this mostly comes about as a spillover rather than a direct effect.

FDI is becoming important in relation to world-wide investment, output, trade, technology and capital flows, and TNCs are playing an increasingly important role in the economic growth of developing countries. Although most developing countries now consider FDI as an important resource for development, its economic effects are almost impossible to either predict or measure with precision. The impact of FDI and TNCs on a country depends on many factors, and varies from country to country, by industry, even by company and over periods of time. This is because government policy tends to have a strong influence on FDI. For instance, different countries may pursue different policies for different industries and over different time periods. Thus, the role of FDI in countries' processes and efforts to meet development objectives can differ greatly across countries, depending particularly on the nature of the country and its government policy. For this reason, it is difficult to separate and quantify the complex TNCs' package of attributes, which likewise vary from one host country to another. Moreover, for obvious reasons, a scientific quantification assessment does not appeal to economic analysis. Consequently, the development effects of FDI end-up being assessed by one of the two general approaches, quantitative and qualitative analyses.

As exemplified by the recent FDI trends in China, large domestic markets remain a powerful magnet for foreign investors. However, although low-cost labour remains a source of competitive advantage for FDI flows to developing countries, its importance is diminishing. Likewise, as exemplified by FDI trends in oil exporting countries, the importance of natural resources is diminishing as new technology now increasingly facilitates the development of substitutes for them. Instead, TNCs are increasingly seeking world-class infrastructure, skilled and productive labour, innovatory capacities and an agglomeration of efficient suppliers, competitors, support institutions and services. In fact, low-cost labour and natural resources no longer provide a base for a sustainable growth process since rising incomes and discovery of substitute products erode the comparative edge they provide. In particular, low-cost labour is only a beginning point for luring FDI and consequently generating static economic benefits. Therefore, developing countries can attain sustained economic growth, through the exploitation of TNCs' dynamic competitive advantages. To achieve this, they have to develop resource bases that can facilitate their progressive shifts up the levels of technological complexity. This involves instituting plans for deepening the content of export activity and building the human capital and macroeconomic capacity to sustain such shifts across a range of tradable activities in response to changing world demand and technologies. Unfortunately, the current unprecedented and accelerating pace of technological change, whose development developing countries have to keep pace with makes any such capacity building more challenging.

Besides resources capacity building, developing countries require to make the investment environment conducive for FDI. The current poor state of affairs particularly in the less advanced developing countries makes it more challenging. Nonetheless, it is the task of the developing countries themselves to sort the country-specific problems. For instance, they should resolve their conflicts at round table discussions, and not through armed confrontations. By doing so, their defence budgets can be reduced and then money allocated to economic growth enhancing departments. Political stability acts as one of the basic 'investment environment improving' requirements. For instance, it plays an instrumental role of building investors' confidence since it reduces the level of risks to which their investments are exposed. In addition, developing countries' leaders should stop playing the hypocrite and lead by example through the institution of policies aimed at reducing corruption and embezzlement. While this is being effected, some effort should be devoted to the liberalisation of the FDI and trade regimes.

Obviously, developing countries are competing for FDI because they want to improve their levels of industrialisation. But in most cases, industrialisation goes hand-in-hand with improvements in human capital, which helps to stimulate productivity. In this event, policies should be directed at mobilising human capital and of course utilising it efficiently. Likewise, industrialisation is complemented by technological advancements. Consequently, necessary conditions are required to capture and diffuse technology. These include the need to strengthen the scientific and technological capacities, and to restructure the existing patterns of international scientific and technological relations. No doubt, it may require linking the world of technical education to the world of work.

Infrastructure not only facilitates the production and marketing of goods, but it also plays a leading role in the diffusion of knowledge. For this reason, developing countries should improve their competitive edge by putting more emphasis on infrastructural services development, and treating them as necessary conditions for the enhancement of the profitability of business enterprises.

The industrialisation process is a kind of revolution, which has the potential to shift developing countries' export bases from natural resource-based products to manufacturing oriented products. In this event, they need to diversify the export base through the identification of the most competitive industries, and through the stimulation of SMEs.

On the macro-economic front, developing countries' weak economic performances and less sound macroeconomic controls, which have hindered large capital inflows need to be reversed. Hence, the necessity to implement macroeconomic policies that lead to the stability of the currencies in real terms and, therefore, promote the competitiveness of production and, hence, confidence of investors.

Regional integration schemes among proximate developing countries, if based on an economic rather than a political foundation, can contribute towards introducing peace and political stability, inducing economic stability, creating a larger resource base, and creating a large economic bargaining unit. They can also lead to maintaining lower relative wage rates, facilitating joint project development, creating a complementary manufacturing region and, hence, attracting FDI and consequently stimulating the growth process. As the developed countries pursue this line of integration, developing countries should also explore its potential benefits.

Minimising the Globalisation Hazards

The economic growth discussed in the foregoing section is not good enough. It needs to be translated into sustainable development. In particular, some of the growth benefits should be diverted to environmental preservation and some should be distributed implying that a new approach to development is required. An approach which gives developing countries a larger role and greater benefits; and which maintains the balance between economic growth and the ecosystem, so that natural resources can support growth over the long-term. There is the need to revive economic growth, particularly in developing countries, as well as on the qualitative aspects of growth. Growth should involve lower energy consumption, more equitable sharing of its benefits, and satisfaction of the essential needs of developing countries. Therefore, there is a need to understand and propose new governance structures and mechanisms at the global and local levels, encompassing political and social needs of the State, social movements and NGOs, grassroots movements, the media, multinationals, organised citizens, the science community and religious movements, among others.

Globalisation should be managed properly so that it does not become merely the survival of the biggest, and the most powerful. The current means of management is via global trade rules. If these rules are fair and transparent for all, not just the most vociferous or historically influential, then globalisation can become a road to prosperity for many. Thus, if the interconnected world is to work for everyone, not only should effective multilateral trade rules be applied for open trade, but the international rules countries play by should also be fair.

Social policies and national governance are more relevant today to make globalisation work for human development and to protect people against its new threats. Therefore, new policies are needed to tackle the negative effects. For instance, the world needs market policies that protect elite labour, and promote job-creating growth, invest in workers' skills, promote labour rights and make informal work more productive and remunerative. Policies should support national cultures, not by shutting out imports but by supporting local culture, arts and artists. All countries need to rethink their social policies for redistribution, for safety nets and for the universal provision of social services. In a nutshell, what is required is an approach that combines human development and poverty eradication with social protection.

Conclusion

Globalisation has come to stay. Most important, however, globalisation has an instrumental role to play in the development process of all countries. What is required are local, national, regional and global policy instruments that can maximise its potential benefits, and yet minimise its potential hazards. Therefore, on the one hand, besides improving the investment environment, developing country governments need to promote domestic capabilities, develop integrated strategies, build educational bases, strengthen technological institutions, encourage firms into export markets to test and advance their competitiveness, and pursue regionalism based on economic rather than political motives. This framework if properly planned and appropriately implemented, will enhance and sustain their economic growth rates. On the other hand, for globalisation to work, the aforementioned economic benefits should be distributed equitably while preserving the environment so that sustainable development for all is achieved. On this note, globalisation should lead to less environmental destruction, less disparity within and between nations, less marginalisation of people and countries, less violation of human rights, less instability of societies, less vulnerability of people, and less poverty and deprivation.

Appendix

Background to the Formation of Regional Economic Blocs

Overview

During the immediate post-World War II period, developed countries realised that economic growth could also be achieved through regional economic integration whose economic advantages would stem from scale economies. In addition, although it was not precisely understood at the time, regional economic integration can generate economic advantages capable of acting as strong determinants of FDI. This involved an economic integration through market agreements among nations in geographical proximity to each other. Consequently, there has been a surge in regional trade arrangements in the past five decades most particularly among developed countries. This has increased developing countries' interest in similar arrangements based on the expectations of benefits such as economies of scale that may accrue from market size, market growth and tariff-discrimination, which act as additional incentives to lure FDI into an economic bloc. Thus, regionalism is also playing a critical role in international economic relations.

This Appendix provides a brief background to the development of, membership of, and objectives for the formation of the respective regional economic blocs that have resulted from countries being in geographic proximity with each other. Some of the literature presented here is drawn from the World Bank web site.

Regional Economic Blocs

Europe

The European Community In 1921, Belgium and Luxembourg decided to form an economic union which was later expanded into a BENELUX union when the Netherlands joined in 1944. In 1951, Belgium, France, Germany, Italy, the Netherlands and Luxembourg (the Six) accepted the Schuman Plan, which had been proposed in 1950, and signed the European Coal and Steel Community (ECSC) Treaty. The signing of the Treaty of Rome in 1957 led to the creation of the European Economic Community (EEC). In 1971, the European Monetary System (EMU) and the European Currency Unit (ECU) were created to provide a measure of monetary stability in the community. In 1973, the European Community (EC) comprising the EEC, the European Atomic Energy Community (EURATOM) and ECSC was formed, and the community enlarged to 9 members by the accession of the UK, the Republic of Ireland and Denmark. Further enlargement to 12 members occurred when Greece was admitted in 1981, and Portugal and Spain were allowed access in 1982. The treaty on the European Union, and economic and monetary union was signed in 1991, and a European Union (EU) created in 1993. Its membership grew to 15 with the accession of Austria,

Finland, and Sweden in 1995.

The purpose of the EEC was to guarantee economic development and political stability in Europe. Its two objectives were to liberalise trade in order to foster a common market, and to ensure the implementation of common economic policies by the member countries. It took the form of a common market, having a common external tariff and making provision for the free movement of labour and capital. A variety of other national policies were also harmonised in order to make the market effective. These policies principally related to agriculture, competition, fiscal matters and regional aid. At the time of the first enlargement, the EC decided to introduce its own regional policy, which was designed to complement national policies and to contribute to a reduction in economic disparities within the community.

The creation of the EU also initiated a campaign regarding the development of an economic union leading to an introduction of a single currency, rather than a common currency preferred by the British. In December 1995, the Madrid Council accepted the 'euro' as the official name of the single currency, and adopted a three phase changeover scenario to the single currency. The interim period (from early 1998 to 31 December 1998) involved the appointment of the management team of the European Central Bank, and adoption of the necessary legislation to facilitate changeover of the banking and financial system to the single currency. By the Spring of 1998, the 11 aspiring candidates (the EU-15 excluding Greece, Denmark, Sweden and the UK.) for the single currency had all passed an 'entrance examination' requirement by meeting the five convergence criteria defined by the Maastricht Treaty. These were price stability, controlled long-term interest rates, limited public deficit and reasonable public debt. The second stage (from 1 January 1999 to 31 December 2001 at the latest) involves all activities up to when the first euro-denominated notes and coins are put into circulation. This period covers the time needed by commercial banks to change over their entire business to the single currency and the time needed to manufacture notes and coins in the single currency. Starting 1 January 1999, the euro became a 'fully fledged currency' in the 11 participant countries when the European Single Currency Board adopted and implemented a single monetary policy denominated in euros. Greece became the twelfth member on 1 January 2001. The third phase will start with the introduction of euro-denominated notes and coins, scheduled to take place at the latest by 1 January 2002. Once these three steps have been completed, the national currency units of the member states of the Economic and Monetary Union will have entirely disappeared. On 28 September 2000, Denmark voted 'no' to the single currency. This might have serious implications for UK and Sweden. The UK has set-up five economic tests, which it has to fulfil before making membership considerations. However, political analysts think this is a cover-up, and a decision may be made as soon as opinion polls show a favourable perception of the euro.

The EU is an economic bloc growing in membership and importance, and moving towards an integrated foreign policy. One of the most significant initiatives of the EU, both politically and economically, is its planned enlargement to ten Central and Eastern European countries (CEECs), namely, Bulgaria, the Czech Republic, Estonia, Hungary, Latvia, Lithuania, Poland, Romania, Slovakia and Slovenia. For instance, in July 1997, the European Commission published 'Agenda 2000', a document examining the economic and political issues that arise from the enlargement of the EU to the CEECs.

The European Free Trade Association (EFTA) EFTA is a second Western European grouping. The seven founding members of EFTA (Austria, Denmark, Norway, Portugal, Sweden, Switzerland and the UK) were members of the Organisation for European

Economic Co-operation (OEEC), which was established in 1947 to implement the Marshall Plan for the economic recovery of war-shattered Europe and to promote economic co-operation between member countries.

The group of seven created EFTA with the signing of the Stockholm Convention in 1960. It was formed for purely trade and hence economic reasons, unlike the EEC which had political objectives as well. For instance, it was concerned with industrial free trade and each country retained its own tariff to outsiders. The formation of a Europe-wide free trade association was originally proposed by the UK in the mid-1950s in order to allow those European countries that, like itself, were not prepared to commit themselves to a Common Agricultural Policy (CAP) or to other political and economic objectives envisaged in the establishment of the EEC at least to enjoy the benefits of free trade in the industrialised products. Although it failed to develop the range of economic policies, which characterise the EEC, EFTA showed a degree of success for its members in terms of macroeconomic performance. Its members became linked to the EEC through a series of agreements aimed at creating a wider European Industrial free trade area. For example, in 1991, the member countries of EFTA and the EEC concluded negotiations to form a European Economic Area (EEA), with an agreement scheduled to enter into force on 1st January 1993. Even before the new agreement, free trade in goods had been established between the two groupings following the creation of a free trade area in 1972.

Liechtenstein became a full EFTA member on 1 September 1991, at the time when some EFTA member countries were considering EC membership. During the first week of March 2001, Switzerland voted not to integrate with the EU. The entry of all its members into the EU apart from Iceland, Liechtenstein, Norway and Switzerland, has however, almost rendered EFTA defunct. Nonetheless, the remaining four EFTA member countries continue to pursue certain trade arrangements with other economic blocs, particularly the EU.

Council for Mutual Economic Assistance (CMEA) Eastern Europe's CMEA is often referred to in the West as COMECON. It was established in January 1949 under the aegis of the Soviet Union in response to the formation of the Committee of European Economic Co-operation in Western Europe in 1948. COMECON's original members were the Soviet Union, Bulgaria, Czechoslovakia, Hungary, Poland and Romania. Albania joined in February 1949 but ceased taking an active part at the end of 1961. The German Democratic Republic became a member in September 1950, and the Mongolian People's Republic in June 1962. In 1964, an agreement was concluded enabling Yugoslavia to participate on equal terms with COMECON members in the areas of trade, finance, currency, and industry. In 1972, Cuba became the 9th full member, while Vietnam became the 10th member when it joined in 1978.

COMECON's objective was to accelerate and co-ordinate economic development and establish a more rational division of labour among member countries. After 1953, it began to promote industrial specialisation and thus reduce 'parallelism' among the member countries. In 1959 the founder countries signed the formal charter of the CMEA, which added to the original purpose of economic co-operation the objectives of 'speeding up economic and technical progress in the member countries' and 'raising the level of industrialisation in industrially less developed countries' (Balassa, 1976).

The economic integration envisaged by COMECON in the early 1960s met with opposition and problems. A major difficulty was posed by the incompatibility of the price systems used in the various member countries. Individual governments set the prices of most goods and commodities disregarding the goods' actual market values, thus, making it difficult for the member states to conduct trade with each other on the basis of relative prices. Instead, trade was conducted mainly on a barter basis through bilateral agreements between governments.

However, the organisation largely lost its purpose and power after the 1989 Eastern Europe democratic revolutions. The collapse of communist governments across Eastern Europe in 1989/90, induced member countries to shift to private enterprise and market-type systems of pricing. By 1991, the member countries had begun to make trade payments in hard, convertible currencies. Under agreements made early in 1991, COMECON was renamed the Organization for International Economic Co-operation. Each nation was deemed free to seek its own trade outlets, and member countries were reduced to a weak pledge to 'co-ordinate' policies on quotas, tariffs, international payments, and relations with other international bodies.

With the collapse of the Soviet Union, the unification of Germany and the disintegration of Czechoslovakia, the CMEA is as good as defunct. Some of its remaining members are seeking entry into the EU.

The Central European Free Trade Agreement (CEFTA) CEFTA was signed in Krakow, Poland on 21 December 1992 by Poland, Hungary, Czech Republic, and Slovak Republic. The free trade agreement between the four countries was created to gradually establish a free trade zone by the year 2001 through the reduction and elimination of tariffs. The objective of CEFTA as outlined in the 1992 document is to promote the development of mutual economic relations between members through the expansion of trade, provision of fair conditions of competition, and expansion of world trade by removing tariff and non-tariff barriers. For instance, CEFTA calls for the gradual elimination of all customs duties on all industrial and agricultural products for members within the regional trading bloc. Its creation was originally an attempt to boost trade among Central European nations after the collapse of the communist-era COMECON trading bloc.

America

North American Free Trade Area (NAFTA) North America constitutes yet another large, but relatively new economic bloc. In 1988, the US and Canada signed a Free Trade Agreement and formed a Free Trade Area (CAFTA). The agreement was designed to strengthen an already existing trading relationship and enhance economic opportunity on both sides of the common boarder. In 1992, the US, Canada and Mexico signed a North American Free Trade Agreement and formed NAFTA. The agreement liberalises barriers to trade and investment between the three partners, while leaving their external barriers *vis-à-vis* third countries under the jurisdiction of each member state. Subsequent to the signing of the NAFTA, two supplementary agreements in the area of environment and labour standards have also been negotiated. NAFTA provides for phased reduction of tariff barriers and tariffication of non-tariff barriers, relaxation of investment restrictions and harmonisation of standards between the three countries over a period of ten to fifteen years. NAFTA has separate agreements for agricultural products for the US and Mexico trade, and Canada and Mexico trade. Provisions contained in the CAFTA agreement govern trade in agricultural products between the US and Canada.

Although several reasons are advanced in the literature as to the motivations of the contracting parties, especially the US and Mexico, to sign a free trade agreement, the main reasons for Mexico are more clear. These include its desire to secure free and preferential access to the vast market of its principal trading partners; the favourable impact of the agreement on attracting foreign investment; and its desire to lock-in the trade liberalising policies, which had been carried out since mid-1980s, including its accession to the General Agreement of Tariffs and Trade (GATT) in 1986.

Latin America and the Caribbean Several regional economic blocs exist in Latin America and the Caribbean. Latin American Free Trade Area (LAFTA) was founded in 1960 by Argentina, Bolivia, Brazil, Chile, Colombia, Ecuador, Mexico, Paraguay, Peru, Uruguay and Venezuela with the aim of promoting the member countries' industrial growth behind regional protective barriers. Its name changed to the Latin American Integration Association (LAIA) under the 1980 Treaty of Montevideo.

The Central American Common Market (CACM) set up under the Manague Treaty in 1960 comprises Costa Rica, El Salvador, Guatemala, Honduras and Nicaragua. The objective of CACM was to establish a common market with a common external tariff, to promote unhindered trade and investment within the group and to foster industrial development of member countries through a regional import-substitution strategy.

The Andean Common Market (ANCOM) established under the Cartagena Agreement of 1969 now comprises Bolivia, Colombia, Ecuador, Peru and Venezuela. Its objective was to enlarge the small domestic markets of member countries and thus promote industrial development via regional rather than domestic import-substitution. The growth of industry in member countries was to be achieved through a common industrial policy consisting of industrial planning at regional level and through trade liberalisation among member states. A parallel objective of the group was to achieve an 'equitable' distribution of cost of benefits of the integration process through micro-management of the industrial policy at regional level and special treatment of less developed members (Bolivia and Ecuador). For example, the latter were granted the right to liberalise their regional imports less rapidly and less fully than the others, and they were chosen to host certain industrial activities. The declaration of Ica in 1989 initiated a process of accelerating integration that resulted in the creation of a free trade area in January 1991 between Bolivia, Colombia and Venezuela, with Ecuador and Peru joining the area in July 1992. This time around, the member countries totally eliminated tariff and non-tariff barriers on internal trade, abolished the preferential regime of the less-developed members, and abandoned the common industrial policy of the past. They also replaced the old Andean Investment code with a new one that granted national treatment to foreign investors.

A Caribbean Community (CARICOM) formed in 1973 now comprises Antigua and Barmuda, Barbados, Belize, Dominica, Grenada, Tobago, St. Kitts-Nevis, St. Lucia and St. Vincent. Its objective was to foster economic co-operation and to integrate the economies of the participating states through the removal of trade barriers. CARICOM is an extension of the Caribbean Free Trade Area (CARIFTA). The East Caribbean Common Market (ECCM) consisting of Guyana, Jamaica, Trinidad and other smaller Islands was formed in 1973. CARICOM and ECCM together formed the Caribbean Community and Common Market (CARACOM). The Association of Caribbean States (ACS) was launched by CARICOM in 1992 with the objective to strengthen its link with the other countries in the Caribbean Basin and Central America. In addition, ASC's aim is to foster functional co-operation among its members rather than promote free trade, although free trade agreements among one or more subsets of member states is acknowledged and even encouraged.

MERCOSUR was established under the treaty of Asuncion signed in March 1991 between Argentina, Brazil, Paraguay and Uruguay to create a Southern Cone Common

Market by 1995. The treaty provides for co-ordination of macroeconomic policies, a common policy towards third countries and the establishment of a common external tariff.

The Group of Three (G3) founded in 1994 comprises Colombia, Mexico and Venezuela. The G3 Treaty provided for an immediate elimination of tariffs on some items and a ten-year transition for others, with the exclusion of agriculture. Mexico's tariff elimination on exports of the other two partners is to proceed more quickly and Venezuela is granted two extra years to dismantle its tariffs on textiles.

Americas Free Trade Area On 22 April 2001, leaders of countries from across the Americas committed their governments to setting up the world's largest free trade zone by 2005, and to halving the number of people living in extreme poverty in the region by 2015. Only those countries with democratic governments will be able to be part of the zone. The leaders also pledged to 'spare no effort to free fellow citizens from the dehumanising conditions of extreme poverty.' The arrangement also committed governments to strengthening 'environmental protection and sustainable use of natural resources with a view to ensuring a balance between economic development, social development and the protection of the environment, as these are interdependent and mutually reinforcing'. The proposed free trade area will eliminate trade barriers from the northern reaches of Canada to Cape Horn in Chile, and become the largest trading bloc in the world once implemented. Cuba stands to be the only nation excluded from the area - as it was from the summit - singled out because of its lack of free elections.

Asia

Southeast Asia The Asian region, populous as it is, has had very limited economic integration. In East Asia, the Association of Southeast Asian Nations (ASEAN) remains the only regional trading arrangement and there is none in the South Asian sub-region. The ASEAN was formed in 1967 by the signing of the Asian Declaration. Its membership initially comprised five countries, i.e. Indonesia, Malaysia, the Philippines, Singapore and Thailand. ASEAN took a giant step towards realising the vision of ASEAN-10 (having all 10 countries in Southeast Asia in ASEAN) with the admission of Brunei in 1984, and Vietnam in 1995. On July 23 1997 Myanmar and Laos were admitted.

ASEAN's main objectives were twofold. First, was to accelerate the economic growth, social progress and cultural development in the region through joint endeavours in the spirit of equality and partnership in order to strengthen the foundation for a prosperous and peaceful community of Southeast Asian nations. Second, was to promote regional peace and stability through abiding respect for justice and the rule of law in the relationship among countries in the region and adherence to the principles of the United Nations Charter.

Economic co-operation was initiated in 1977 with the establishment of specialist economic committees covering tourism and trade, industry, minerals and energy, food, agriculture and forestry, transport and communication, and banking, and with the adoption of the preferential trade agreement. The aim of the preferential trade area was to encourage intra-regional trade through the granting of trade preferences on a product by product basis. Additional programmes, which have contributed to preferential trading include the ASEAN Industrial Joint Ventures and the ASEAN Industrial Complementation schemes. During the Manila Summit in December 1987, the ASEAN members endorsed a 5 year target of intra-regional trade liberalisation, shortening of the exclusion list, deepening of the margin of preferences, and a standstill and rollback of non-tariff barriers. Early in 1992, the proposal for an ASEAN Free Trade Area (AFTA), with a common external tariff to be introduced within a fifteen year period, was adopted. The mechanism to achieve this is the Common Effective Preferential Tariff (CEPT), which took effect on 1 January 1993. It seeks closer economic integration and co-operation through the establishment of complementary industries and investment incentives to non-member countries. Today, ASEAN economic co-operation covers trade, investment, industry, services, finance, agriculture, forestry, energy, transportation and communication, intellectual property, small and medium enterprises, and tourism.

The Middle East The Regional Co-operation for Development (RDC) created in 1964, was an ad hoc arrangement for industrial integration between Iran, Pakistan and Turkey. It was, however, short lived. The Arab Common Market (ACM) consisting of Iraq, Jordan, Syria and Kuwait all from the Middle East, and Egypt from North Africa has been in existence since 1964. The Gulf Co-operation Council (GCC) was established in 1981 as a common market consisting of Saudi Arabia, Bahrain, Qatar, Oman, Kuwait and United Arab Emirates. It was meant to institutionalise a long history of informal co-operation that had long existed among the six member countries. Although political changes in the region played an important role in accelerating the formation of GCC, the idea of a formal regional grouping predated the political developments. The rules governing economic integration of GCC partners were spelt out in the so-called Unified Economic Agreement, signed in June 1982. The agreement foresaw the creation of a customs union with a common external tariff and free trade for all goods originating in GCC members. Recently, there have been fresh attempts at defining a deadline for the adoption of a common external tariff, which is supposed to facilitate negotiations with the EU for the creation of a free trade area or customs union between the two entities. The GCC's interest in such a union derives from its desire to open the European markets to its petrochemical exports.

Asia-Pacific

Asia-Pacific Economic Co-operation (APEC) APEC was established in 1989 in response to the growing interdependence among Asia-Pacific economies. Begun as an informal dialogue group, APEC has since become the primary regional vehicle for promoting open trade and practical economic co-operation. Its goal is to advance Asia-Pacific economic dynamism and sense of community. The founder members are Australia, Brunei, Canada, Indonesia, Japan, Republic of Korea, Malaysia, New Zealand, the Philippines, Singapore, Thailand and Unites States. The People's Republic of China, Hong Kong and Taipei, China (Taiwan) joined in November 1991. In November 1993, APEC accepted Mexico and Papua New Guinea as new members. At the same time, APEC decided that Chile would become a full member in November 1994. Peru, Russia and Vietnam became formal members in November 1998.

During their informal discussions in November 1993, the APEC economic leaders envisioned a community of Asia-Pacific economies based on the spirit of openness and partnership; of co-operative efforts to solve the challenges of change; of free exchange of goods, services and investment; of broadly based economic growth and higher living and educational standards; and, of sustainable growth that respects the natural environment. At the second meeting in 1994 the vision of an open trading system became the ambitious goal of free and open trade and investment in the Asia-Pacific region by 2010 for developed member economies and 2020 for developing member economies.

In 1995, APEC leaders adopted the Osaka Action Agenda, which firmly established the three pillars of APEC activities: trade and investment liberalisation, business facilitation and, economic and technical co-operation. APEC leaders also instructed that high attention be given to the following six areas of economic and technical co-operation: developing human capital, fostering safe and efficient capital markets, strengthening economic infrastructure, harnessing technologies of the future; promoting environmentally sustainable growth, and encouraging the growth of small and medium-sized enterprises.

Africa

West Africa   Numerous economic blocs exist in Africa. In West Africa, West African Economic Community (WAEC), was set up in 1974 by Burkina Faso (then Upper Volta), Ivory Coast, Mali, Mauritania, Niger and Senegal. CEAO is an extension of the French West African Federation (FWAF) that collapsed in 1959. Its membership grew when Benin joined in 1985 followed by Togo. CEAO's objective was to create a customs union among the partners and to promote 'equitable and balanced' economic growth of all its members. To achieve the latter objective, the CEAO Treaty envisaged a made-to-measure structure of tariff and tax preferences on intra-CEAO trade in industrial products to suit the 'protection needs' of various member states. This created a distorted structure of effective protection that did not conform to any economic criterion and prevented effective market integration to take root. It changed its name to Union Economique et Monaitaire Ouest-Africaine (UEMOA) in 1994. Guinea Bissau joined in May 1997. CEAO/UEMOA represents the third and the fourth attempts, respectively, by West African States that belonged to the former federation of French Western Africa to maintain the arrangements for monetary and economic co-operation, which were established during the colonial era. All its members except Mauritania belong to the French Franc Zone and use a common currency, the CFA franc.

In 1973, the Mano River Union (MRU) was established under agreement between Liberia and Sierra Leone. Guinea joined it in 1980. Established as a customs union, MRU's objective was, among others, co-operation in the establishment of 'union' industries.

The Economic Community of West African States (ECOWAS) constitutes 16 members, namely Benin, Burkino Faso, Cape Verde, the Gambia, Ghana, Guinea, Guinea Bissau, Ivory Coast, Liberia, Mali, Mauritania, Niger, Nigeria, Senegal, Sierra Leone and Togo. It is a customs union with an objective of liberalising trade and establishing a common external tariff. ECOWAS is the most populous and economically, as well as culturally, the most diversified of Sub-Sahara Africa groupings. The original idea of a community embracing all of West Africa goes back to 1963. However, the negotiations that led directly to the formation of ECOWAS began only after the end of Nigeria's civil war in early 1970s. The ECOWAS Treaty envisaged the creation of a common market among member countries with a phased reduction of tariffs and non-tariff barriers on products of community origin until their complete elimination by 1989. In addition, it sought the establishment of a common external tariff, fiscal and monetary harmonisation, and close co-operation in all areas of economic activity. However, the lack of currency convertibility for countries outside the French Franc Zone, marked differences in the level of economic development of the member states within ECOWAS. In addition, the generally protective and import-substituting trade regimes followed by most member countries considerably slowed the process of integration. Thus, despite its declared objective of creating an economic community, ECOWAS has to date failed to achieve free trade in goods, let alone in factor services.

Equatorial and Central Africa   Three regional economic blocs exist in Equatorial and

Central Africa. The Union Douaniere et Economique de l'Afrique Centrale (UDEAC), or the Customs and Economic Union of Central Africa, was established in 1964 by the Republic of Congo, Gabon, Cameroon, and the Economic Union of Equatorial and Central Africa (EUECA). It links the member countries in a monetary union. The French Central African countries share a long history of co-operation and common institutions beginning with the creation of French Equatorial Africa in 1910. The Treaty of Brazzaville formally founded UDEAC in 1966. Its member countries also belong to the French Franc Zone with the CFA franc as their common currency. The original Treaty of Brazzaville envisaged a customs and monetary union with the complete removal of internal tariffs and non-tariff trade barriers among the member countries, and the establishment of a common external tariff and common customs administration for trade with the rest of the world. However, the Treaty was extensively revised in 1974, de facto abolishing the common effective tariff and restricting the intra-union trade in manufactured goods to those produced by firms enjoying the privileges of the Taxe Unique (TU) system. The TU regime in UDEAC aimed at tailoring the structure of tariff preferences on internal trade to the desire of the participants to protect their limited industrial capacity, resulting in an extremely distorted and complex structure of domestic and trade taxes that bore no relation to any economic logic. UDEAC changed its name to Comunauté Economique et Monetaire d'Afrique Centrale (CEMAC) in 1994.

The Afro-Malagasy Economic Union (AMEU) was formed in 1974. Its membership to date comprises Cameroon, the Central African Republic, Chad, Congo Brazzaville, Dahomey, Ivory Coast, Mali, Mauritania, Niger, Senegal, Togo, and Burkino Faso.

In 1976, Burundi, Rwanda and Zaire established the Communaute Economique des Pays des Grands Lacs (CEPGL) or the Economic Community of the Great Lakes Countries. The Communaute Economique des Etats de l'Afrique Central (CEEAC) or the Economic Community for Central African States comprising of the members of UDEAC and CEPGL together with Chad, Equatorial Guinea and the states of Sao Thome et Principe was formed in 1983.

North Africa In North Africa, there is the Maghreb Economic Community, functioning under common market principles, whose membership includes Algeria, Libya, Morocco and Tunisia. There is also the Casablanca group that formed a Free Trade Area, consisting of Egypt, Ghana, Guinea and Morocco.

Eastern and Southern Africa In Eastern and Southern Africa, the East African Common Market (EACM) comprising Kenya, Tanzania and Uganda was the most successful in the late-1960s and early-1970s. Its economic integration was based on a customs union, a common market and a common currency. However, it de-integrated in 1978. Currently, there is an effort to revive it. The East African Customs Union (EACU) was founded in 1967 by Ethiopia, Kenya, Sudan, Tanzania, Uganda and Zambia under the Treaty of the East African Co-operation. On 15 January 2001, the presidents of Kenya, Uganda and Tanzania re-launched the East African Community (EAC), aiming at creating a customs union and then a common market along the EU lines. However, with Uganda and Tanzania reluctant to expose their fragile industries to competition from abroad, negotiations on the more controversial details relating to the removal of trade barriers were postponed for a while. Rwanda and Burundi have expressed interest in joining the scheme.

Founded in 1910 by Botswana, Lesotho, Namibia, South Africa and Swaziland, the Southern African Customs Union (SACU) is the oldest, and by most accounts the most effective, integration scheme in Africa. Its goods and factors markets are well integrated.

Trade in goods and services (other than agriculture) within the union is totally free of barriers, but imports from the rest of the world face a common external tariff and a common excise tax the proceeds of which flow into a consolidated revenue fund. The union partners then share the revenues using a complicated revenue-sharing formula. All SACU members except Botswana are also members of the Rand Monetary Area with the central Bank of South Africa acting as the central Bank of the Area as a whole.

The South African Development Community (SADC) was set up by Angola, Botswana, Congo (D. R.), Lesotho, Malawi, Mauritius, Mozambique, Namibia, Seychelles, Swaziland, Tanzania, Zambia and Zimbabwe to provide a counter to South Africa's economic hegemony on the region. SADC's first meeting was held in Arusha in 1979 with the aim of harmonising development plans to reduce the region's economic dependence on South Africa. Following the collapse of the Apartheid regime, South Africa has since become a member.

The Preferential Trading Area (PTA) was formally borne by the Treaty of Lusaka in 1981. By the early 1990s, its membership comprised Angola, Burundi, Comoro, Djibuti, Ethiopia, Kenya, Lesotho, Malawi, Mauritius, Mozambique, Namibia, Rwanda, Sudan, Swaziland, Uganda, Tanzania, Zambia and Zimbabwe. The Treaty of Lusaka envisaged an ambitious program of internal trade liberalisation; the development of industry, agriculture, human resources and communications within and between member countries; and ultimately the creation of an economic community in the sub-region. Initial action concentrated on trade promotion through tariff preferences and the establishment of the PTA Clearing-House to minimise the use of scarce foreign exchange for internal transactions.

Dissatisfaction with the PTA's progress and the new wave of regionalism in the continent led its members to draw up a new treaty establishing the Common Market for Eastern and Southern Africa (COMESA) in December 1993, which effectively replaced the PTA in December 1994. The objective of COMESA is once again to create a free trade zone that will evolve into a customs union with a common external tariff by the year 2004 and into a common market thereafter. The treaty signed in Kampala in 1992 places binding obligations on member countries with the aim of promoting integration towards a fully developed common market for East and Southern Africa. Congo (D. R.), Egypt, Eritrea, Madagascar, Mauritius and Seychelles have also become members. The sixth summit of COMESA, held in Cairo, endorsed a programme for the attainment of its Common External Tarrif and Customs Union by December 8, 2004.

Conclusion

The objectives behind the formation of regional blocs have been almost uniform. For instance, they relate to co-operation on trade and project development, economic growth of the regions, and peace and stability. However, there are instances when the political agenda has surpassed the economic agenda. Moreover, numerous as they are, most of the regional blocs particularly those comprising developing countries have had little, if any impact in the international social, political and economic arena. They have not met with the same degree of success as those with between industrial countries with market economies.

Bibliography

Abdel Rahman, I. H. (1979), 'Science and Technology, The Development Dilemma', *The Unesco Courier*, New York, Geneva, UNESCO, November 1979.

Agodo, O. (1978), 'The Determinants of US Private Manufacturing Investments in Africa', *Journal of International Business Studies*, Winter 1978, pp. 95-107.

Agosin, M. R., and Benavente, J. M. (1998), Canadian foreign direct investment in Chile, unpublished paper prepared for the Centre for International Studies, University of Toronto.

Alun, J. (1988), 'ASEAN Production-Factor Mobility: Some Thoughts', in Esmara, H., (ed.), *ASEAN - Co-operation: A New Perspective*, Singapore, Chopmen, pp. 43-53.

Aquino, T. G., and Bolanos, B. B. (1993), 'Foreign Investment Inflows and Political Stability in the Philippines', in *The New Wave of Foreign Direct Investment in Asia*, Singapore, Nomura Research Institute and Institute of Southeast Asian Studies, pp. 174-196.

Arndt, H. W., and Garnaut, R. (1979), 'ASEAN and The Industrialisation of East Asia', *Journal of Common Market Studies*, Vol. XVII, No. 3, March 1979, pp. 191-212.

Arrow, K. J. (1962), 'The economic implications of learning by doing', *Review of Economic Studies*, 29, 155-173.

Balassa, B. (1961), *The Theory of Economic Integration*, Homewood, Richard, D. I.

Balassa, B. (1976), Types of Economic Integration World Wide, Regional, Sectoral in Machlup, F., (ed.), *International Economic Association*, New York, Wiley, pp. 1-31.

Balassa, B. (1978), 'Exports and Economic Growth', *Journal of Development Economics*, Vol. 5, 1978, pp. 181-189.

Balassa, B., and Stoutjesdijk, A. (1976), 'Economic Integration Among Developing Countries', *Journal of Common Market Studies*, Vol. XIV, pp. 37-55.

Balasubramanyam, V. N., and Greenaway, D. (1992), 'Economic Integration and Foreign Direct Investment: Japanese Investment in the EC', *Journal of Common Market Studies*, Vol. XXX, No. 2, June 1992, pp. 175-193.

Balasubramanyam, V. N., Sapsford, D., and Salisu, M. A. (1996), 'Foreign Direct Investment and Growth: New Hypothesis and Evidence', *Discussion Paper (EC7/96), The Management School, Lancaster University*.

Bandera, V. N, and White, J. T (1968), 'US Direct Investments and Domestic Markets in Europe', *Economia Internazionale*, 21, pp. 117-133.

Barker, D., Barlow, M., Bello, W., Bertrand, A., Blackwelder, B., Cavanagh, J., Clarke, T., Goldsmith, E., Hayes, R., Hines, C., Khor, M., Kimbrell, A., Korten, D., Larrain, S., Mander, J., Menotti, V., Mittal, A., Norberg-Hodge, H., Ritchie, M., Shiva, V., Shrybman, S. and Wallach, L. (1999), 'Alternatives to Economic Globalization: A Preliminary Report' in Gueneau, S., Biagiotti, I. and Mongruel, S. (1998), '*Globalization and Sustainable Development: 12 fact sheets*' - retrieved from website http://www.envirodev.org/librairie/ pedago/mond_1999/trade/

Barro, R. J. (1991), 'Economic Growth in a Cross Section of Countries', *The Quarterly*

Journal of Economics, Vol. CVI, Issue 2, May 1991, pp. 407-443.

Barro, R. J. (1989), 'Economic growth in a cross section of countries', *NBER Working Paper, no. 3120, Cambridge, Mass, National Bureau of Economic Research*.

Barro, R. J. (1997), *Determinants of economic growth: a cross-country empirical study*, Cambridge, Mass; London, MIT Press.

Barro, R. J., and Sala-i-Martin, X. (1995), *Economic Growth*, New York, London, McGraw - Hill.

Beghin, J., Roland-Holst, D., and Van der Mensbrugghe, D. (1998), 'Outward orientation and the environment in the Pacific Basin: Coordinated trade and environmental policy reform in Mexico', in in Hiro Lee and Roland-Holst, D. W., (eds.), *Economic Development & cooperation in the Pacific Basin, Cambridge*, pp. 446-467, Cambridge University Press.

Bende-Nabende, A. (1995), The Role and Determinants of Foreign Direct Investment in Least Developed Countries, with Special Reference to Uganda - unpublished MBA dissertation.

Bende-Nabende, A. (1999), *FDI, Regionalism, Government Policy and Endogenous Growth*, Aldershot, Ashgate.

Bende-Nabende, A. (2000), 'Foreign Direct Investment in ASEAN: an Historical Perspective', in Strange, R., Slater, J. and Molteni, C., (eds.), *The European Union and ASEAN*, pp. 33-62, Macmillan, Chippenham, Wiltshire.

Bende-Nabende, A. and Ford, J. L. (1998), 'FDI, Policy Adjustments and Endogenous Growth: Multiplier Effects from a Small Dynamic Model for Taiwan, 1959-1995', *World Development*, Vol. 26, No. 7, pp. 1315-1330.

Bende-Nabende, A., Ford, J. L., and Sen, S (2000a), 'Productivity analysis in Asia-Pacific Economic Cooperation region: A multi-country translog comparative analysis', 1965-97 *Birmingham Department of Economics Discussion Paper no. 00-03*.

Bende-Nabende, A., Ford, J. L., Sen, S., and Slater, J. (2000b), Long-run dynamics of FDI and its spillovers onto output: Evidence from the Asia-Pacific economic cooperation region, *Birmingham Department of Economics Discussion Paper no. 00-10*.

Bende-Nabende, A., Ford, J. L., and Slater, J. R. (1997a), 'The Impact of FDI and Regional Economic Integration on the Economic Growth of the ASEAN-5 Economies, 1970-1994: A Comparative Analysis from a Small Structural Model', *Birmingham University Department of Economics Discussion Paper no. 97-13*.

Bennell, P. (1994), 'British Manufacturing Investment in Sub-saharan Africa: Corporate Responses During Structural Adjustments', *Working Paper 13, Institute of Development Studies*.

Bhagwati, J. (1971), 'Trade-Diversity, Customs Union and Welfare-Improved; A Classification', *Economic Journal*, September, Vol. 81, pp. 580-587.

Borensztein, Eduardo, Jose de Gregorio and Jong-Wha Lee (1995), 'How does foreign direct investment affect economic growth?' *National Bureau of Economic Research Working paper No. 5057*, Cambridge, MA.

Boserup, E. (1981), *Population and technical change: A study of long-term trends*, Chicago, University of Chicago Press.

Brown, A. J. (1961), 'Customs Union verses Economic Separation in Developing Countries', *Yorkshire Bulletin*, Vol. I and II, May 1961.

Cantwell, J. (1987), 'The Reorganisation of European Industries After Integration; Selected Evidence on the Role of Multinational Enterprise Activities', *Journal of Common Market Studies*, Vol. XXXI, No. 2, Dec. 1987, pp. 127-181.

Cantwell, J. (1994), 'The Theory of Technological Competence and its Application to International Production', in Cantwell, J., (ed.), *The United Nations Library on Transnational Corporations, Transnational Corporations and Innovatory Activities*, Vol. 17, London, Routledge, 1994, pp. 107-143.

Chen, E. K. Y., and Wong, T. Y. C. (1995), 'Two-Way FDI Flow Between Hong Kong and Mainland China', in *The New Wave of Foreign Direct Investment In Asia*, Singapore, Nomura Research Institute and Institute of Southeast Asian Studies, pp. 243-277.

Chen-Min Hsu (1995), 'Debit Financing, Public Investment, and Economic Growth in Taiwan', in Ito Takatoshi and Krueger, A. O., (ed.), *Growth Theories in light of The East Asian Experience*, Chicago, London, University of Chicago Press, National Bureau of Economic Research, pp. 129-152.

Chou, J. (1995), 'Old and New Development Models: The Taiwanese Experience', in Ito Takatoshi and Krueger, A. O., (ed.), *Growth Theories in Light of the East Asian Experience*, Chicago, London, University of Chicago Press, National Bureau of Economic Research, pp. 105-128.

Christensen, L. R. and Jorgenson, D. W. (1969), 'Measurement of US real capital input: 1929-1967', *Review of Income and Wealth*, 15: pp. 293-320.

Christensen, L. R., Cummings, D. and Jorgenson, D. W. (1980), 'Economic growth, 1947-73: an international comparision', in Kendrick, J. W. and Vaccara, B. N., (eds), *New Development in Productivity Measurement and Analysis*, Chicago: University of Chicago Press.

Chudnovsky, D. (1993), 'Introduction: Transnational Corporations and Industrialisation', in Chudnovsky, D., (ed.), *The United Nations Library on Transnational Corporations, Transnational Corporations and Industrialisation*, Vol. 11, London, Routledge, pp. 1-28.

Chudnovsky, D. B., Lopez, A., and Porta, F. (1997), 'Market or policy driven? Foreign direct investment boom in Argentina', *Oxford Development Studies*, 25, 2, pp. 173-188.

Cooper, C. A., and Massell, B. I. F. (1965), 'Towards A General Theory of Customs Union for Developing Countries', *Journal of Political Economy*, Vol. LXXIII, Feb.-Dec. 1965, pp. 461-476.

Cynn, J. W. (1999), 'The political economy of technical learning: a case study of Korea's electronics industry', University of Oxford, unpublished dissertation mimeo.

De Long, B. J. (1988), 'Productivity growth, convergence, and welfare', *American Economic Review*, 78, pp. 1138-1154.

De Long, B. J., and Summers, H. L. (1991), 'Equipment Investment and Economic Growth', *The Quarterly Journal of Economics*, Vol. CVI, Issue 2, May 1991, pp. 445-502.

Denison, E. F. (1962), *Sources of Economic Growth in the United States and the Alternatives before us*. New York: Committee for Economic Development.

Denison, E. F. (1985), *Trends in American Economic Growth, 1929-1982*, Washington D. C., The Brookings Institution.

Domar, E. (1947), 'Expansion and employment', *American Economic Review*, 37, pp. 34-55.

Dowrick, S., and Nguyen, D. (1989), 'OECD comparative economic growth 1950-85: Catch-up and convergence', *American Economic Review*, 79, pp. 1010-1030.

Dunning, J. D. (1981), *International Production and The Multinational Enterprise*, London,

George, A. and Unwin.

Dunning, J. H. (1986), *Japanese Participation in British Industry*, London, Croom Helm.

Dunning, J. H., (ed.) (1972), *International Investment: selected readings*, Harmondsworth, Middlesex: Penguin Books.

Dunning, J. H. (1980), 'Towards an Eclectic Theory of International Production: Some Empirical Tests', *Journal of International Business Studies*, 11, pp. 9-31.

Dunning, J. H., and Robson, P. (1987), 'Multinational Corporate Integration and Regional Economic Integration', *Journal of Common Market Studies*, Vol. XXVI, No. 2, December 1987, pp. 103-125.

Edwards, S. (1992), 'Trade Orientation, Distortions and growth in Developing Countries', *Journal of Development Economics*, Vol. 39, pp. 31-57.

EFTA (1992), *The Trade Effects of EFTA and the EEC 1959-1967*, Geneva, European Free Trade Association.

El Agraa, A. M., and Jones, A. J. (1981), *Theory of Customs Union*, Deddington, Philip Allan.

Enos, J. C., and Park, W. H. (1988), *The Adoption and Diffusion of Imported Technology: The case of Korea*, London, Croom Helm.

Ernst, D., Ganiatsos, T., and Mytelka, L., (eds), (1998a), *Technological capabilities and export success in Asia*, London, Routledge.

Eskeland, G., and Harrison, A. (1997), 'Moving to greener pastures? Multinationals and the pollution haven hypothesis', The World Bank unpublished mimeo.

Feder, G. (1982), 'On Exports and Economic Growth', *Journal of Development Economics*, Vol. 12, pp. 59-74.

Fong Chan Onn (1989), 'Malaysia: In Pursuit of Newly Industrialising Economy Status', *Asian Development Review*, Vol. 7, No. 2, pp. 68-87.

Frank, R. (2001), Asia's Investment Spotlight Sweeps North, *The Wall Street Journal*, February 28.

Franko, L. G. (1994), 'Trends in Direct Employment in Multinational enterprises in Industrialised Countries', in Enderwick, P., (ed.), *The United Nations Library on Transnational Corporations, Transnational Corporations and Human Resources*, Vol. 16, London, Routledge, pp. 87-118.

Fukuda, Shin-ichi and Hideki Toya (1993), 'Conditional convergence in East Asian countries: The role of exports for economic growth', *Discussion Paper no. 57, Economic Research Institute, Economic Planning Agency, Tokyo.*

GATT (1992), *Trade Policy Review, Singapore*, Vol. 1, No. 1, Geneva, GATT.

Georgion, G. C., and Weinhold, S. (1992), 'Japanese Direct Investment in the US', *The World Economy*, Vol. 15, No. 6, Nov. 1992, pp. 761-778.

Goldberge, M. A. (1972), 'The Determinants of US Direct Investment in the EEC: A Comment', *American Economic Review*, Vol. 62, September 1972, pp. 692-699.

Grossman, G. M., and Krueger, A. B. (1992), 'Environmental impacts of a NAFTA', *CEPR Discussion Paper series no. 644*, London.

Grossman, G., and Helpman, E. (1991), *Innovation and growth in the global economy*, Cambridge, MIT Press.

Gueneau, S., Biagiotti, I. and Mongruel, S. (1998), '*Globalization and Sustainable Development: 12 fact sheets*' - retrieved from website http://www.envirodev.org/ librairie/pedago/mond_1999/trade/

Gupta, V. K. (1983), 'A Simultaneous determination of structure, conduct and performance in Canadian manufacturing' *Oxford Economic Papers*, 35, pp. 281-301.

Hall, S. (1991), 'Marketing Barriers Facing Developing Country Manufactured Exports: A Conceptual Note', *The Journal of Development Studies*, Vol. 27, No. 4, July 1991, pp. 137-150.

Hamad, K. (1995), 'Comment', in Ito Takatoshi and Krueger, A. O., (ed.), *Growth Theories in Light of the East Asian Experience*, Chicago, London, University of Chicago Press, National Bureau of Economic Research, pp. 33-36.

Harrod, R. F. (1939), 'An essay in dynamic theory', *Economic Journal*, 49, pp. 14-33.

Heckscher, E. (1919), 'The Effects of Foreign Trade on Distribution of Income' *Economisc Tidskrift*, pp. 497-512.

Heitger, B. and Stehn, R. (1990), 'Japanese Direct Investment in the EC - Response to the Internal Market 1993?', *Journal of Common Market Studies*, Vol. XXIX, No. 29, September, pp. 1-15.

Herbert-Copley, B. (1998), 'innovation, regulation and environmental management in the Chilean and Canadian pulp and paper industries' unpublished dissertation, Carleton University, Ottawa.

Hill, H. and Lindsey, C. W. (1987), 'Multinationals from Larger and Small Countries: A Philippine Case Study', *Banca Nazionale del Lavoro*, XL, March 1987, pp. 77-92.

Hummels, D. L., and Stern, R. M. (1994), 'Evolving Patterns of North American Merchandise Trade and Foreign Direct Investment, 1960-1990'; *The World Economy*, Vol. 17, No. 1, January 1994, pp. 5-29.

Humphrey, J. (1993), 'Japanese production management and labour relations in Brazil', *Journal of Development Studies*, 30, 1, pp. 92-114.

ILO (1977), *Social and Labour Practices of Multinational Enterprises in the Petroleum Industry*, Geneva, ILO.

ILO (1981), *Multinational's Training Practices and Development*, Geneva, ILO.

ILO (1994), 'International Labour Organisation, Multinationals' Training Practices and Development', in Enderwick, P., (ed.), *The United Nations Library on Transnational Corporations, Transnational Corporations and Human Resources*, Vol. 16, London, Routledge, pp. 216-234.

Johnson, H. G. (1964), *Money, Trade, and Economic Growth: Survey Lectures in Economic Theory, Comparative Costs and Commercial Policy: Theory of Customs Union*, London, Unwin University Books.

Jorgenson, D. (1990), 'Productivity and economic growth', in Berndt, E. R., and Triplett, J. E., (eds.), *Fifty years of economic measurement: The jubilee of the Conference on Research in Income and Wealth*, chapter 3, Chicago, University of Chicago Press.

Kehoe, J. T. (1995), 'A Review of Mexico's Trade Policy from 1982 to 1994', *The World Economy,* ' pp. 173-189.

Khambata, D. and Ajami, R. (1992), *International Business, Theory and Practice*, New York, Oxford, Maxwell-Macmillan Publishing.

Kim Jong-Il and Lau, L. J. (1992), 'Human Capital and Aggregate Productivity: Some Empirical Evidence from the Group-of-Five Countries', *Working Paper, Stanford, CA: Department of Economics, Stanford University*.

Kim Jong-Il and Lau, L. J. (1994), 'The Sources of economic Growth in the East Asian Newly Industrialized Countries', *Journal of Japanese and International Economies*, 8: 235-271.

Kim Jong-Il and Lau, L. J. (1995), 'The Role of Human Capital in the Economic Growth of the East Adian Newly Industrialised Countries', *Asia-Pacific Economic Review*, 1: pp 3-22.

Kindleberger, C. P. (1993), 'European Integration and the International Corporation', in Robson, P., (ed.), *United Nations Library on Transnational Corporations, Transnational Corporations and Regional Economic Integration*, Vol. 9, London, Routledge, pp. 87-98.

King, M. A. and Robson, M. H. (1992), 'Investment and Technical Progress', *Oxford Review of Economic Policy*, Vol. 8, No. 4, pp. 43-46.

Kiyohiko Fukushima and Kwan, C. H. (1995), 'Foreign Direct Investment and Regional Industrial Restructuring in Asia', in *The New Wave of Foreign Direct Investment in Asia*, Singapore, Nomura Research Institute of Southeast Asian studies, pp. 1-42.

Knickerbocker, F. (1973), *Oligopolistic Reaction and Multinational Enterprise*, Boston, Harvard University Press.

Kokko, A. (1994), 'Sweden: Effects of EU Membership on Investment and Growth', *The World Economy*, Vol. 17, No. 5, Sept. 1994, pp. 667-677.

Koldor, N., and Mirrlees, J. (1962), 'A new model of economic growth', *Review of Economic Studies*, 29, 174-192.

Kormendi, R. C. and Meguire, P. G. (1985), 'Macroeconomic Determinants of Growth: Cross Country Evidence', *Journal of Monetary Economics*, Vol. 16, pp. 141-163.

Krajewski, S., Bank, S., and Yu., H. S. (1994), 'North American Business Integration', *Business Quarterly*, Vol. 58, No .3, Spring 1994, pp. 55-61.

Krueger, A. O. (1980), 'Trade Policy as an Input to Development', *American Economic Review*, Vol. 70, May 1980, pp. 288-292.

Krugman, P. (1994), The myth of Asia's miracle', *Foreign Affairs*, 73: pp. 62-78.

Kuznets, S. (1966), *Modern economic growth: Rate, structure and spread*, New Haven, Conn, Yale University Press.

Kyriacou, G. (1991), 'Level and growth effects of human capital', *C. V. Starr Center Working Paper no. 91-26, New York University*.

Lall, S. (1995a), 'Employment and foreign investment: Policy options for developing countries', *International Labour Review*, 134, pp. 521-540.

Lateef, A. (1997), 'Linking up with the global economy: a case study of the Bangalore softeare industry', *Discussion paper no. DP/96/1997, International Institute of Labour Studies*.

Lee, H., and Roland-Holst, D. (1997), 'Trade and the environment', in Francois, J. F., and Reinert, K. A., (eds.), *Applied methods for trade policy analysis: A handbook*, Cambridge, Cambridge University Press.

Levin, R. and Renelt, D. (1992), 'A Sensitivity Analysis of Cross-Country Growth Regression', *American Economic Review*, Vol. 82, September 1992, pp. 942-963.

Lim, L. Y. C. and Fong, E. F. (1993), 'Vertical Linkages and Multinational Enterprises in Developing Countries', in Chudnovsky, D., (ed.), *The United Nations Library on Transnational Corporations, Transnational Corporations and Industrialisation*, Vol. 11, London, Routledge, pp. 82-99.

Lim, L. Y. C., and Pang, P. F. (1991), *Foreign Direct Investment and Industrialisation in Malaysia, Singapore, Taiwan and Thailand*, Paris, OECD.

Little, J. S. (1988), 'The Effects of Foreign Direct Investment on United States Employment During Recession and Structural Change', *New England Economic Review*, July/August 1988.

Lucas, R. E. (1988), 'On the Mechanics of Economic Development', *Journal of Monetary Economics*, Vol. 22, pp. 3-42.

Lunn, J. L. (1980), 'Determinants of US Direct Investment in the EEC', *European Economic*

Review, Vol. 13, January, pp. 93-101.

Mahalanobis, P. C. (1955), 'The approach of operational research to planning in India', *Sankhya, Indian Journal of Statistics*, 16, pp. 3-62.

Mansfield, E. (1994), 'Technology and Technological Change', in Cantwell, J., (ed.), *The United Nations Library on Transnational Corporations, Transnational Corporations and Innovatory Activities*, Vol. 17, London, Routledge, pp. 37-72.

Manson, R. H. (1994), in ILO, 'An Introduction Based on an Overview of the Literature', in Enderwick, P., (ed.), *The United Nations Library on Transnational Corporations, Transnational Corporations and Human Resources*, Vol. 16, London, Routledge, pp. 216-234.

Molle, W. (1990), *The Economics of European Integration: Theory, Practice, Policy*, Aldershot, Darthmouth.

Mondy, Ashota and Fung-Yi Wang (1997), 'Explaining industrial growth in coastal China: Economic reforms.. and what else?, *World Bank Economic Review*, 11, 2, pp. 293-325.

Neumann, V. (1945), 'A model of general equilibrium', *Review of Economic Studies*, 13, pp. 1-9.

OECD (1978), *Investing in Developing Countries*, 4th ed., Paris, OECD.

OECD (1995), *Foreign Direct Investment, Trade and Employment*, Paris, OECD.

Ohlin, Bertil (1933), *Inter-regional and International Trade*, Cambridge, MA: Harvard University Press.

Panagariya, A. (1998), 'Should East Asia go regional?', in Hiro Lee and Roland-Holst, D. W., (eds.), *Economic Development & cooperation in the Pacific Basin, Cambridge*, Cambridge University Press.

Pang Eng Fong (1993), 'Staying Global and Going Regional: Singapore's Inward and Outward Direct Investments', in *The New Wave of Foreign Direct Investment in Asia*, Singapore, Nomura Research Institute and Institute of Southeast Asian Studies, pp. 111-129.

Park, Y. C. (1988), *Korea in the Open Economy*, Dornbusch, R. and Helmers, F., (ed.), New York, Oxford University Press.

Pina, C. (1994), 'Direct Employment Effects of MNEs in Developing Countries', in Enderwick, P., (ed.), *The United Nations Library on Transnational Corporations, Transnational Corporations and Human Resources*, Vol. 16, London, Routledge.

Plummer, M. G. (1997), Regional Economic Integration and Dynamic Policy Reform: The 'special' case of developing Asia, *Asia-Pacific Development Journal*, pp. 158-183.

Pyo, H. K. (1995), 'A time-series test of the endogenous growth model with human capital', in Ito Takatoshi and Krueger, A. O., (ed.), *Growth Theories in Light of the East Asian Experience*, Chicago, London, University of Chicago Press, National Bureau of Economic Research, pp. 229-245.

Ramsey, F. P. (1928), 'A mathematical theory of savings', *Economic Journal*, 38, pp. 543-559.

Ramstetter, E. D. (1993), 'Prospects for Foreign Firms in Developing Economies of the Asia and Pacific Region', *Asian Development Review*, Vol. 11, No. 1.

Rana, P. B. (1985), 'Foreign Direct Investment and Economic Growth in the Asian and Pacific Regions', *Asian Development Review*, Vol. 5, No. 1, pp. 100-115.

Raut, L., and Srinivasan, T. N. (1991), 'Endogenous fertility, technical change and growth in a model of overlapping generations', *Economic Growth Center Discussion Paper, no. 628,* Yale University.

Repetto, R. (1995), *Jobs, competitiveness and environmental regulations: What are the real*

314 *Globalisation, FDI, Regional Integration and Sustainable Development*

issues?, Washington D. C., World Resources Institute.

Ribeiro, M. S., Contemporary Issues on Foreign Direct Investment Statistics and Promotion Policies: A Research Paper - retrieved from web site http://www.gwu.edu/~ibi/minerva/Spring2000/Ribeiro.pdf

Ricardo, D. (1948), *The Principles of Political Economy and Taxation*, New York: E. P. Dutton & Co.

Riedel, J. (1991), 'Intra-Asian Trade and Foreign Direct Investment', *Asian Development Review*, Vol. 9, No. 1, pp. 111-146.

Ritchie, B., Zhuang, L. and Whitworth, T. (2001), Experiences of JV Companies in China: Management and Operational issues, in Thorp, R. and Little, S., *Global Change: The impact of Asia in the 21st century*, pp. 255-272.

Riveros, L., Vatter, J., and Agosin, M. R. (1996), 'La inversion extranjera directa en Chile, 1987-93: aprovechamiento de ventajas comparativas y conversion de deuda' in Agosin, (ed.) Inversion, extranjera Directa en America Latin: Su Contribucion al Desarrollo, Santiago de Chile and Mexico City, Fondo de Cultura Economica.

Romer, P. M. (1986), 'Increasing Returns and Long Run Growth', *Journal of Political Economy*, Vol. 94, pp. 1002-1037.

Romer, P. M. (1990), 'Endogenous Technological Change', *Journal of Political Economy*, Vol. 98, No. 5, pp. S71-S102.

Root, F .R. and Ahmed, A. A. (1979), 'Empirical Determinants of Manufacturing Direct Foreign Investment in Developing Countries', *Economic Development and Cultural Change*, Vol. 27, July 1979, pp. 751-767.

Saad, I. (1995), 'Foreign direct investment, structural change, and deregulation in Indonesia', in *The New Wave of Foreign Direct Investment in Asia*, Singapore, Nomura Research Institute and Institute of Southeast Asian Studies, pp. 197-219.

Scaperlanda, A., and Balough, R. (1983), 'Determinants of US direct investment in the EEC revisited', *European Economic Review*, 21, pp. 381-390.

Scarperlanda, A. E. and Mauer, L. J. (1969), 'The Determinants of US Direct Investment in the EEC', *American Economic Review*, Vol. 59, September 1969, pp. 558-568.

Scheider, F. and Frey, B. S. (1985), 'Economic and Political Determinants of Foreign Direct Investment', *World Development*, Vol. 13, February 1985, pp. 161-175.

Schin-ichi Fukunda and Hideki Toya (1995), 'Conditional Convergence in East sian Countries: The Role of Exports in Economic Growth', in Ito Takatoshi and Krueger, A. O., (ed.), *Growth Theories in light of The East Asian Experience*, Chicago, London, University of Chicago Press, National Bureau of Economic research, pp. 247-266.

Schive, C. (1993), 'Foreign Investment and Technology Transfer in Taiwan', in Lall, S., (ed.), *The United Nations Library on Transnational Corporations, Transnational Corporations and Economic Development*, Vol. 3.

Schmitt, N. (1990), 'New International Trade Theories and Europe 1992: Some Results Relevant for EFTA Countries', *Journal of Common Market Studies*, Vol. XXIX, No.29, September 1990-1991, pp. 53-73.

Schmitz, A. and Bieri, J. (1972), 'EEC Tariffs and US Direct Investment', *European Economic Review*, Vol. 80, pp. 259-270.

Schultz, T. W. (1971), *Investing in Human Capital: The Role of Education and of Research*, New York, London, Collier-Macmillan.

Scott, M. F. G., *A new view of economic growth*, Oxford, Oxford University Press.

Shang Jim Wei (1995), 'The Open Door Policy and China's Rapid Growth: Evidence from City Level Data', in Ito Takatoshi and Krueger, A. O., (ed.), *Growth Theories in Light of*

The East Asian Experience, Chicago, London, University of Chicago Press, National Bureau of Economic Research, pp. 73-104.

Simon, J. L. (1981), Princeton, Princeton University Press.

Smith, Adam (1776), *The Wealth of Nations,* New York.

Solow, R. M. (1956), 'A Contribution to the Theory of Economic Growth', *The Quarterly Journal of Economics,* Vol. 70, pp. 65-94.

Solow, R. M. (1957), 'Technical Change and the Aggregate Production Function', *Review of Economics and Statistics*, Vol. 39, No. 3, pp. 312-320.

Srinivasan, T. N. (1995), Long-run growth theories and empirics: Anything new?', in Ito Takatoshi and Krueger, A. O., (eds.), *Growth Theories in Light of the East Asian Experience*, Chicago, London, University of Chicago Press, National Bureau of Economic Research, pp. 37-66.

Stokey, N. L. (1991), 'Human Capital, Product Quality, and Growth', *The Quarterly Journal of Economics,* Vol. CVI, Issue 2, May 1991, pp. 587-616.

Streeten, P. (1974), 'The theory of development policy', in Dunning, J., H., (ed.), *Economic analysis and the multinational enterprise*, London, George Allen & Unwin.

Taylor, P. (1999), 'A growing for and going places', *Financial Times*, 2 June.

The Economic Development Board (1993), *Thirty Years of Economic Development*, Singapore, EDB.

Thompson, A. J. (1994), 'Canada-United States Free Trade and Investment', *The World Economy,* Vol. 17, No. 1, January 1994, pp. 63-73.

Torris, C. R. (1985), 'The Determinants of Direct Foreign Investment in a Small LDC', *Journal of Economic Development*, Vol. 10, No. 2, July 1985, pp. 29-45.

UN (1992), *World Investment Report 1992, Transnational Corporations as Engines of Growth*, New York, UN.

UN, *UNESCO Statistical Yearbook*, New York, Paris, UNESCO (various years).

UNCTAD (1992), *World Investment Directory 1992, Vol. 1, Asia and the Pacific*, Division of Transnational Corporations and Investment, New York, UN.

UNCTAD (1993), 'The Role of Transnational Enterprise in Latin American Integration', in Robson, P., (ed.), *The United Nations Library on Transnational Corporations, Transnational Corporations and regional Economic Integration*, Vol. 9, London, Routledge, pp. 241-264.

UNCTAD (1994), *The Least Developed Countries 1993-1994 Report*, Division of Transnational Corporations and Investment, New York, UN.

UNCTAD (1995), *Foreign Direct Investment in Africa*, Division of Transnational Corporations and Investment, New York, UN.

UNCTAD (1996), *World Investment Report, Investment, Trade and International Policy Arrangements*, New York, UN.

UNCTAD (1997a), *World Investment Report, Transnational corporations, market structure and policy competition*, New York, UN.

UNCTAD (1999), *World Investment Report, Foreign Direct Investment and the Challenge of Development*, New York, UN.

UNCTAD (2000), *World Investment Report, Cross-border Mergers and Acquisitions and Development*, New York, UN.

UNCTC (1989), *Impact of Technological Change on Patterns of International Trade*, Division of Transnational Corporations and Investment, New York, UN.

UNCTC (1992), *The Determinants of Foreign Direct Investment, A Survey of the Evidence*, Division of Transnational Corporations and Investment, New York, UN.

UNCTMD (1992), *World Investment Report 1992, Transnational Corporations as Engines of Growth*, New York, UN.

UNTCMD (1993), 'The Effects of Integration on the Activities of Transnational Corporations in the European Community: Theory and Empirical Tests', in Robson, P., (ed.), *The United Nations Library on Transnational Corporations, Transnational Corporations and Regional Economic Development*, Vol. 9, London, Routledge, pp. 99-123.

Uzawa, H. (1965), 'Optimal technical change in an aggregative model of economic growth', *International Economic Review*, 6, pp. 18-31.

Van den Bulcke, D. (1993), 'European Economic Integration and the Process of Multinationals', in Robson, P., (ed.), *United Nations Library on Transnational Corporations, Transnational Corporations and Regional Economic Integration*, Vol. 9, London, Routledge, pp. 163-172.

Van der Phoeg, F., and Tang, J. G. (1992), 'The Macroeconomics of Growth: An International Perspective', *Oxford Review of Economic Policy*, Vol. 8, No. 4, pp. 15-28.

Vernon, R. (1966), 'International Investment and International Trade in the Product Life Cycle.' *Quarterly Journal of Economics*, 190-207.

Viner, J. (1950), *The Customs Union Issue*, New York: Carnegie endowment for International Peace.

Wallis, K. (1968)., 'The EEC and US Foreign Investment: Some Empirical Evidence Re-examined', *Economic Journal*, Vol. 78, September 1968, pp. 717-719.

Warhurst, A. (1999), 'The transfer and diffusion of clean technology', Final report to the Economic Social Research Council, University of Bath.

Wilson, D., (ed.) (1997), *Investing in China*, London, Financial Times Publication, Pearson Professional.

World Bank (1995), *Global Economic Prospects and the Developing Countries*, Washington D. C., Oxford University Press, The World Bank.

World Bank (1995), *The World Development Report 1995, Workers in an Integrating World*, Washington D. C., Oxford University Press, The World Bank.

World Wide Fund for Nature (1998, 1999a), WWF mimeos.

Yannopoulos, G. N. (1990), 'Foreign Direct Investment and European Integration: The Evidence from the Formative Years of the European Community', *Journal of Common Market Studies*, Vol. XXXIII, No. 28, March 1990, pp. 235-259.

Young, A. (1991), 'Learning by Doing and The Dynamic Effects of International Trade', *The Quarterly Journal of Economics,* Vol. CVI, Issue 2, May 1991, pp. 369-406.

Young, A. (1993), 'Accumulation, exports and growth in the high performing Asian economies, *Carnegie-Rochester Conference Seminar on Public Policy*, 40.

Author Index

Subject Index